F or this cover illustration, I've decided to try something new and focus on a single character. I've always wanted to draw in a slightly realistic manner. At first I thought I'd feature Eve, but since the 10th volume is such a milestone, I decided on Train.

—Kentaro Yabuki, 2002

Kentaro Yabuki made his manga debut with *Yamato Gensoki*, a short series about a young empress destined to unite the warring states of ancient Japan and the boy sworn to protect her. His next series, *Black Cat*, commenced serialization in the pages of *Weekly Shonen Jump* in 2000 and quickly developed a loyal fan following. *Black Cat* has also become an animated TV series, first hitting Japan's airwaves in the fall of 2005.

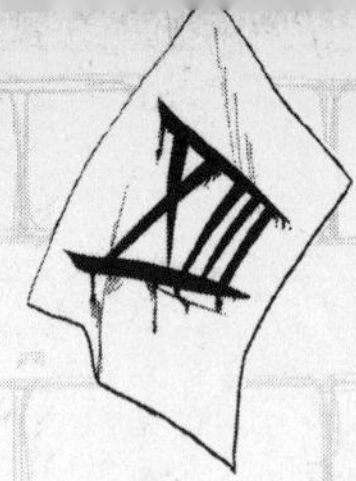

BLACK CAT VOL. 10
The SHONEN JUMP Manga Edition

STORY AND ART BY
KENTARO YABUKI

English Adaptation/Kelly Sue DeConnick
Translation/JN Productions
Touch-up Art & Lettering/Gia Cam Luc
Design/Courtney Utt
Editor/Jonathan Tarbox

Editor in Chief, Books/Alvin Lu
Editor in Chief, Magazines/Marc Weidenbaum
VP of Publishing Licensing/Rika Inouye
VP of Sales/Gonzalo Ferreyra
Sr. VP of Marketing/Liza Coppola
Publisher/Hyoe Narita

BLACK CAT © 2000 by Kentaro Yabuki
All rights reserved. First published in Japan in 2000 by
SHUEISHA Inc., Tokyo. English translation rights in the United
States of America and Canada arranged by SHUEISHA Inc.
The stories, characters and incidents mentioned in this
publication are entirely fictional.

Printed in the U.S.A.

Published by VIZ Media, LLC
P.O. Box 77010
San Francisco, CA 94107

SHONEN JUMP Manga Edition
10 9 8 7 6 5 4 3 2 1
First printing, September 2007

T 251363

VIZ MEDIA™
www.viz.com

THE WORLD'S
MOST POPULAR MANGA
SHONEN JUMP
www.shonenjump.com

SHONEN JUMP MANGA EDITION

BLACK CAT™

ブラック・キャット

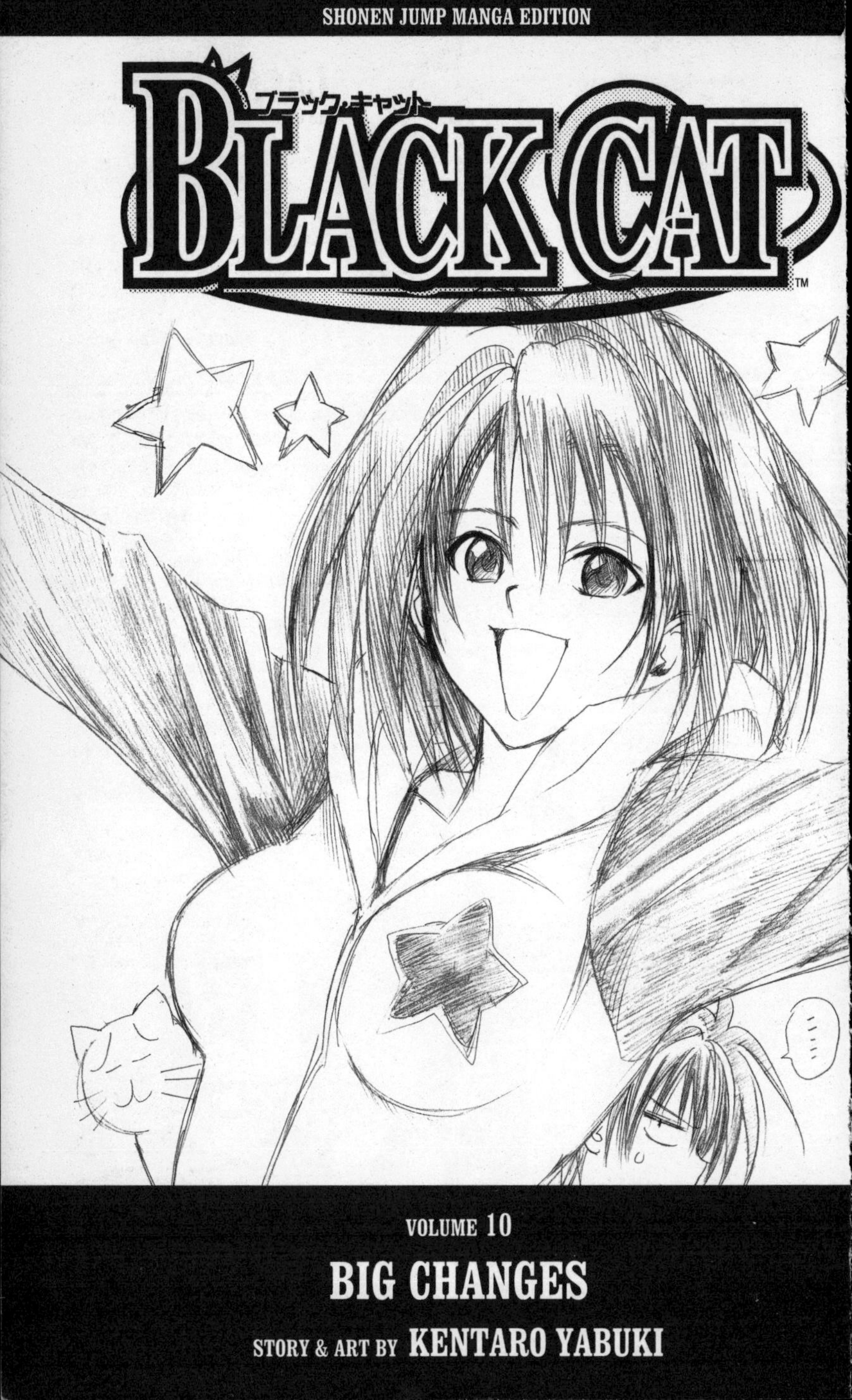

VOLUME 10

BIG CHANGES

STORY & ART BY **KENTARO YABUKI**

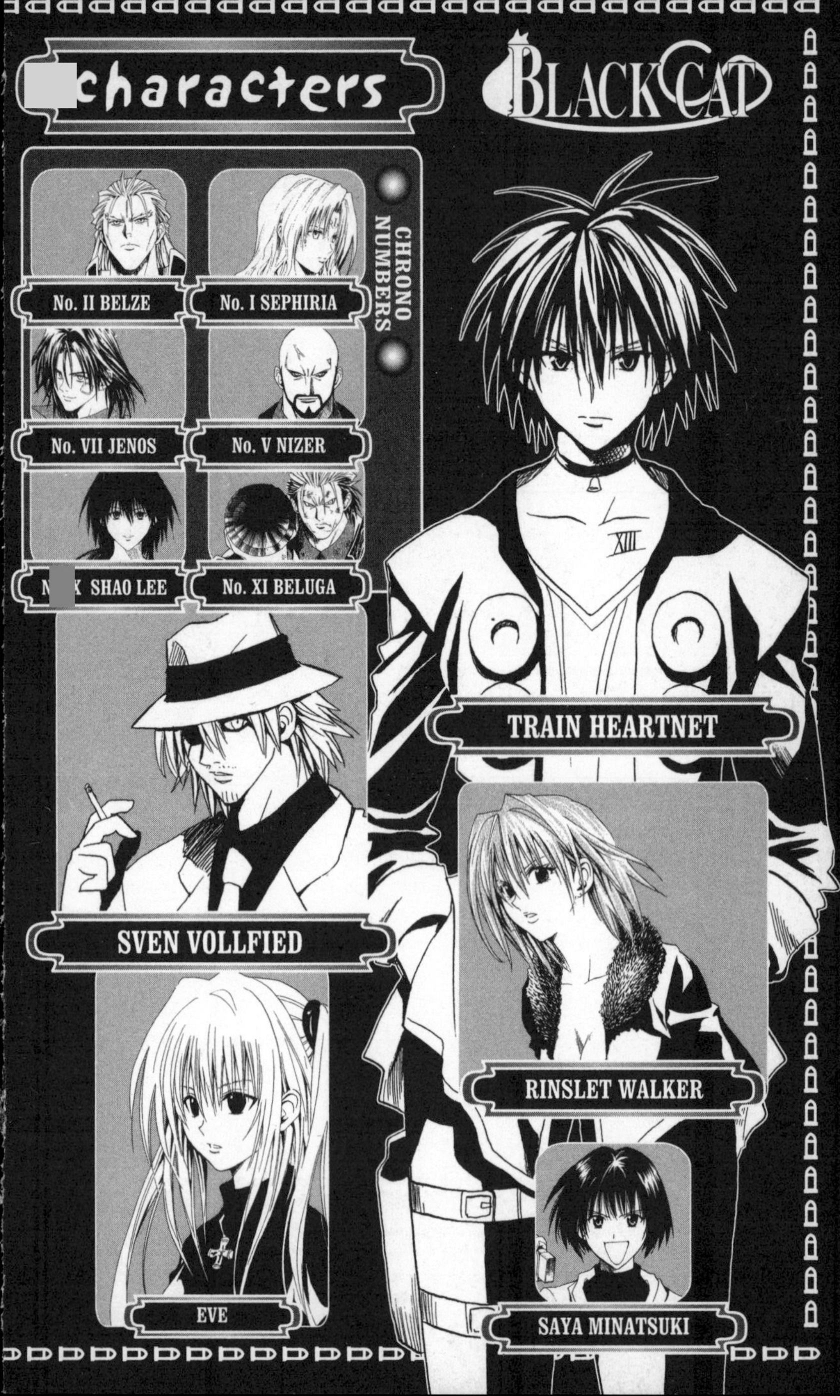

[redacted] characters
BLACK CAT
CHRONO NUMBERS
No. II BELZE
No. I SEPHIRIA
No. VII JENOS
No. V NIZER
N[redacted]X SHAO LEE
No. XI BELUGA
TRAIN HEARTNET
SVEN VOLLFIED
RINSLET WALKER
EVE
SAYA MINATSUKI

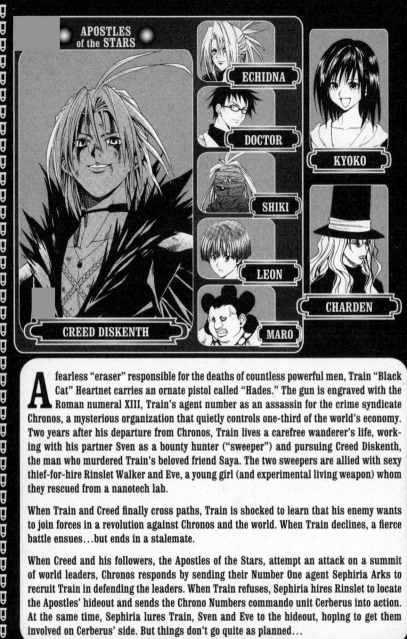

APOSTLES of the STARS

ECHIDNA

DOCTOR

SHIKI

LEON

MARO

CREED DISKENTH

KYOKO

CHARDEN

A fearless "eraser" responsible for the deaths of countless powerful men, Train "Black Cat" Heartnet carries an ornate pistol called "Hades." The gun is engraved with the Roman numeral XIII, Train's agent number as an assassin for the crime syndicate Chronos, a mysterious organization that quietly controls one-third of the world's economy. Two years after his departure from Chronos, Train lives a carefree wanderer's life, working with his partner Sven as a bounty hunter ("sweeper") and pursuing Creed Diskenth, the man who murdered Train's beloved friend Saya. The two sweepers are allied with sexy thief-for-hire Rinslet Walker and Eve, a young girl (and experimental living weapon) whom they rescued from a nanotech lab.

When Train and Creed finally cross paths, Train is shocked to learn that his enemy wants to join forces in a revolution against Chronos and the world. When Train declines, a fierce battle ensues...but ends in a stalemate.

When Creed and his followers, the Apostles of the Stars, attempt an attack on a summit of world leaders, Chronos responds by sending their Number One agent Sephiria Arks to recruit Train in defending the leaders. When Train refuses, Sephiria hires Rinslet to locate the Apostles' hideout and sends the Chrono Numbers commando unit Cerberus into action. At the same time, Sephiria lures Train, Sven and Eve to the hideout, hoping to get them involved on Cerberus's side. But things don't go quite as planned...

BLACK CAT

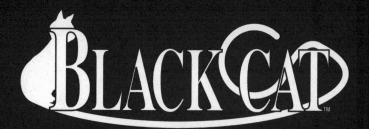

VOLUME 10 BIG CHANGES

CONTENTS

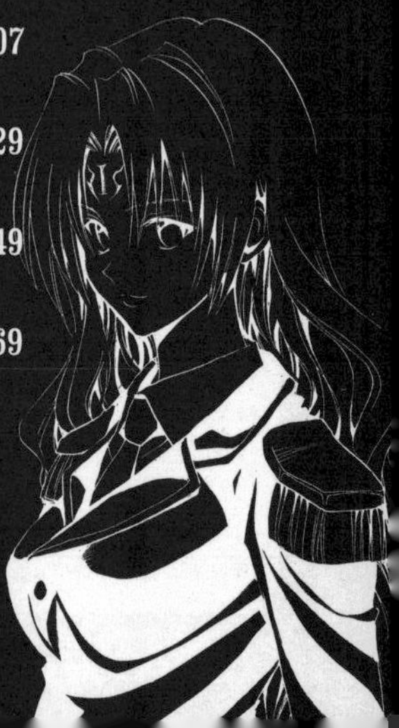

Chapter 85:
A Random Encounter

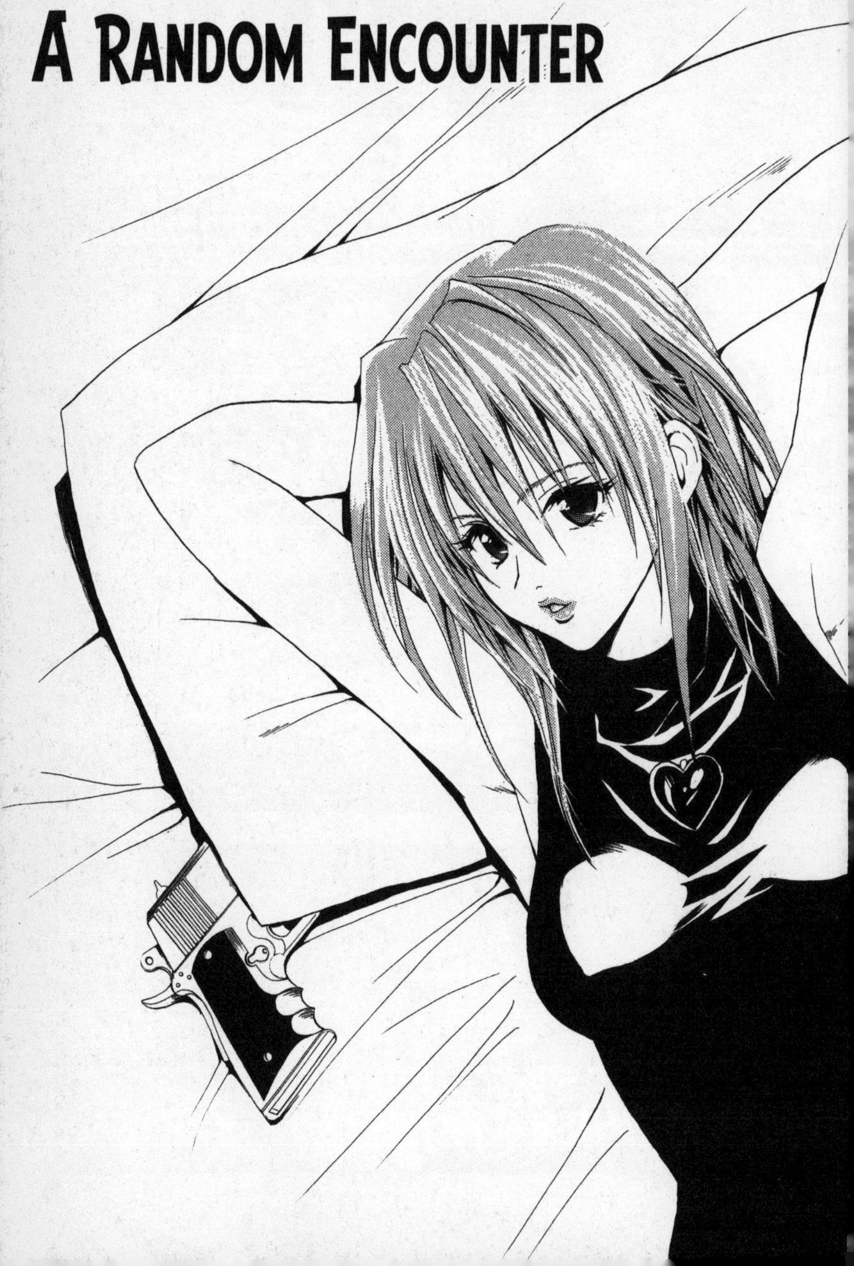

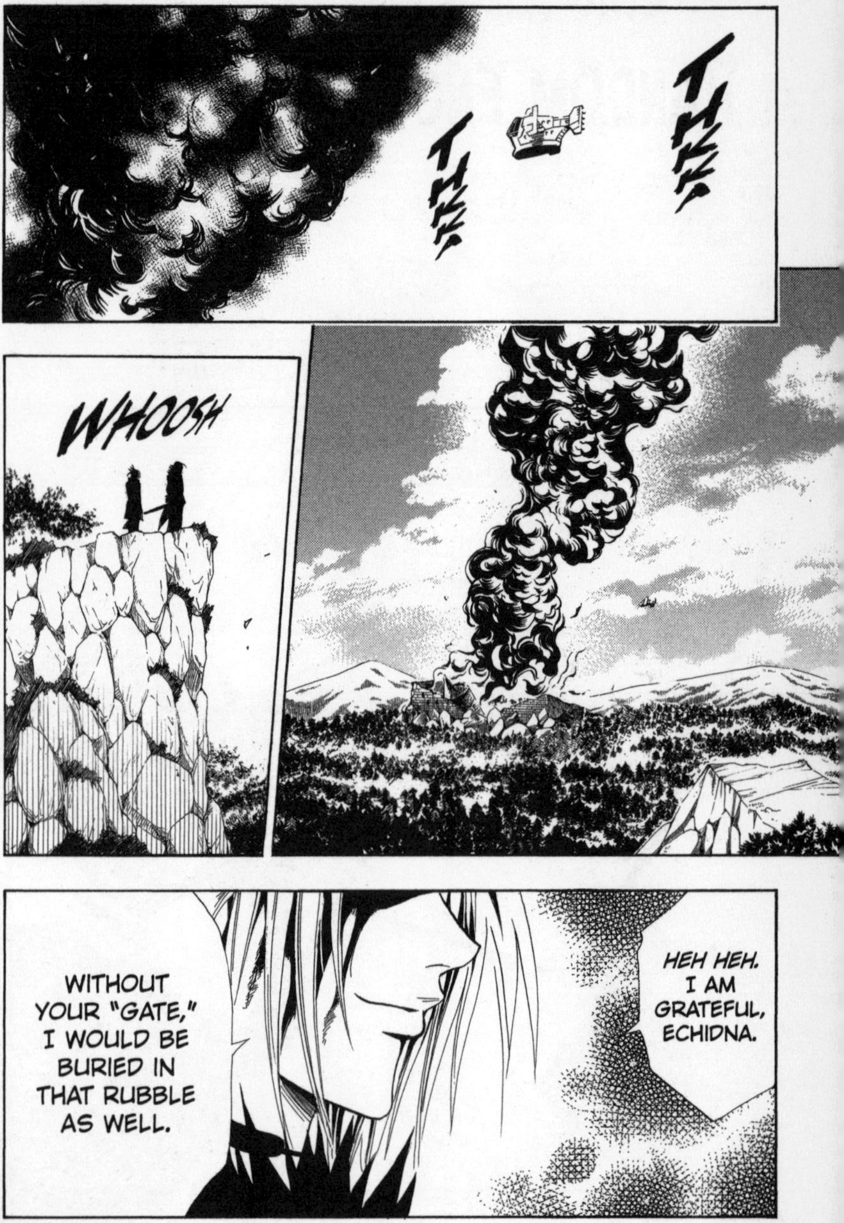
THKK
THKK
WHOOSH
HEH HEH. I AM GRATEFUL, ECHIDNA.
WITHOUT YOUR "GATE," I WOULD BE BURIED IN THAT RUBBLE AS WELL.

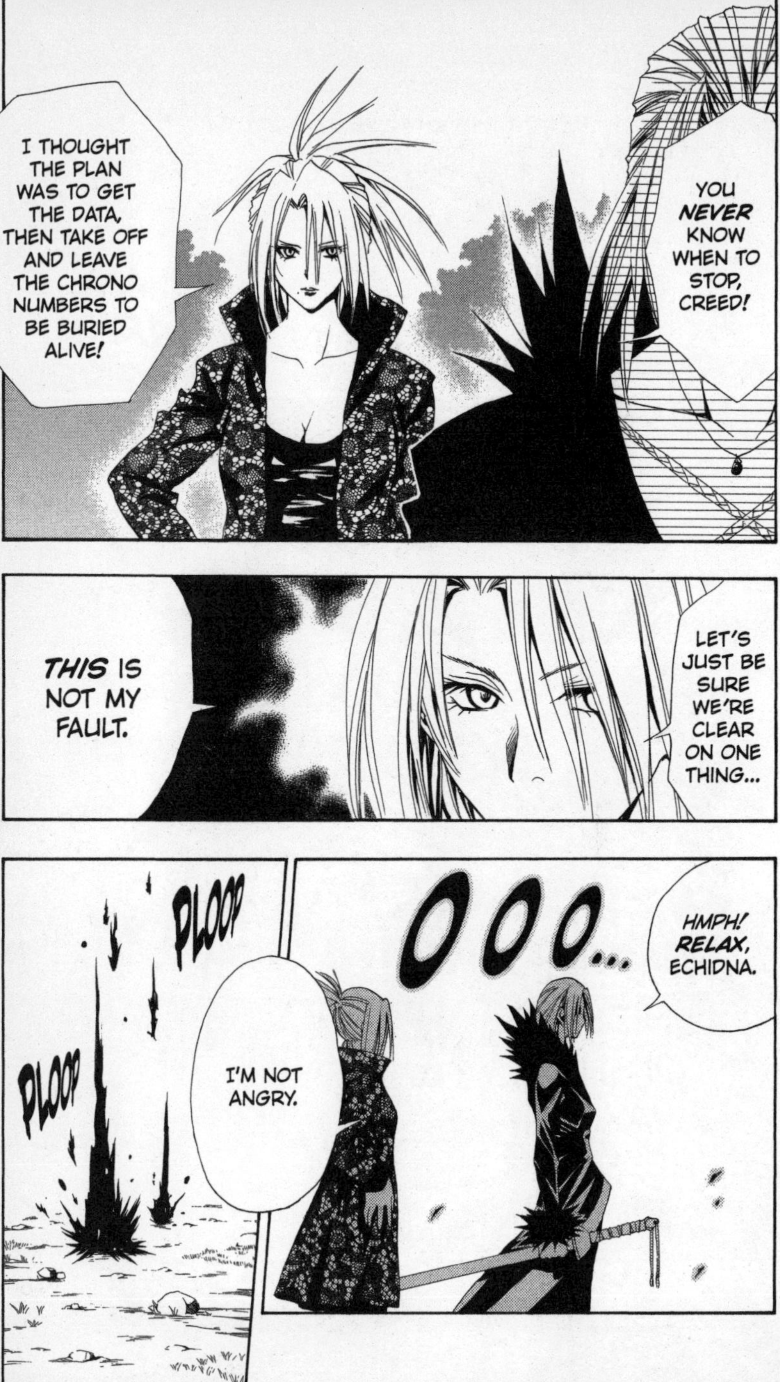
YOU NEVER KNOW WHEN TO STOP, CREED!
I THOUGHT THE PLAN WAS TO GET THE DATA, THEN TAKE OFF AND LEAVE THE CHRONO NUMBERS TO BE BURIED ALIVE!
LET'S JUST BE SURE WE'RE CLEAR ON ONE THING...
THIS IS NOT MY FAULT.
HMPH! RELAX, ECHIDNA.
OOO...
I'M NOT ANGRY.
PLOOP
PLOOP

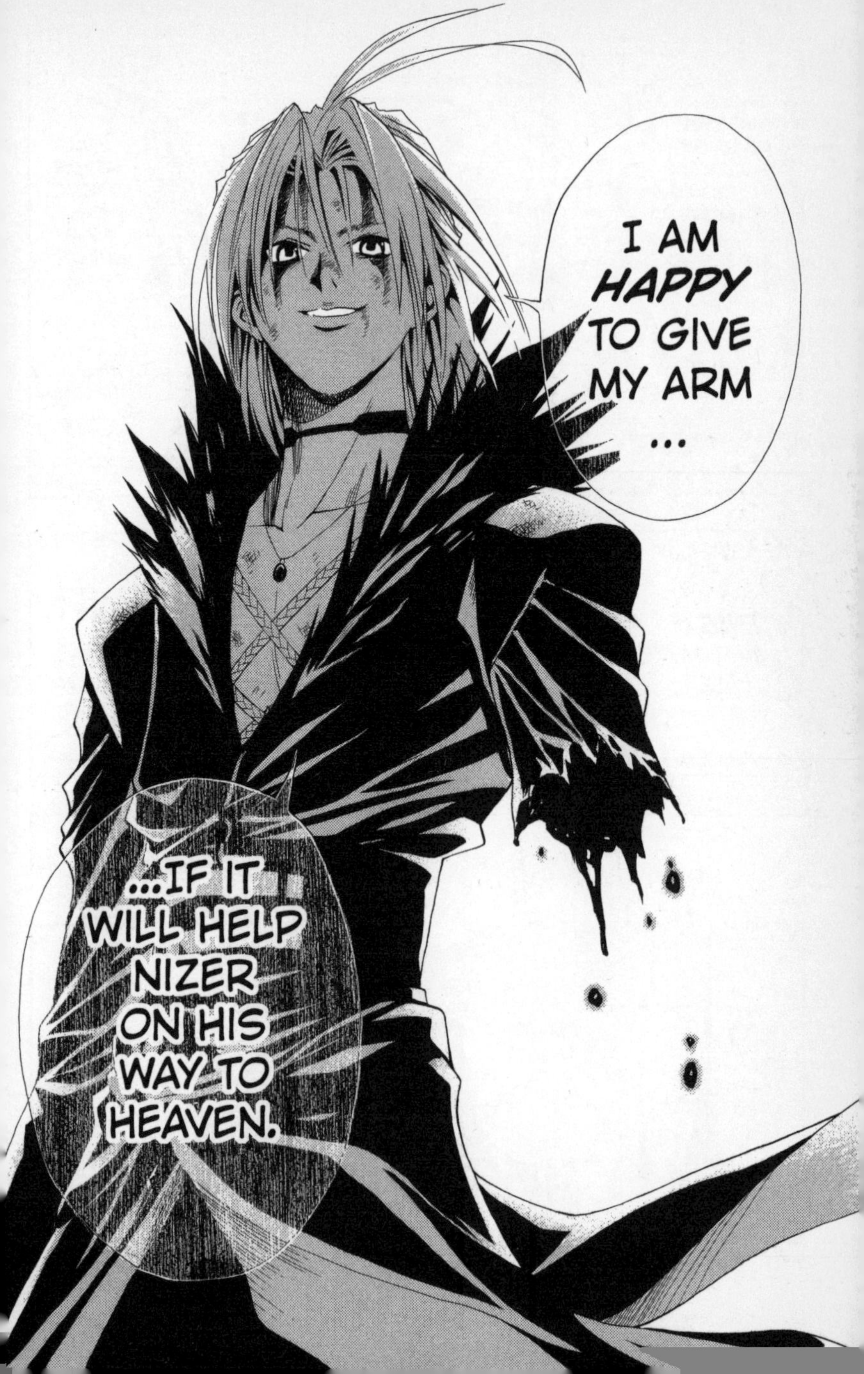
I AM *HAPPY* TO GIVE MY ARM ...
...IF IT WILL HELP NIZER ON HIS WAY TO HEAVEN.

READ THIS WAY

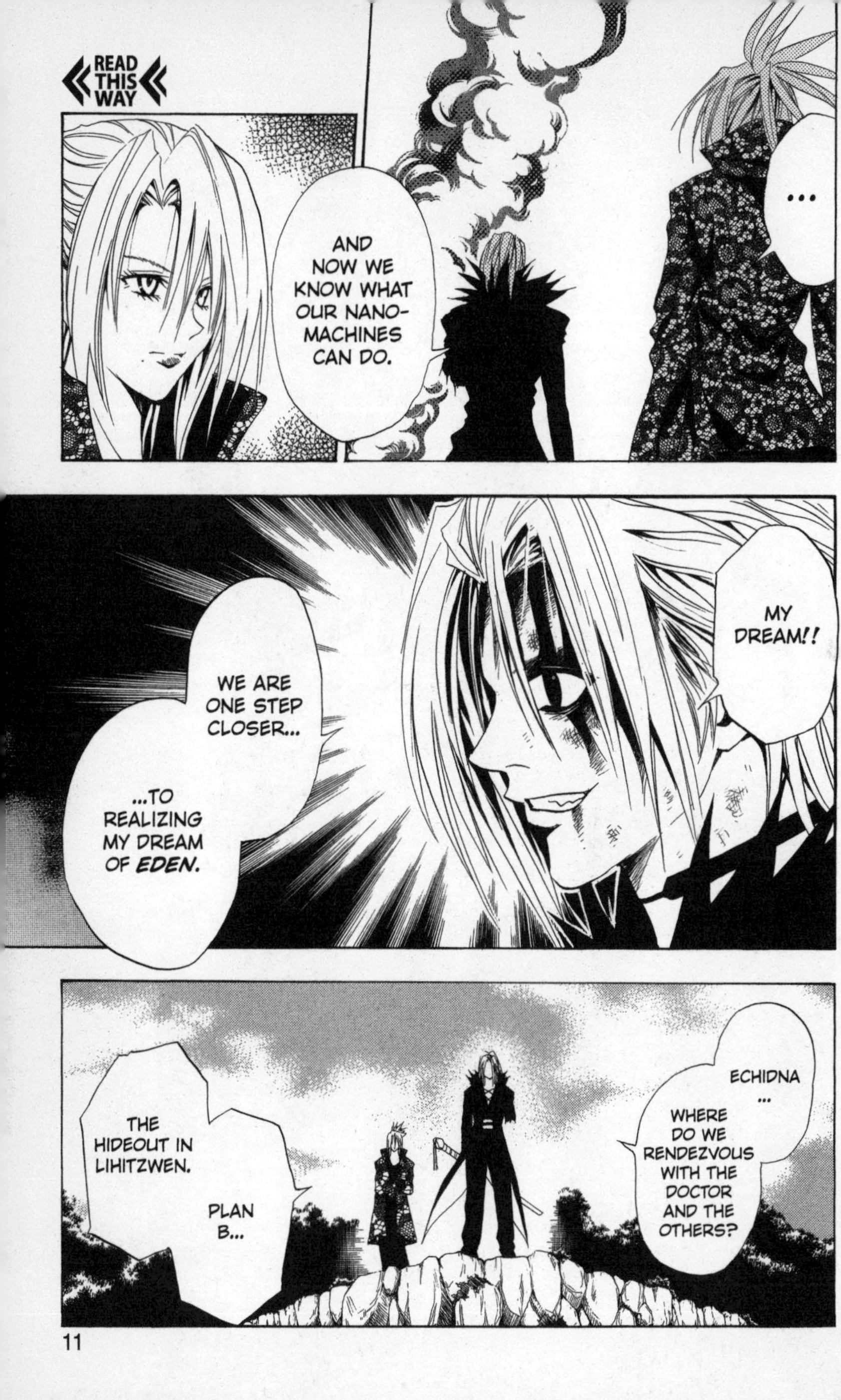
...
AND NOW WE KNOW WHAT OUR NANO-MACHINES CAN DO.
MY DREAM!!
WE ARE ONE STEP CLOSER...
...TO REALIZING MY DREAM OF *EDEN*.
ECHIDNA ... WHERE DO WE RENDEZVOUS WITH THE DOCTOR AND THE OTHERS?
THE HIDEOUT IN LIHITZWEN.
PLAN B...

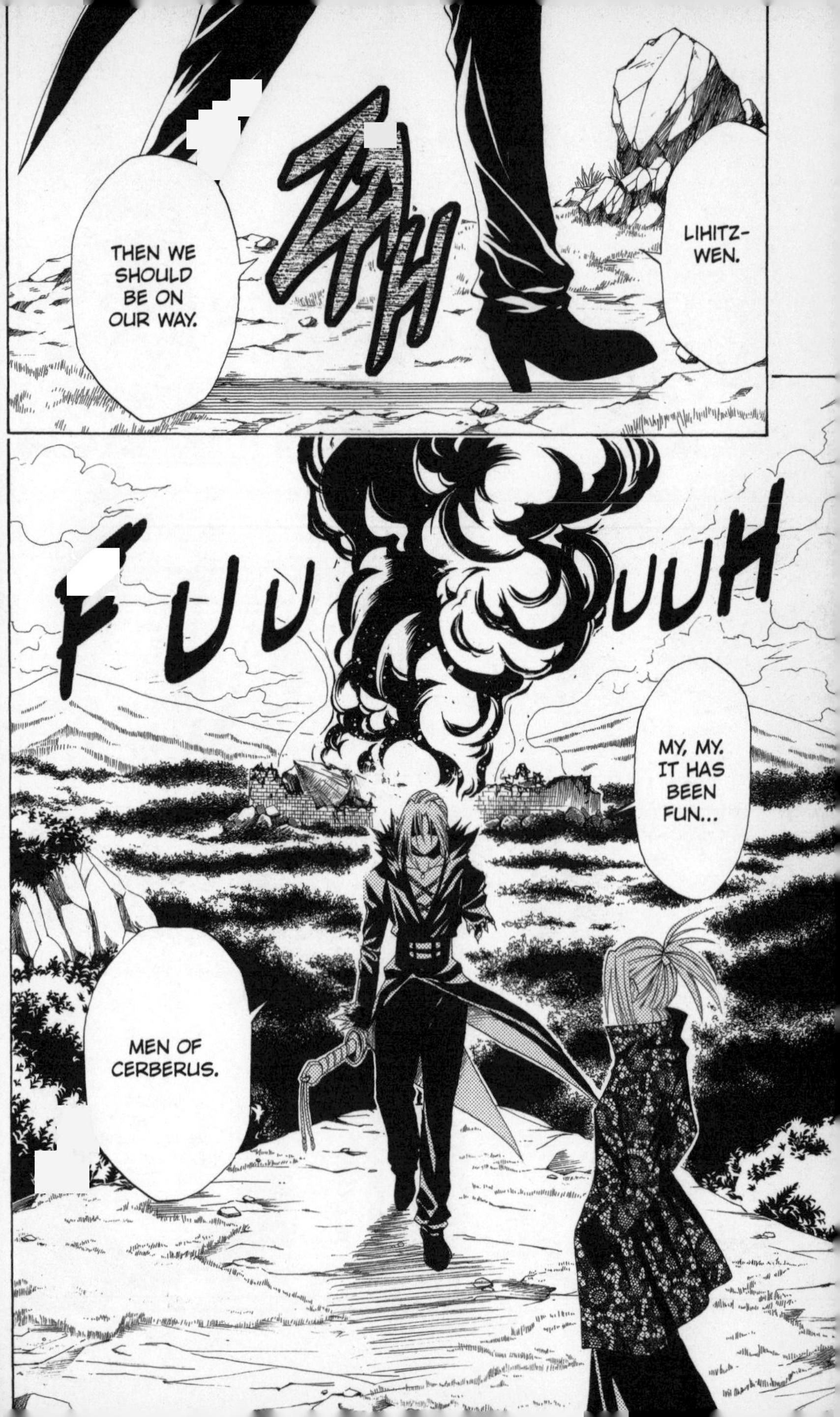
LIHITZ-WEN.
THEN WE SHOULD BE ON OUR WAY.
MY, MY. IT HAS BEEN FUN...
MEN OF CERBERUS.

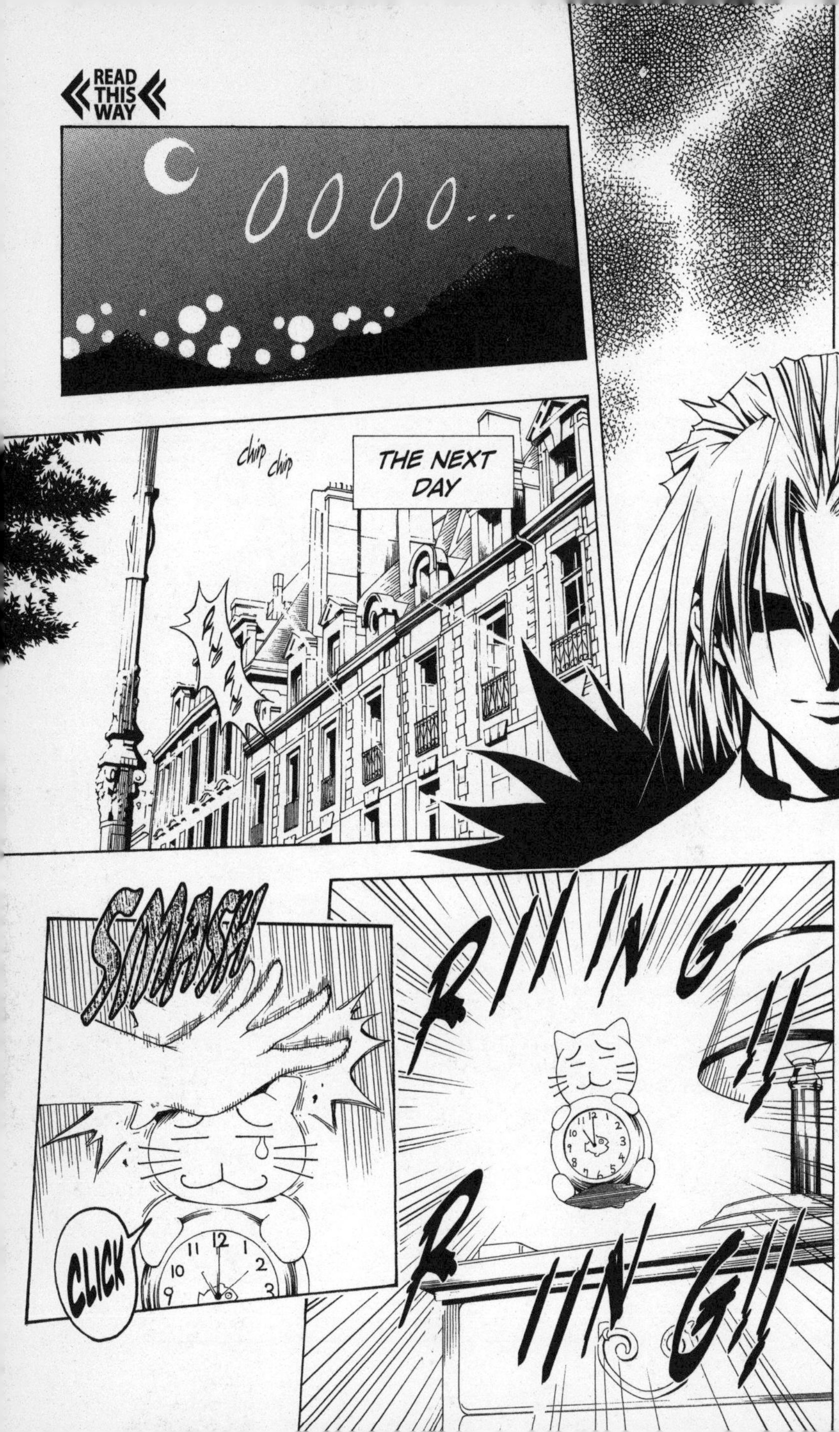
READ THIS WAY
Oooo...
THE NEXT DAY
chirp chirp
RIIING!!
RIIING!!
SMASH
CLICK

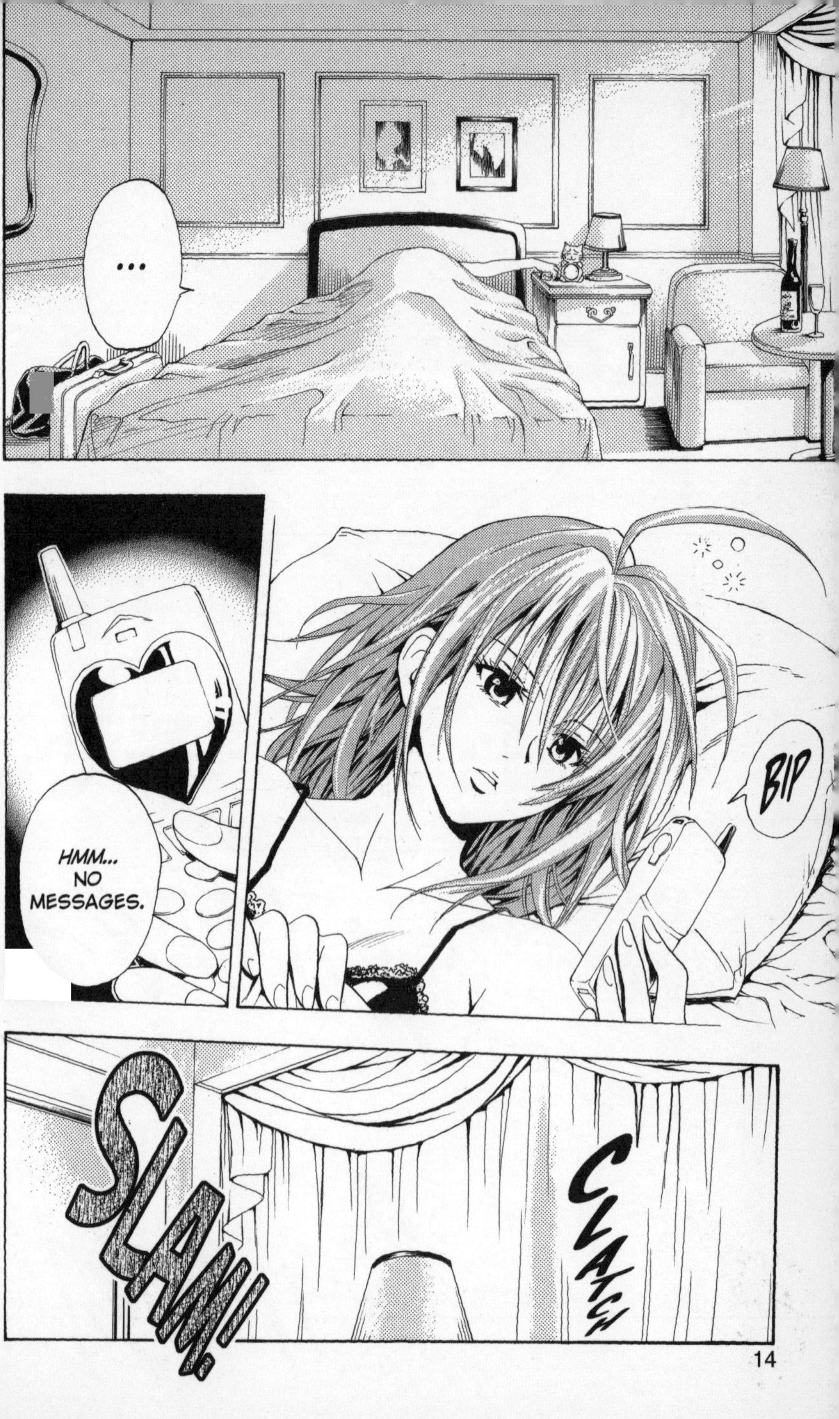
...
BIP
HMM... NO MESSAGES.
CLATCH
SLAM!!

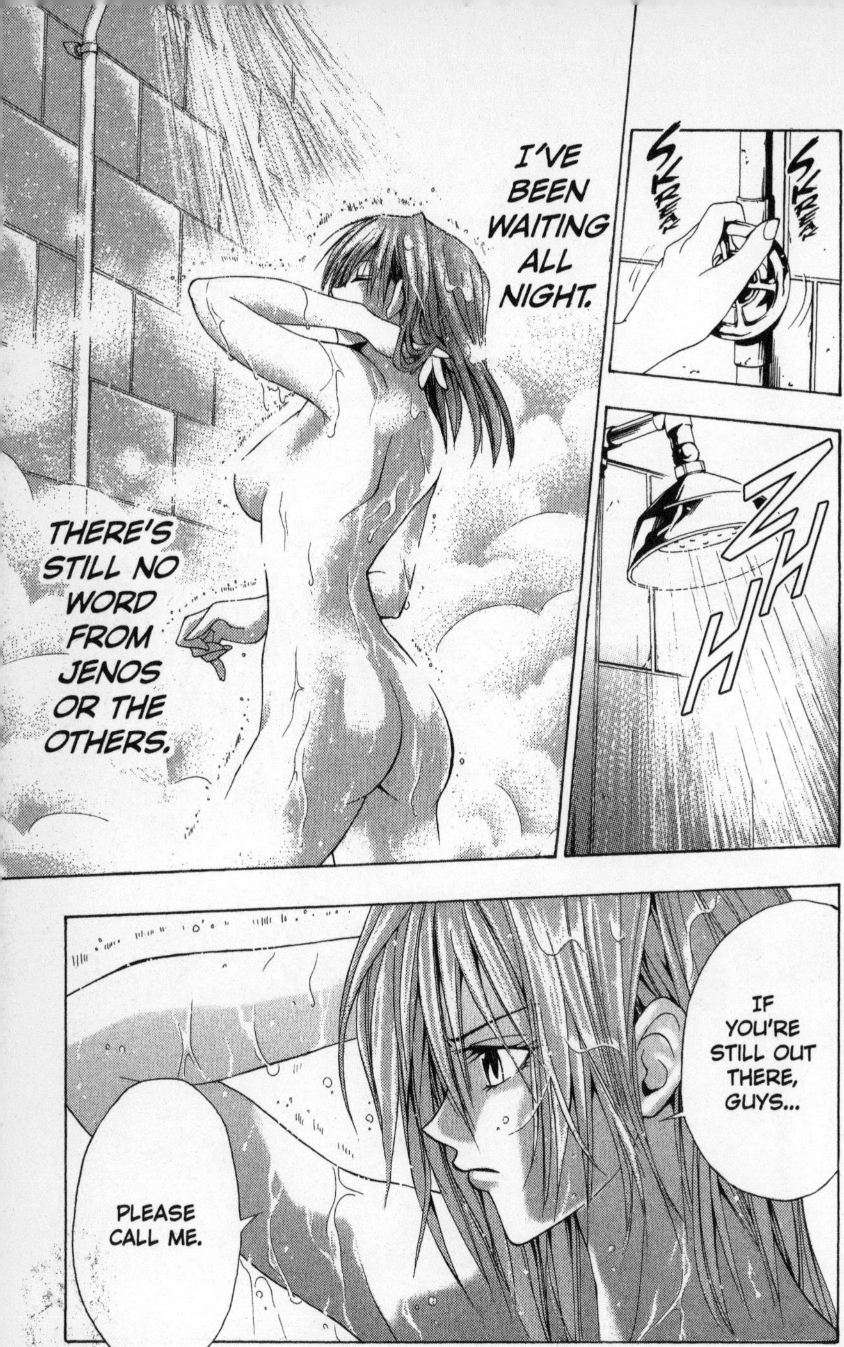
SKREE
SKREE
ZHHHH
I'VE BEEN WAITING ALL NIGHT.
THERE'S STILL NO WORD FROM JENOS OR THE OTHERS.
IF YOU'RE STILL OUT THERE, GUYS...
PLEASE CALL ME.

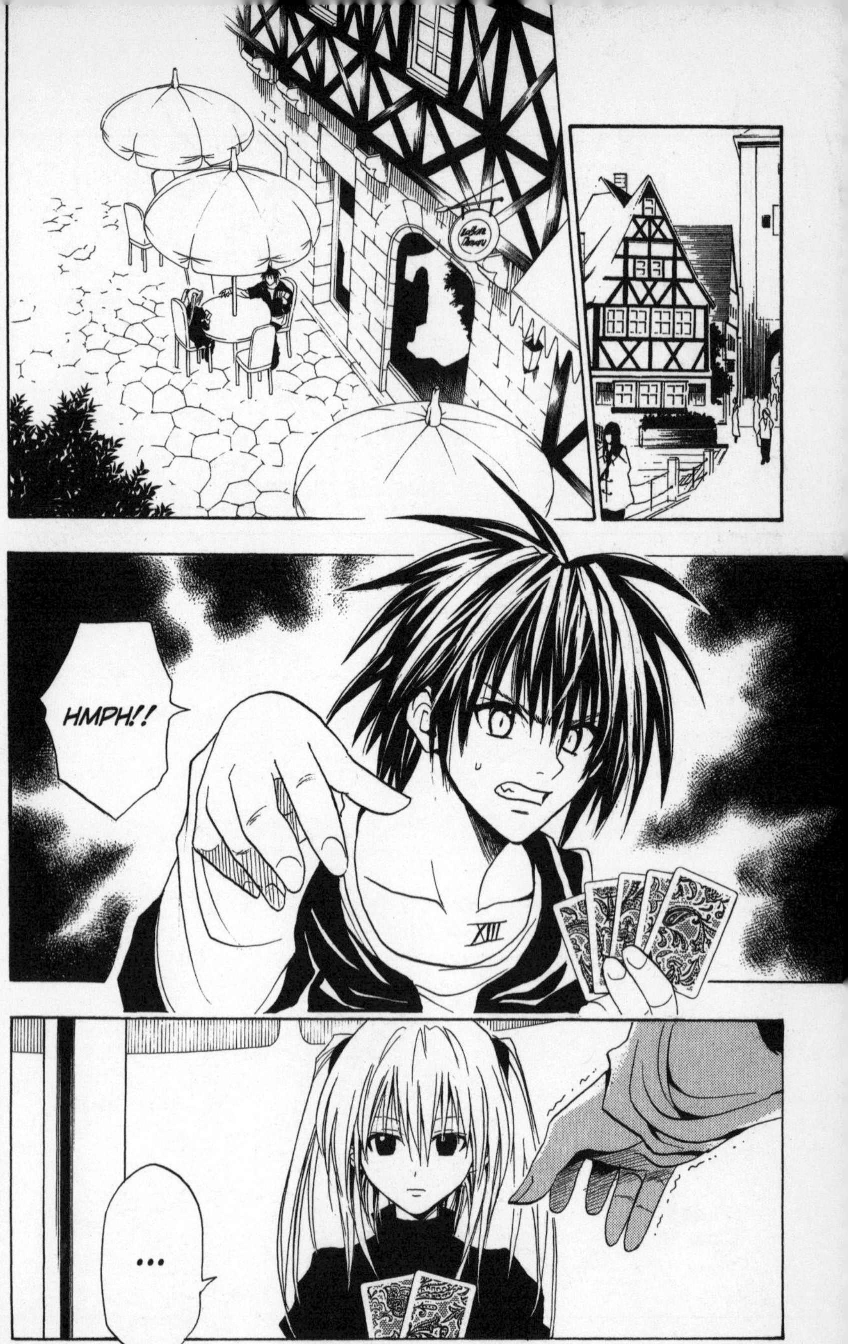
HMPH!!
...

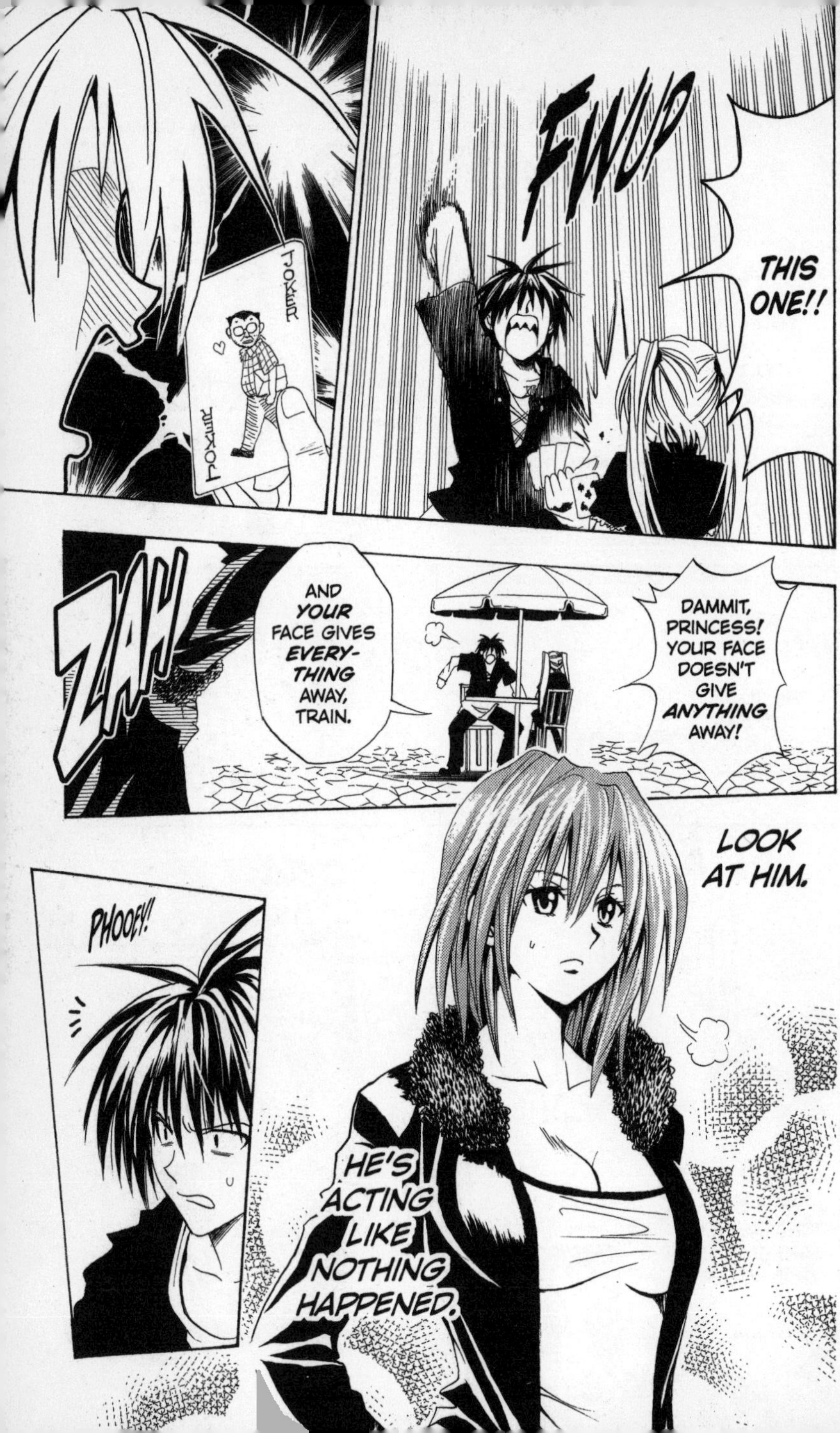

FWUP
THIS ONE!!
JOKER
JOKER
DAMMIT, PRINCESS! YOUR FACE DOESN'T GIVE ANYTHING AWAY!
AND YOUR FACE GIVES EVERYTHING AWAY, TRAIN.
ZAH
LOOK AT HIM.
HE'S ACTING LIKE NOTHING HAPPENED.
PHOOEY!

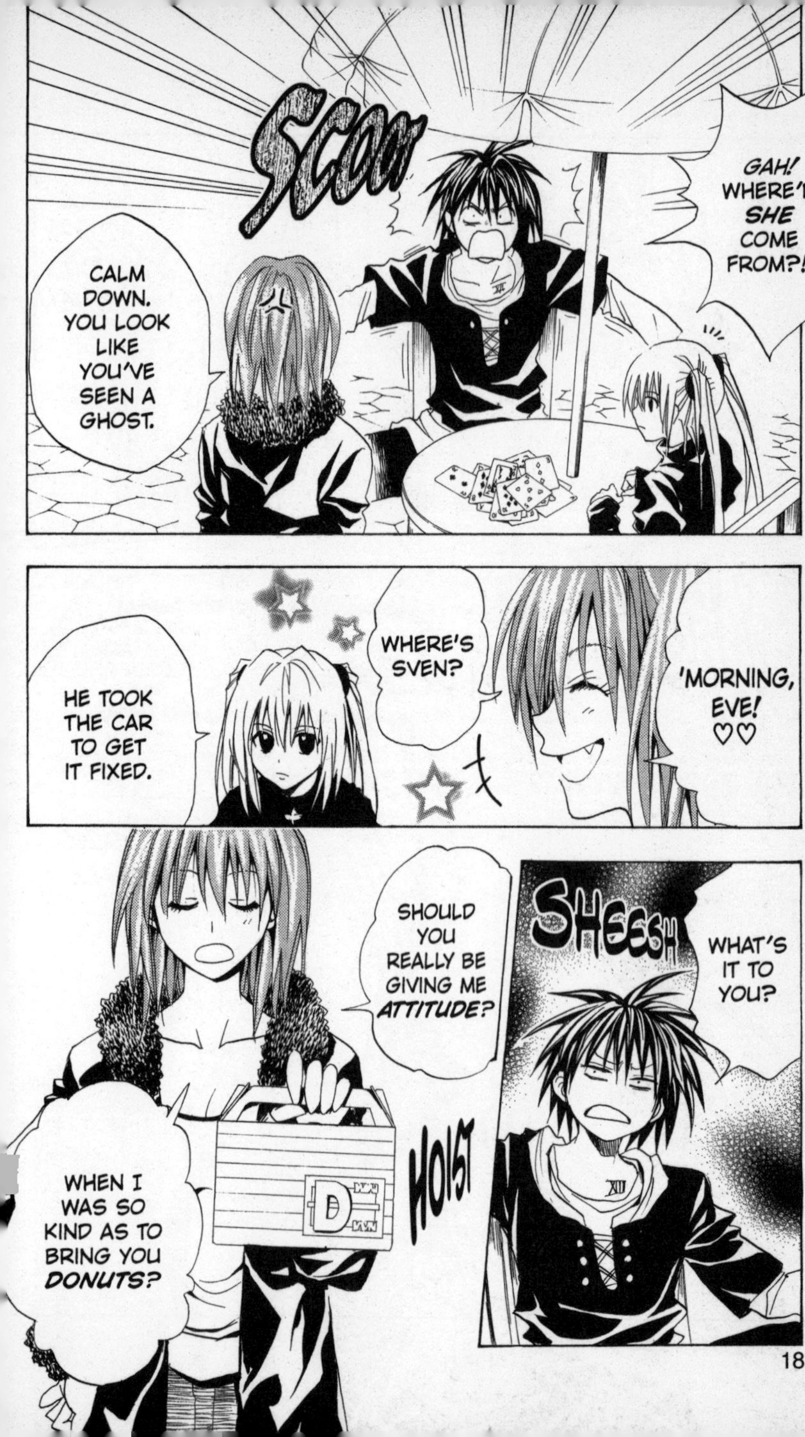
SCOM
GAH! WHERE'D SHE COME FROM?!
CALM DOWN. YOU LOOK LIKE YOU'VE SEEN A GHOST.
'MORNING, EVE! ♡♡
WHERE'S SVEN?
HE TOOK THE CAR TO GET IT FIXED.
SHEESH
WHAT'S IT TO YOU?
SHOULD YOU REALLY BE GIVING ME ATTITUDE?
HOIST
WHEN I WAS SO KIND AS TO BRING YOU DONUTS?

READ THIS WAY

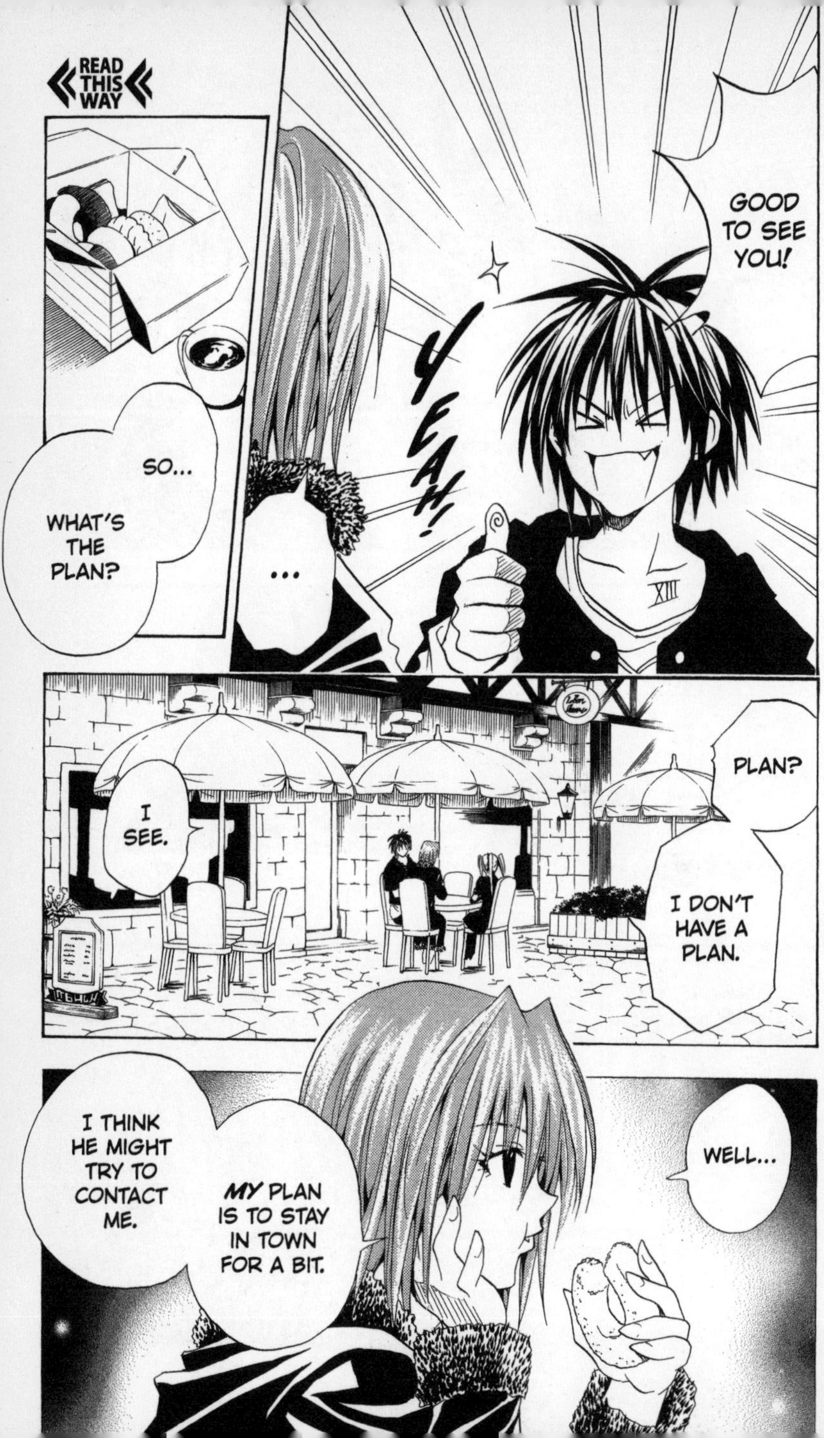
GOOD TO SEE YOU!
YEAH!
...
SO...
WHAT'S THE PLAN?
PLAN?
I DON'T HAVE A PLAN.
I SEE.
WELL...
MY PLAN IS TO STAY IN TOWN FOR A BIT.
I THINK HE MIGHT TRY TO CONTACT ME.

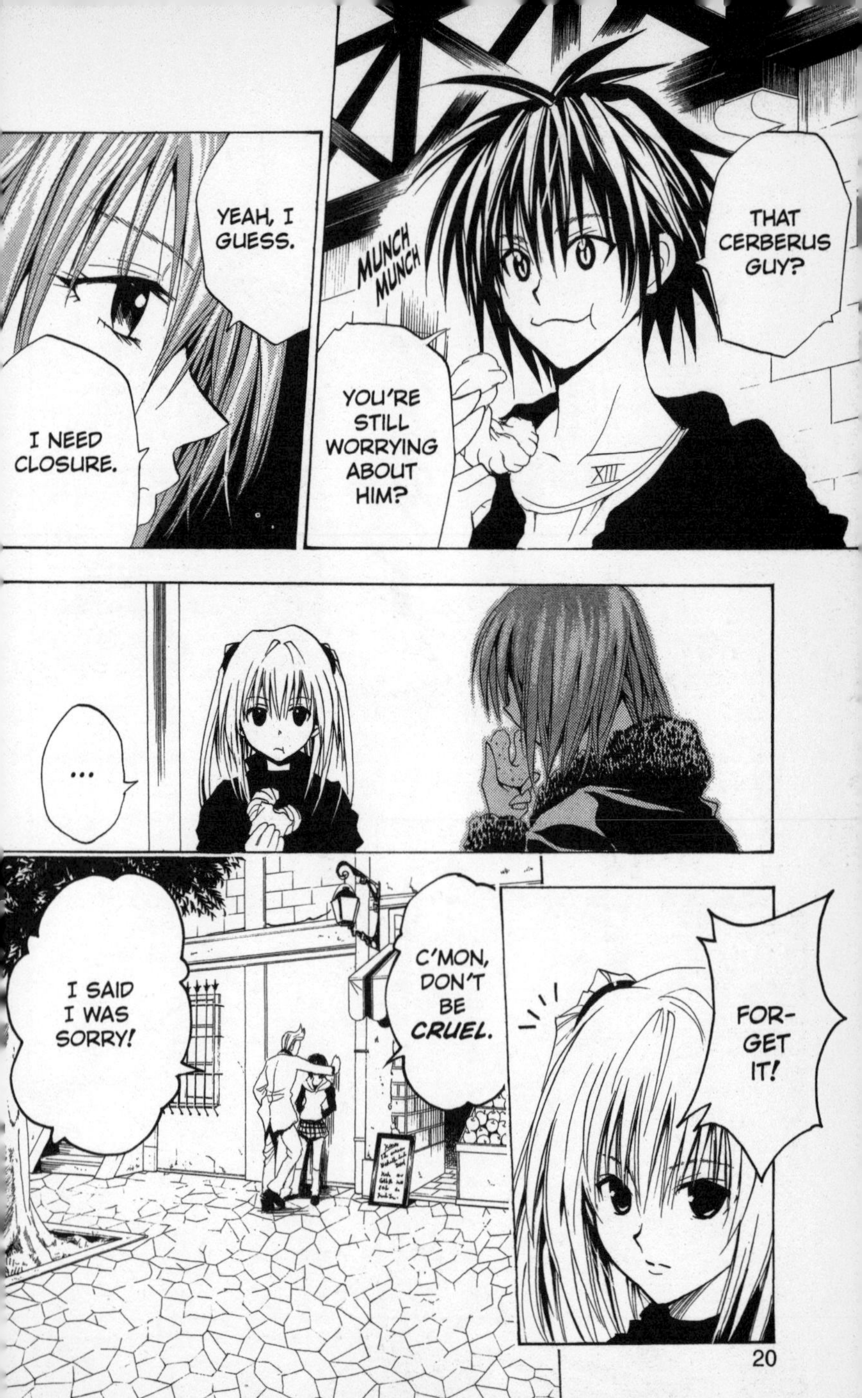
THAT CERBERUS GUY?
MUNCH MUNCH
YOU'RE STILL WORRYING ABOUT HIM?
YEAH, I GUESS.
I NEED CLOSURE.
...
FOR-GET IT!
C'MON, DON'T BE CRUEL.
I SAID I WAS SORRY!

READ THIS WAY

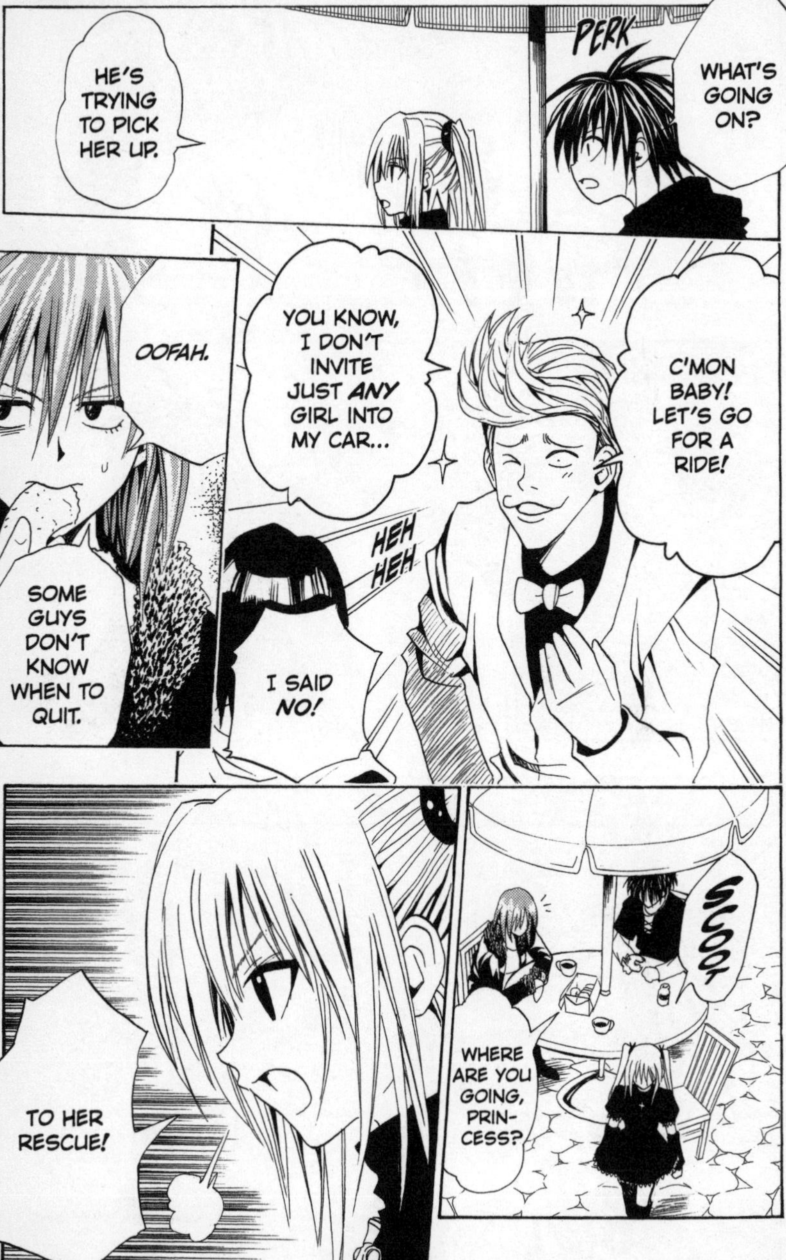
PERK
WHAT'S GOING ON?
HE'S TRYING TO PICK HER UP.
C'MON BABY! LET'S GO FOR A RIDE!
YOU KNOW, I DON'T INVITE JUST ANY GIRL INTO MY CAR...
HEH HEH
I SAID NO!
OOFAH.
SOME GUYS DON'T KNOW WHEN TO QUIT.
SCOOT
WHERE ARE YOU GOING, PRINCESS?
TO HER RESCUE!

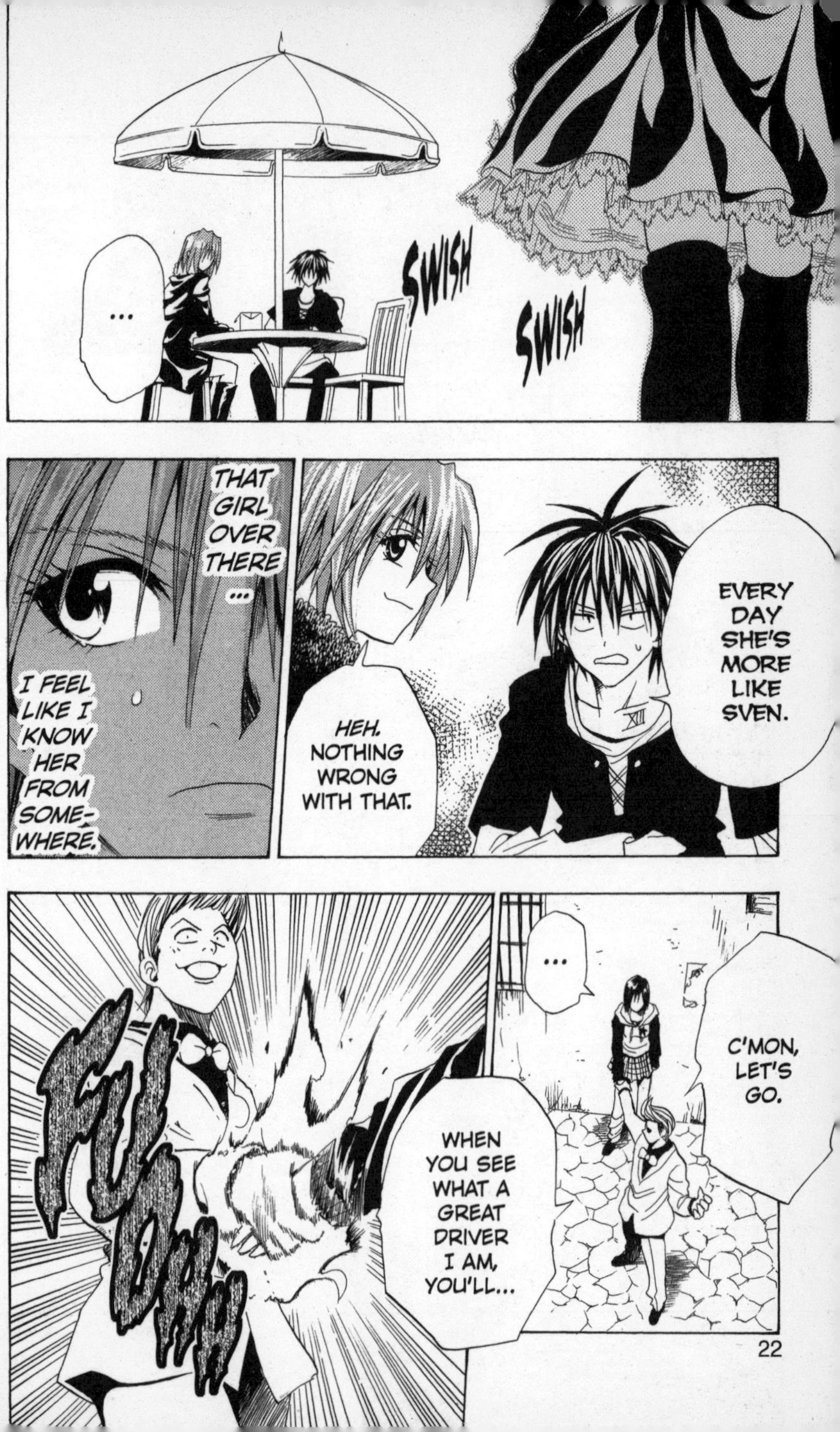
SWISH
SWISH
...
EVERY DAY SHE'S MORE LIKE SVEN.
HEH. NOTHING WRONG WITH THAT.
THAT GIRL OVER THERE...
I FEEL LIKE I KNOW HER FROM SOME-WHERE.
C'MON, LET'S GO.
...
WHEN YOU SEE WHAT A GREAT DRIVER I AM, YOU'LL...

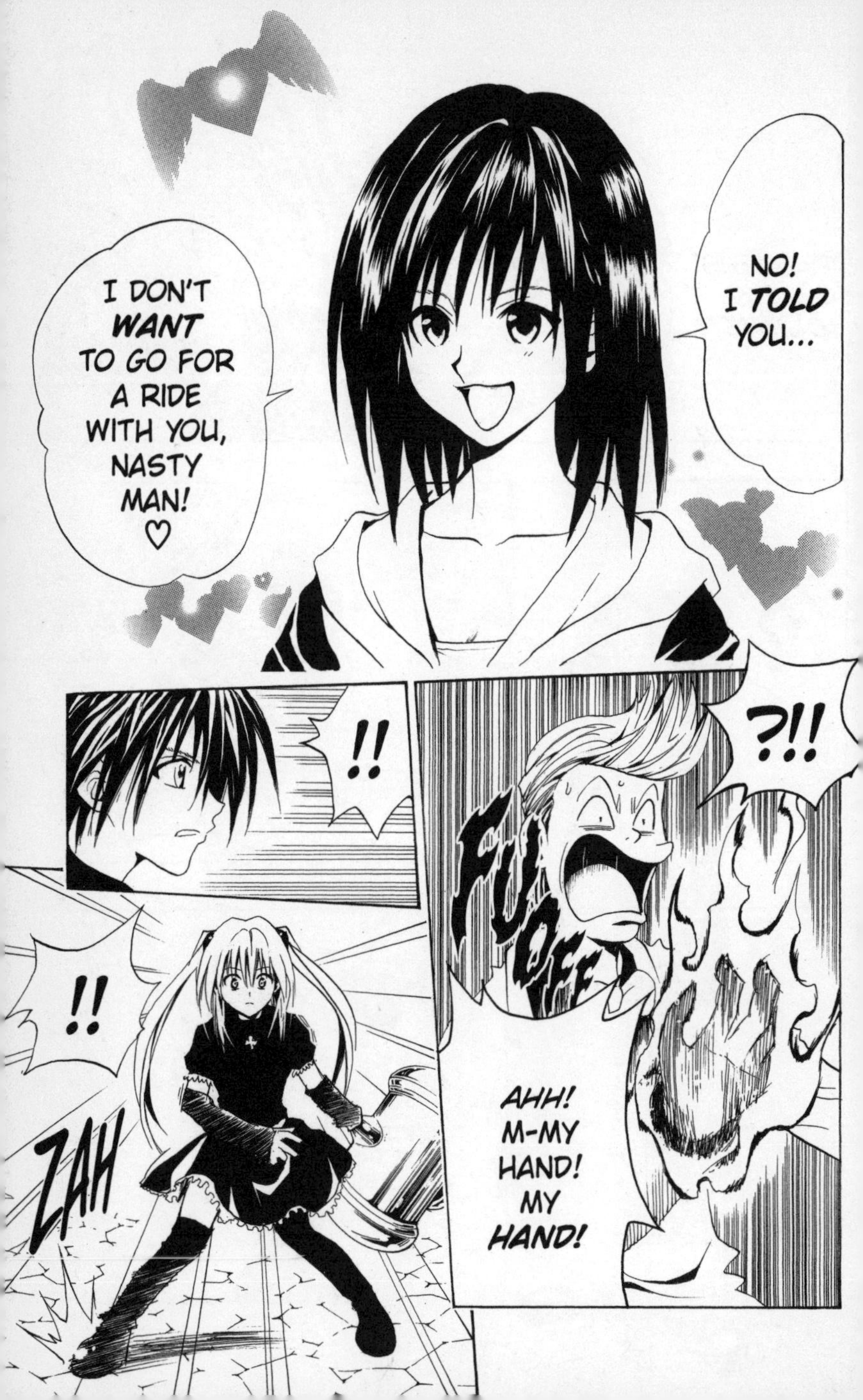
NO! I *TOLD* YOU...
I DON'T *WANT* TO GO FOR A RIDE WITH YOU, NASTY MAN! ♡
?!!
FUOFF
AHH! M-MY HAND! MY *HAND!*
!!
!!
ZAH

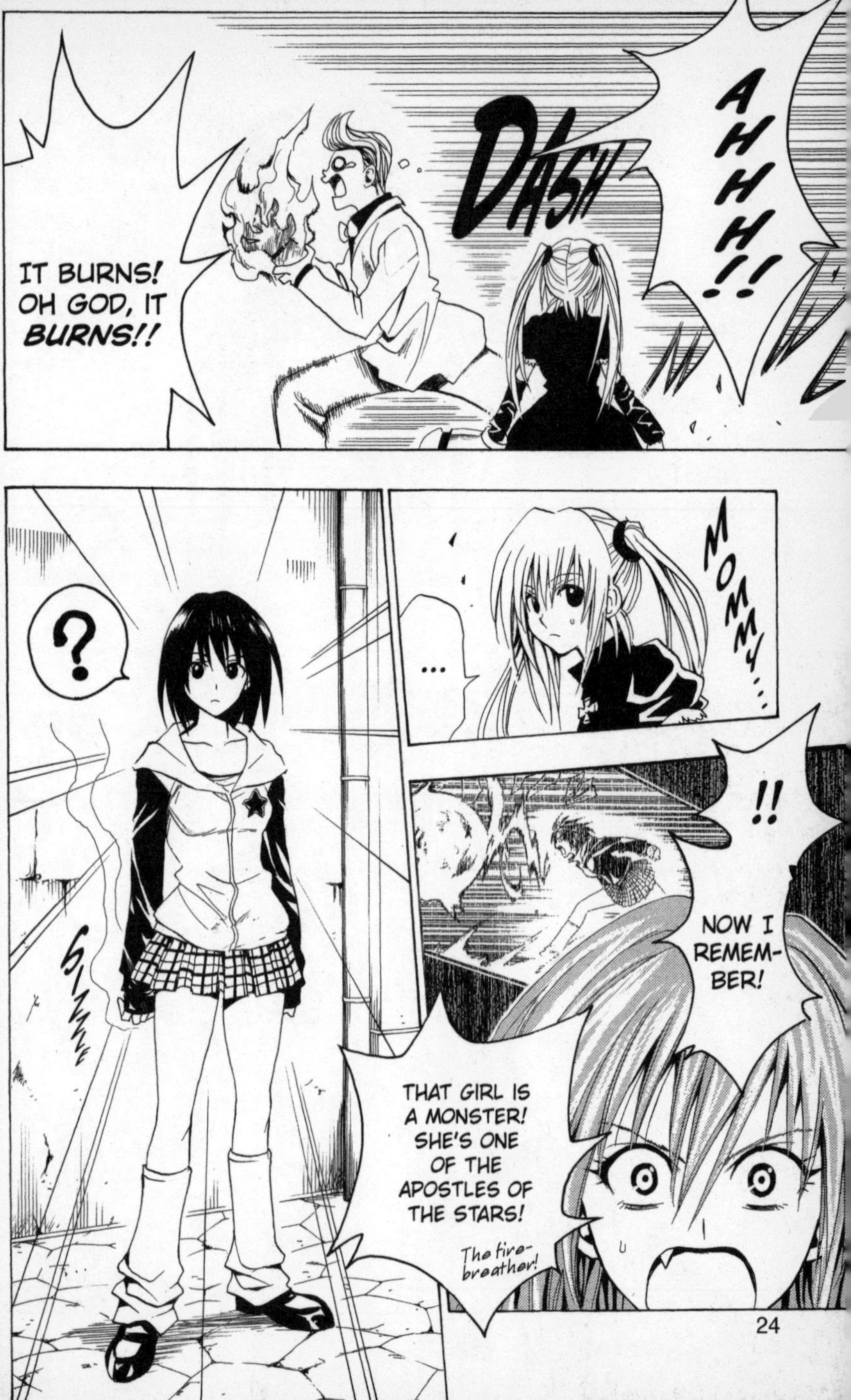
AHHHH!!
DASH
IT BURNS! OH GOD, IT BURNS!!
MOMMY...
...
!!
NOW I REMEMBER!
THAT GIRL IS A MONSTER! SHE'S ONE OF THE APOSTLES OF THE STARS!
The fire-breather!
?
SIZZZZ

READ THIS WAY

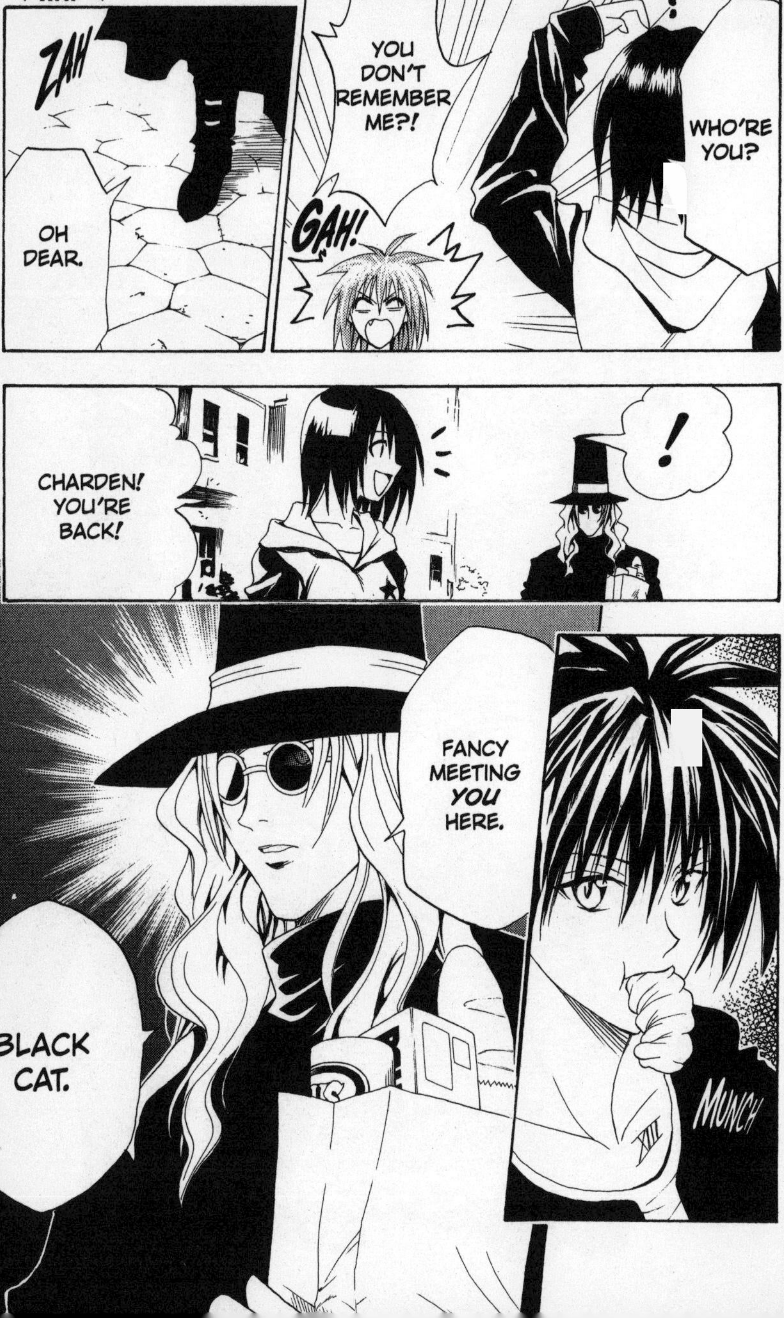
?
WHO'RE YOU?
YOU DON'T REMEMBER ME?!
GAH!
ZAH
OH DEAR.
!
CHARDEN! YOU'RE BACK!
FANCY MEETING YOU HERE.
MUNCH
BLACK CAT.

SKETCHES: PART 1

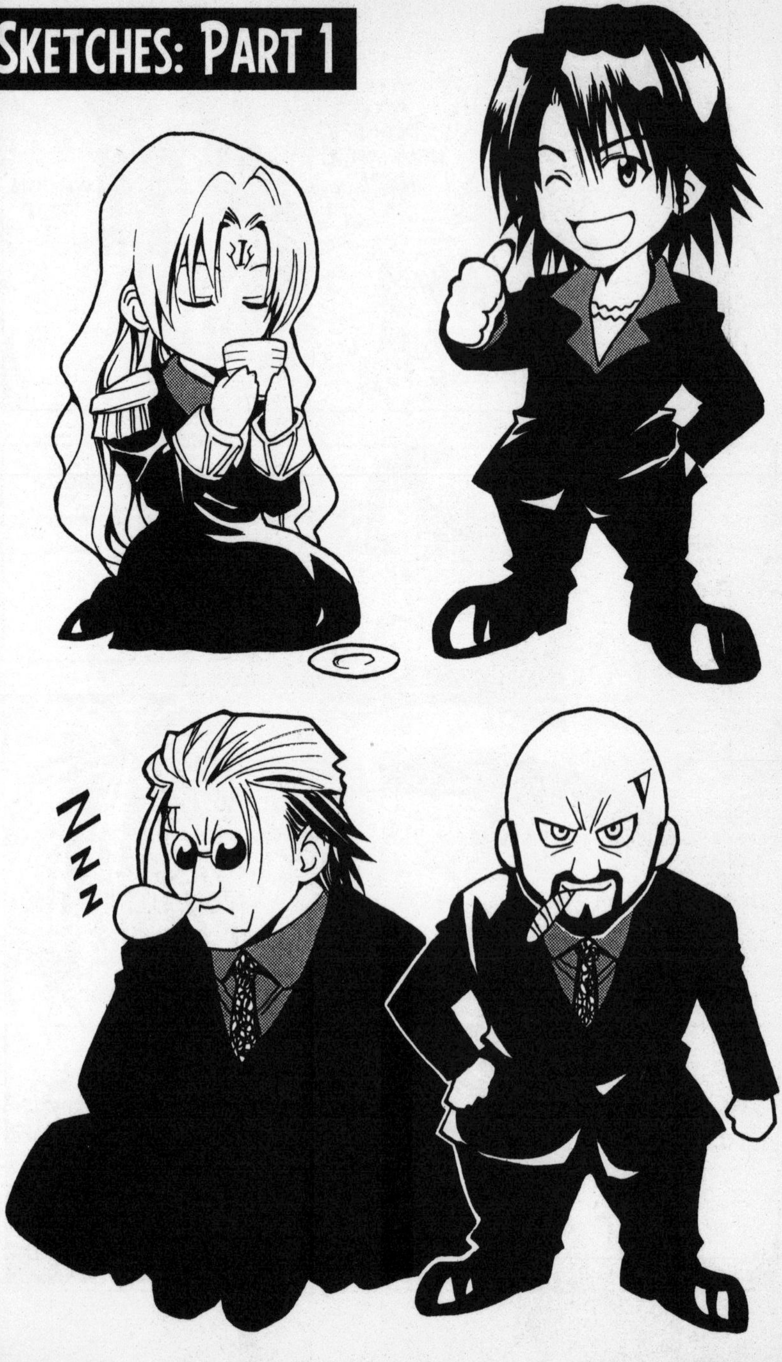
NNN

Chapter 86: Kyoko's Crush

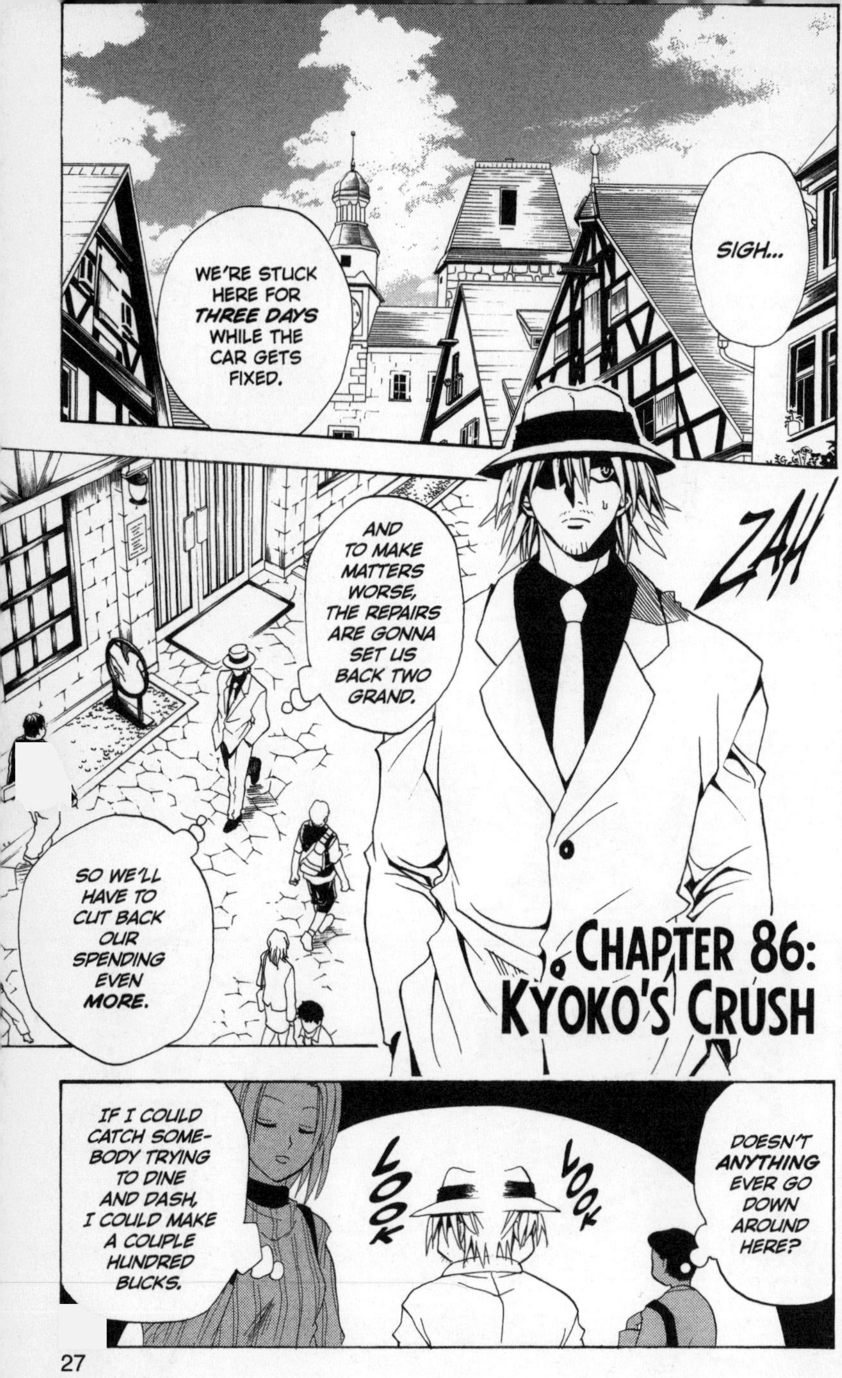
SIGH...
WE'RE STUCK HERE FOR THREE DAYS WHILE THE CAR GETS FIXED.
ZAH
AND TO MAKE MATTERS WORSE, THE REPAIRS ARE GONNA SET US BACK TWO GRAND.
SO WE'LL HAVE TO CUT BACK OUR SPENDING EVEN MORE.
CHAPTER 86: KYOKO'S CRUSH
DOESN'T ANYTHING EVER GO DOWN AROUND HERE?
VOOK
LOOK
IF I COULD CATCH SOMEBODY TRYING TO DINE AND DASH, I COULD MAKE A COUPLE HUNDRED BUCKS.

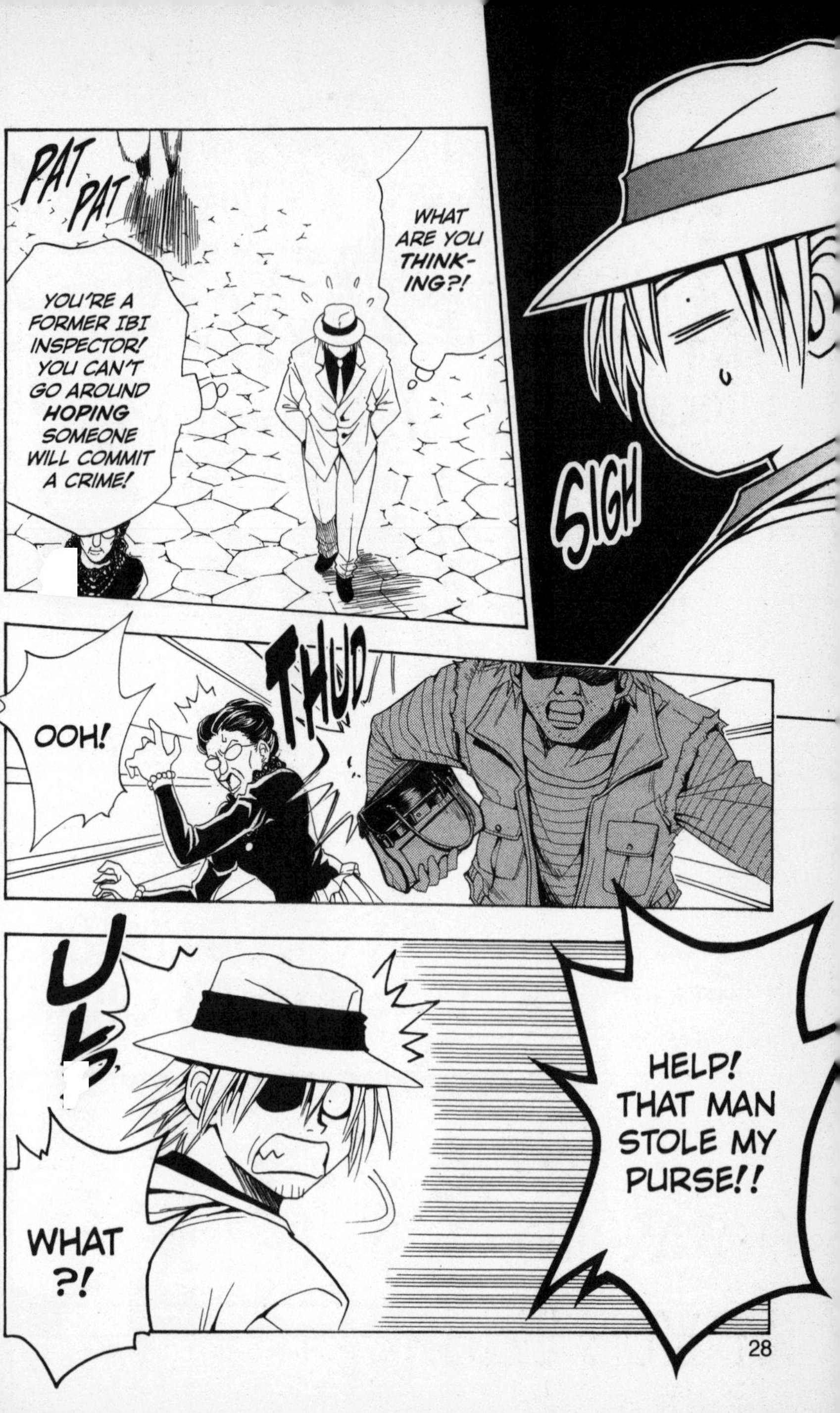

SIGH
PAT PAT
WHAT ARE YOU THINKING?!
YOU'RE A FORMER IBI INSPECTOR! YOU CAN'T GO AROUND **HOPING** SOMEONE WILL COMMIT A CRIME!
THUD
OOH!
HELP! THAT MAN STOLE MY PURSE!!
WHAT ?!

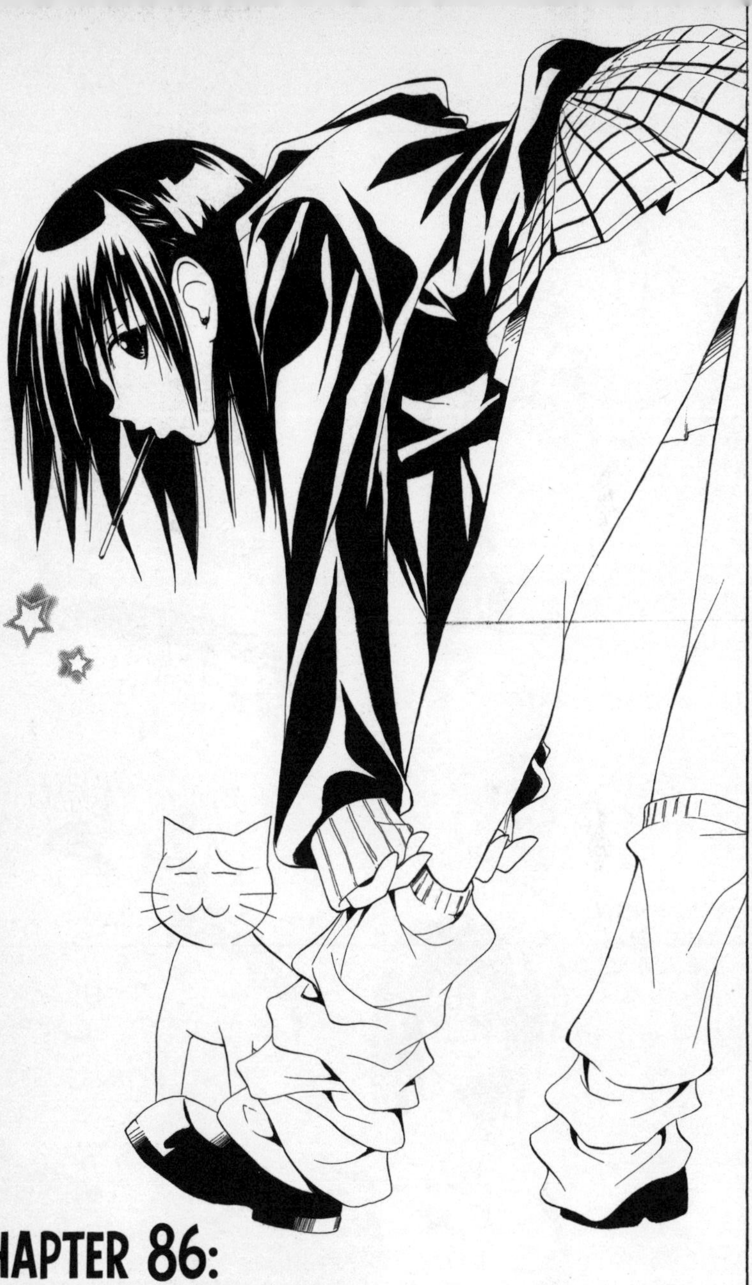

Chapter 86:
Kyoko's Crush

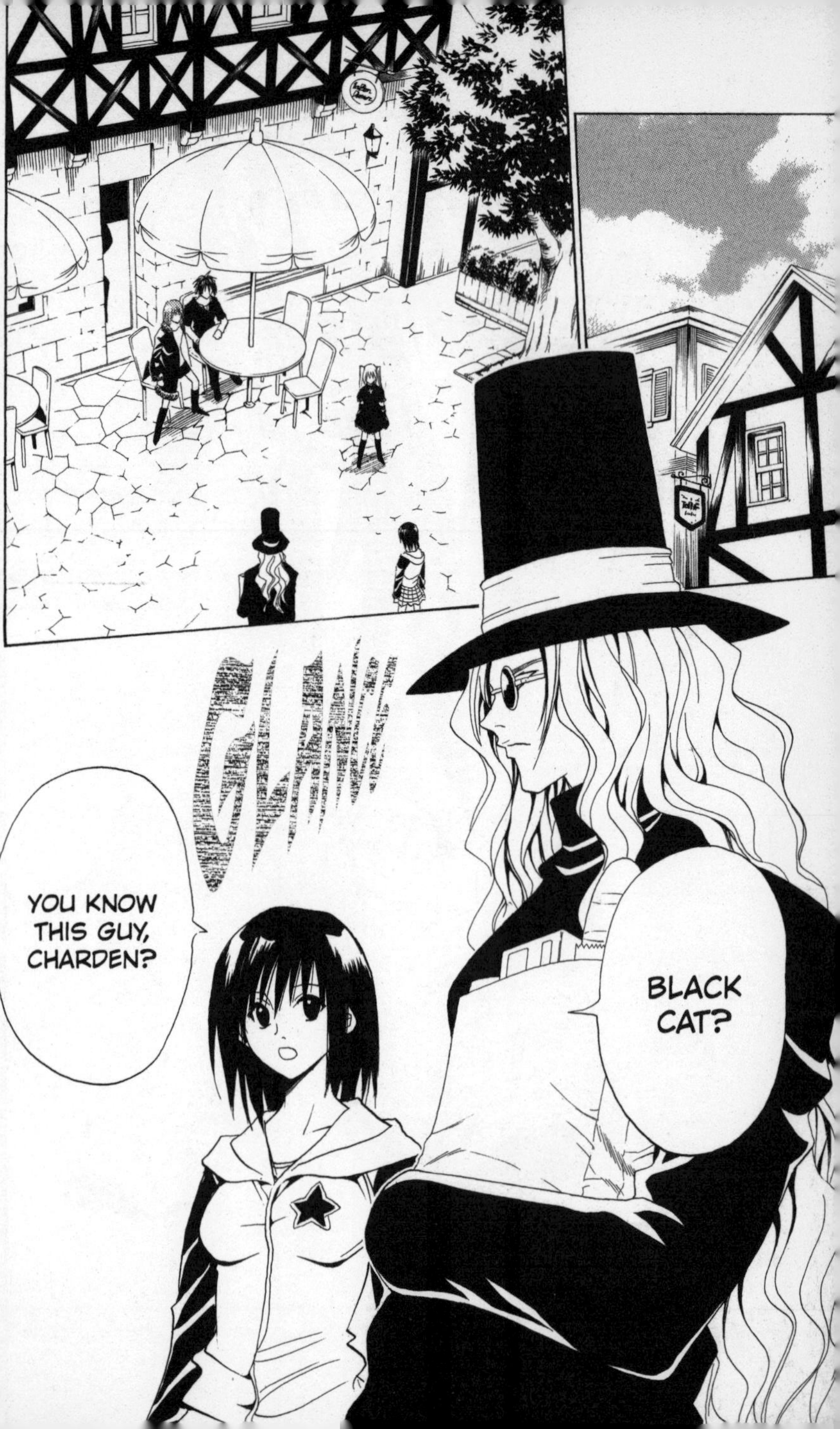
GLANCE
BLACK CAT?
YOU KNOW THIS GUY, CHARDEN?

READ THIS WAY

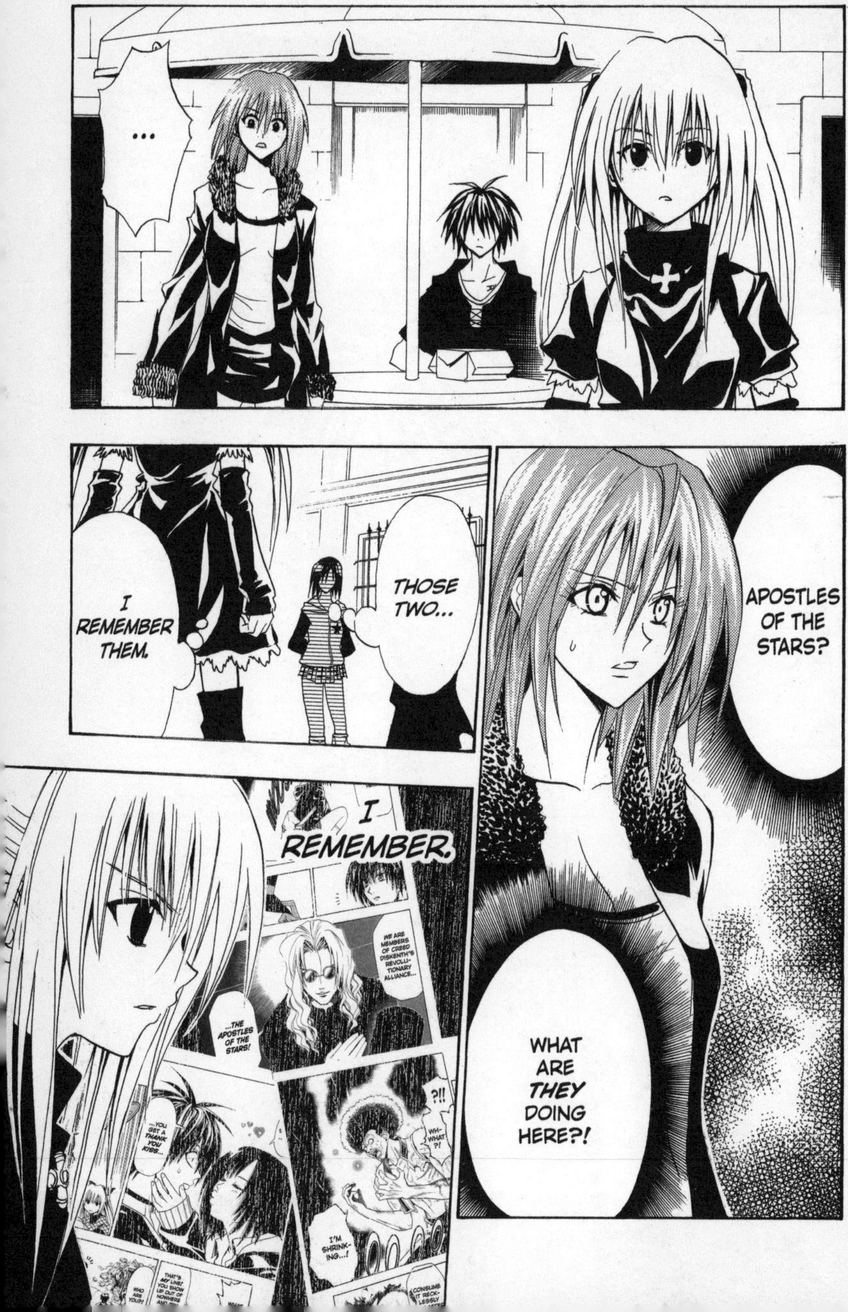
...
APOSTLES OF THE STARS?
WHAT ARE *THEY* DOING HERE?!
THOSE TWO...
I REMEMBER THEM.
I REMEMBER.
WE ARE MEMBERS OF CREED DISKENTH'S REVOLU-TIONARY ALLIANCE...
...THE APOSTLES OF THE STARS!
?!!
WH-WHAT?!
I'M SHRINK-ING...!
CONSUME IT RECK-LESSLY
...YOU GET A *THANK YOU* KISS...
THAT'S *MY* LINE! YOU SHOW UP OUT OF NOWHERE
WHO ARE YOU?!

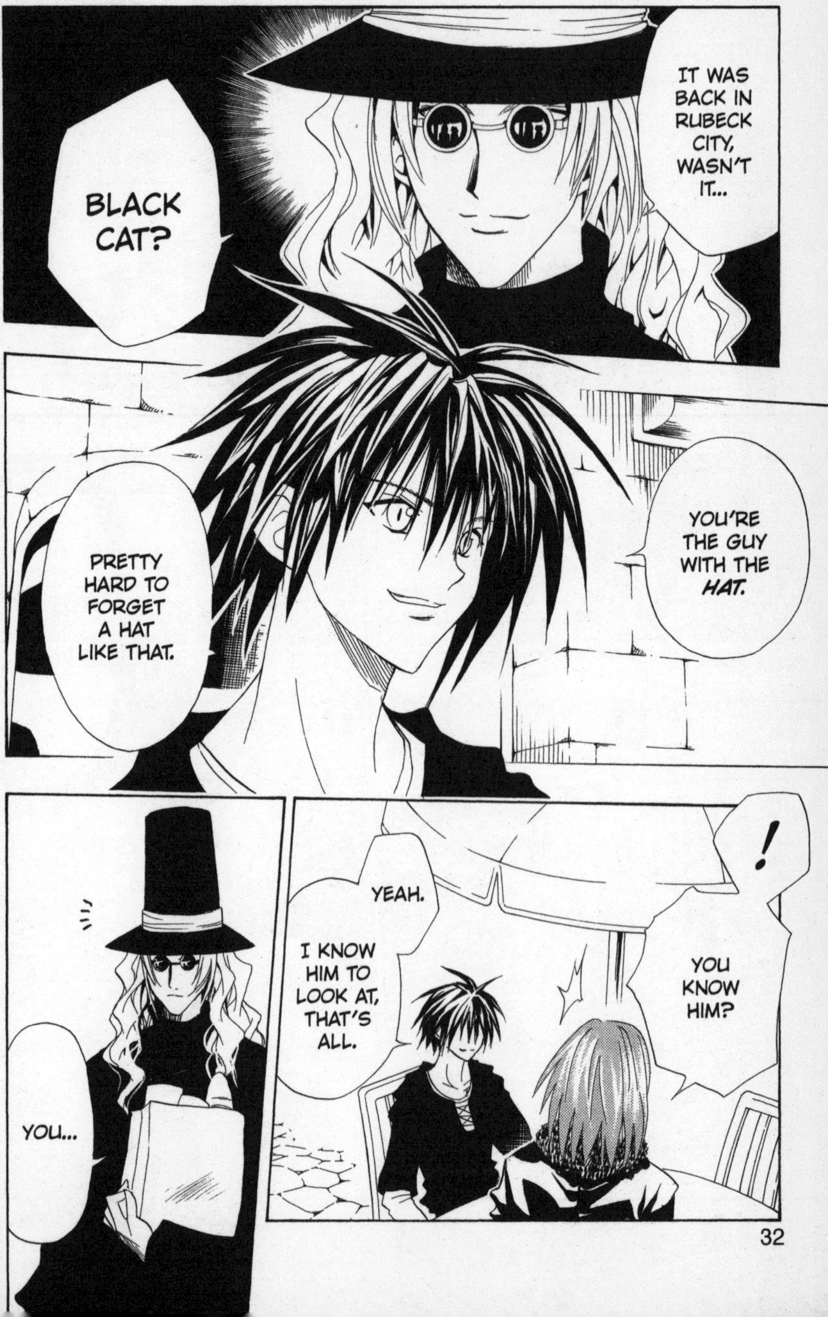
IT WAS BACK IN RUBECK CITY, WASN'T IT...
BLACK CAT?
YOU'RE THE GUY WITH THE *HAT.*
PRETTY HARD TO FORGET A HAT LIKE THAT.
!
YOU KNOW HIM?
YEAH.
I KNOW HIM TO LOOK AT, THAT'S ALL.
YOU...

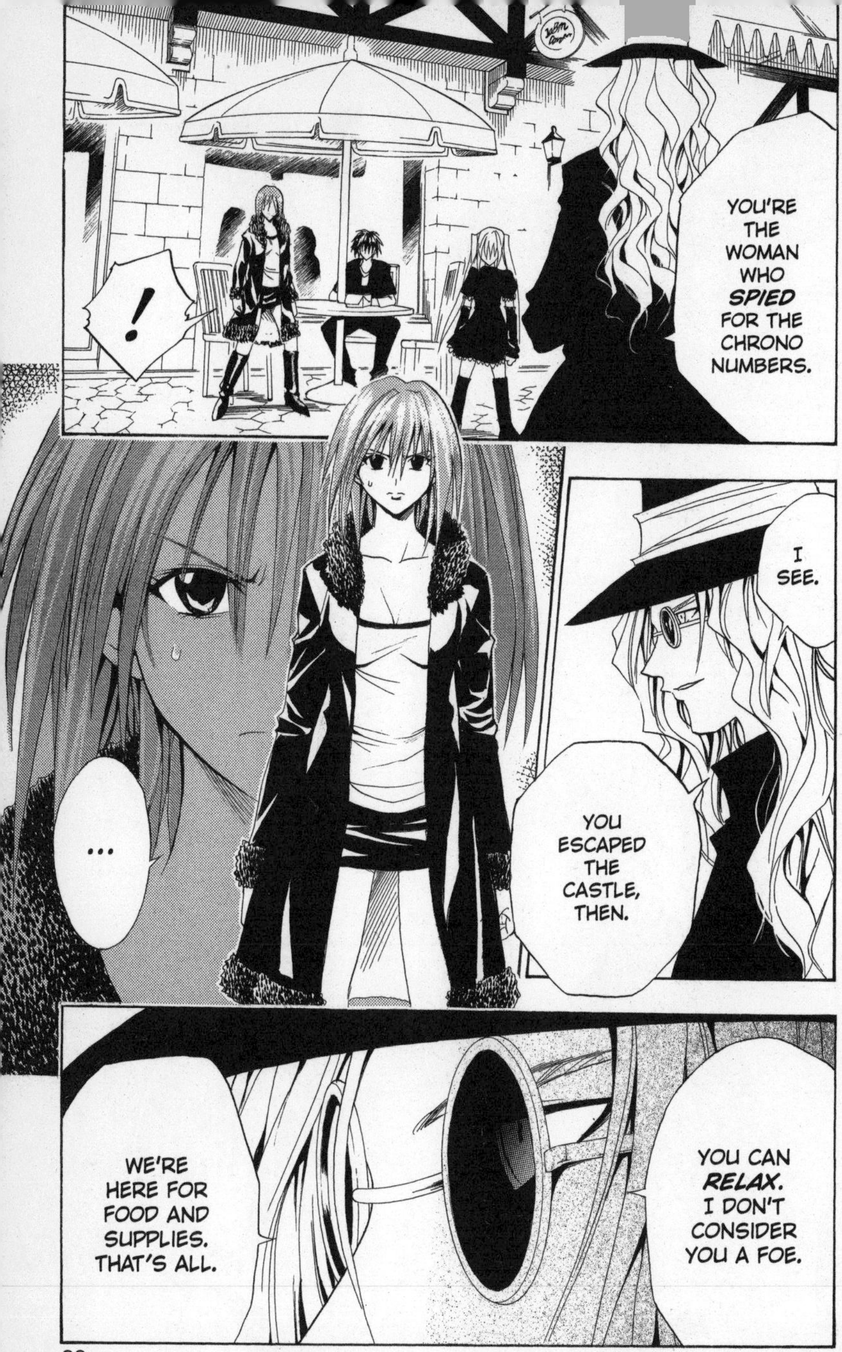
YOU'RE THE WOMAN WHO ***SPIED*** FOR THE CHRONO NUMBERS.
!
I SEE.
YOU ESCAPED THE CASTLE, THEN.
...
YOU CAN ***RELAX.*** I DON'T CONSIDER YOU A FOE.
WE'RE HERE FOR FOOD AND SUPPLIES. THAT'S ALL.

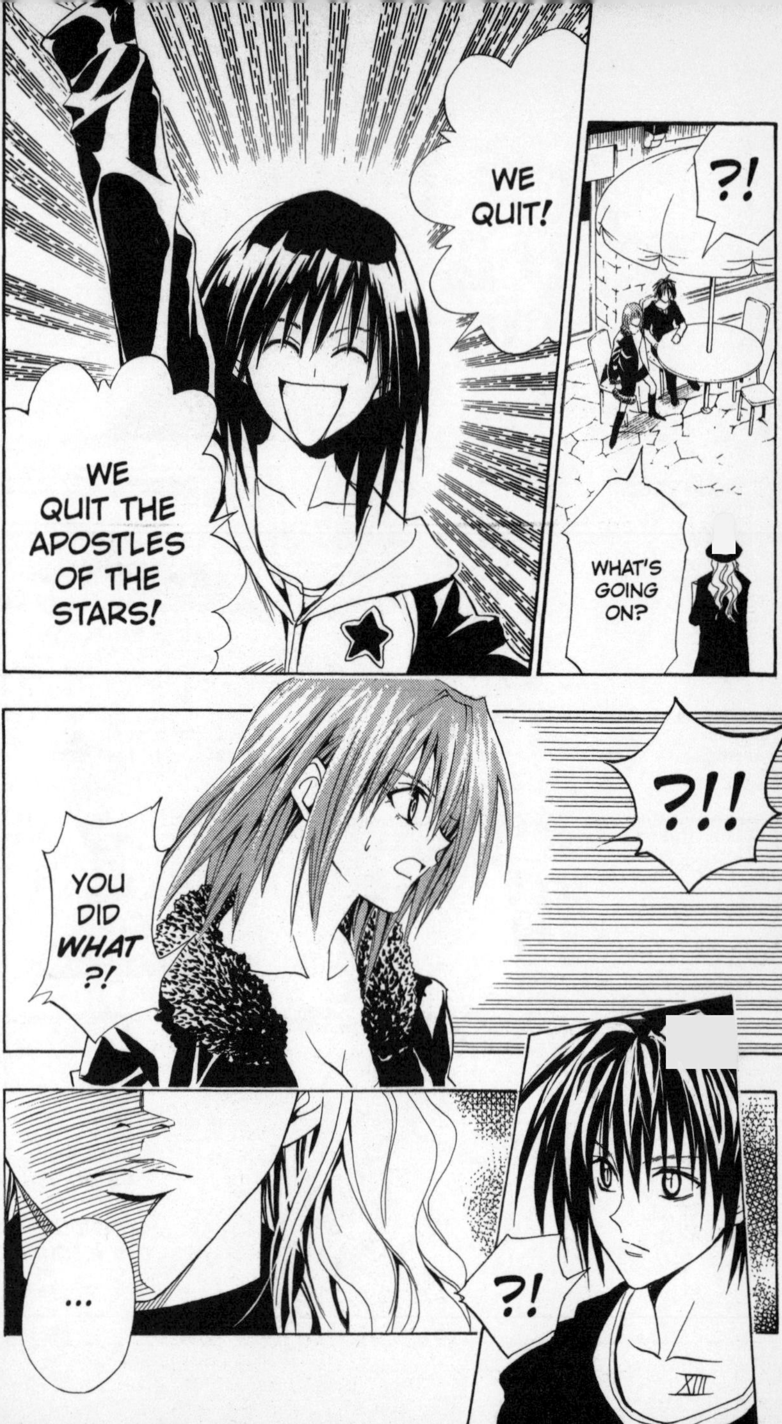
?!
WHAT'S GOING ON?
WE QUIT!
WE QUIT THE APOSTLES OF THE STARS!
?!!
YOU DID *WHAT* ?!
?!
...

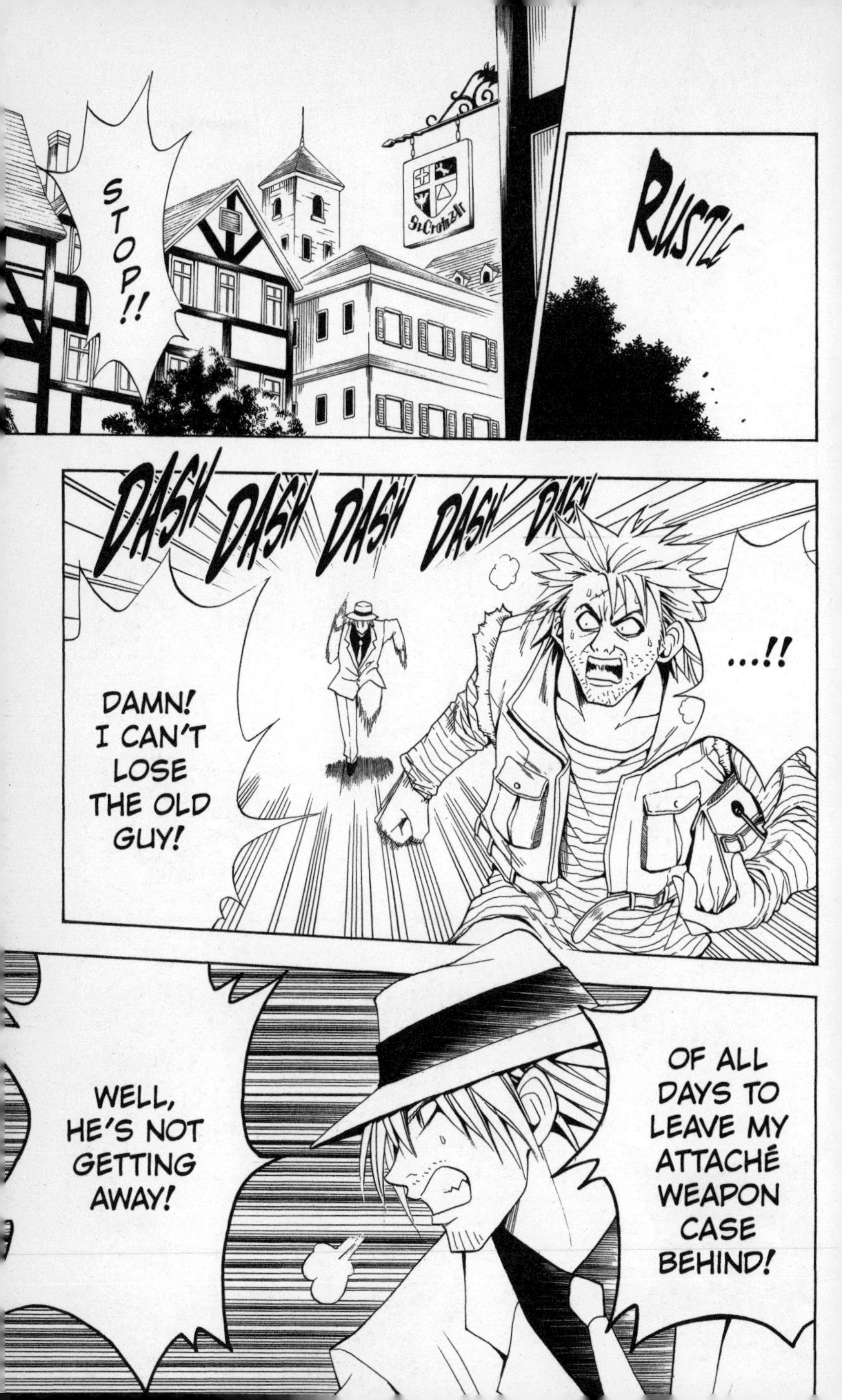

RUSTLE
STOP!!
DASH DASH DASH DASH DASH
...!!
DAMN! I CAN'T LOSE THE OLD GUY!
OF ALL DAYS TO LEAVE MY ATTACHÉ WEAPON CASE BEHIND!
WELL, HE'S NOT GETTING AWAY!

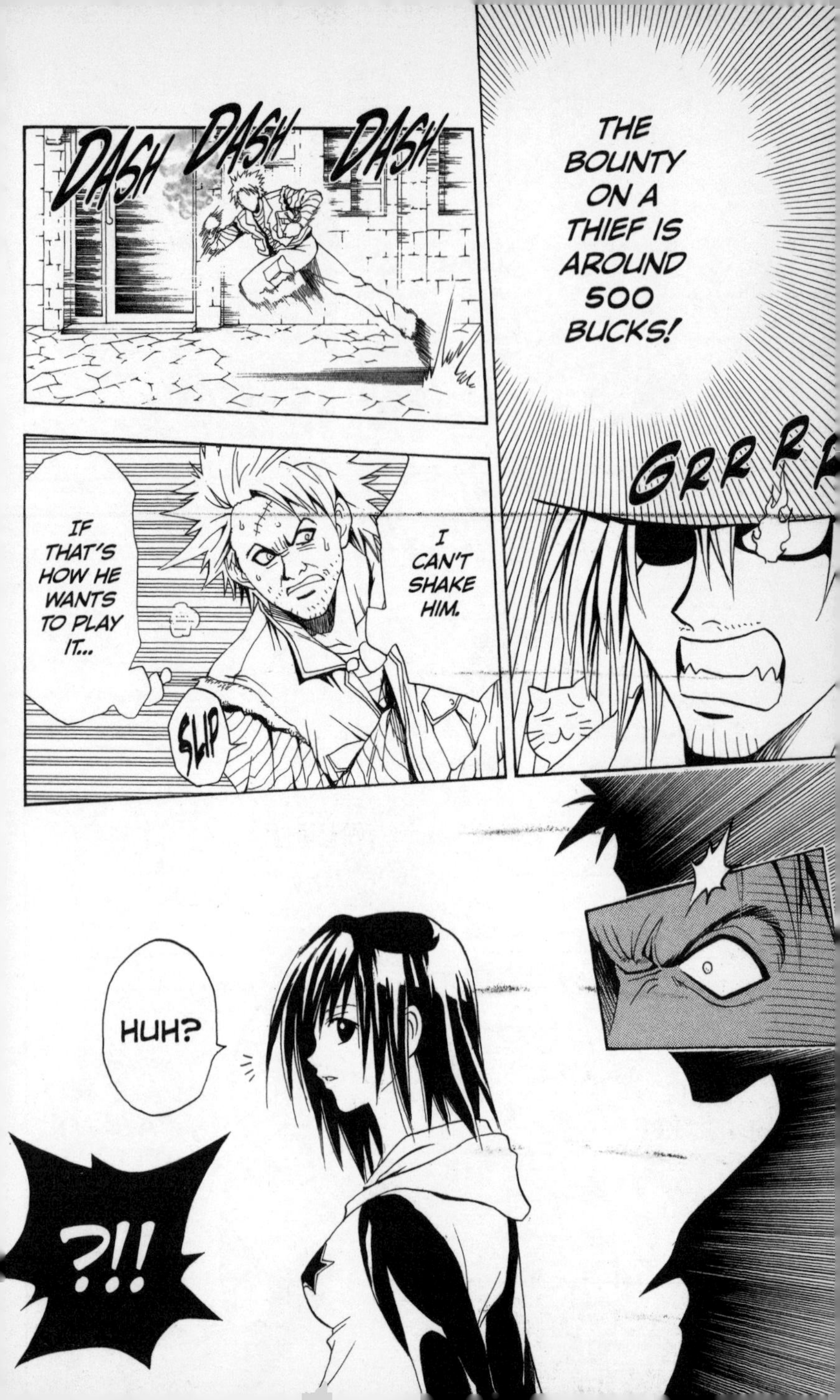
THE BOUNTY ON A THIEF IS AROUND 500 BUCKS!
GRRRR
DASH DASH DASH
I CAN'T SHAKE HIM.
IF THAT'S HOW HE WANTS TO PLAY IT...
SLIP
HUH?
?!!

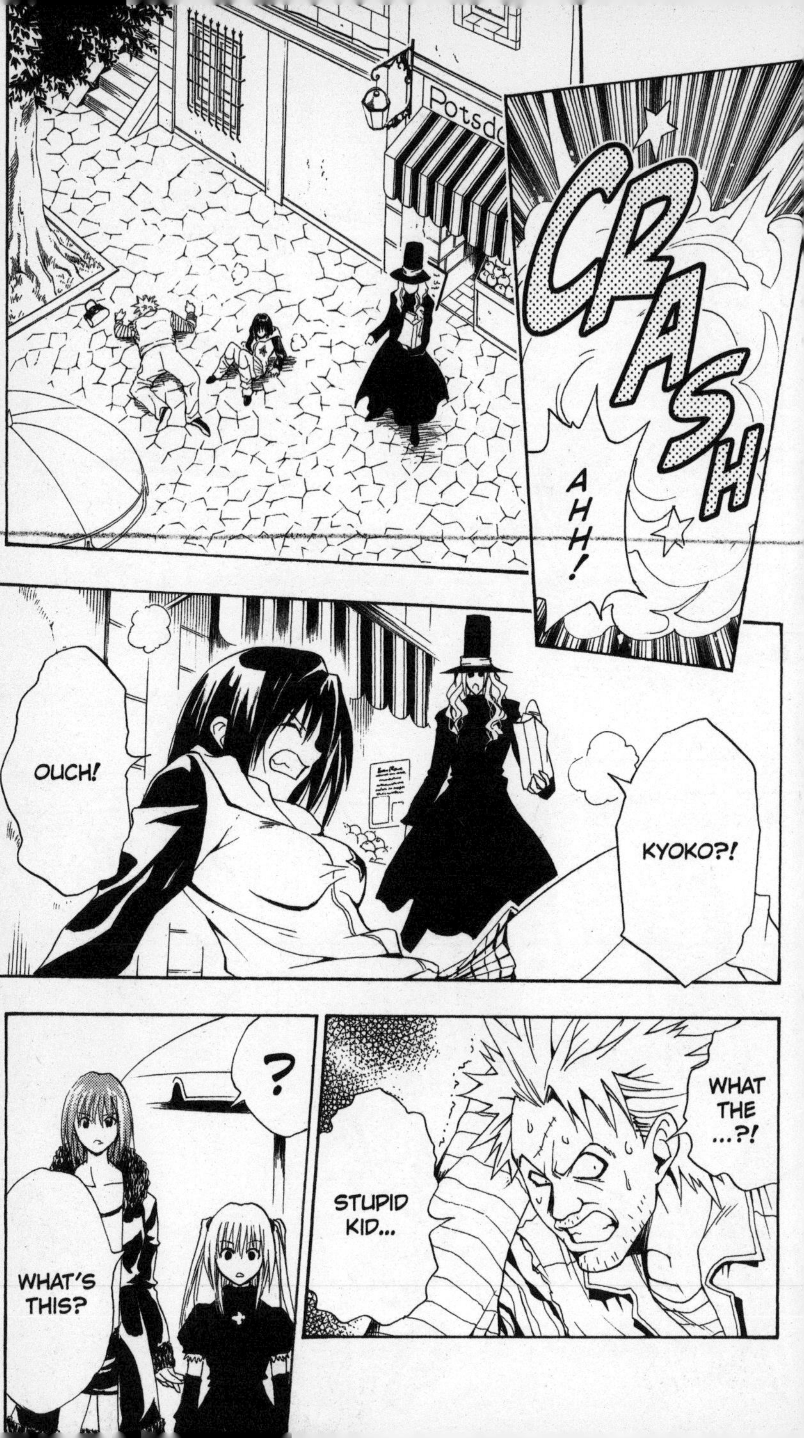
CRASH
AHH!
KYOKO?!
OUCH!
WHAT THE ...?!
STUPID KID...
?
WHAT'S THIS?

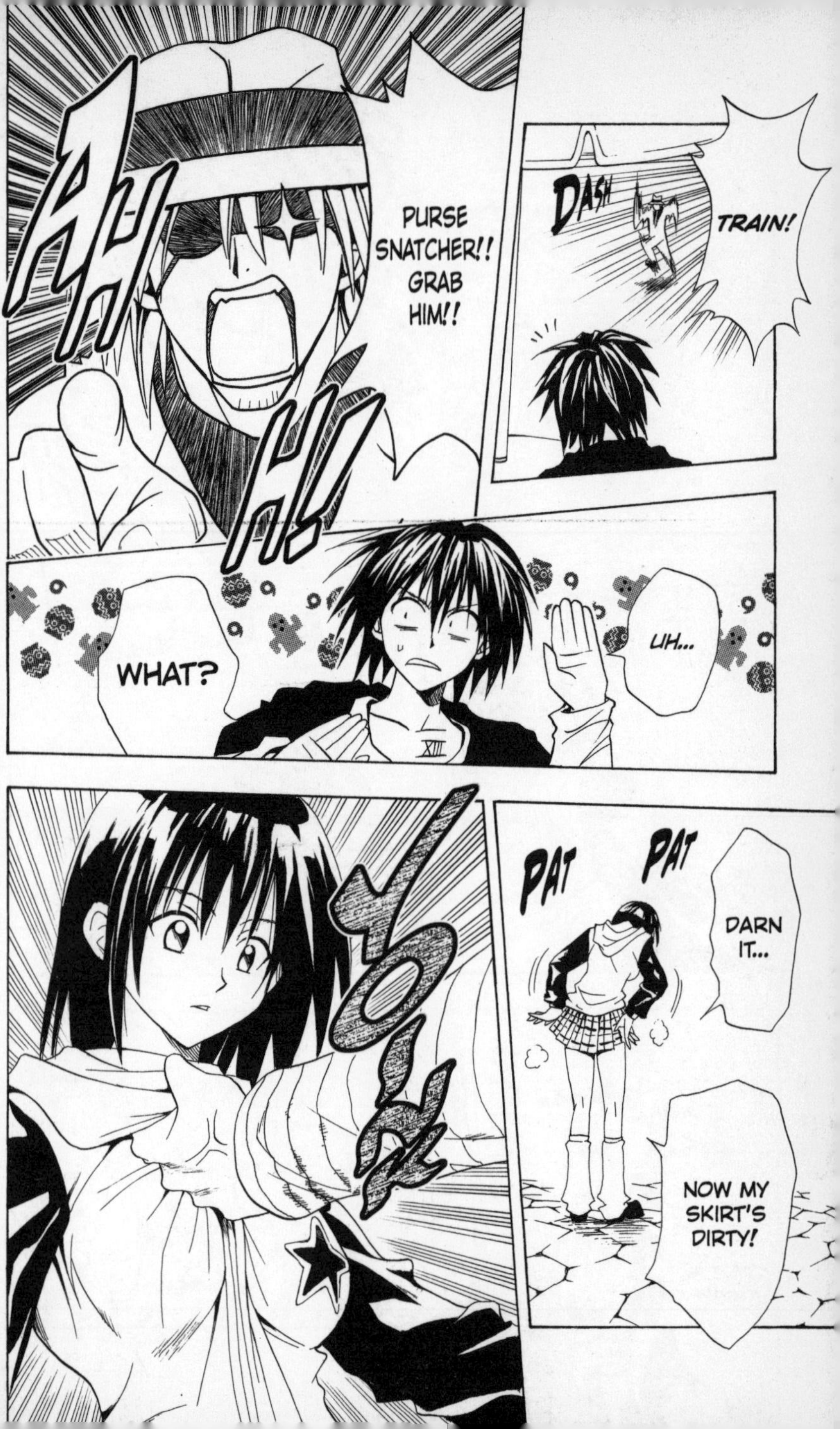
DASH
TRAIN!
PURSE SNATCHER!! GRAB HIM!!
UH...
WHAT?
PAT PAT
DARN IT...
NOW MY SKIRT'S DIRTY!

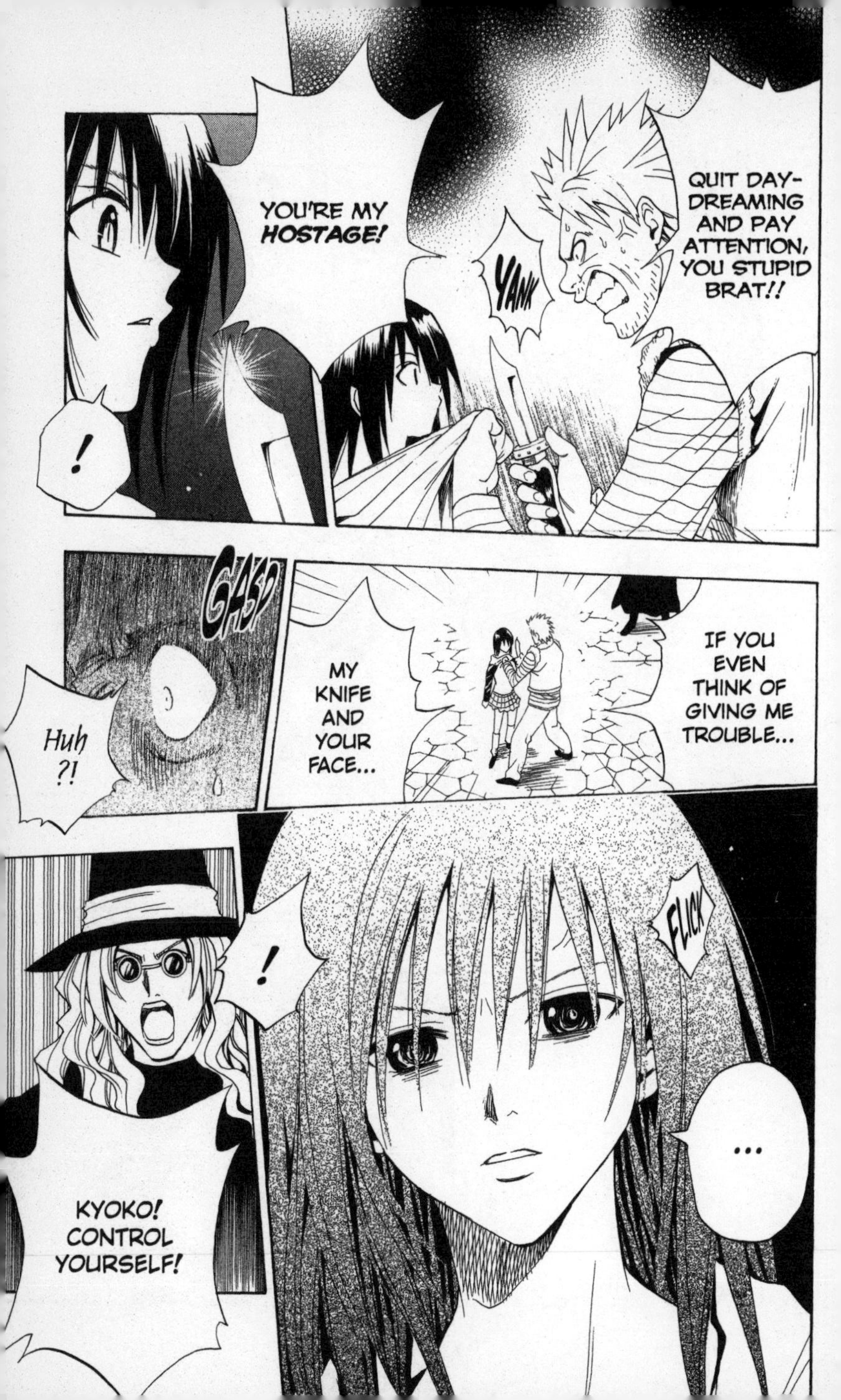
QUIT DAY-DREAMING AND PAY ATTENTION, YOU STUPID BRAT!!
YANK
YOU'RE MY *HOSTAGE!*
!
IF YOU EVEN THINK OF GIVING ME TROUBLE...
MY KNIFE AND YOUR FACE...
GASP
Huh ?!
FLICK
...
!
KYOKO! CONTROL YOURSELF!

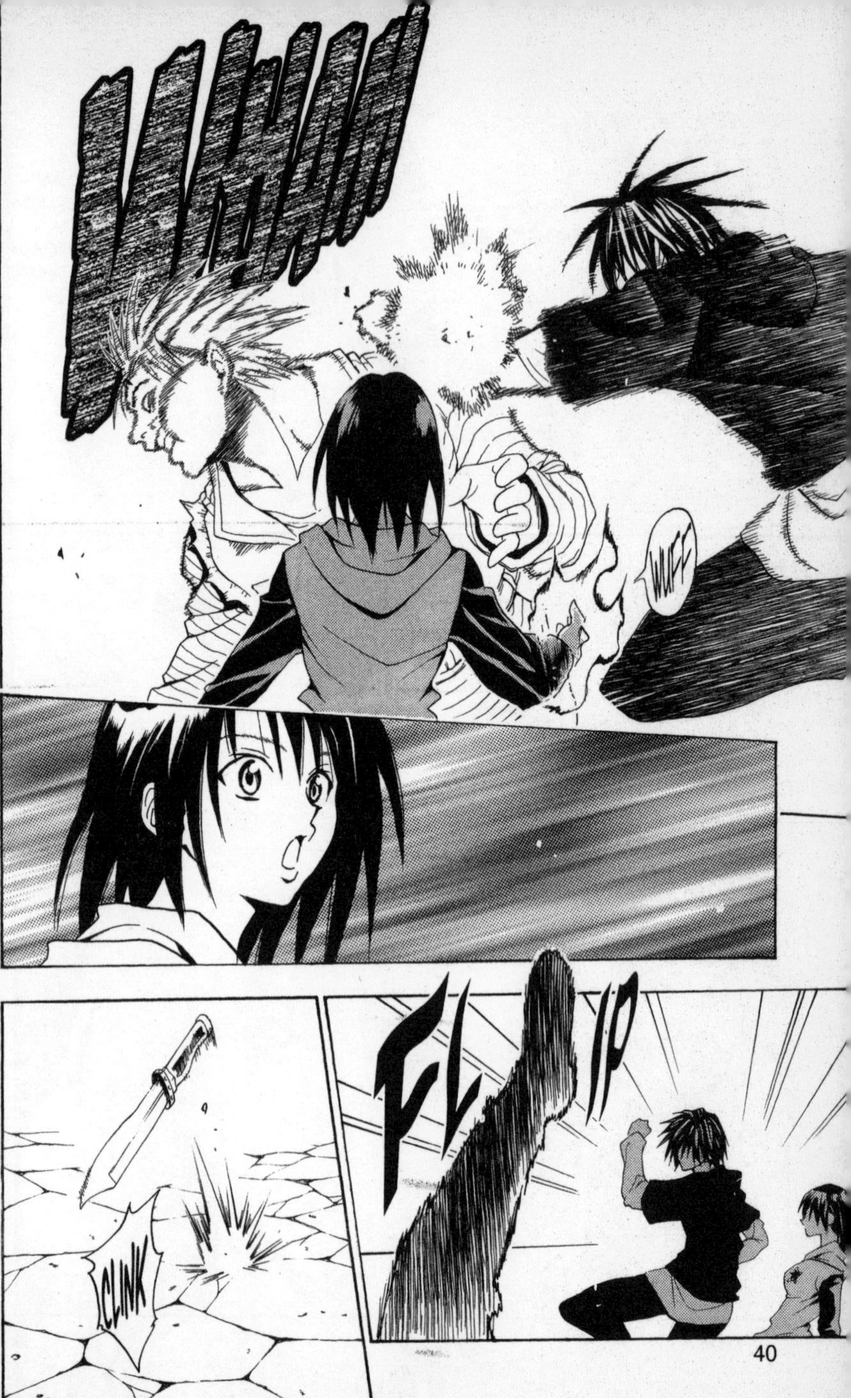
WUFF
FLIP
CLINK

READ THIS WAY

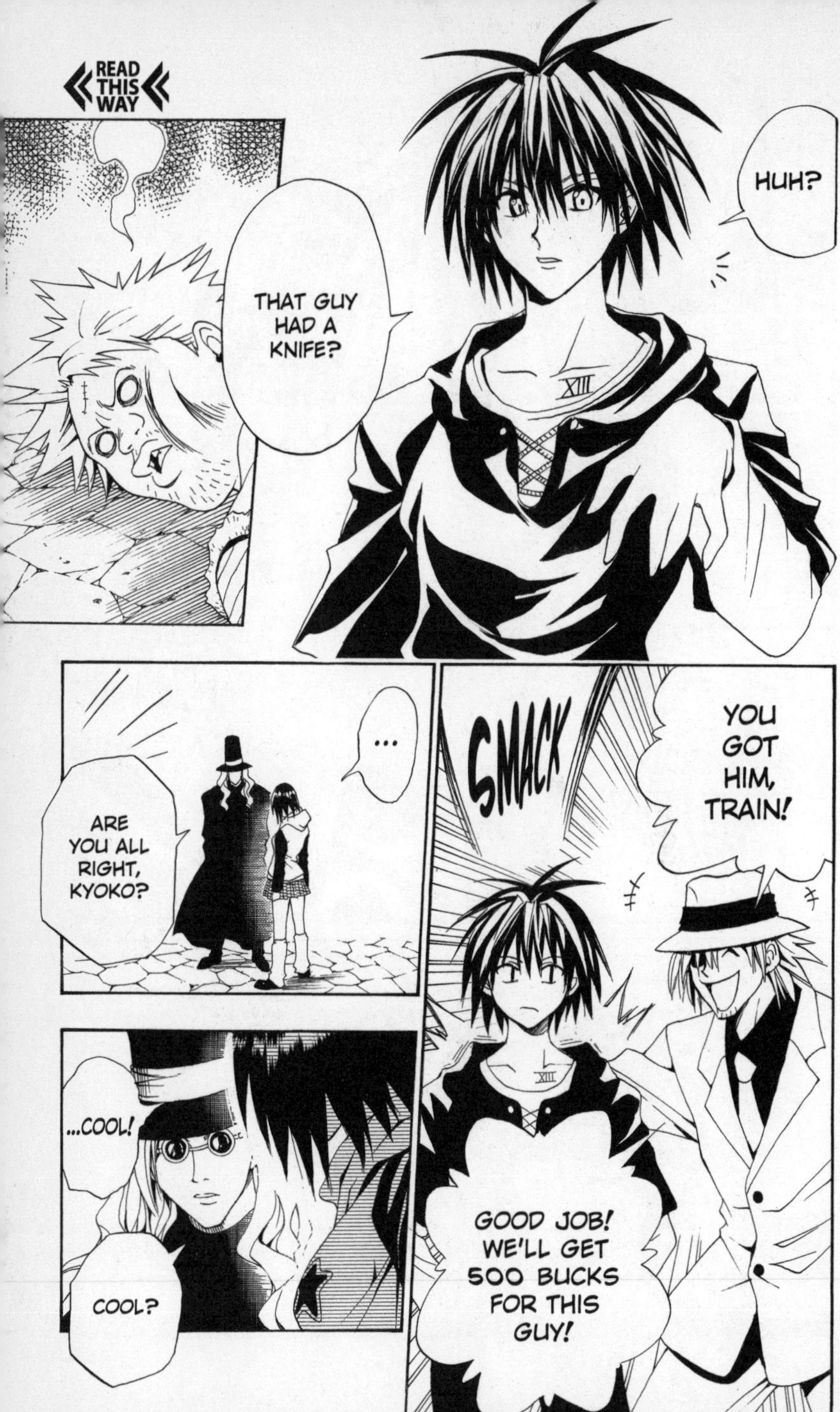
HUH?
THAT GUY HAD A KNIFE?
SMACK
YOU GOT HIM, TRAIN!
GOOD JOB! WE'LL GET 500 BUCKS FOR THIS GUY!
...
ARE YOU ALL RIGHT, KYOKO?
...COOL!
COOL?

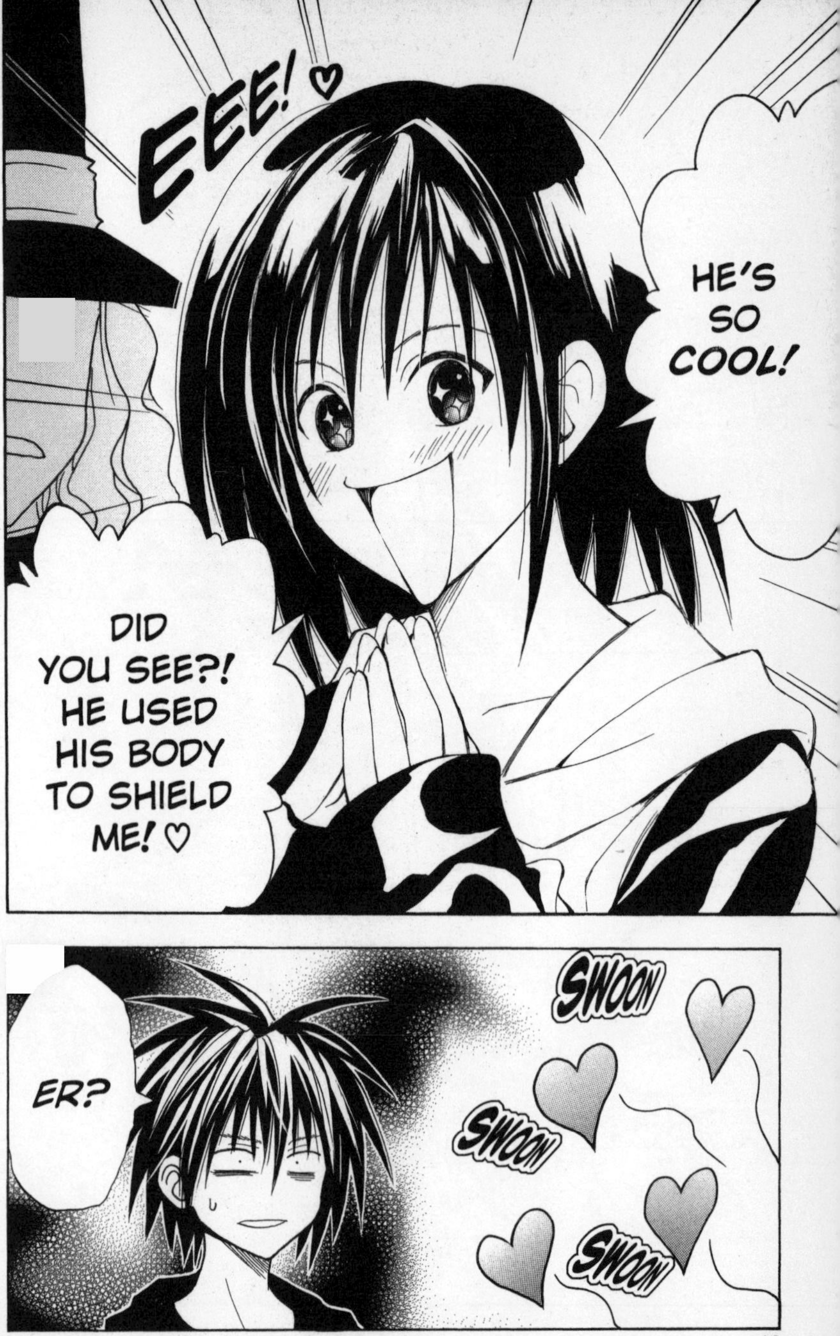
EEE! ♡
HE'S SO COOL!
DID YOU SEE?! HE USED HIS BODY TO SHIELD ME! ♡
SWOON
SWOON
SWOON
ER?

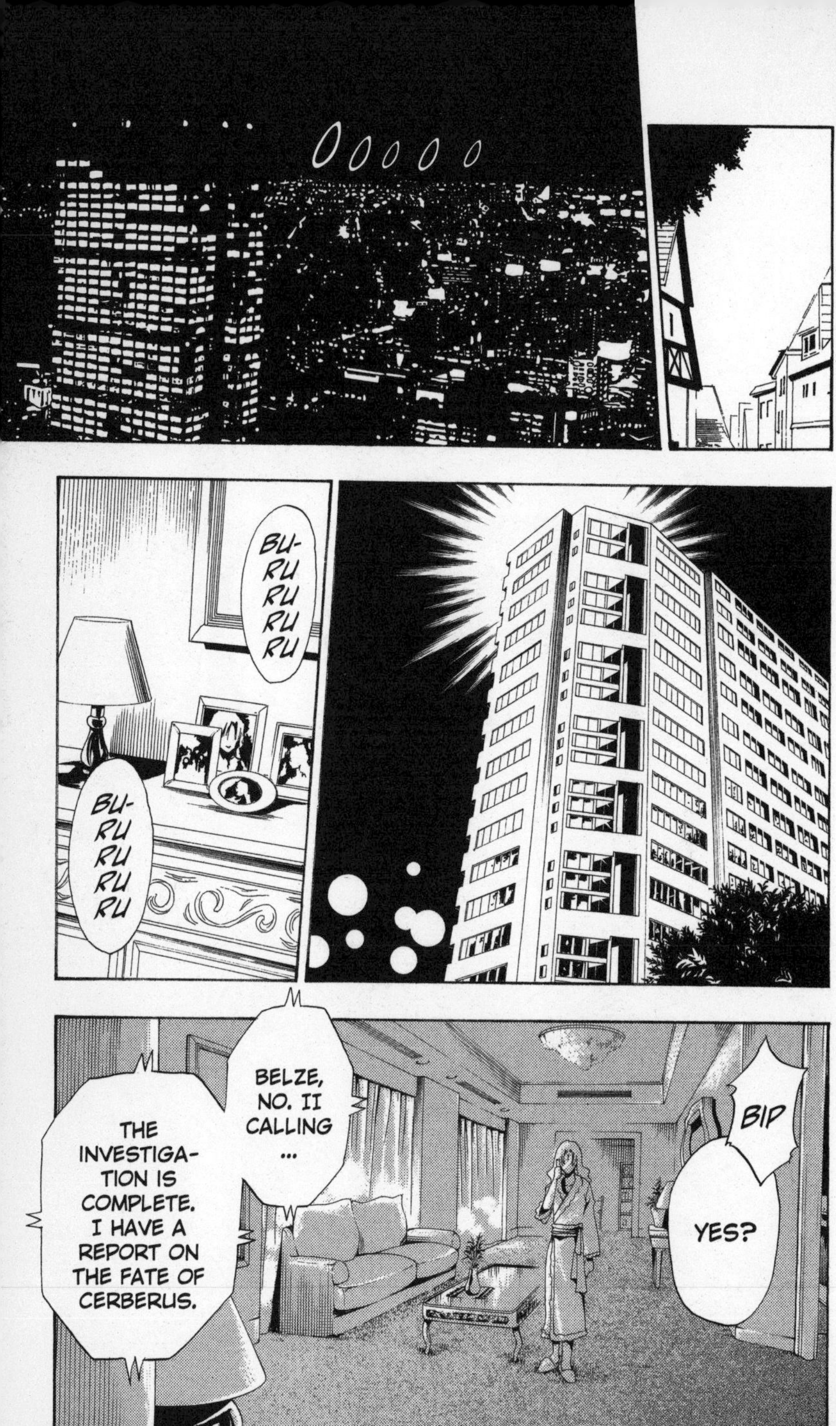
Ooooo
BU-RU RU RU RU
BU-RU RU RU RU
BIP
YES?
BELZE, NO. II CALLING ...
THE INVESTIGATION IS COMPLETE. I HAVE A REPORT ON THE FATE OF CERBERUS.

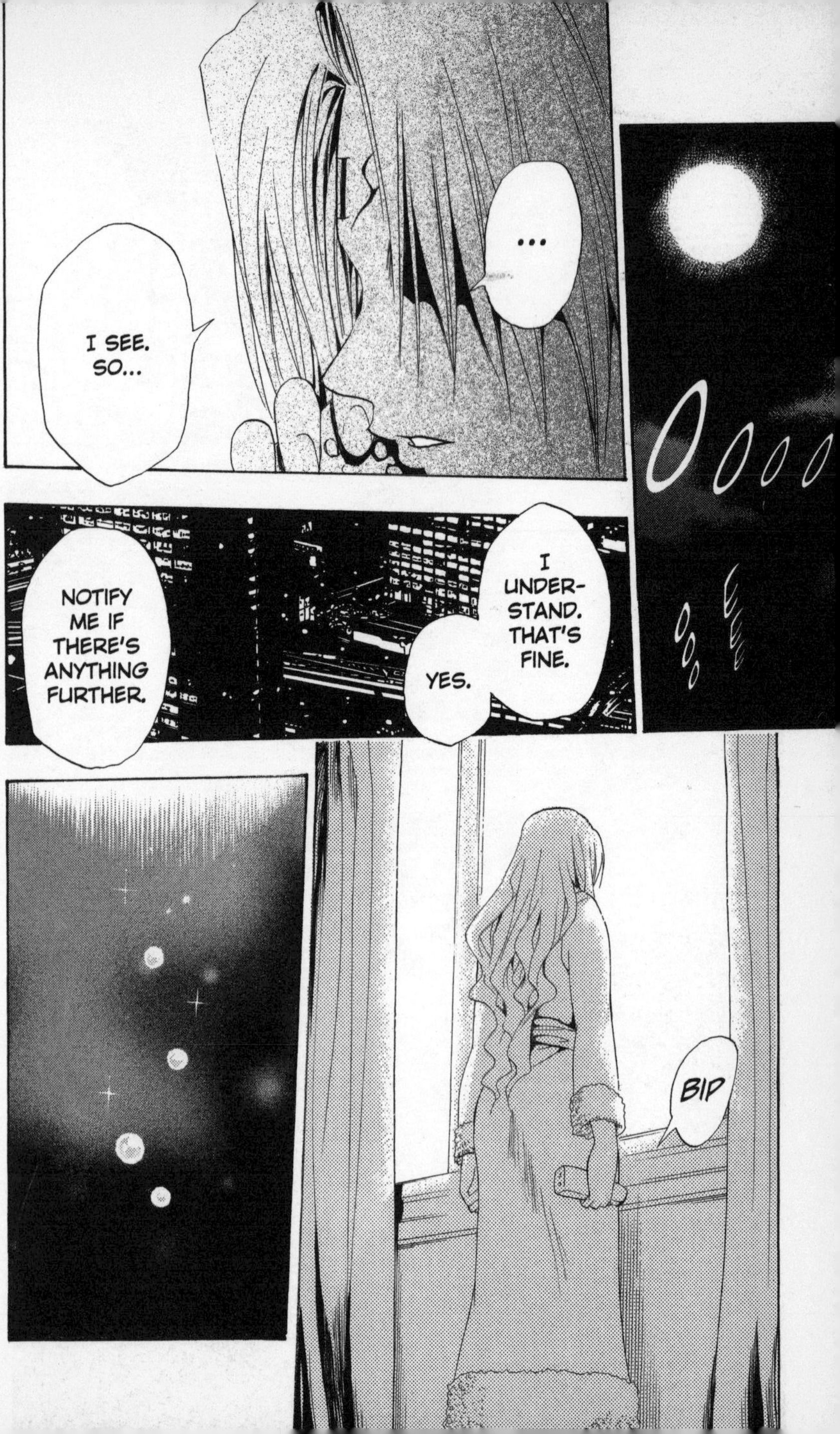
...
I SEE. SO...
I UNDER-STAND. THAT'S FINE.
YES.
NOTIFY ME IF THERE'S ANYTHING FURTHER.
BIP

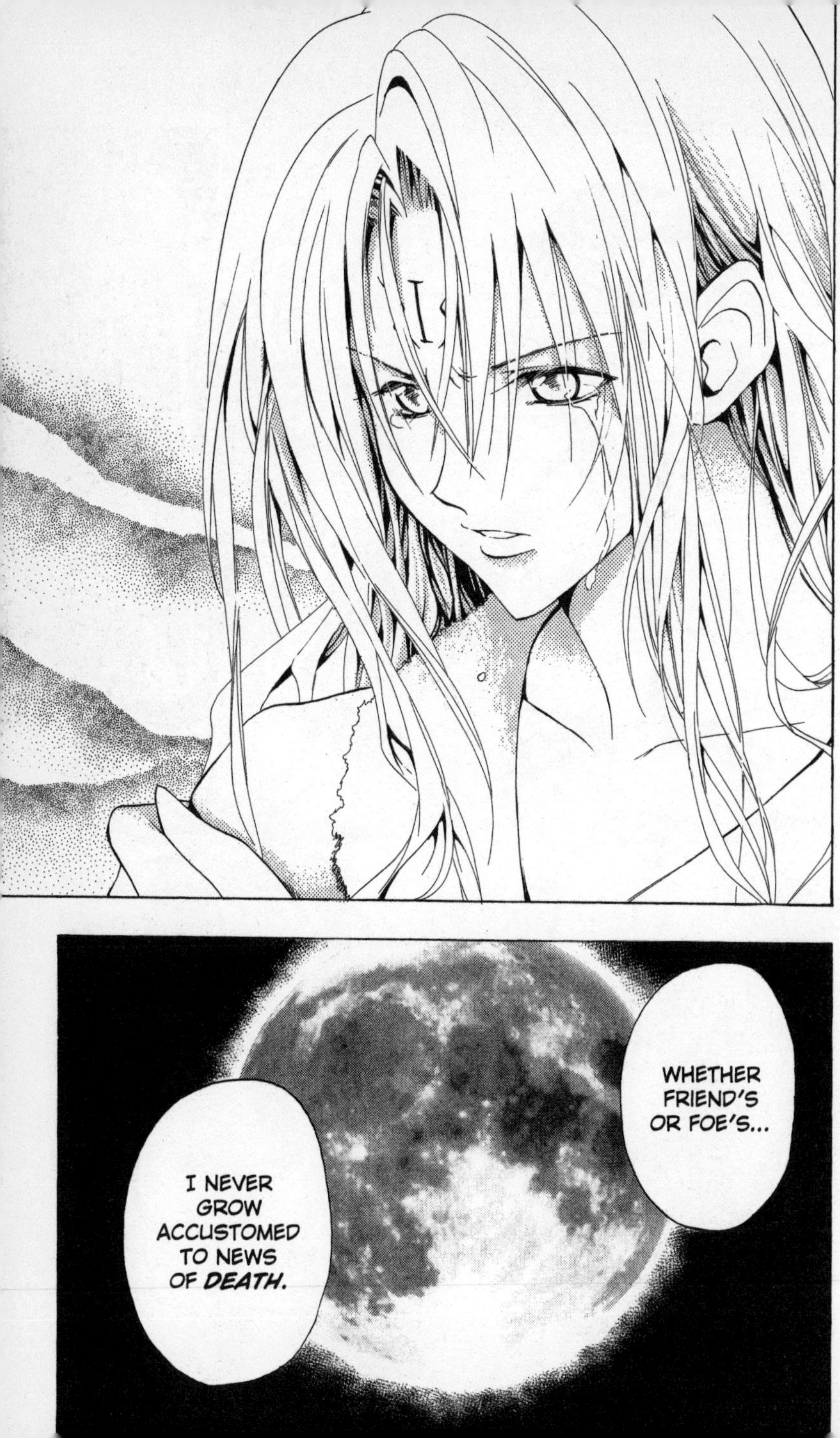
WHETHER FRIEND'S OR FOE'S...
I NEVER GROW ACCUSTOMED TO NEWS OF *DEATH*.

SKETCHES: PART 2

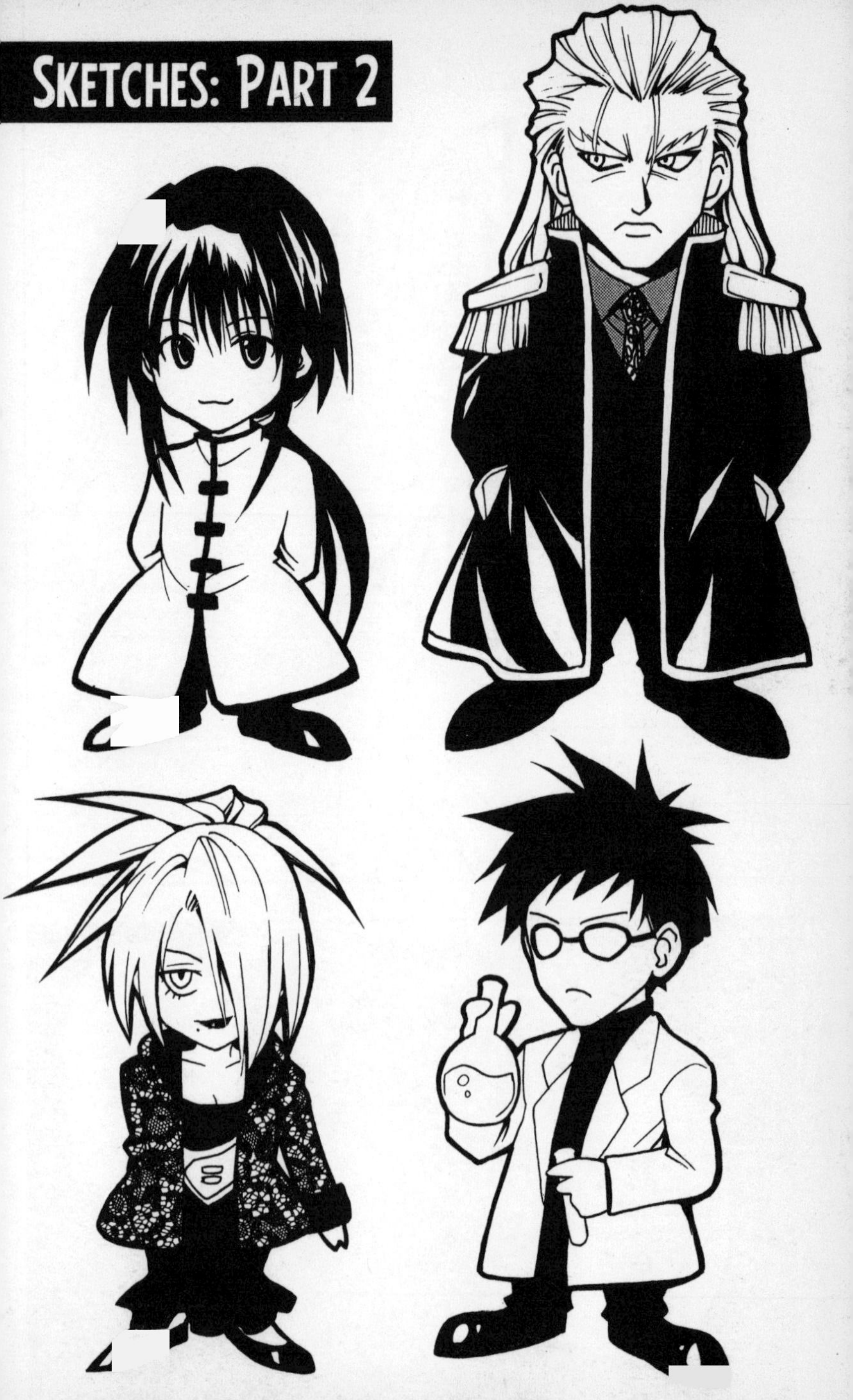

Chapter 87: Jenos's Resolve

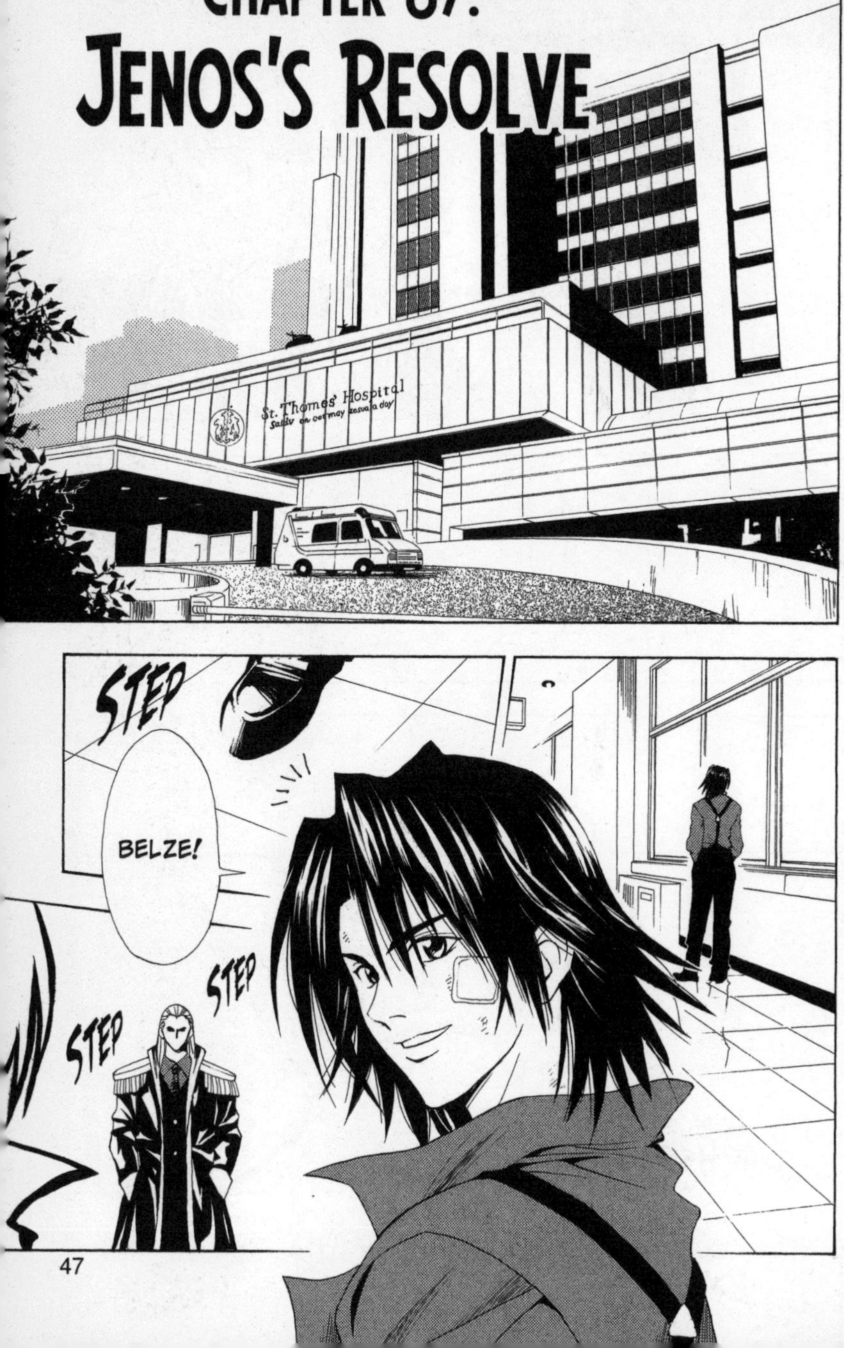
St. Thomes' Hospital
STEP
BELZE!
STEP
STEP

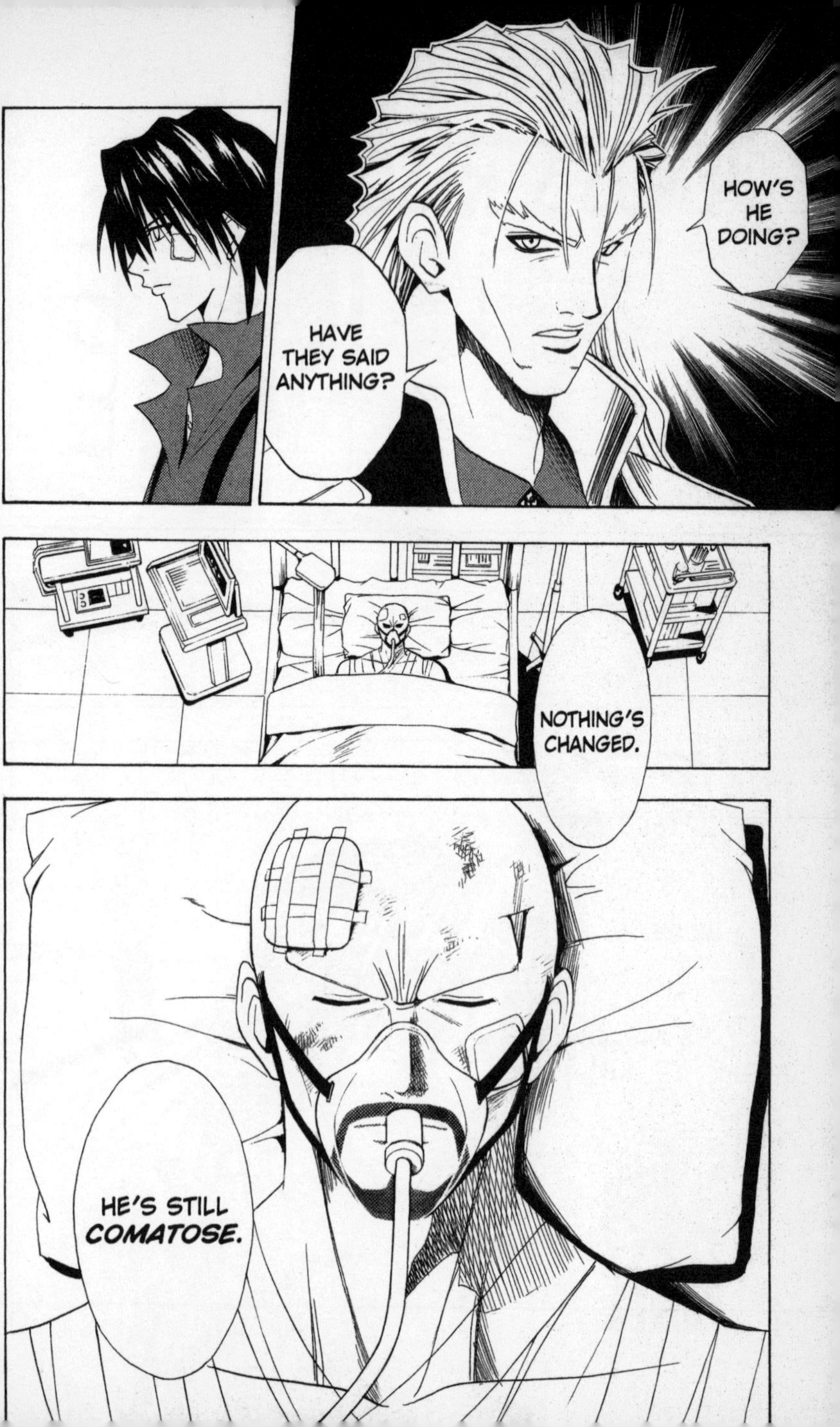
HOW'S HE DOING?
HAVE THEY SAID ANYTHING?
NOTHING'S CHANGED.
HE'S STILL COMATOSE.

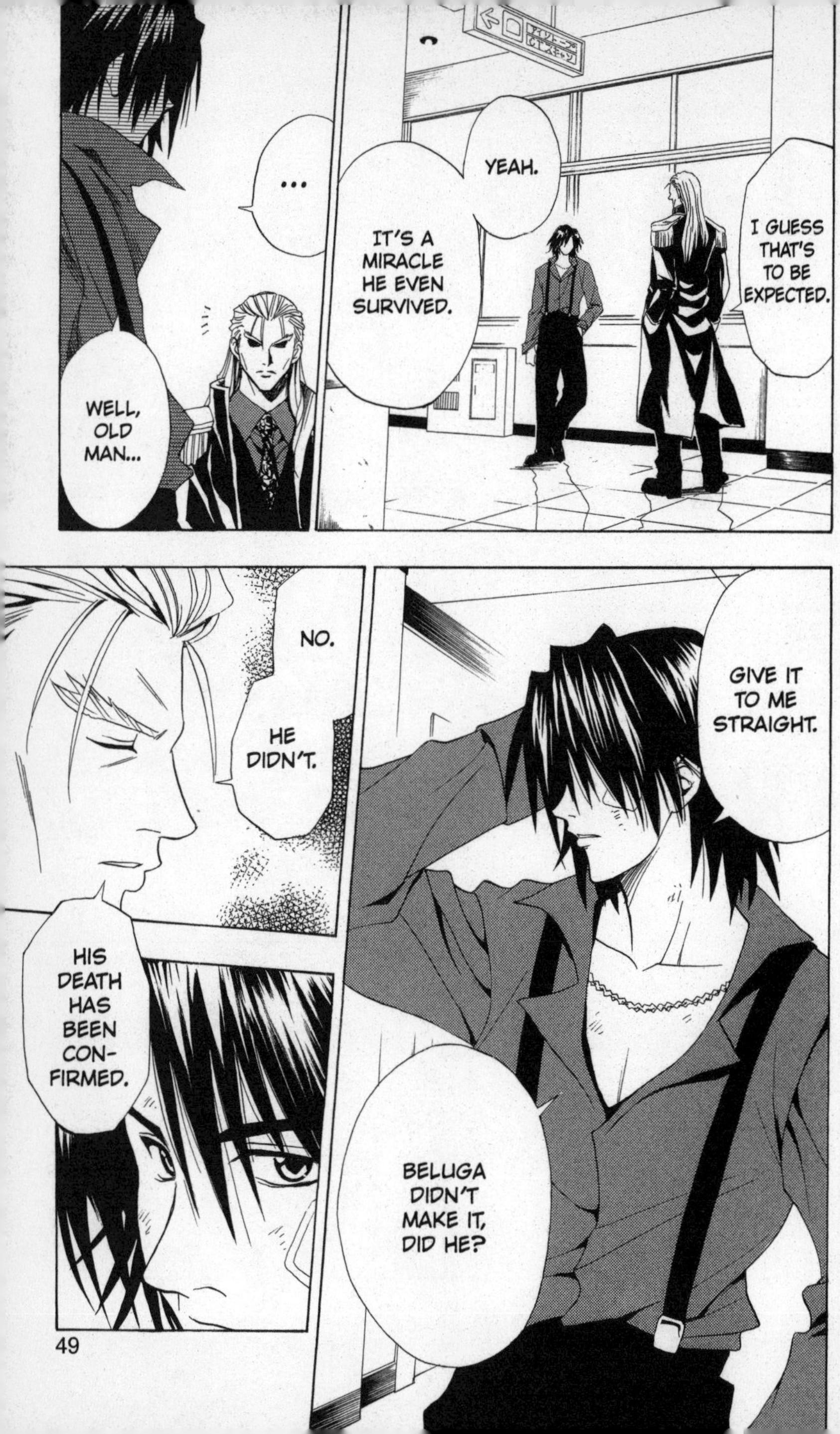
I GUESS THAT'S TO BE EXPECTED.
YEAH.
IT'S A MIRACLE HE EVEN SURVIVED.
...
WELL, OLD MAN...
GIVE IT TO ME STRAIGHT.
BELUGA DIDN'T MAKE IT, DID HE?
NO.
HE DIDN'T.
HIS DEATH HAS BEEN CON-FIRMED.

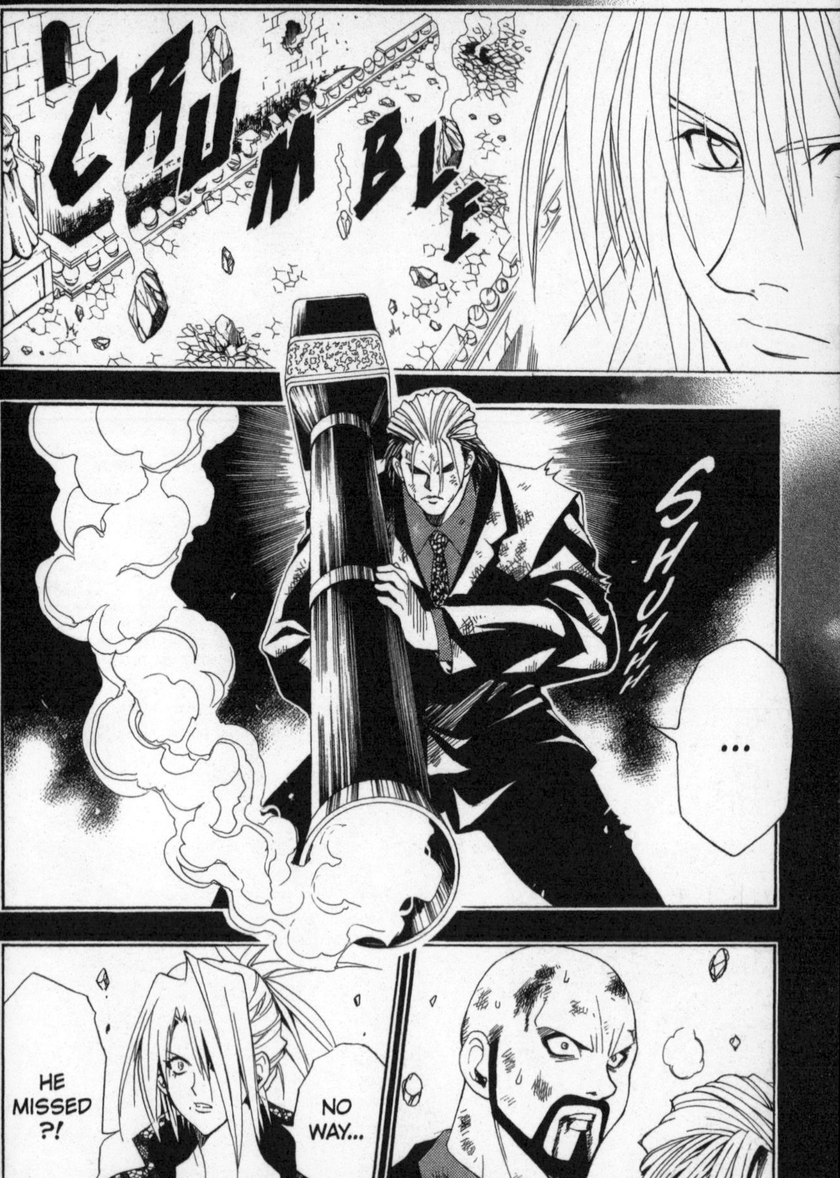
CRUMBLE
SHUHHH
...
NO WAY...
HE MISSED ?!

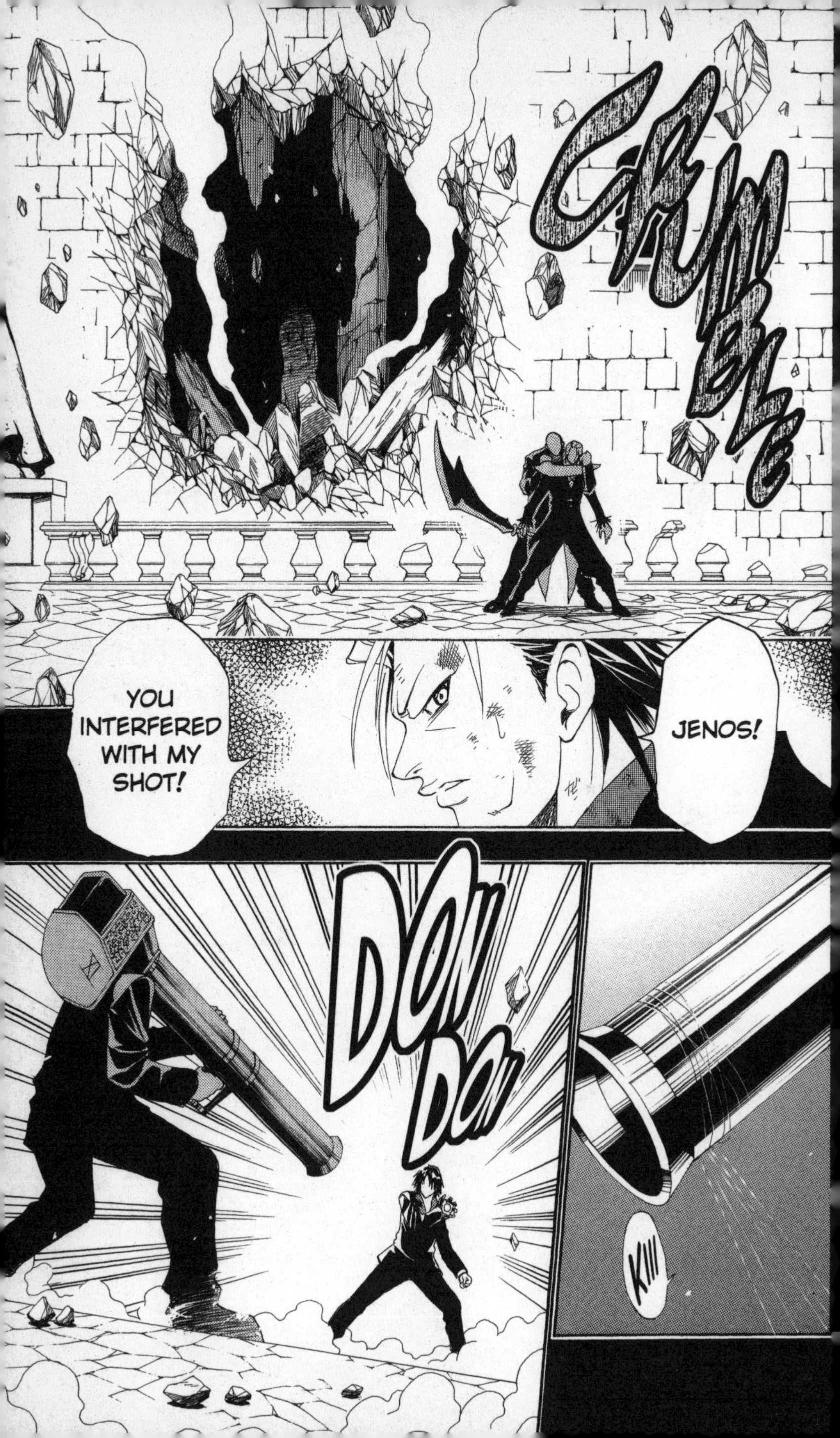
CRUMBLE
JENOS!
YOU INTERFERED WITH MY SHOT!
DON DON

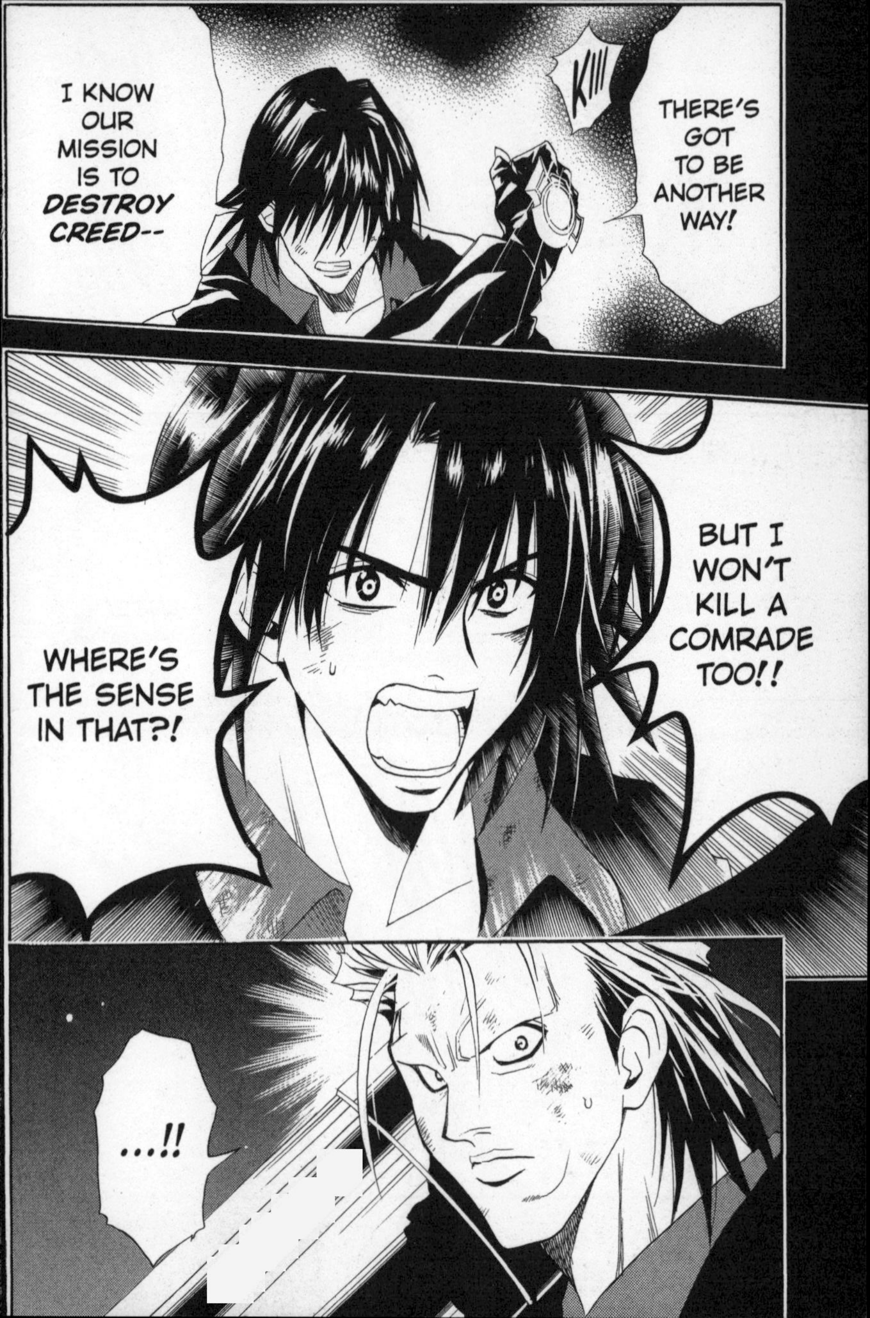

KIII
THERE'S GOT TO BE ANOTHER WAY!
I KNOW OUR MISSION IS TO DESTROY CREED--
BUT I WON'T KILL A COMRADE TOO!!
WHERE'S THE SENSE IN THAT?!
...!!

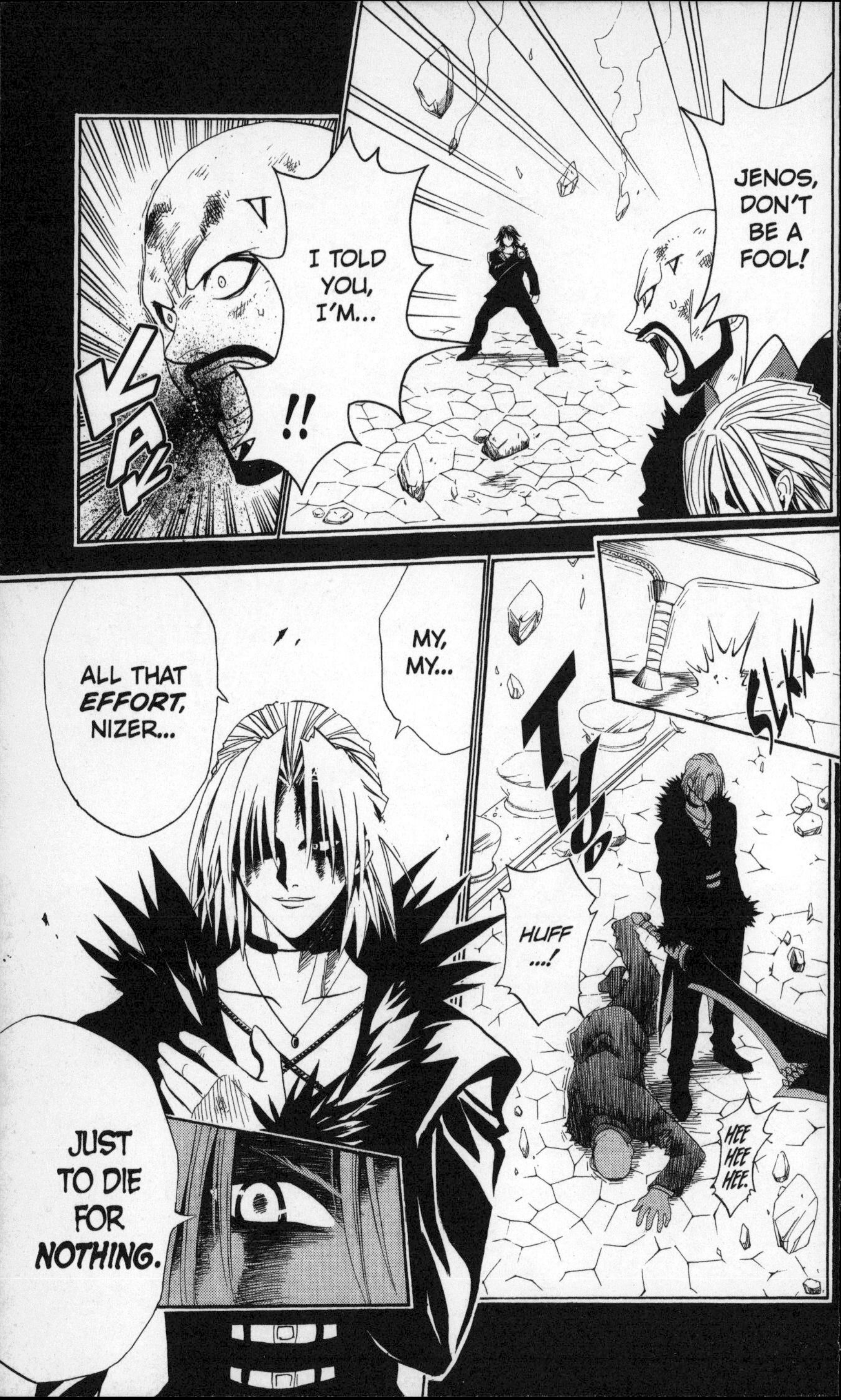
JENOS, DON'T BE A FOOL!
I TOLD YOU, I'M...
!!
SLKK
THUD
HUFF ...!
HEE HEE HEE.
MY, MY...
ALL THAT *EFFORT,* NIZER...
JUST TO DIE FOR **NOTHING.**

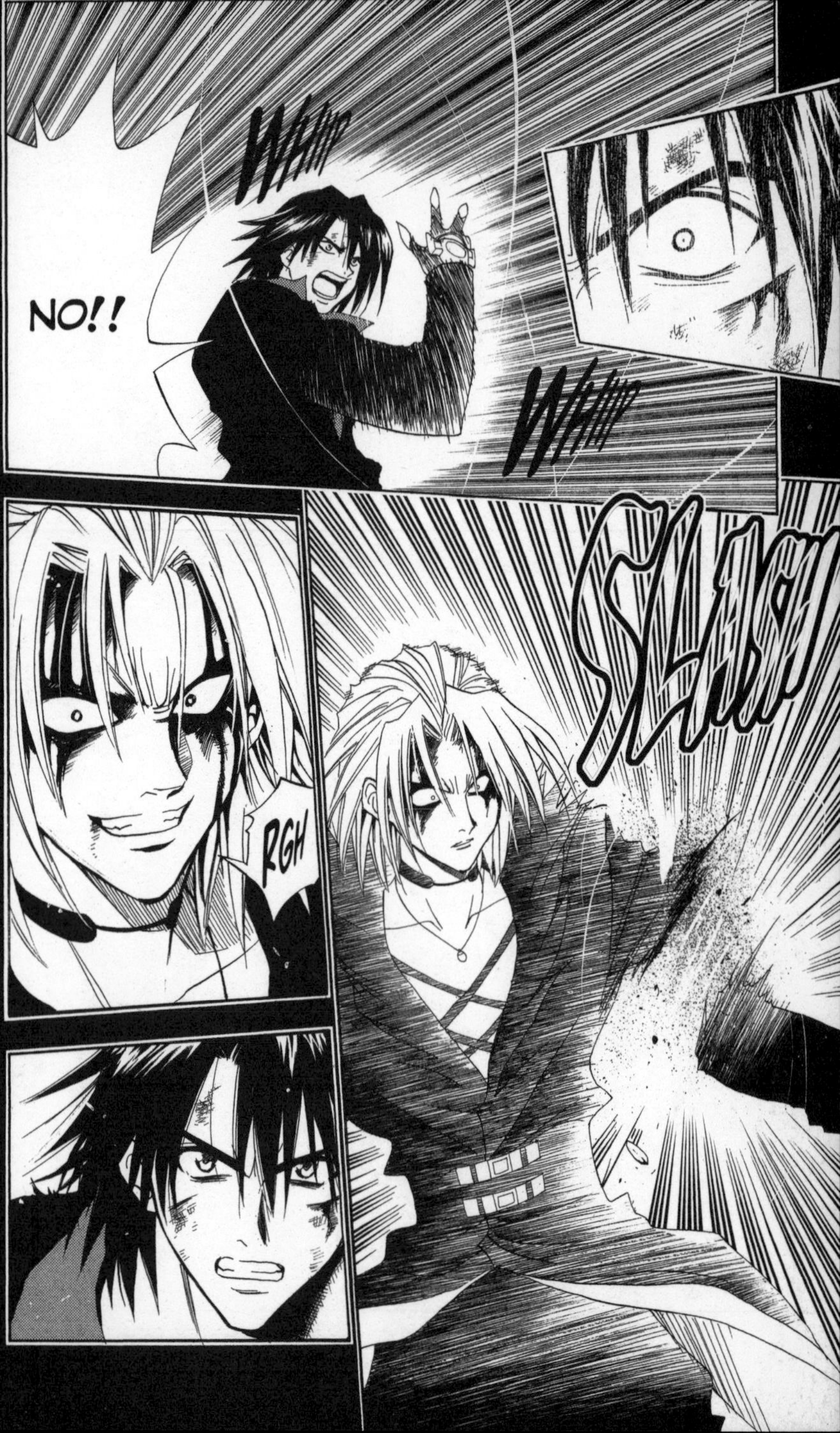
WHIP
NO!!
WHIP
SLASH
RGH

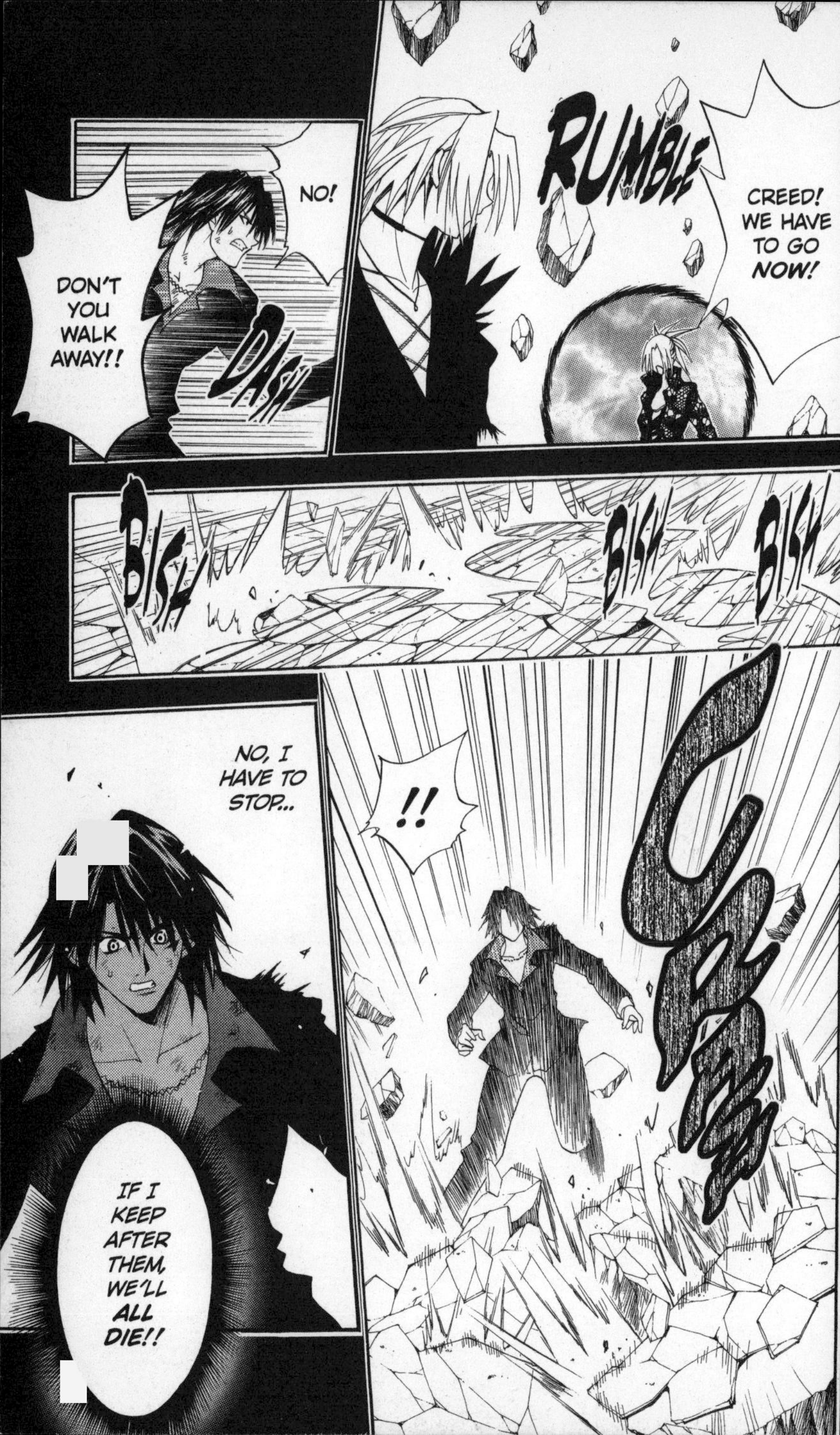
CREED! WE HAVE TO GO NOW!
RUMBLE
NO!
DON'T YOU WALK AWAY!!
DASH
BISH
BISH
BISH
!!
NO, I HAVE TO STOP...
IF I KEEP AFTER THEM, WE'LL ALL DIE!!

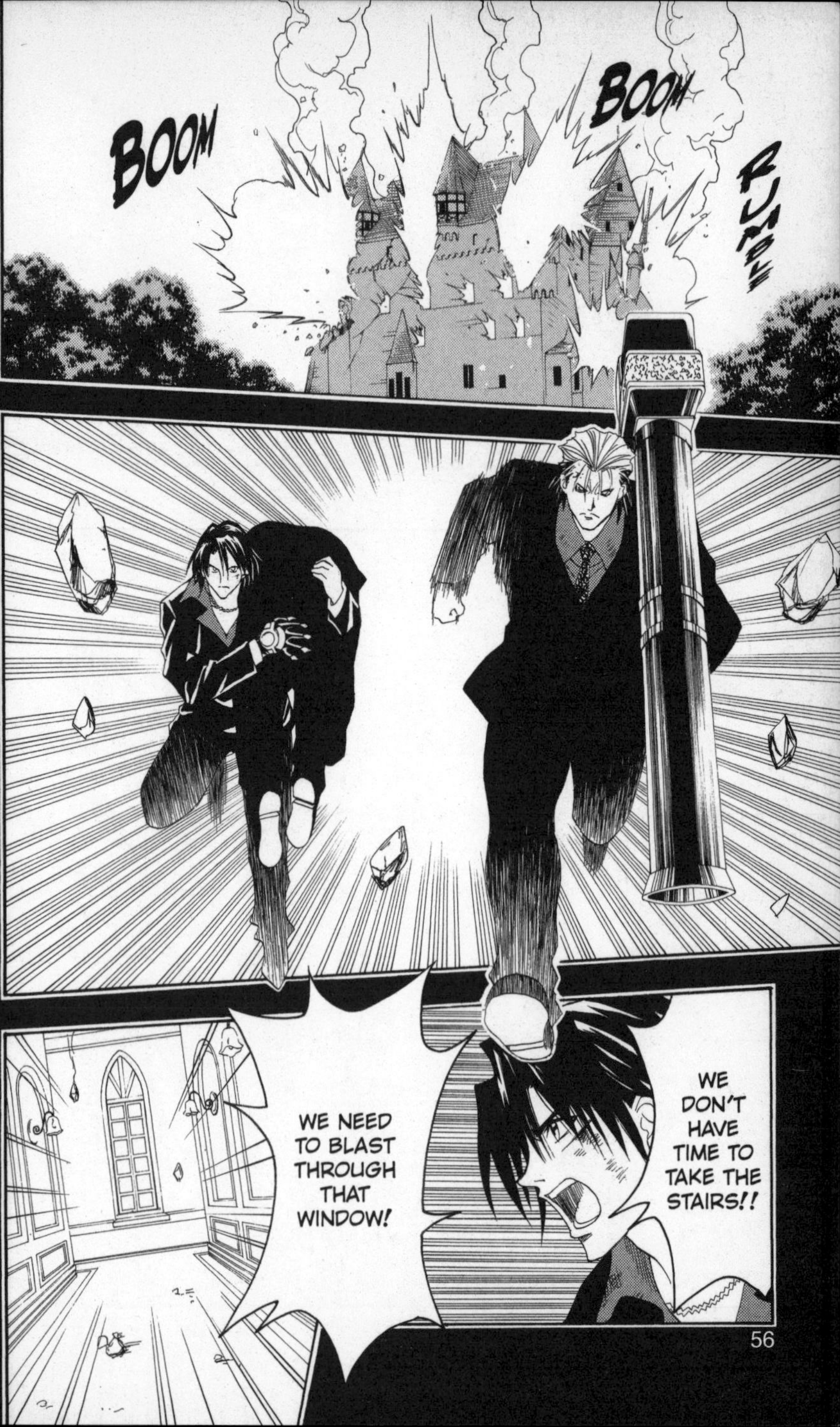
BOOM
RUMBLE
BOOM
WE DON'T HAVE TIME TO TAKE THE STAIRS!!
WE NEED TO BLAST THROUGH THAT WINDOW!

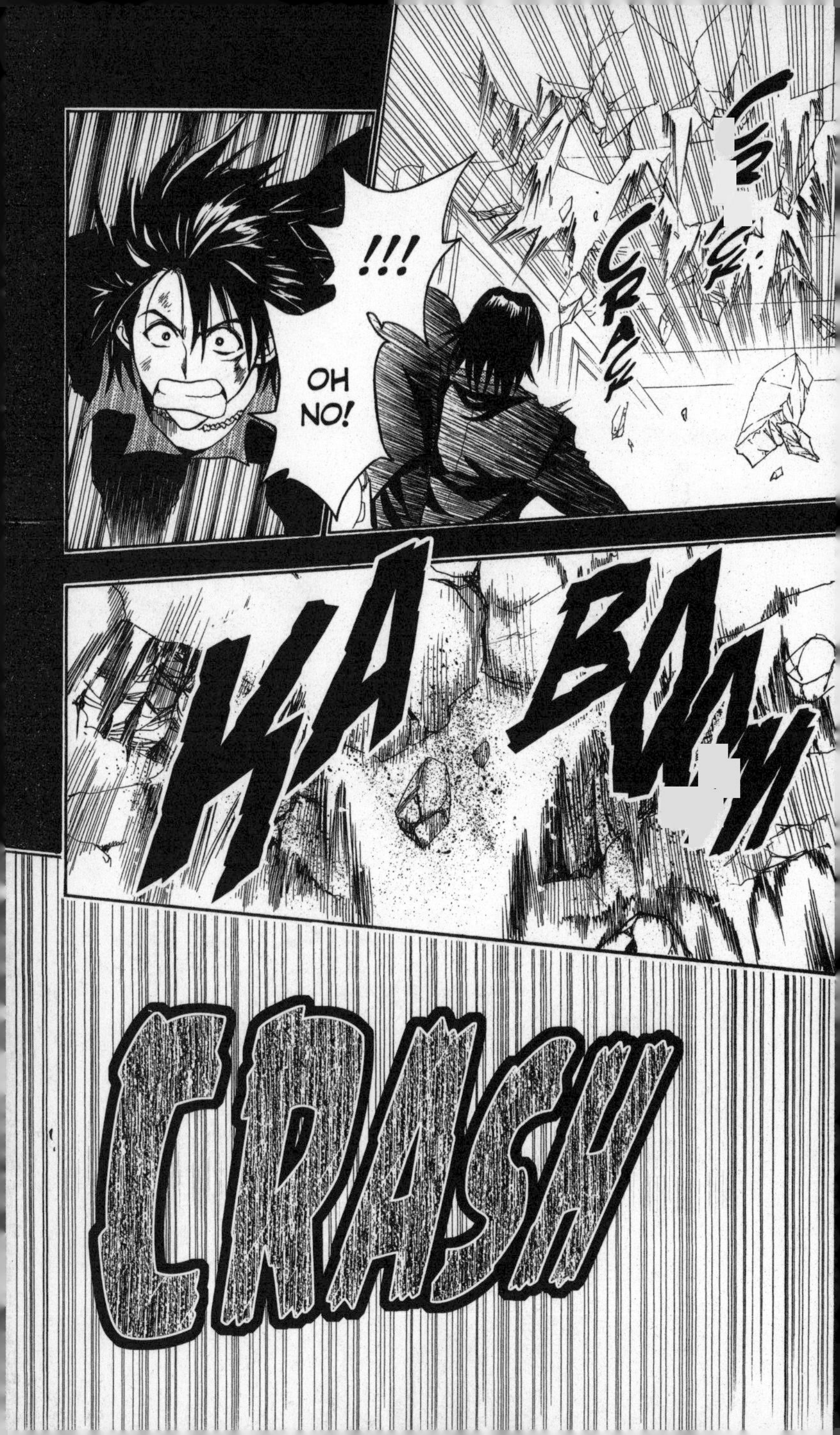
CRACK
!!!
OH NO!
KA BAM
CRASH

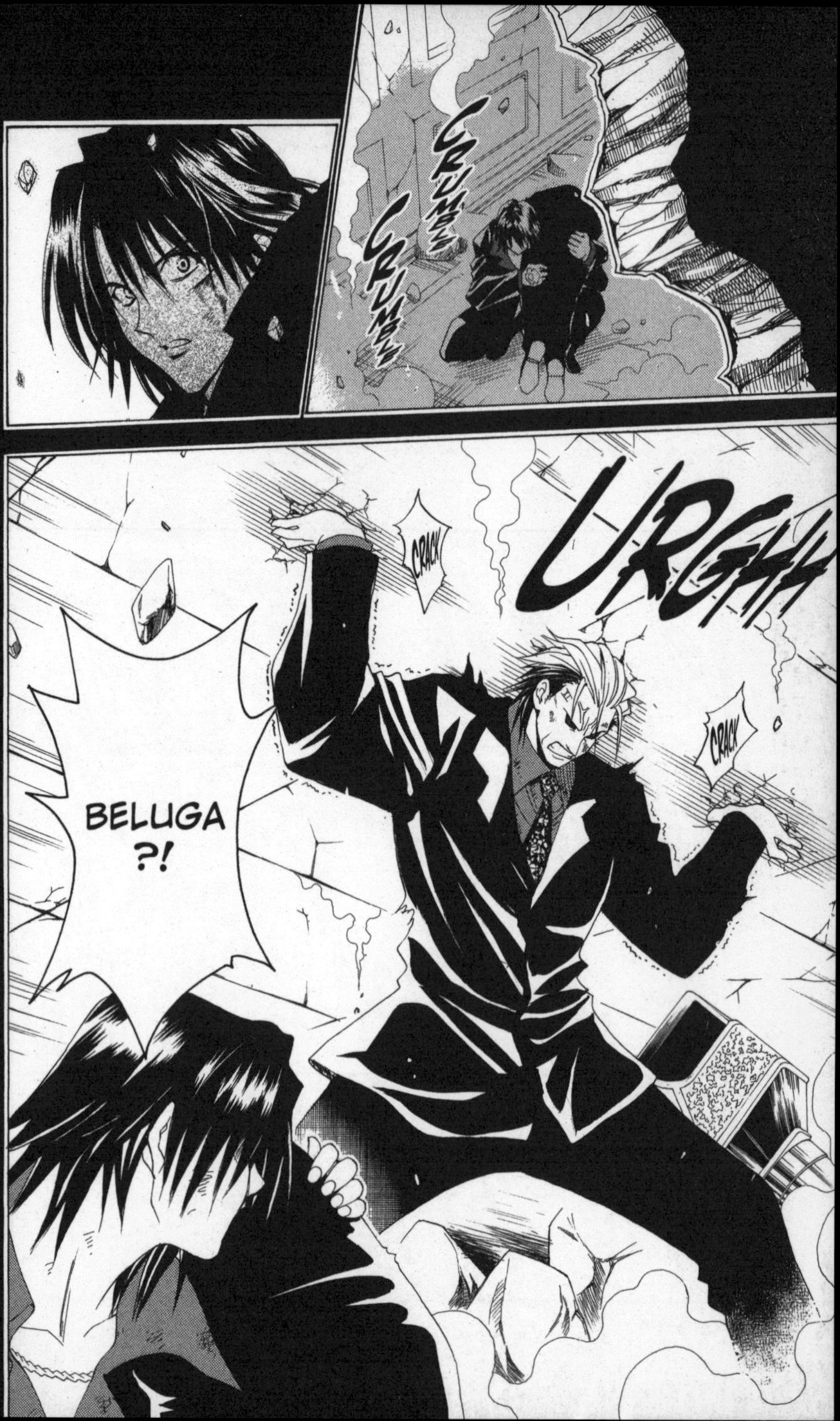
CRUMBLE
CRUMBLE
URGHH
CRACK
CRACK
BELUGA ?!

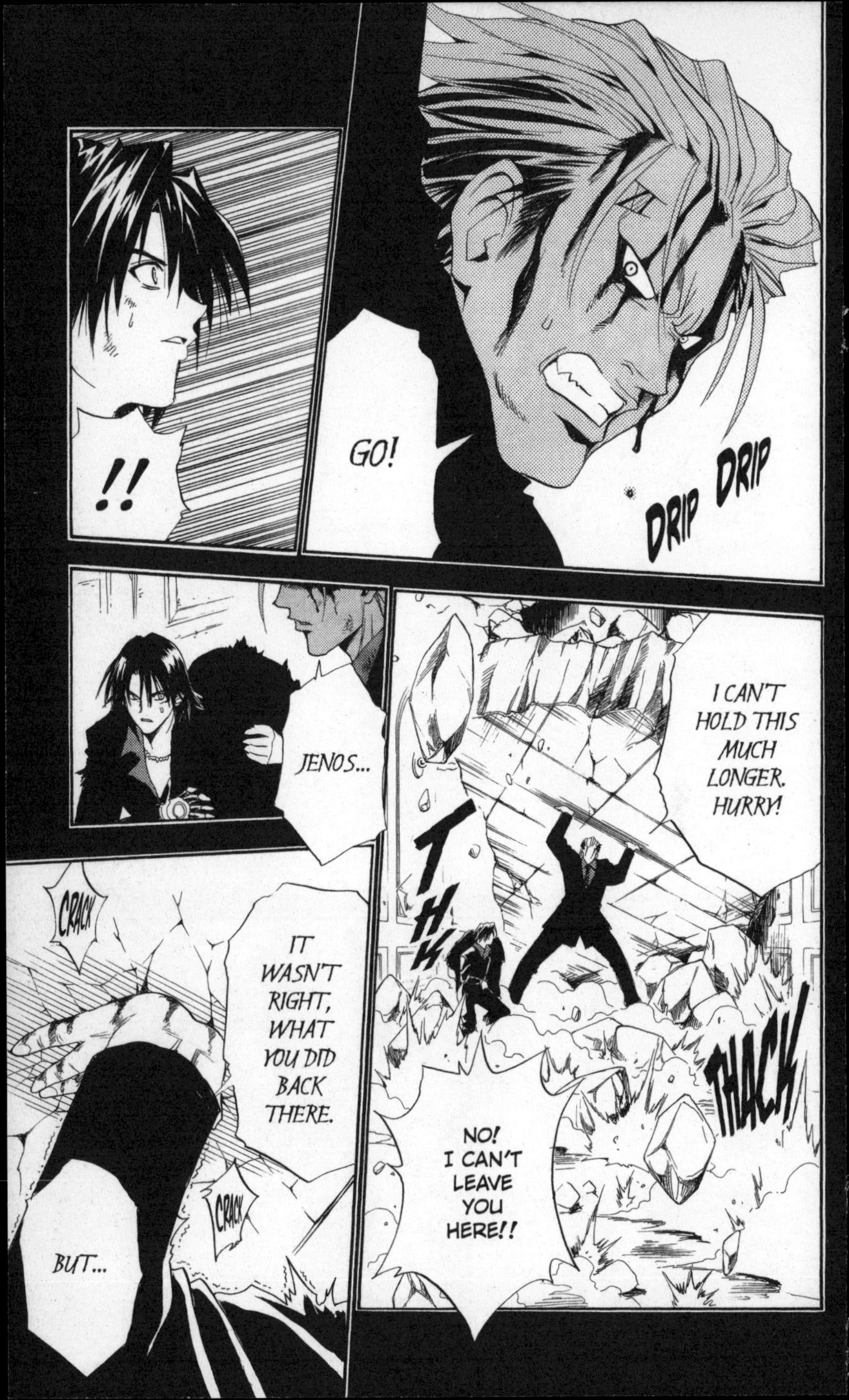
GO!
DRIP DRIP
!!
I CAN'T HOLD THIS MUCH LONGER. HURRY!
THACK
NO! I CAN'T LEAVE YOU HERE!!
JENOS...
CRACK
IT WASN'T RIGHT, WHAT YOU DID BACK THERE.
CRACK
BUT...

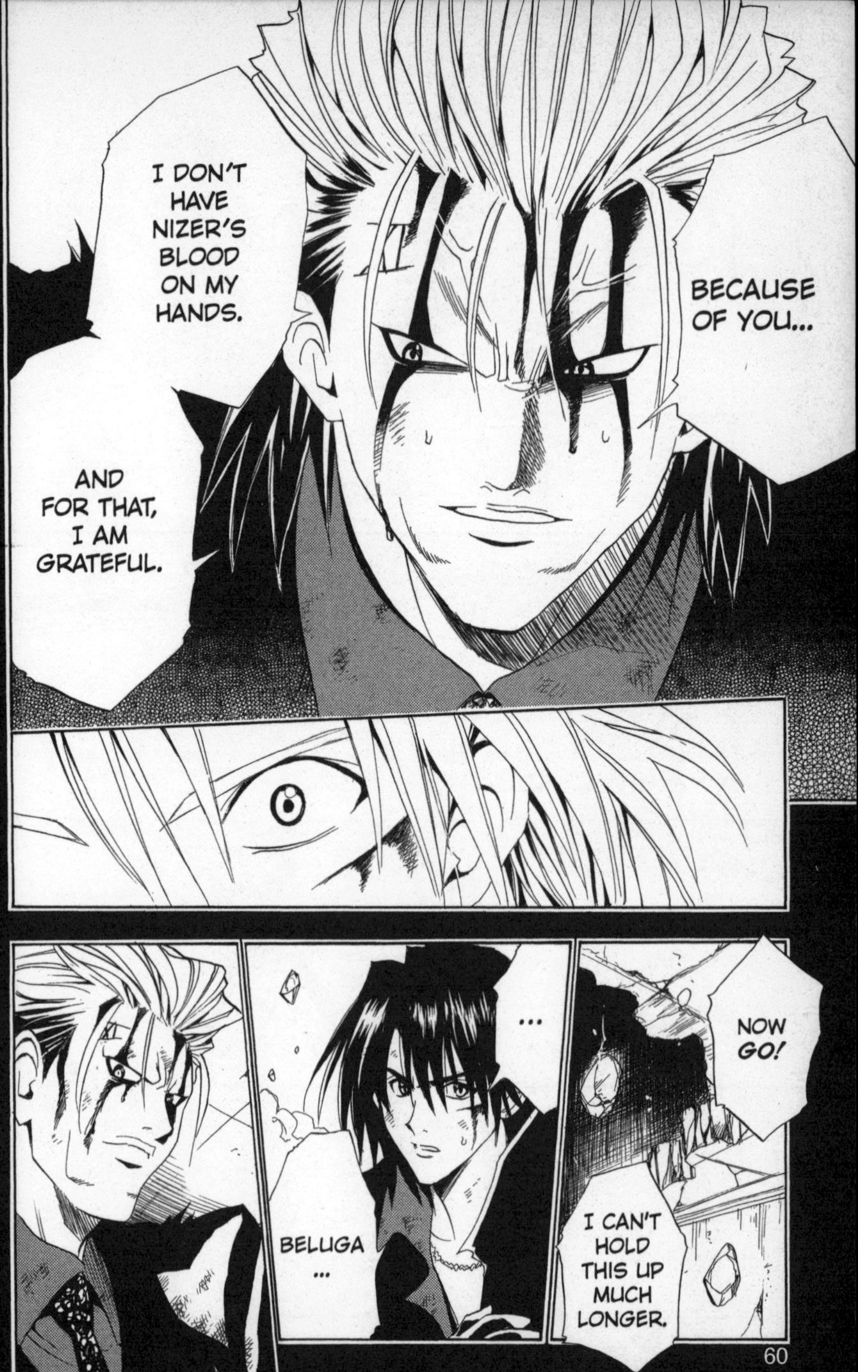
BECAUSE OF YOU...
I DON'T HAVE NIZER'S BLOOD ON MY HANDS.
AND FOR THAT, I AM GRATEFUL.
NOW GO!
I CAN'T HOLD THIS UP MUCH LONGER.
...
BELUGA ...

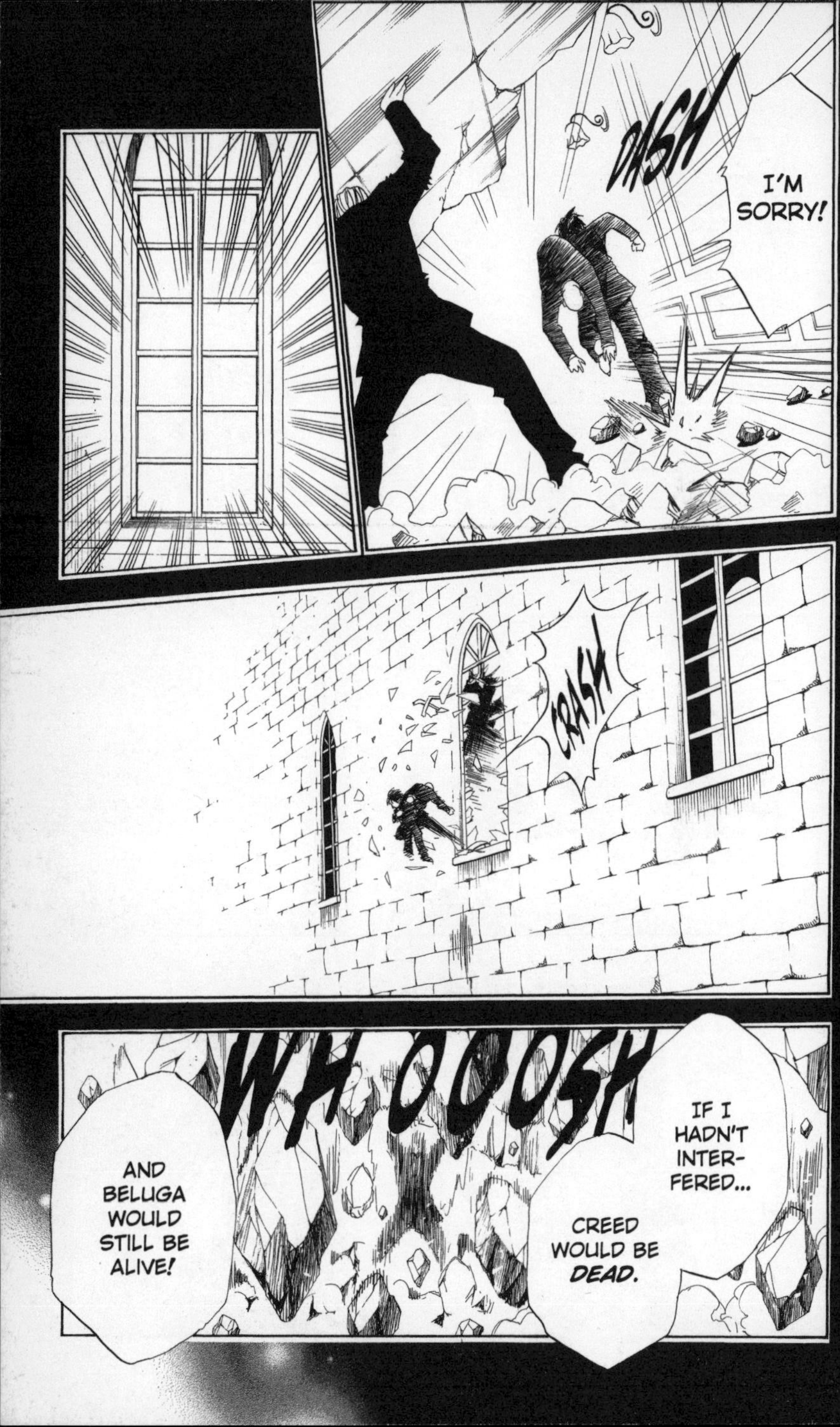
DASH
I'M SORRY!
CRASH
IF I HADN'T INTER-FERED...
CREED WOULD BE DEAD.
WHOOOSH
AND BELUGA WOULD STILL BE ALIVE!

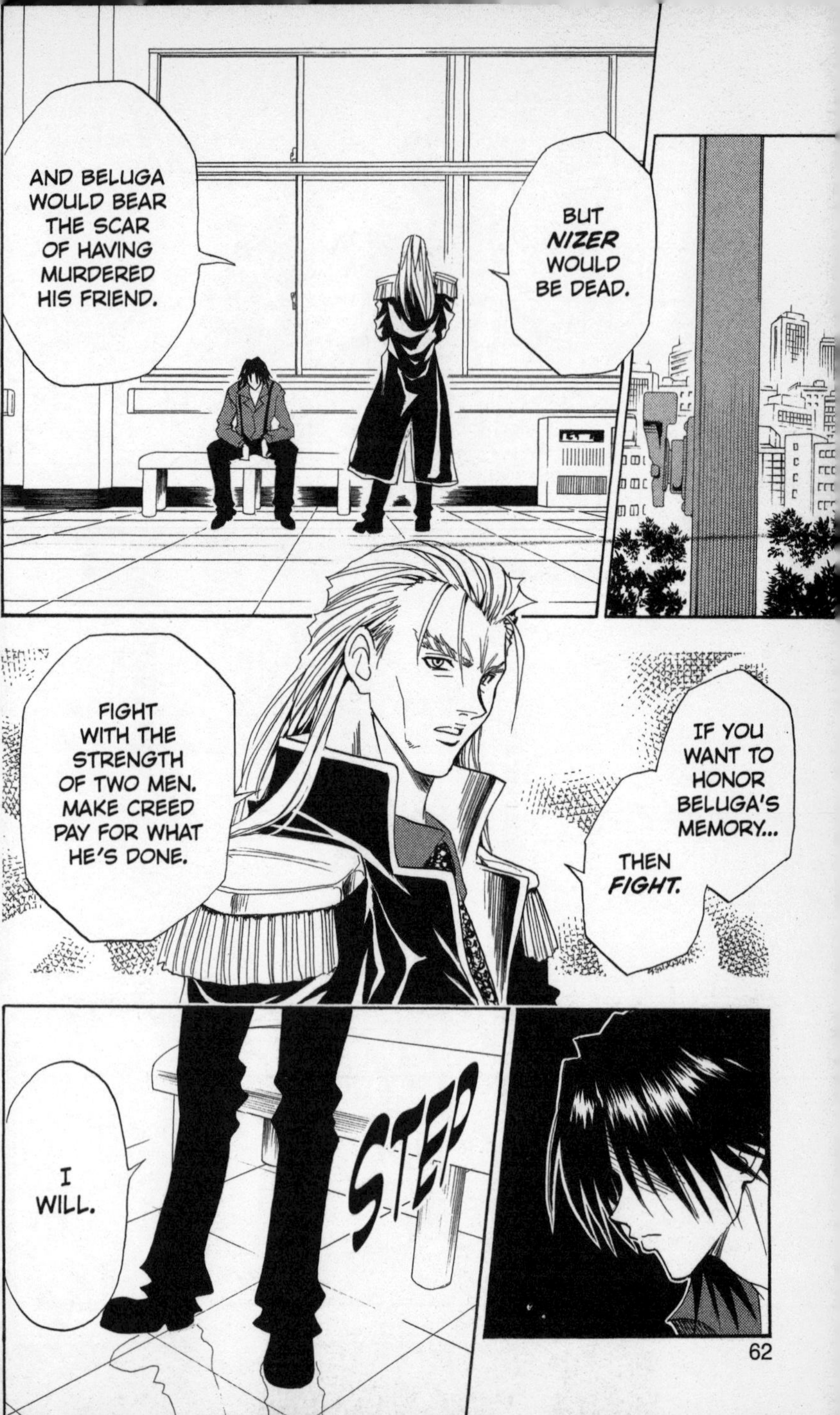
BUT *NIZER* WOULD BE DEAD.
AND BELUGA WOULD BEAR THE SCAR OF HAVING MURDERED HIS FRIEND.
IF YOU WANT TO HONOR BELUGA'S MEMORY...
THEN *FIGHT*.
FIGHT WITH THE STRENGTH OF TWO MEN. MAKE CREED PAY FOR WHAT HE'S DONE.
STEP
I WILL.

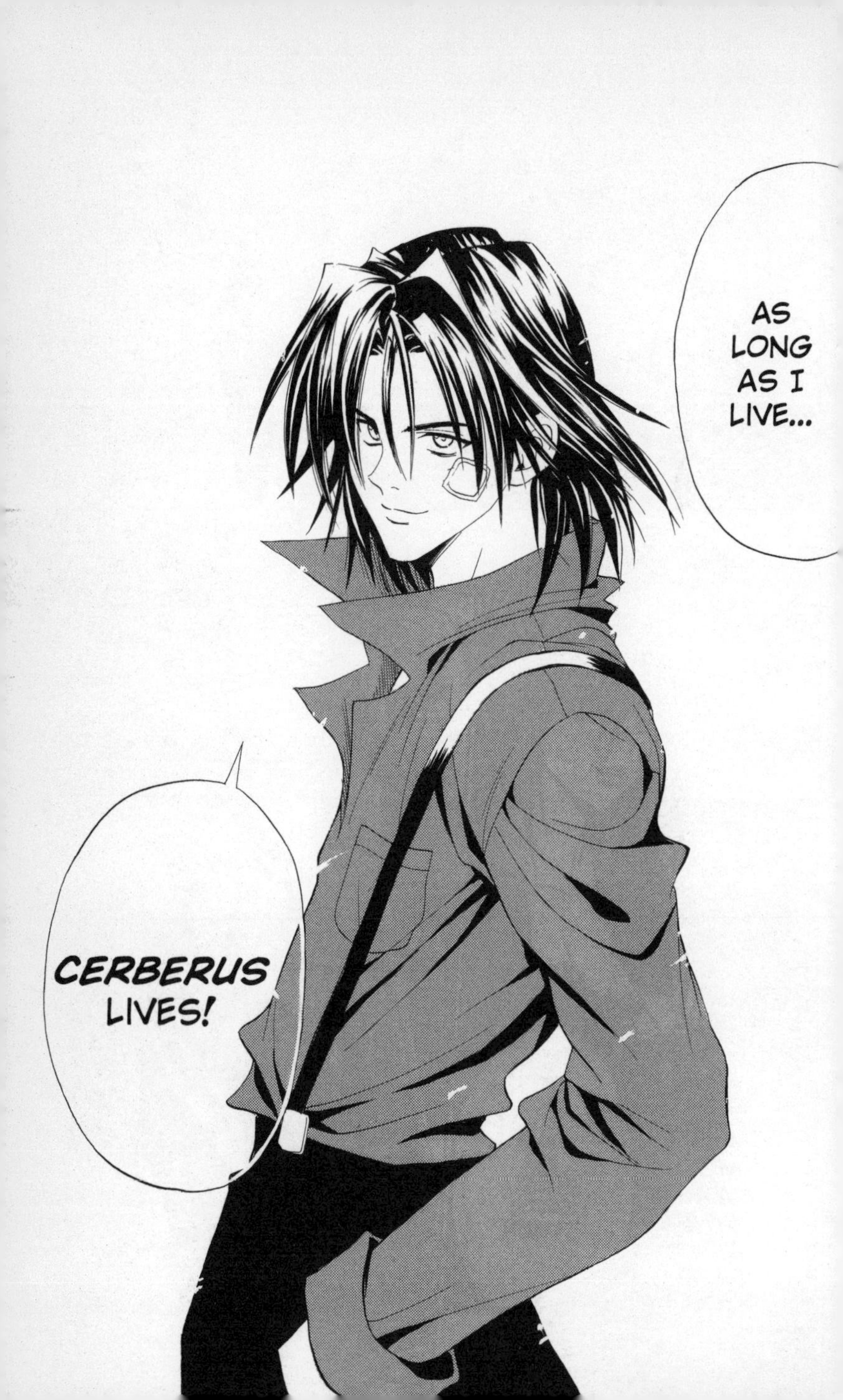
AS LONG AS I LIVE...
CERBERUS LIVES!

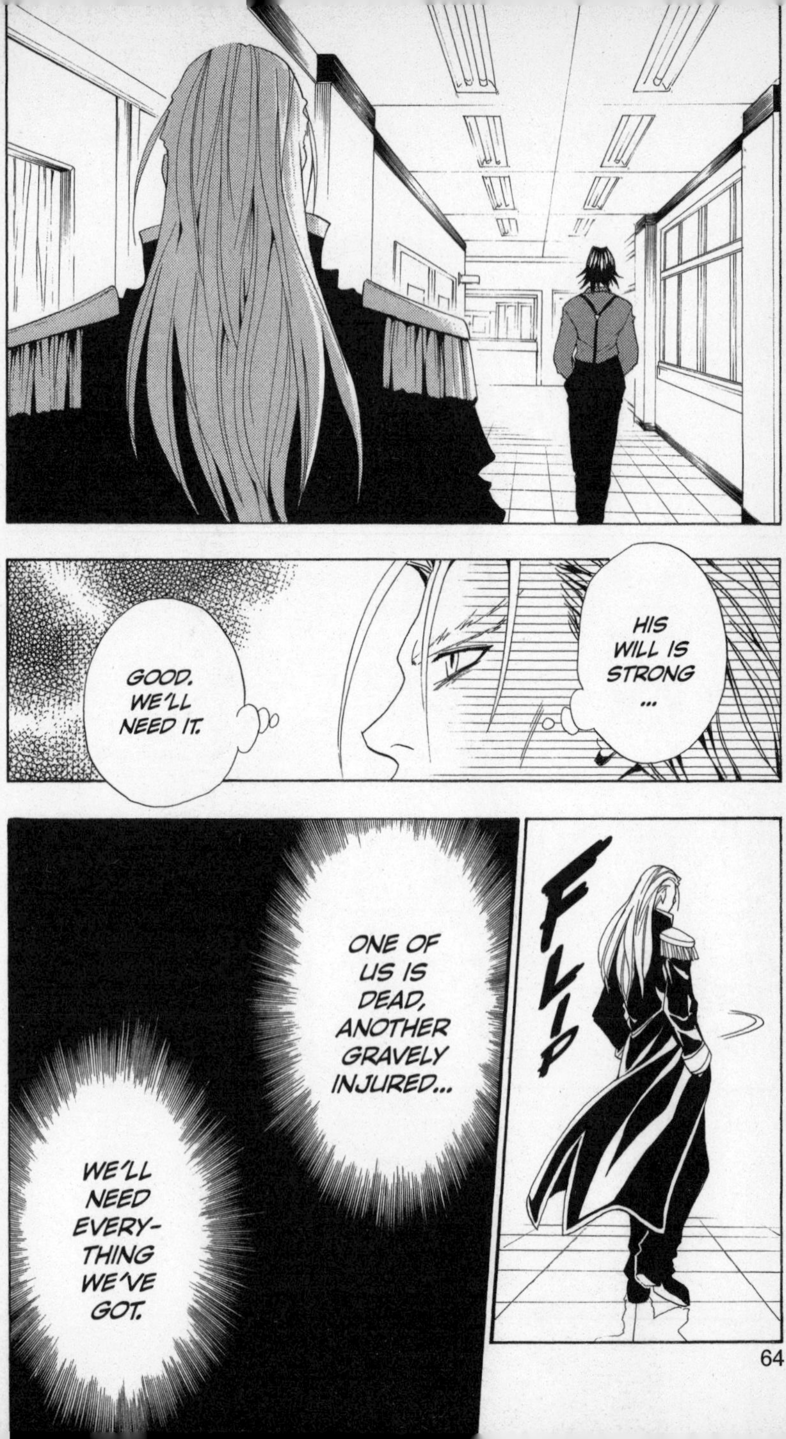
HIS WILL IS STRONG ...
GOOD. WE'LL NEED IT.
FLIP
ONE OF US IS DEAD, ANOTHER GRAVELY INJURED...
WE'LL NEED EVERY-THING WE'VE GOT.

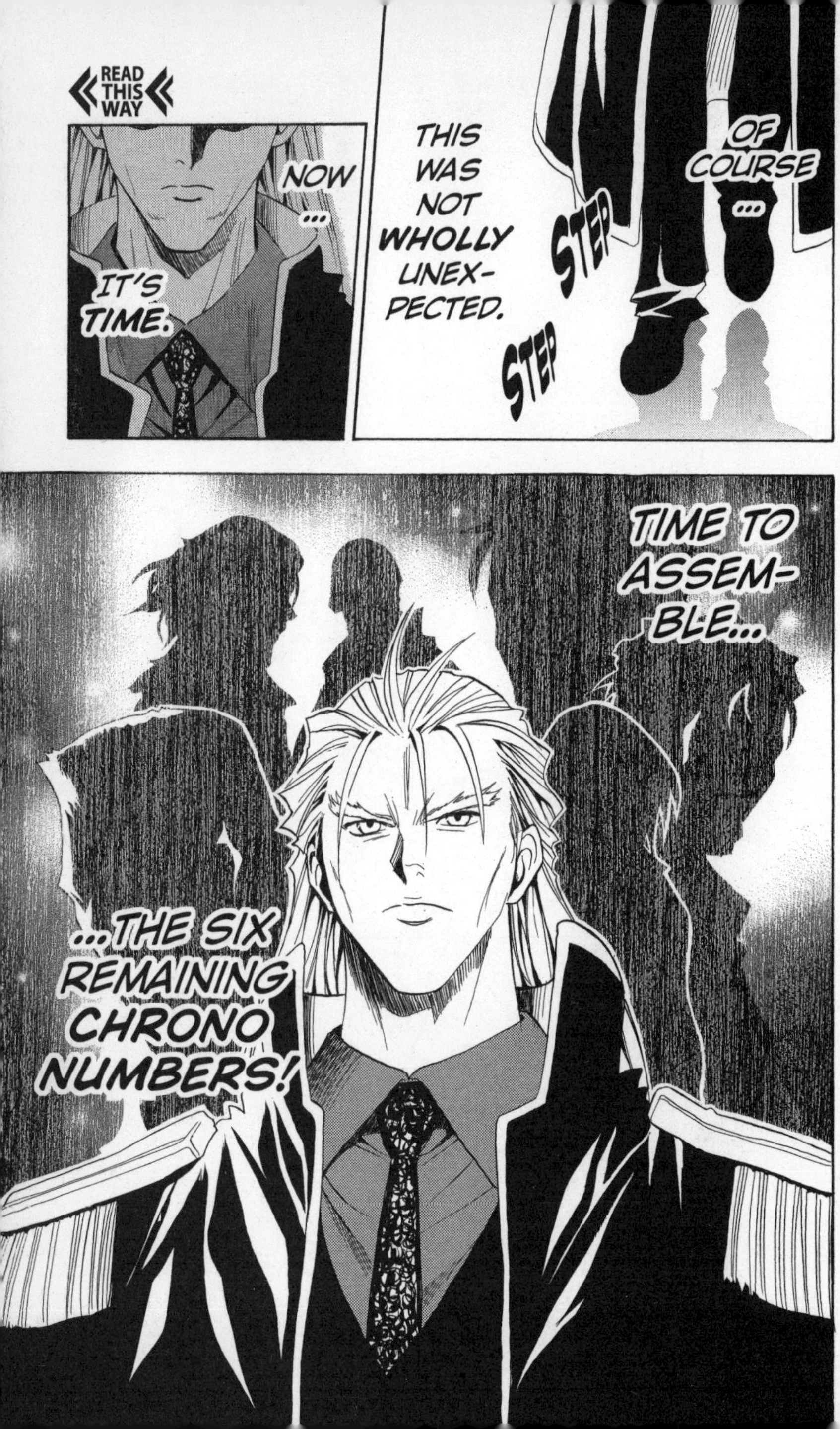
READ THIS WAY
OF COURSE ...
STEP STEP
THIS WAS NOT WHOLLY UNEXPECTED.
NOW ...
IT'S TIME.
TIME TO ASSEMBLE...
...THE SIX REMAINING CHRONO NUMBERS!

SKETCHES: PART 3

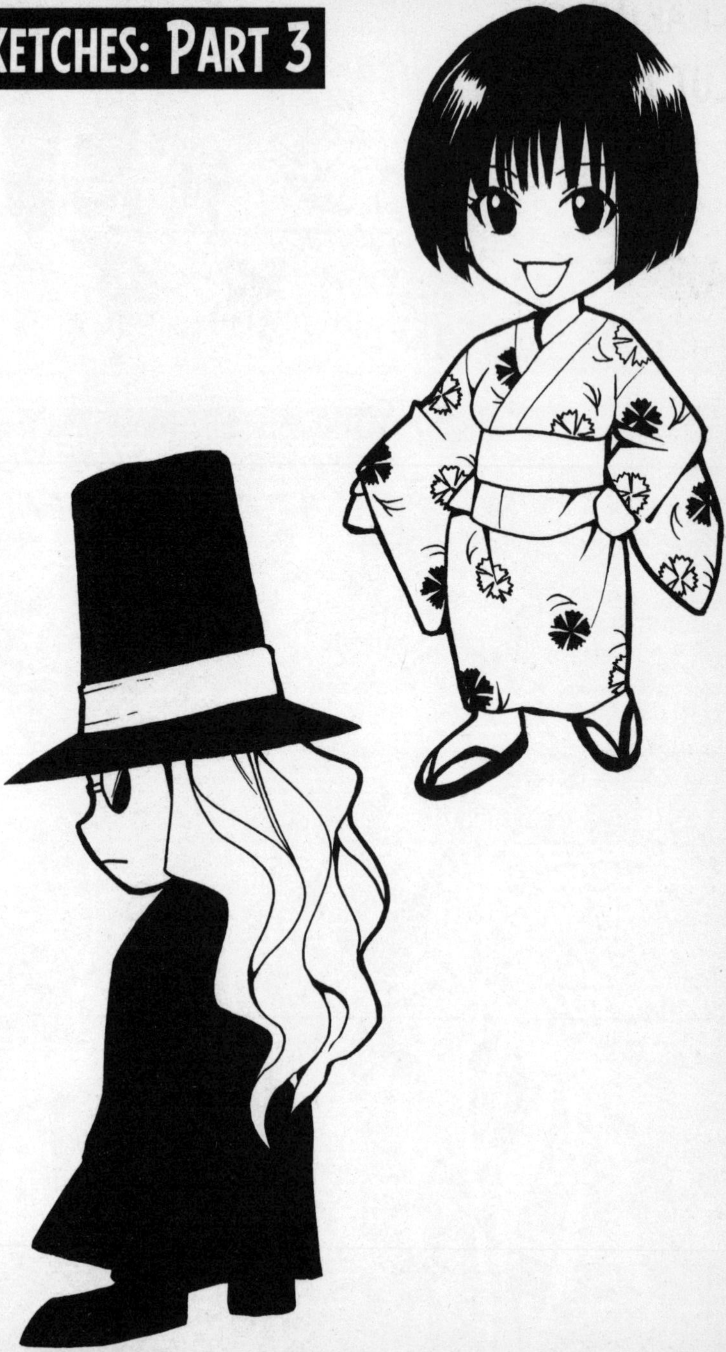

Chapter 88: Cut and Run

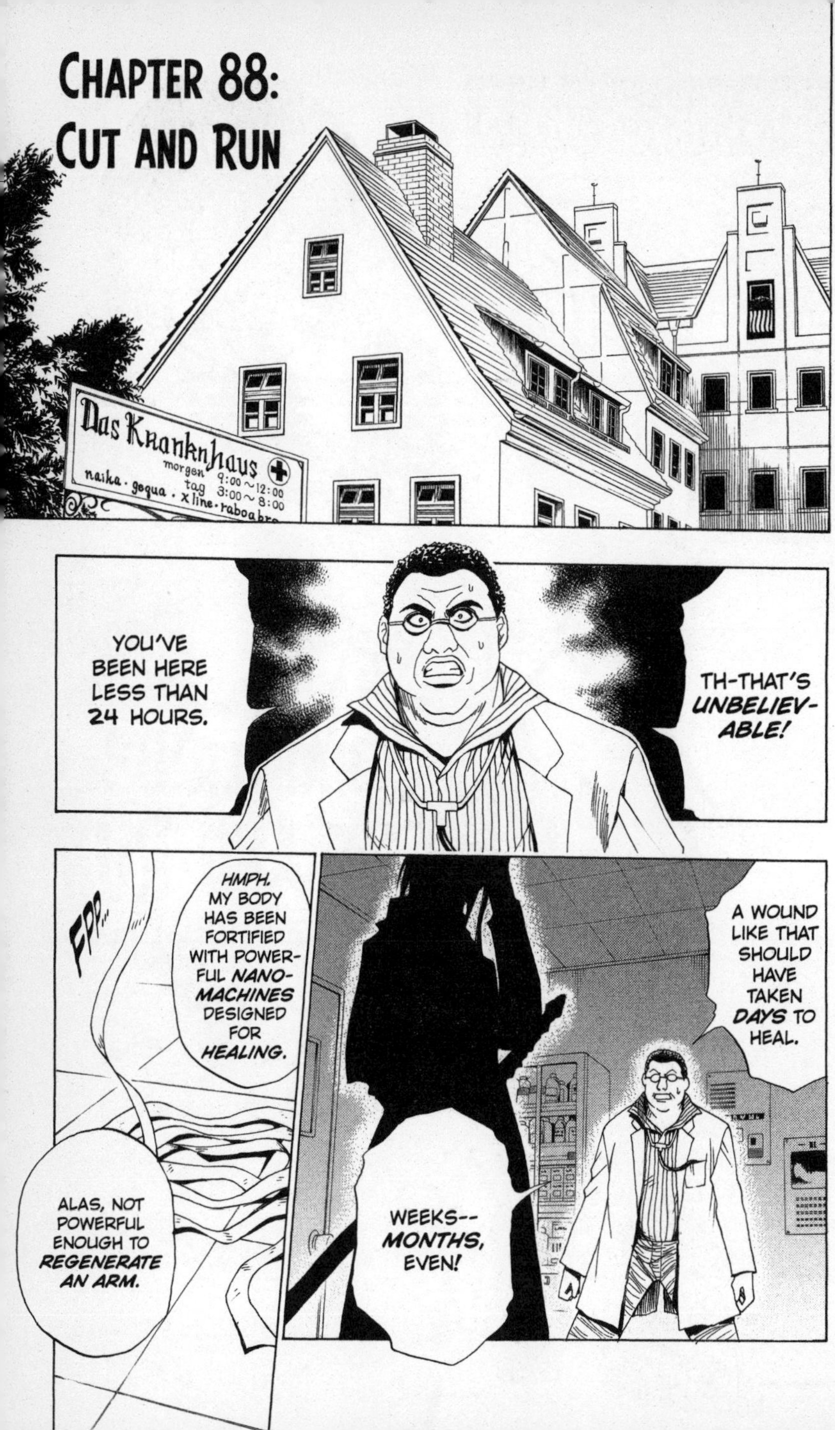
Das Kranknhaus
morgen 9:00 ~ 12:00
tag 3:00 ~ 8:00
naika . gequa . x line .
TH-THAT'S *UNBELIEV-ABLE!*
YOU'VE BEEN HERE LESS THAN 24 HOURS.
A WOUND LIKE THAT SHOULD HAVE TAKEN *DAYS* TO HEAL.
WEEKS-- *MONTHS,* EVEN!
HMPH. MY BODY HAS BEEN FORTIFIED WITH POWERFUL *NANO-MACHINES* DESIGNED FOR *HEALING.*
FPP...
ALAS, NOT POWERFUL ENOUGH TO *REGENERATE AN ARM.*

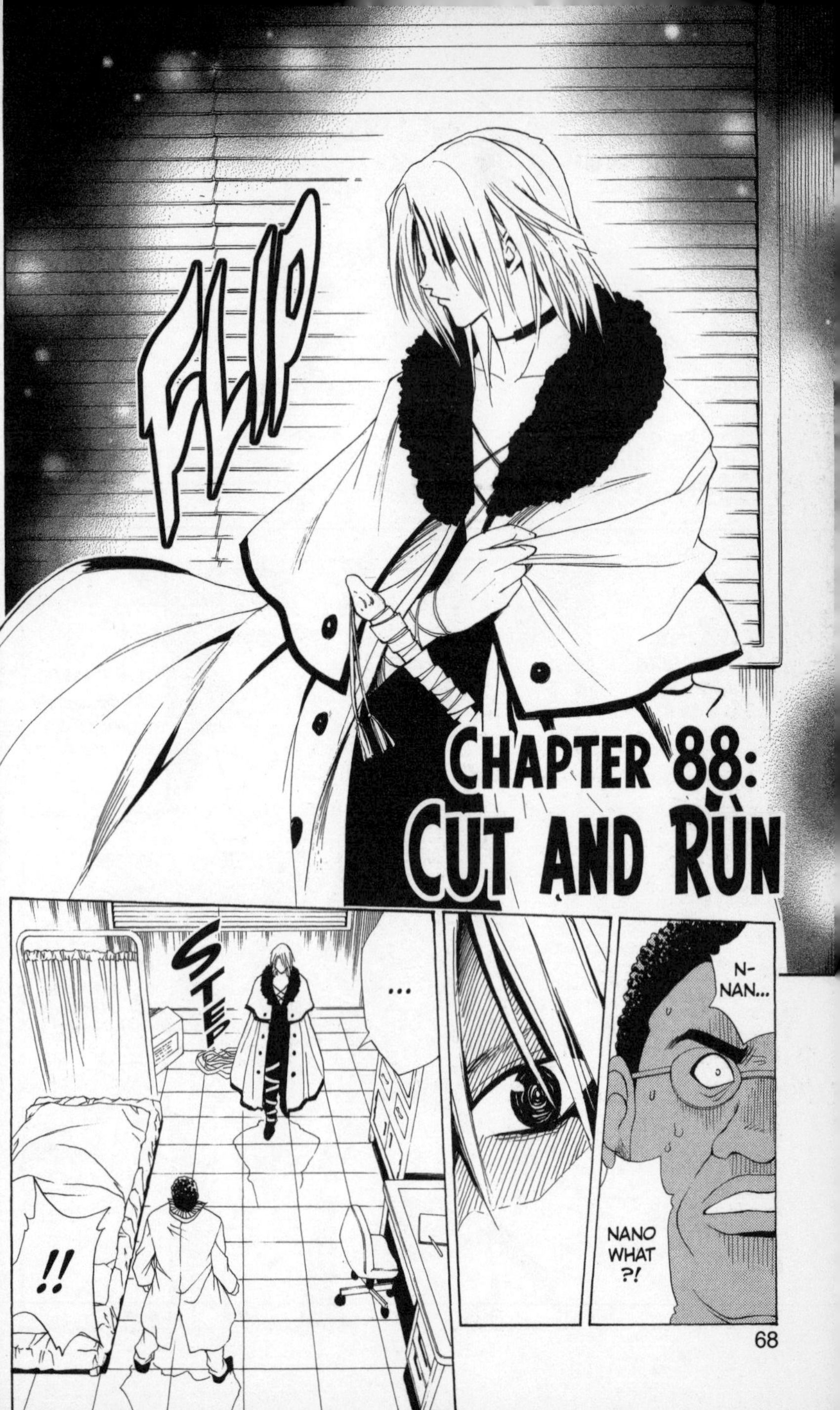
FLIP
CHAPTER 88:
CUT AND RUN
N- NAN...
NANO WHAT ?!
...
STEP
!!

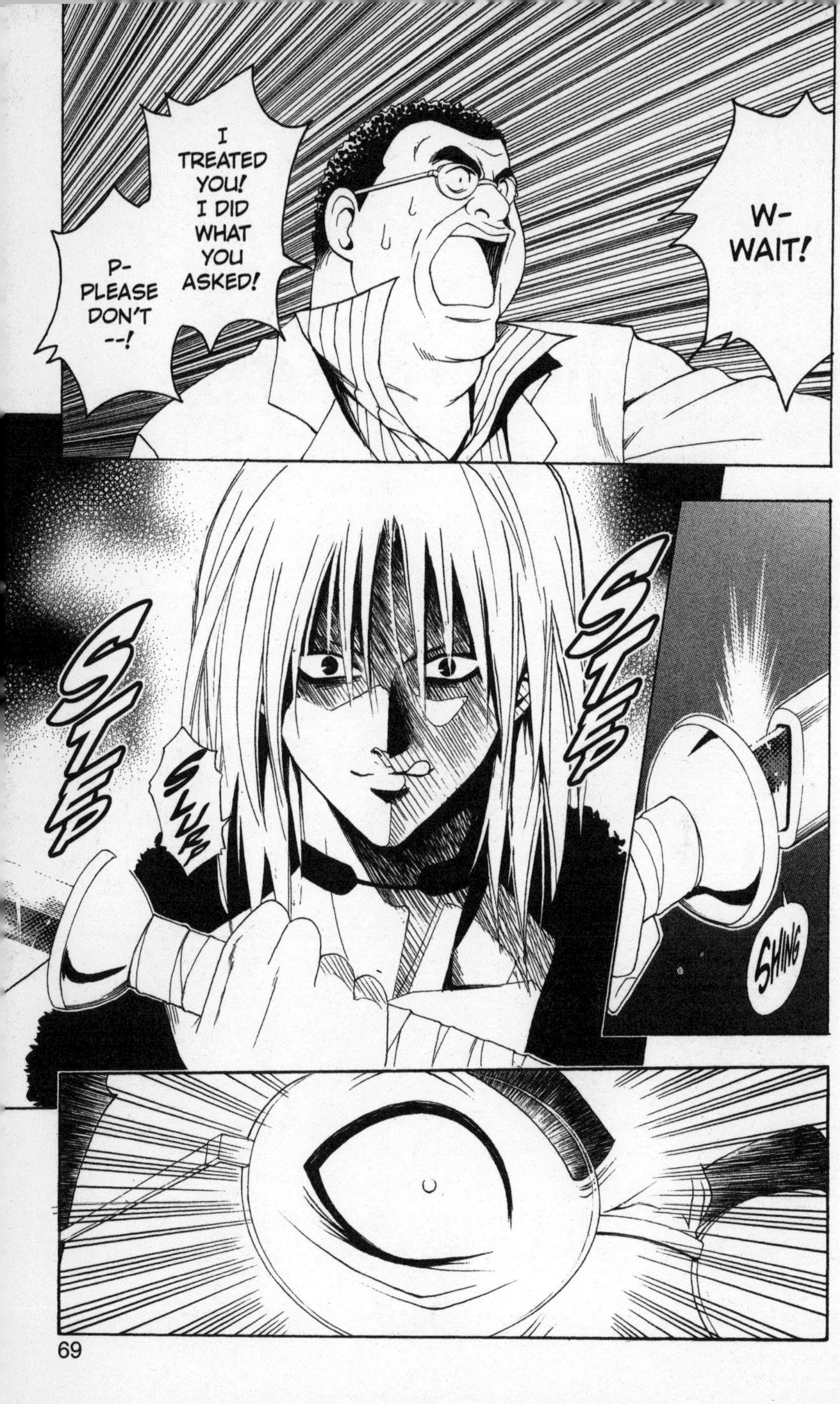

W-WAIT!
I TREATED YOU! I DID WHAT YOU ASKED!
P-PLEASE DON'T --!
SHING
SLURP
SLURP
SLURP

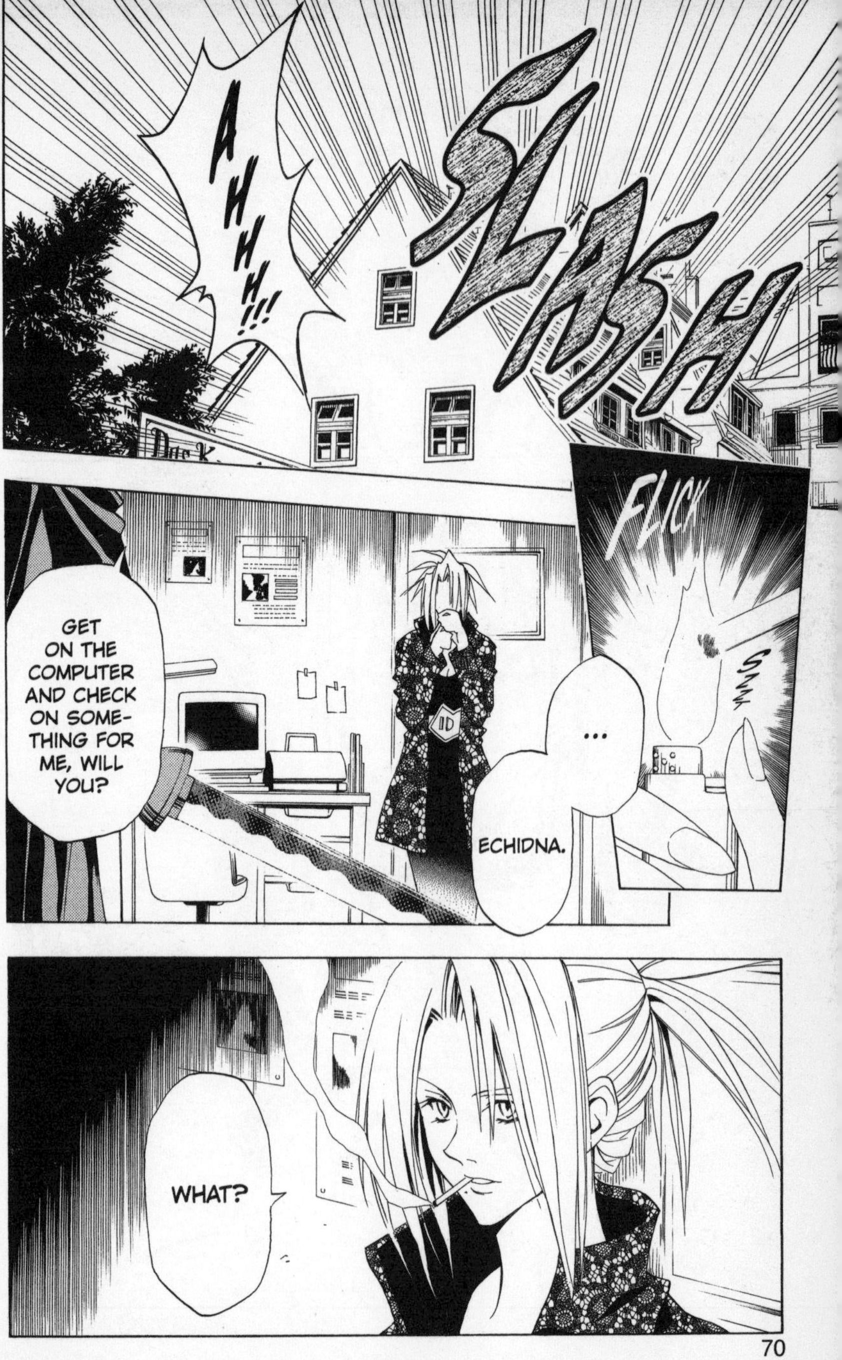
SLASH
AHHHH!!!
FLICK
...
ECHIDNA.
GET ON THE COMPUTER AND CHECK ON SOME-THING FOR ME, WILL YOU?
WHAT?

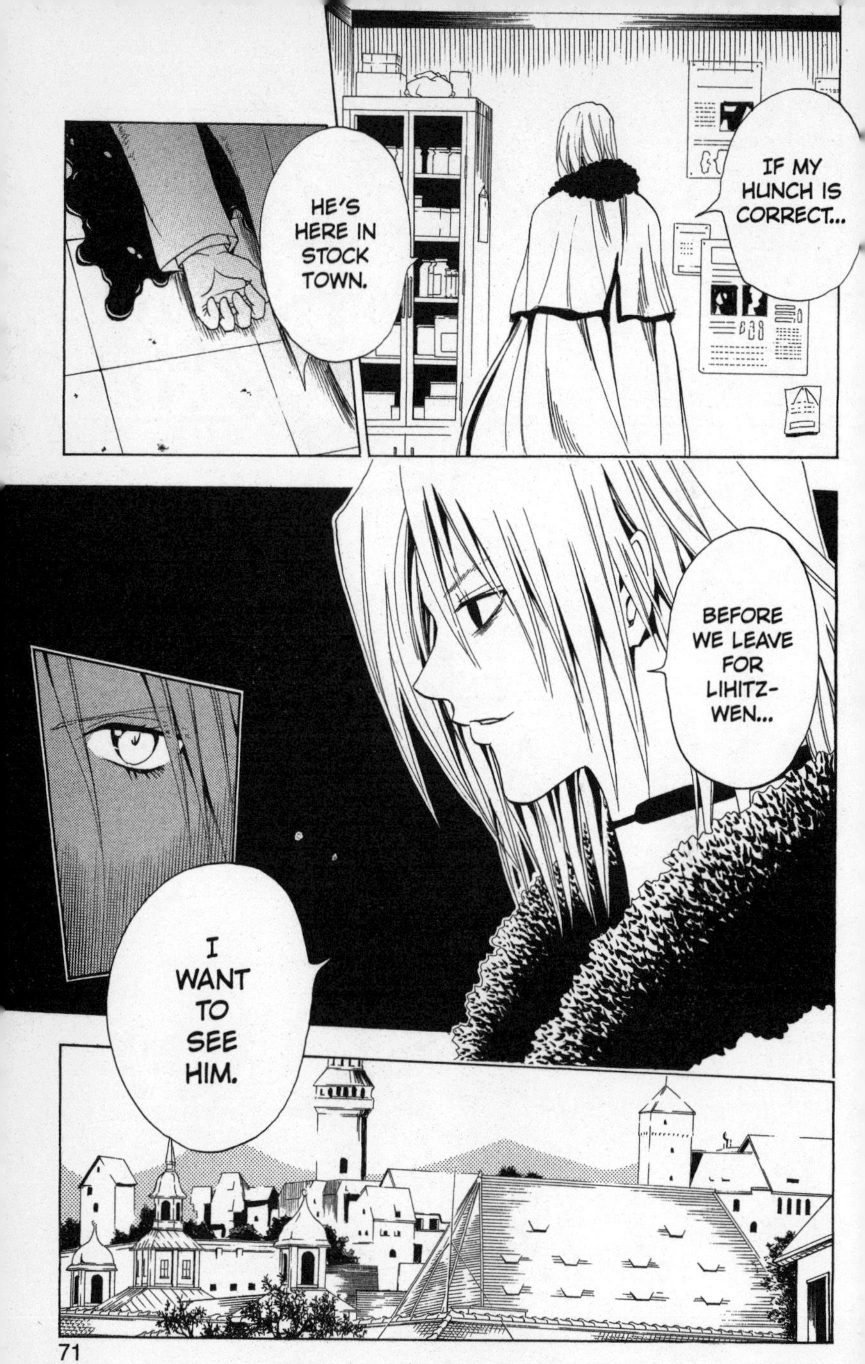
IF MY HUNCH IS CORRECT...
HE'S HERE IN STOCK TOWN.
BEFORE WE LEAVE FOR LIHITZ-WEN...
I WANT TO SEE HIM.

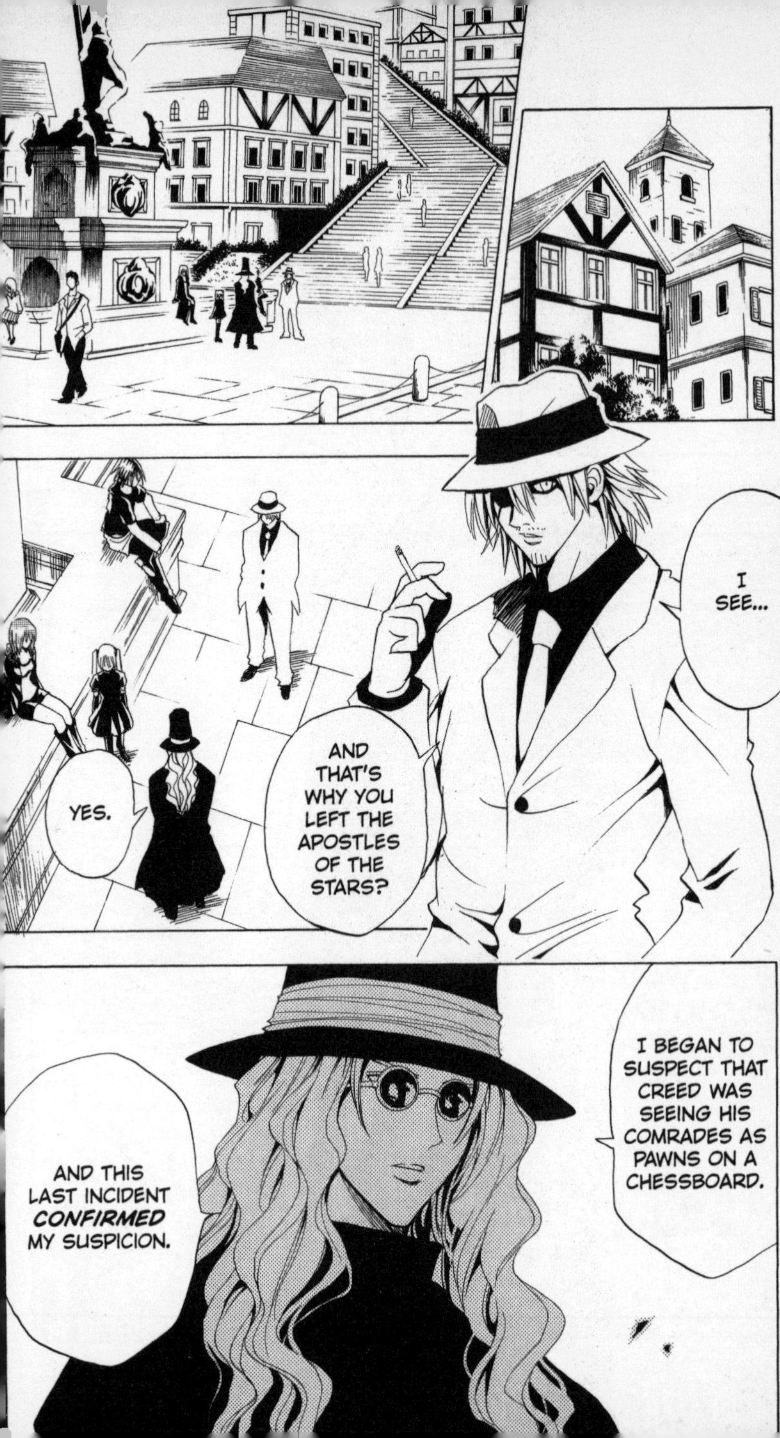
I SEE...
AND THAT'S WHY YOU LEFT THE APOSTLES OF THE STARS?
YES.
I BEGAN TO SUSPECT THAT CREED WAS SEEING HIS COMRADES AS PAWNS ON A CHESSBOARD.
AND THIS LAST INCIDENT *CONFIRMED* MY SUSPICION.

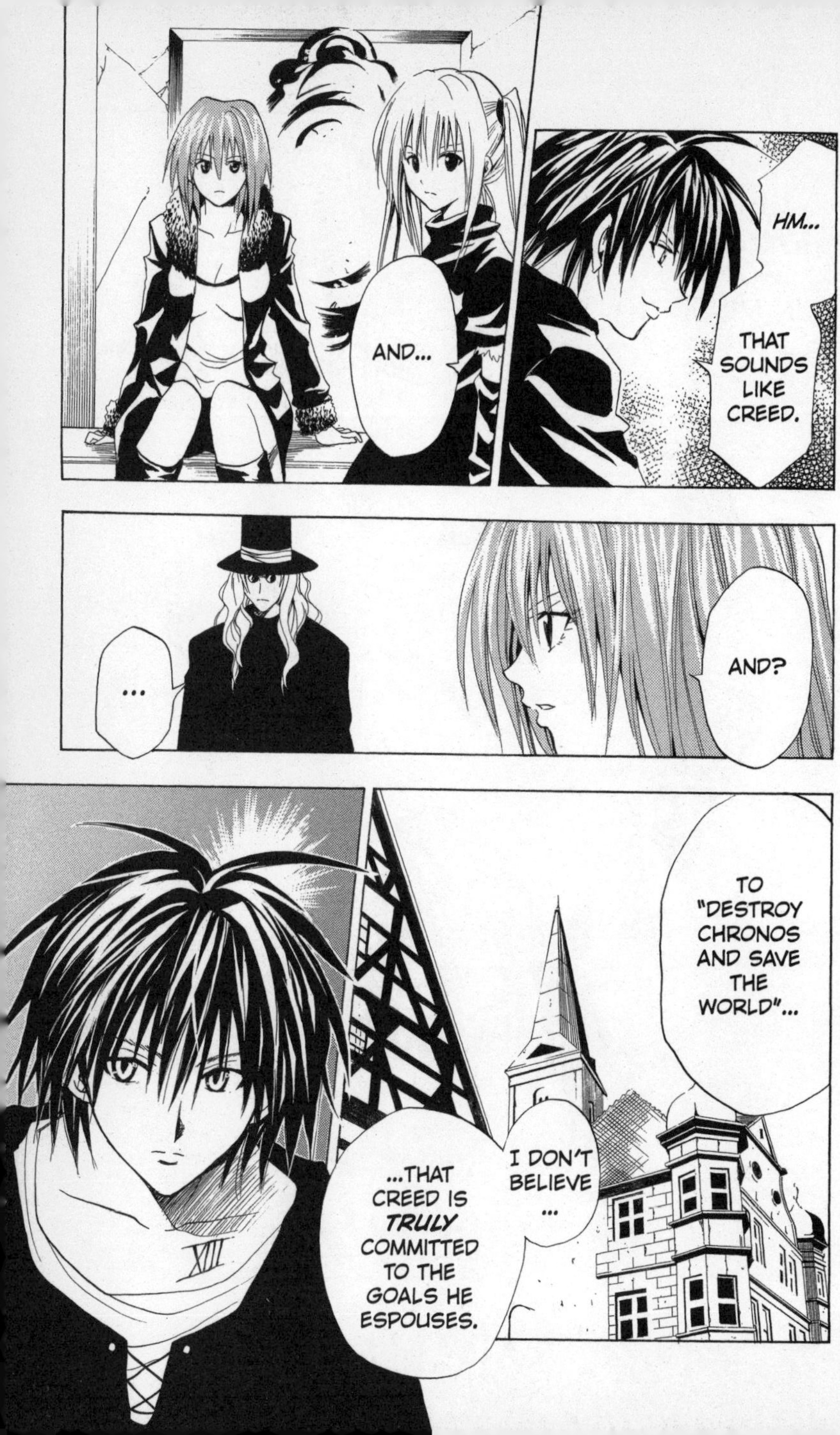
HM...
THAT SOUNDS LIKE CREED.
AND...
AND?
...
TO "DESTROY CHRONOS AND SAVE THE WORLD"...
I DON'T BELIEVE ...
...THAT CREED IS TRULY COMMITTED TO THE GOALS HE ESPOUSES.

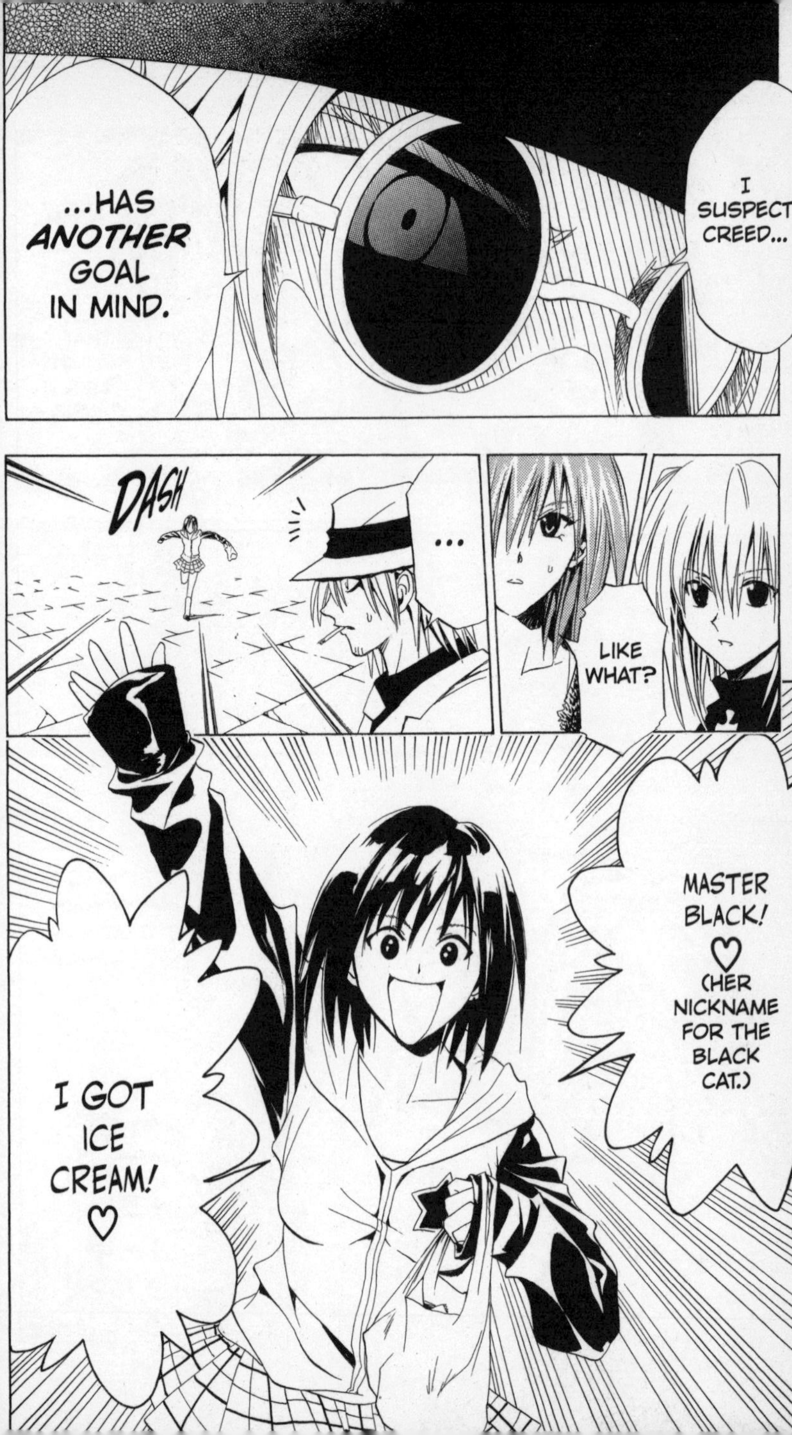
I SUSPECT CREED...
...HAS *ANOTHER* GOAL IN MIND.
LIKE WHAT?
DASH
...
MASTER BLACK! ♡
(HER NICKNAME FOR THE BLACK CAT.)
I GOT ICE CREAM! ♡

READ THIS WAY

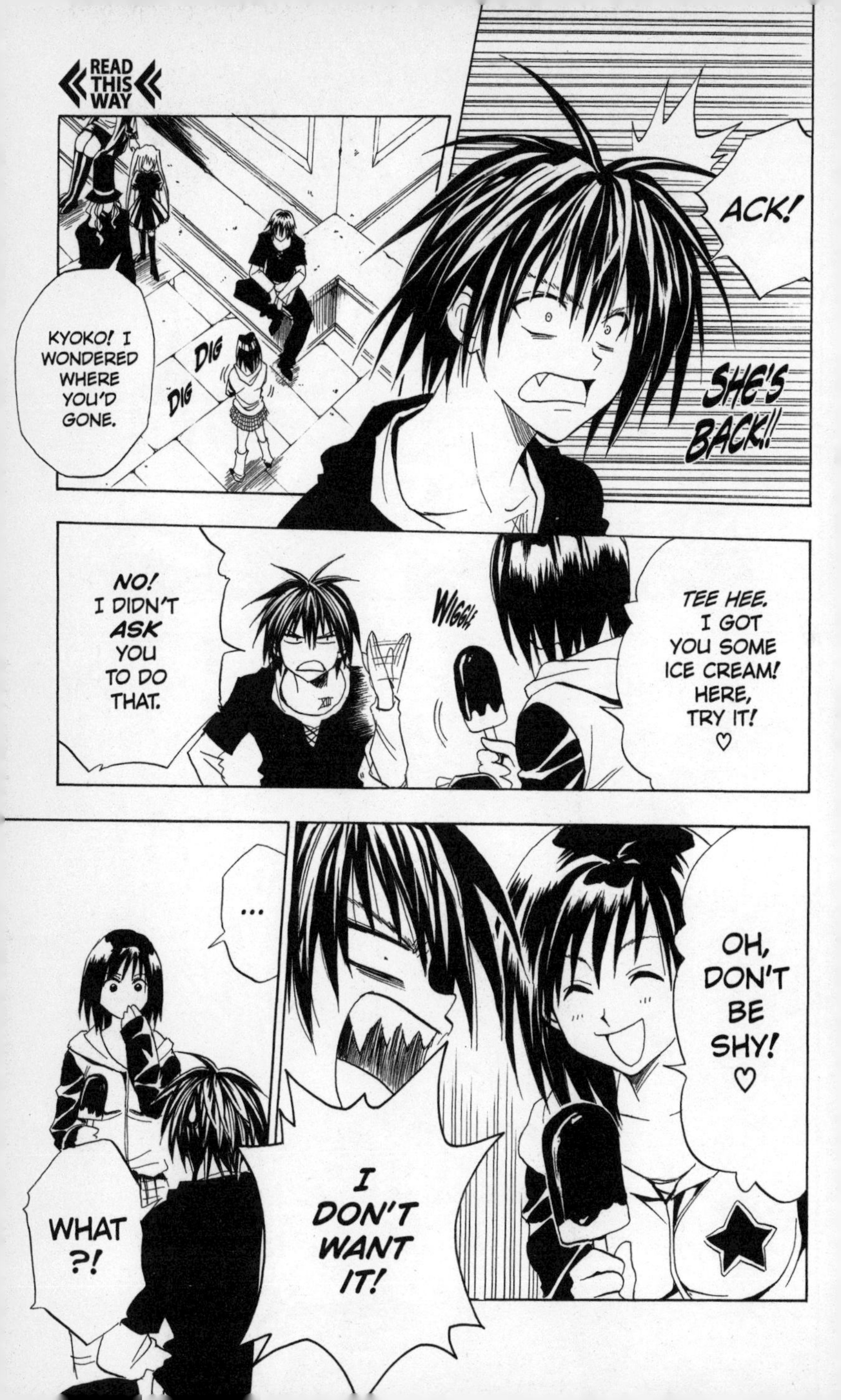
ACK!
SHE'S BACK!!
KYOKO! I WONDERED WHERE YOU'D GONE.
DIG
DIG
TEE HEE. I GOT YOU SOME ICE CREAM! HERE, TRY IT! ♡
WIGGLE
NO! I DIDN'T ASK YOU TO DO THAT.
OH, DON'T BE SHY! ♡
I DON'T WANT IT!
...
WHAT?!

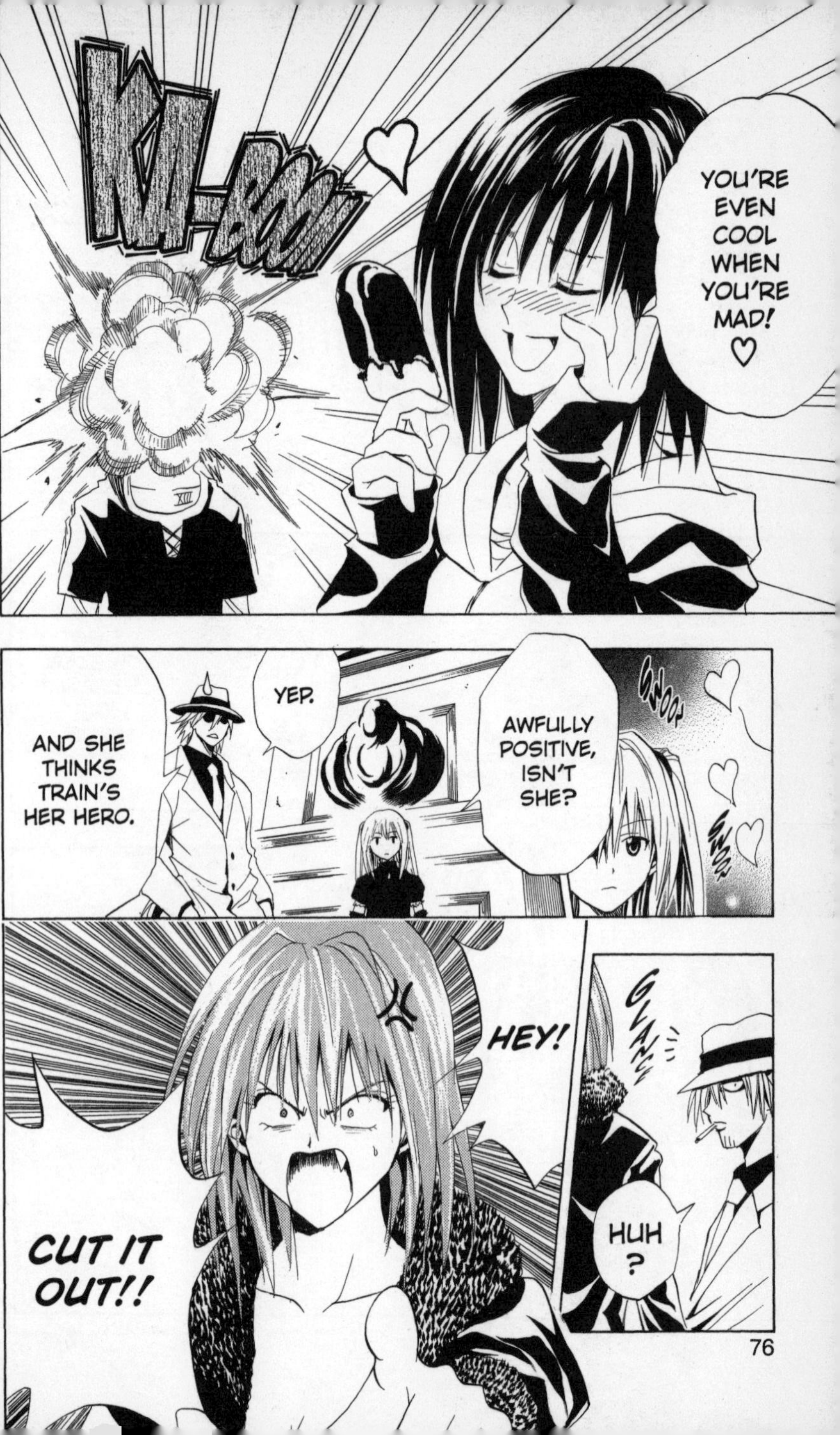
KA-BOOM
YOU'RE EVEN COOL WHEN YOU'RE MAD! ♡
AWFULLY POSITIVE, ISN'T SHE?
YEP.
AND SHE THINKS TRAIN'S HER HERO.
GLANCE
HUH?
HEY!
CUT IT OUT!!

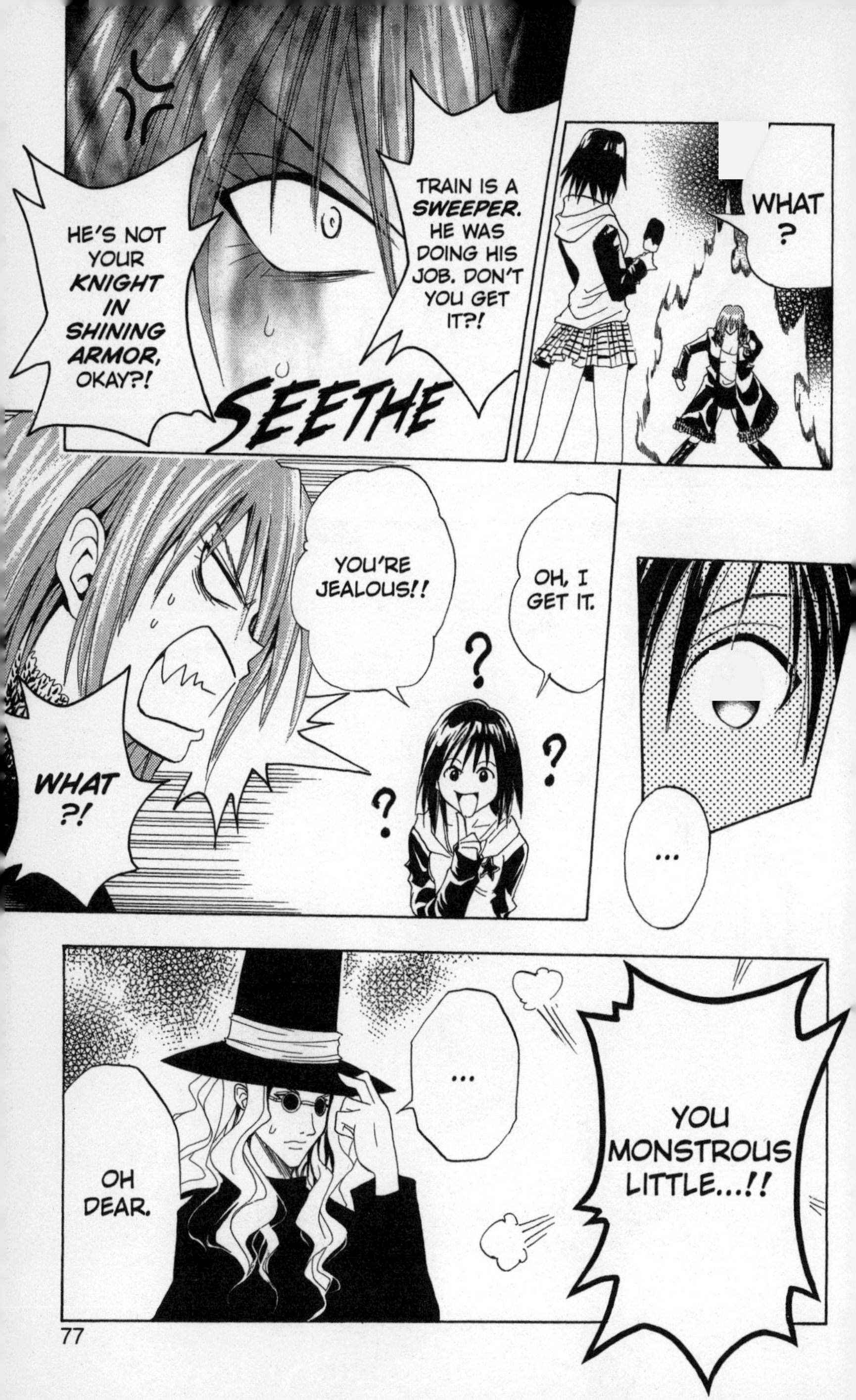
WHAT ?
TRAIN IS A SWEEPER. HE WAS DOING HIS JOB. DON'T YOU GET IT?!
HE'S NOT YOUR KNIGHT IN SHINING ARMOR, OKAY?!
SEETHE
...
OH, I GET IT.
YOU'RE JEALOUS!!
?
?
?
WHAT ?!
YOU MONSTROUS LITTLE...!!
...
OH DEAR.

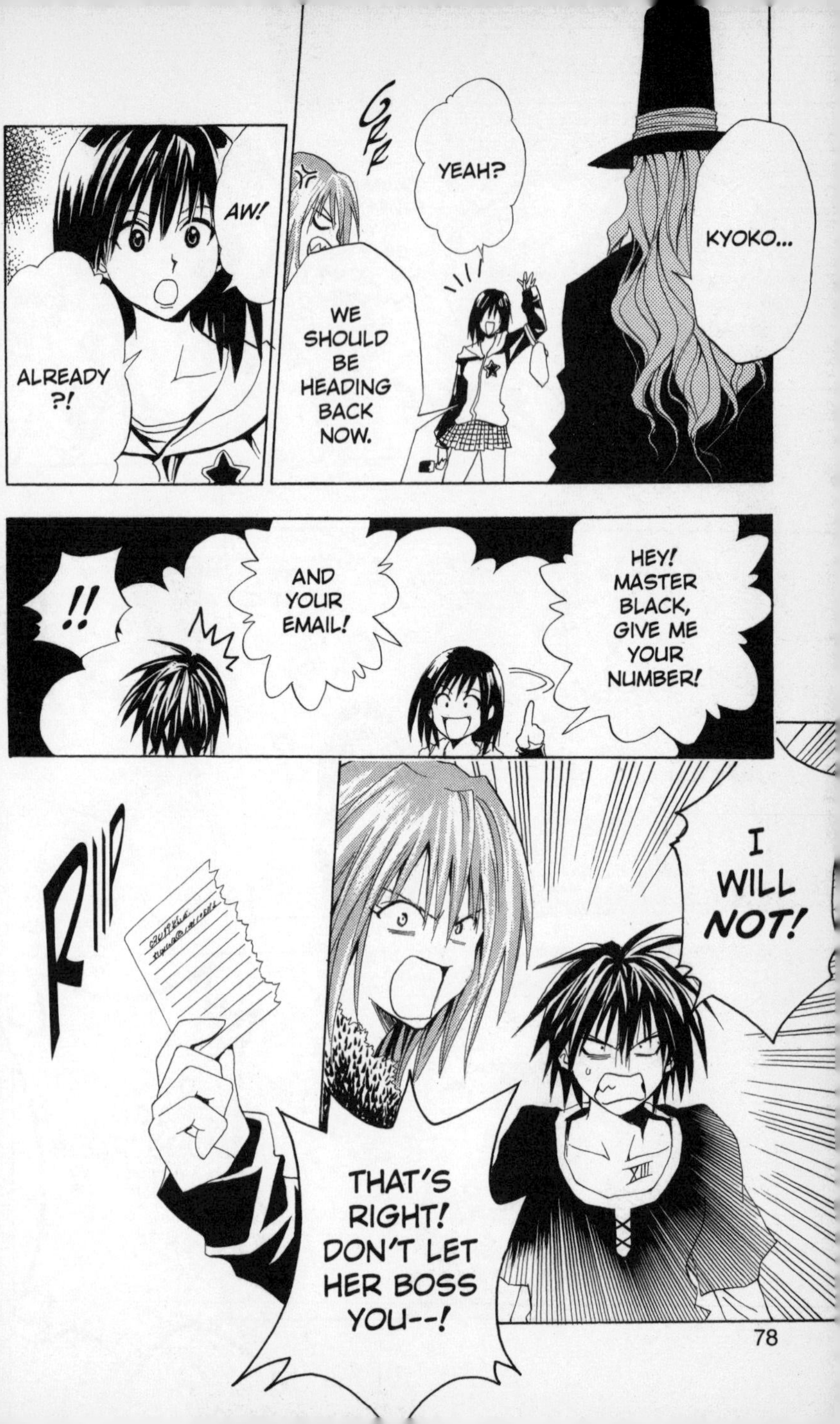
KYOKO...
YEAH?
GRR
WE SHOULD BE HEADING BACK NOW.
AW!
ALREADY?!
HEY! MASTER BLACK, GIVE ME YOUR NUMBER!
AND YOUR EMAIL!
!!
I WILL NOT!
RIP
THAT'S RIGHT! DON'T LET HER BOSS YOU--!

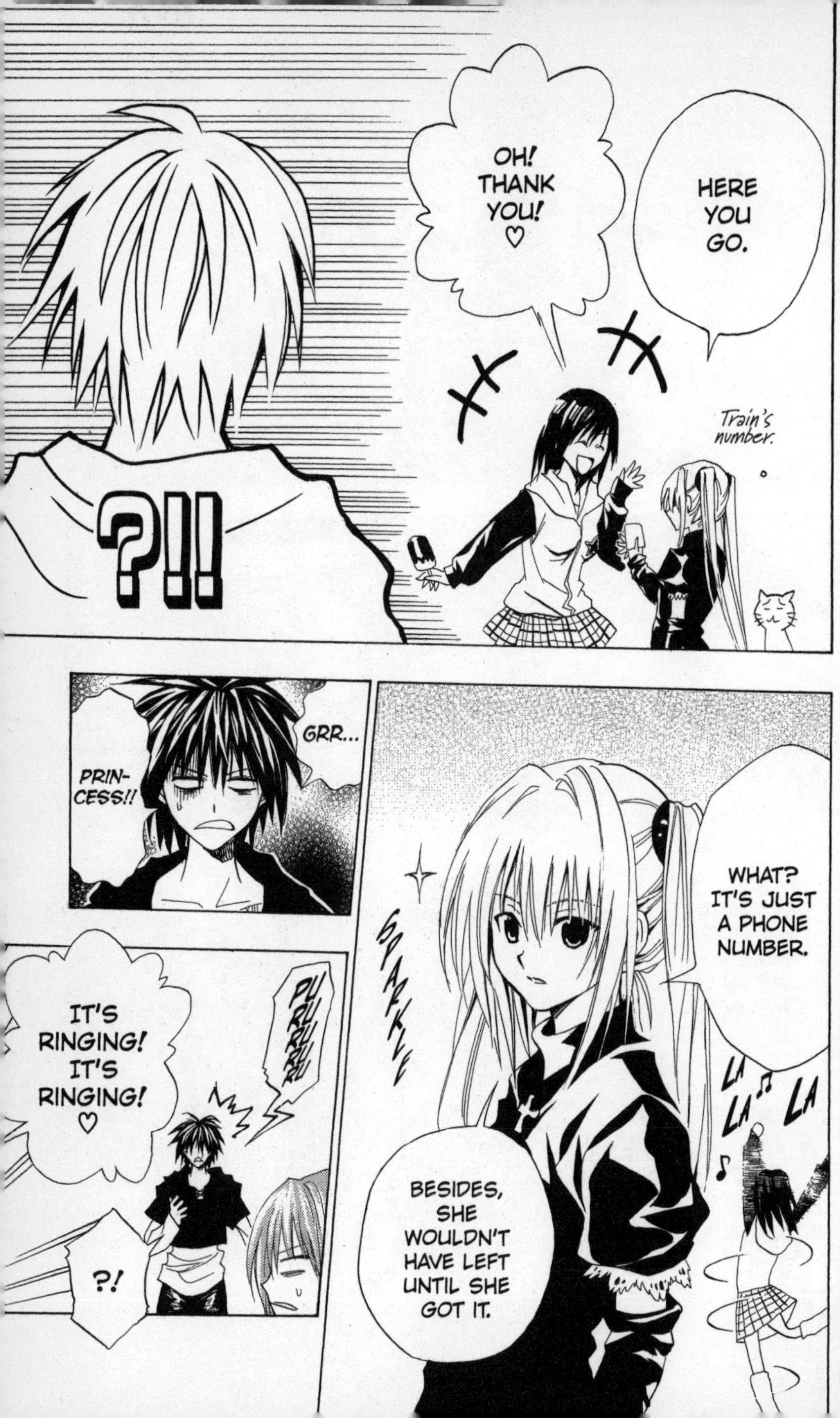
HERE YOU GO.
OH! THANK YOU! ♡
Train's number.
?!!
WHAT? IT'S JUST A PHONE NUMBER.
SPARKLE
LA LA ♪ LA ♪
BESIDES, SHE WOULDN'T HAVE LEFT UNTIL SHE GOT IT.
GRR...
PRIN-CESS!!
PURURURURU
IT'S RINGING! IT'S RINGING! ♡
?!

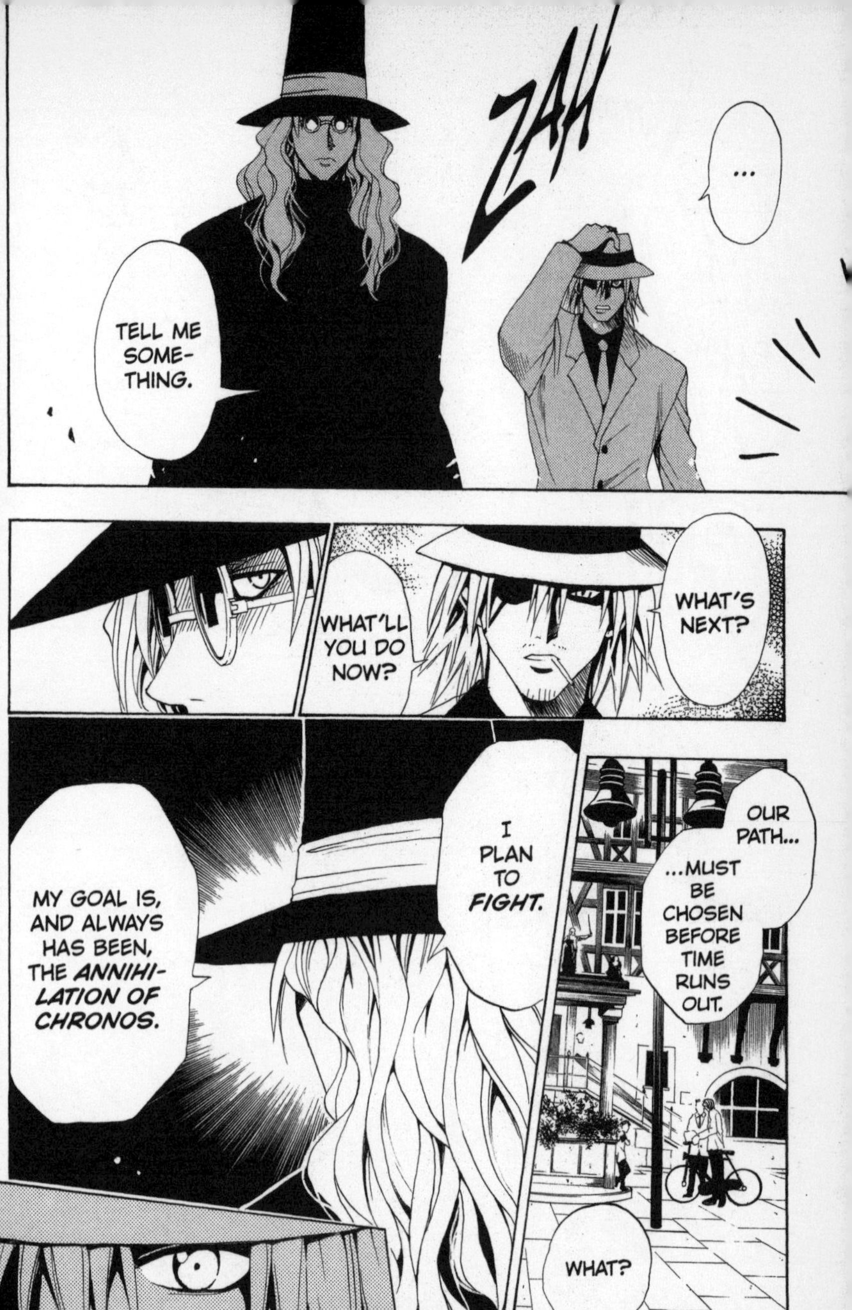
...
ZAH
TELL ME SOME-THING.
WHAT'S NEXT?
WHAT'LL YOU DO NOW?
OUR PATH...
...MUST BE CHOSEN BEFORE TIME RUNS OUT.
WHAT?
I PLAN TO *FIGHT*.
MY GOAL IS, AND ALWAYS HAS BEEN, THE *ANNIHILATION OF CHRONOS*.

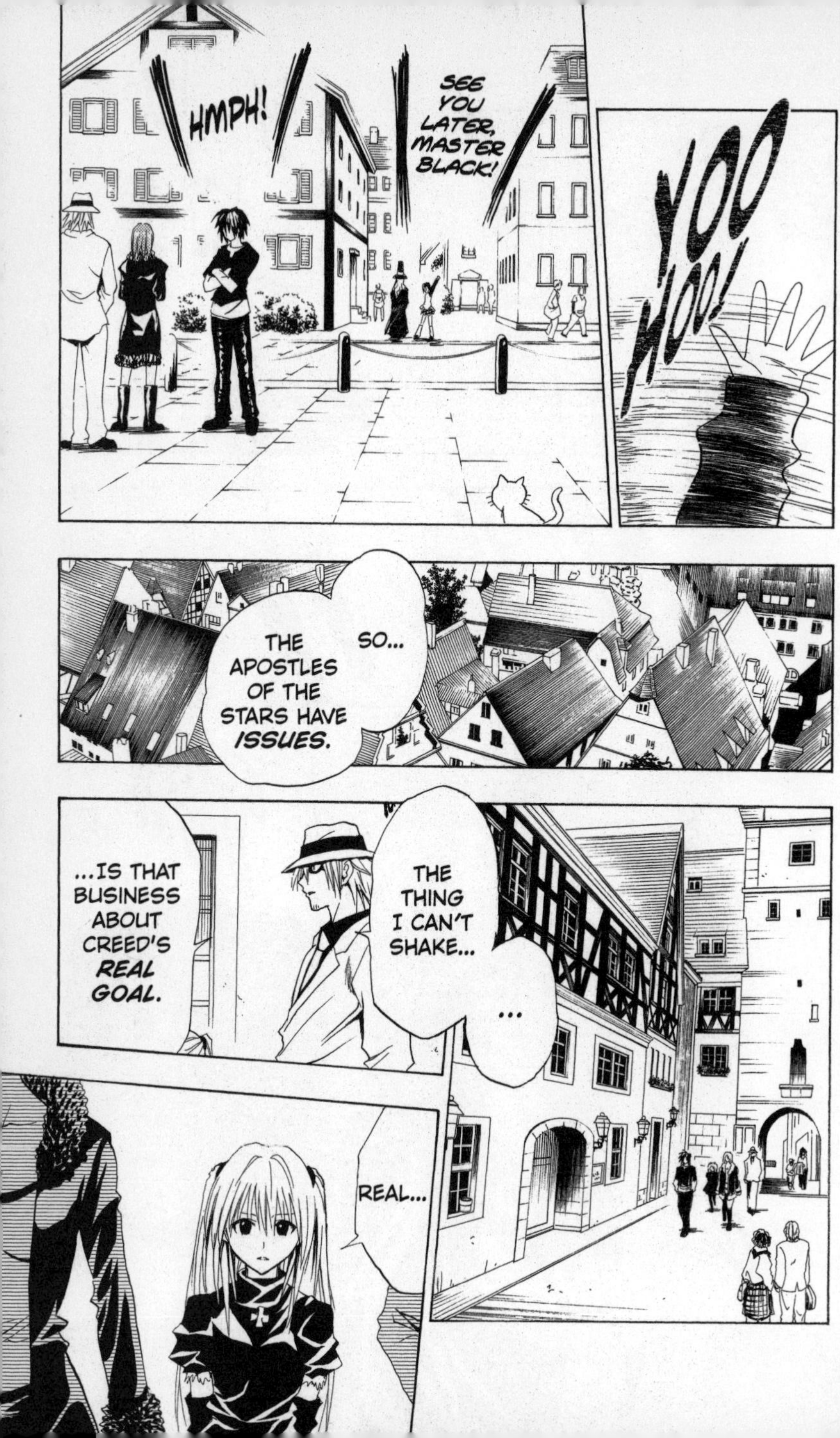
YOO HOO!
SEE YOU LATER, MASTER BLACK!
HMPH!
SO...
THE APOSTLES OF THE STARS HAVE *ISSUES.*
THE THING I CAN'T SHAKE...
...IS THAT BUSINESS ABOUT CREED'S *REAL* GOAL.
...
REAL...

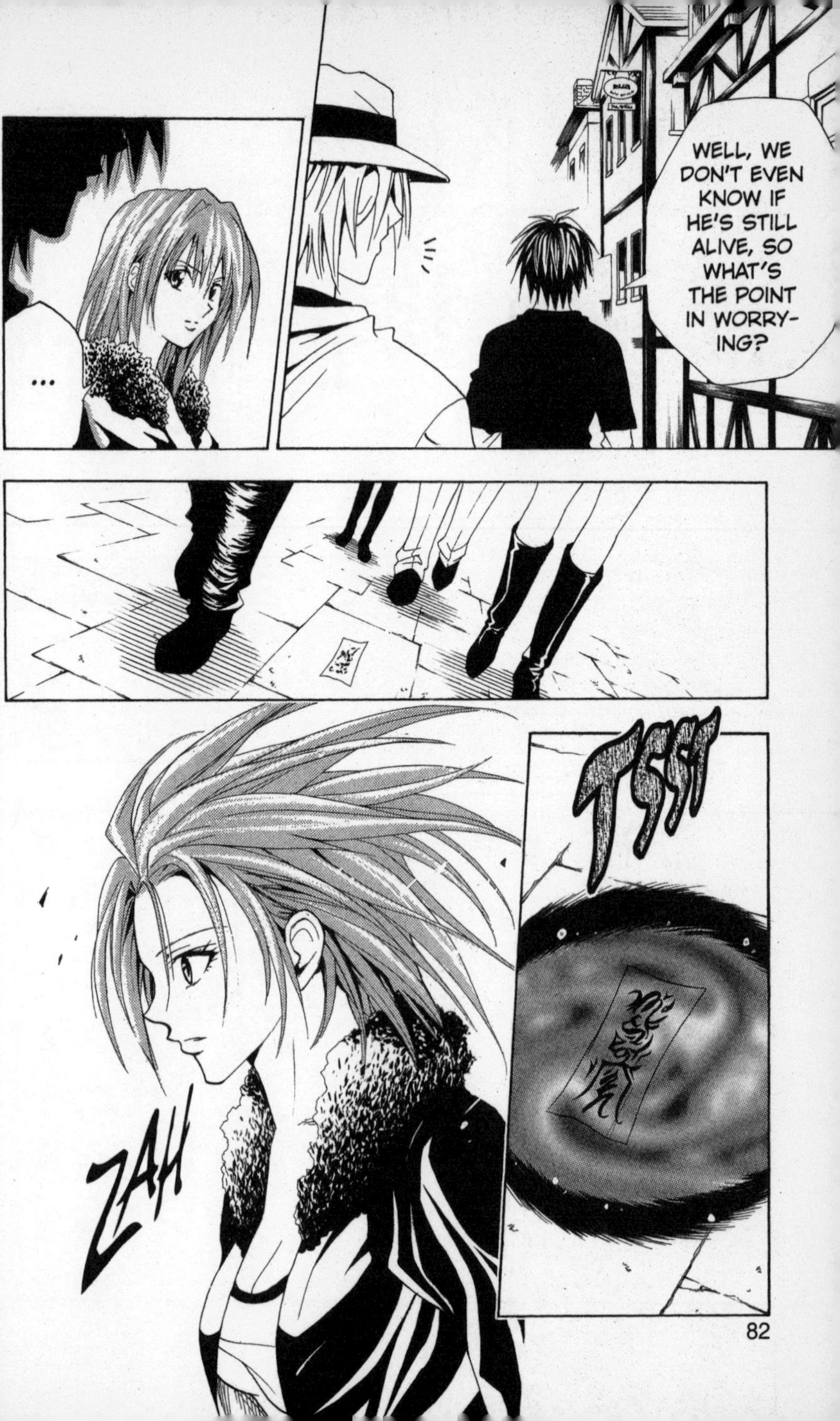
WELL, WE DON'T EVEN KNOW IF HE'S STILL ALIVE, SO WHAT'S THE POINT IN WORRY-ING?
...
TSST
ZAH

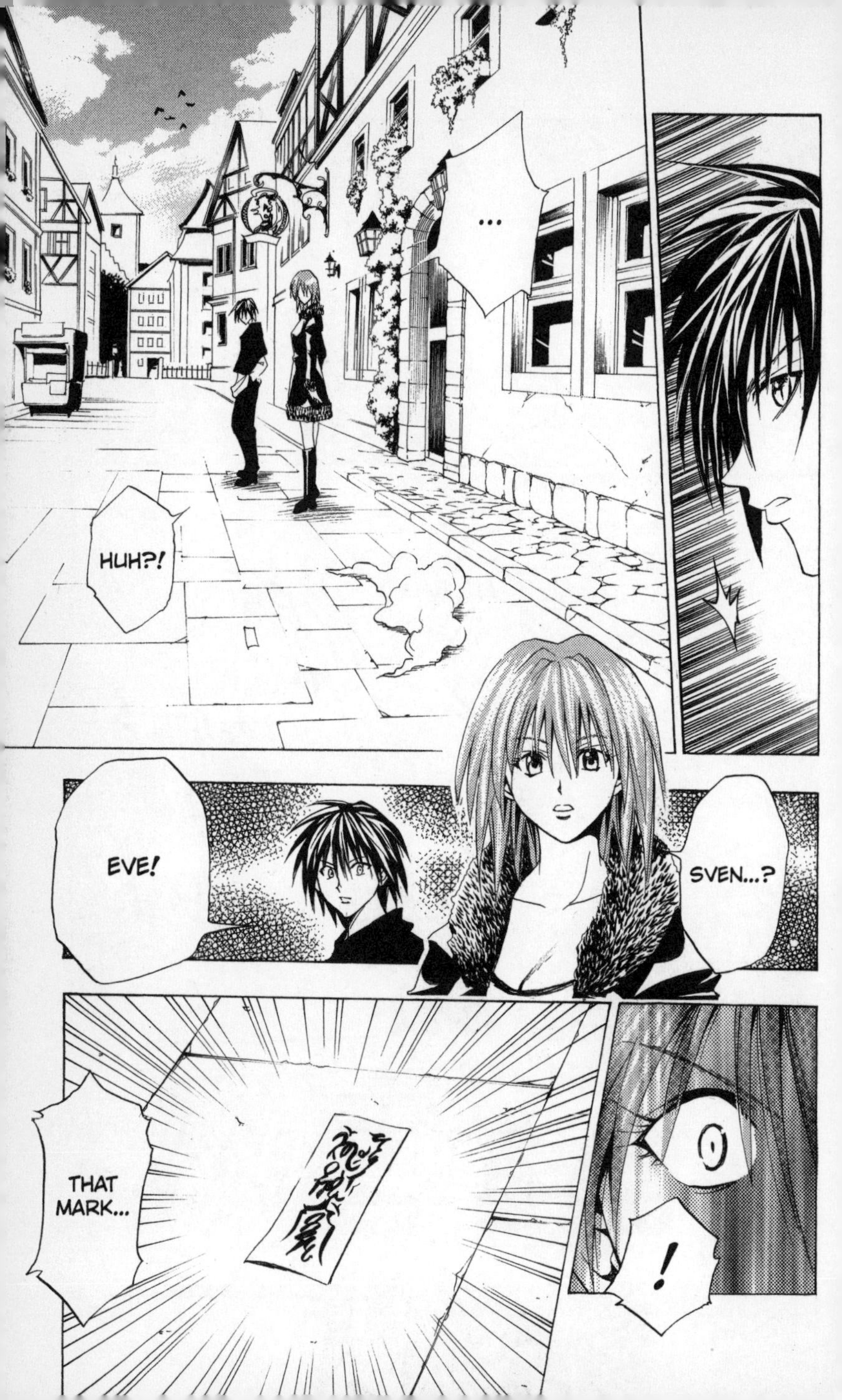
...
HUH?!
SVEN...?
EVE!
!
THAT MARK...

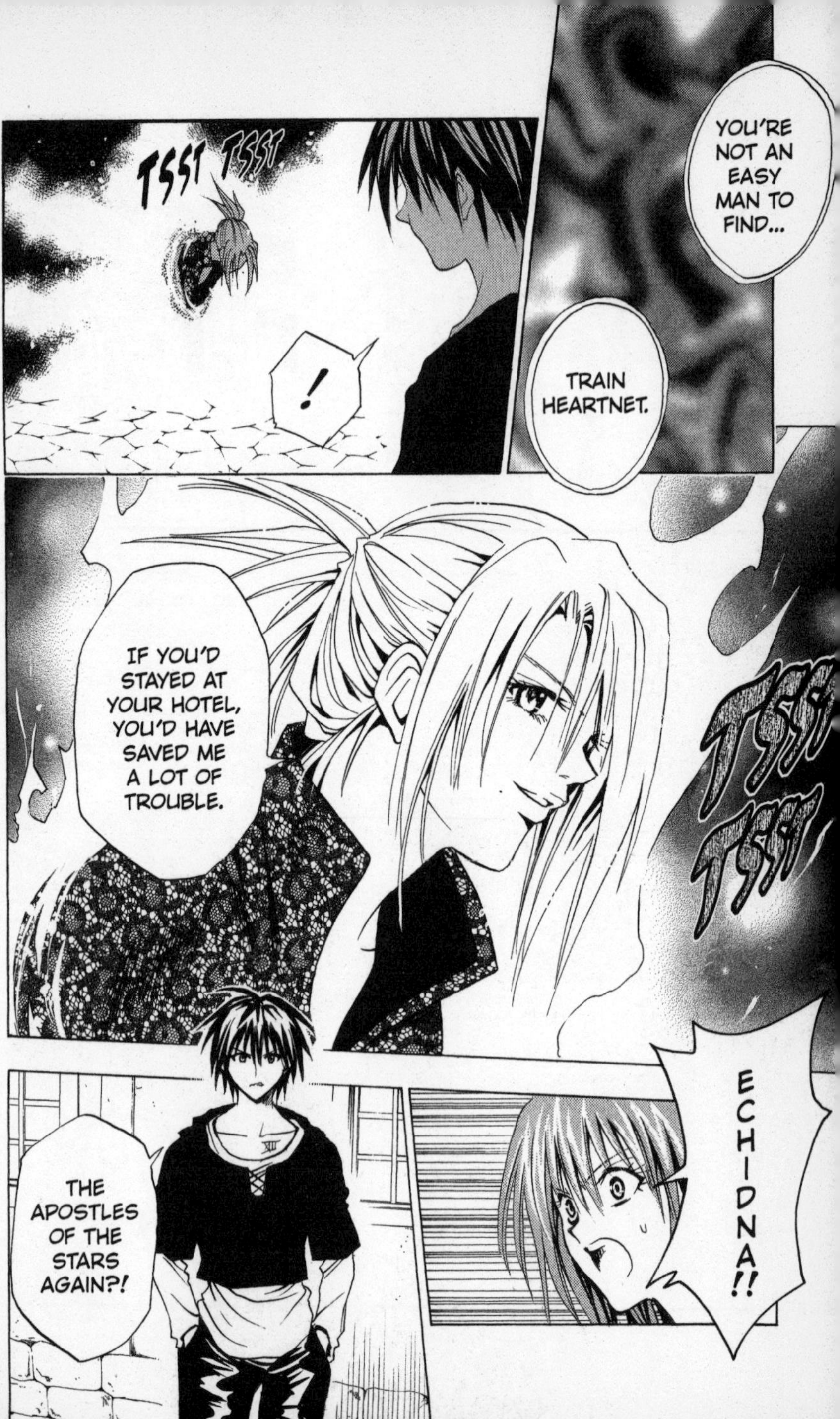
YOU'RE NOT AN EASY MAN TO FIND...
TRAIN HEARTNET.
TSST TSST
!
TSST TSST
IF YOU'D STAYED AT YOUR HOTEL, YOU'D HAVE SAVED ME A LOT OF TROUBLE.
ECHIDNA!!
THE APOSTLES OF THE STARS AGAIN?!

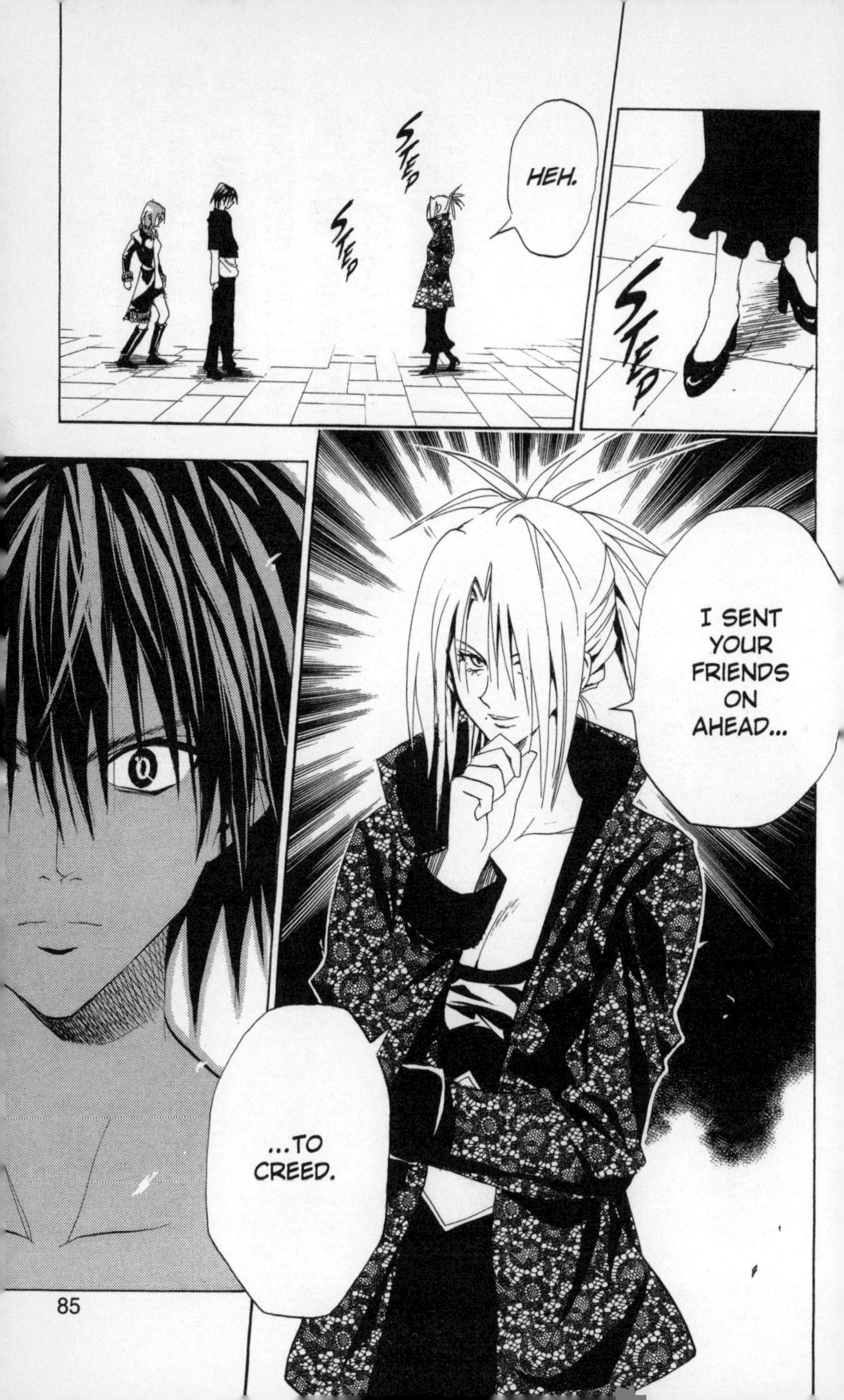
STEP
HEH.
STEP
STEP
I SENT YOUR FRIENDS ON AHEAD...
...TO CREED.

◎ *Akamaru Jump* Poster design of Eve
The theme was "Sexy Summer,"
so I wasn't sure whom to feature,
but I decided on Eve.
(I considered Rinslet and
Kyoko both, but Eve seemed
the most refined.)
The medium was colored ink.

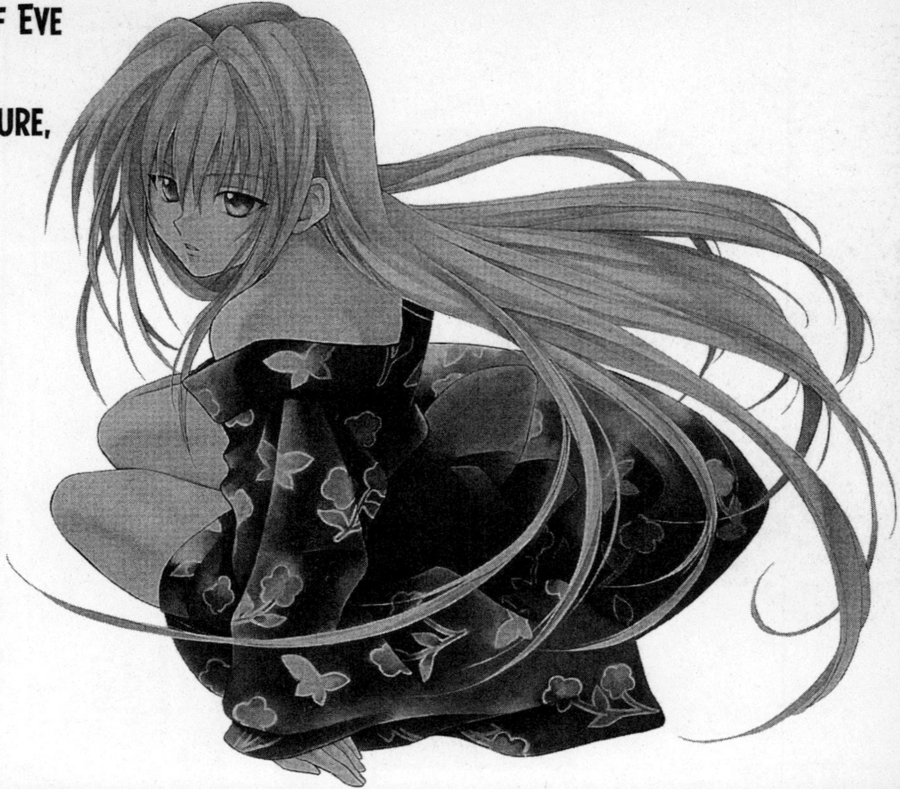

Chapter 89: Creed's Doubt

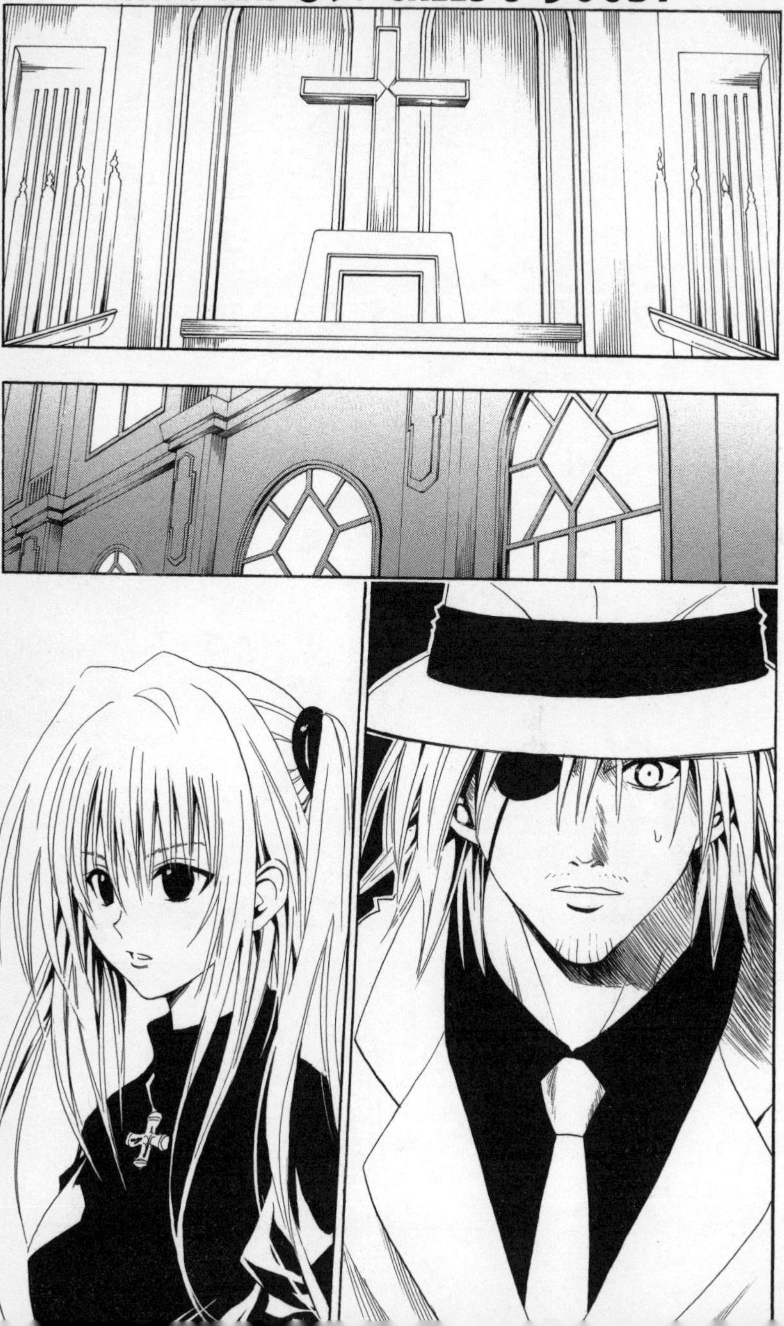

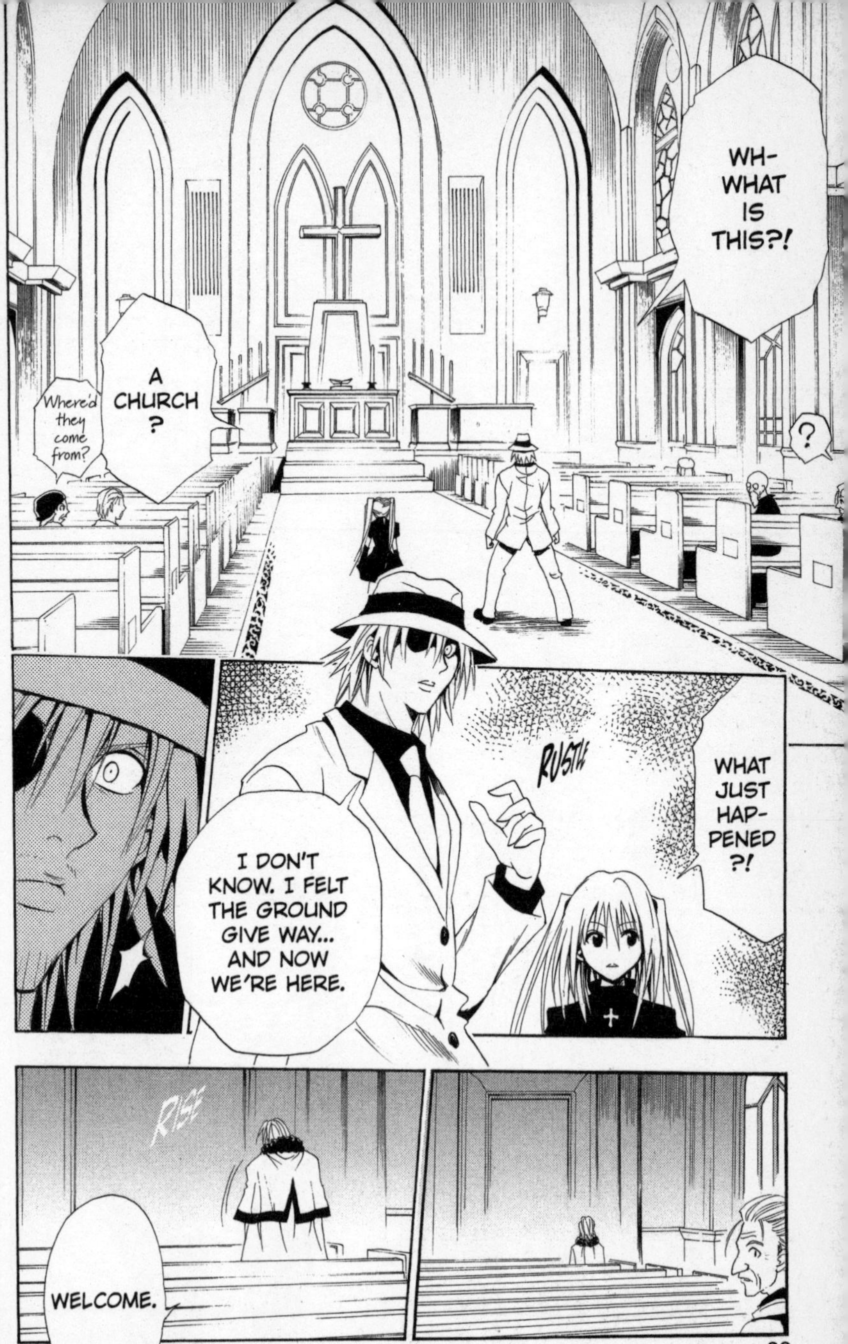
WH-WHAT IS THIS?!
?
A CHURCH?
Where'd they come from?
WHAT JUST HAP-PENED?!
RUSTLE
I DON'T KNOW. I FELT THE GROUND GIVE WAY... AND NOW WE'RE HERE.
RISE
WELCOME.

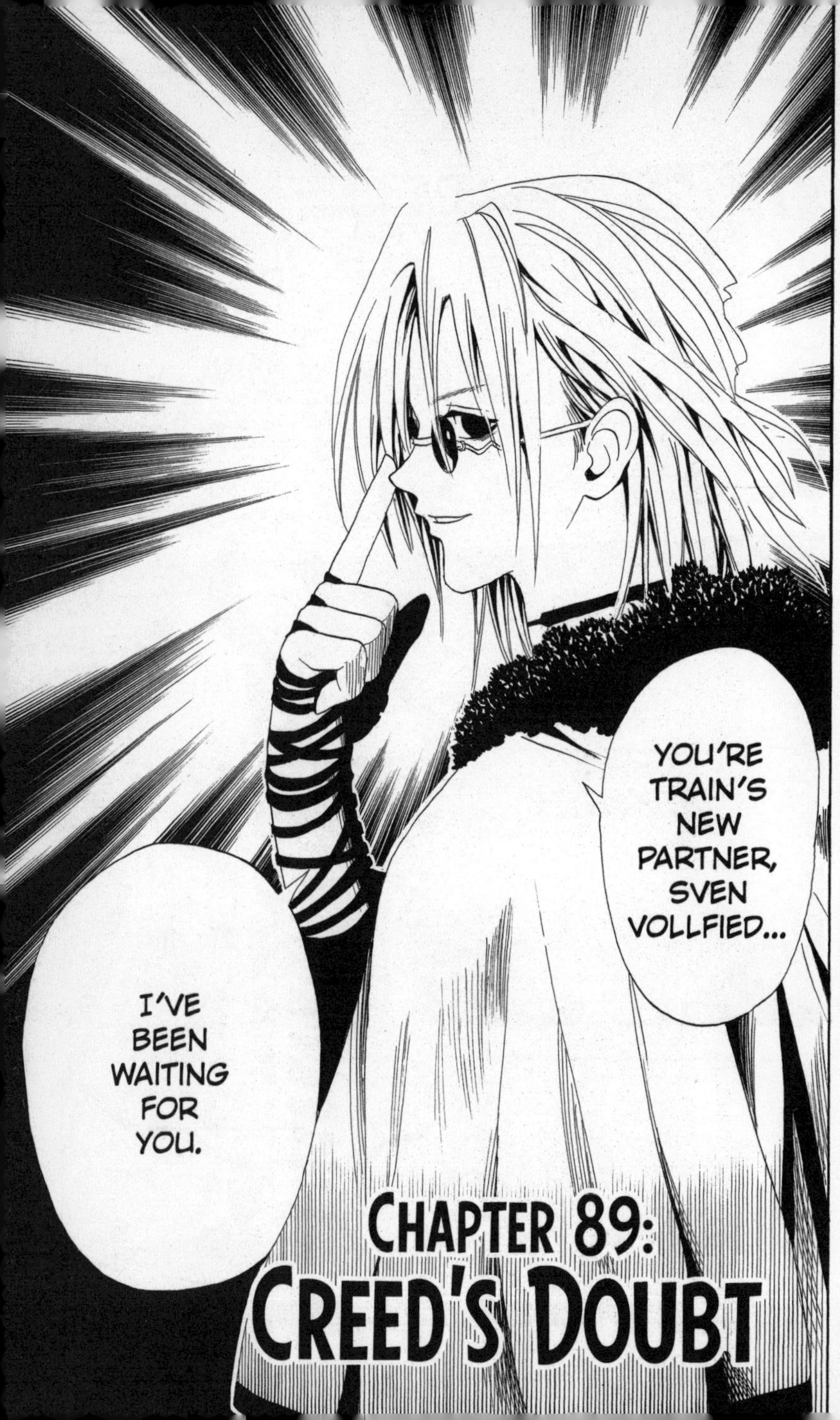
YOU'RE TRAIN'S NEW PARTNER, SVEN VOLLFIED...
I'VE BEEN WAITING FOR YOU.

CHAPTER 89: CREED'S DOUBT

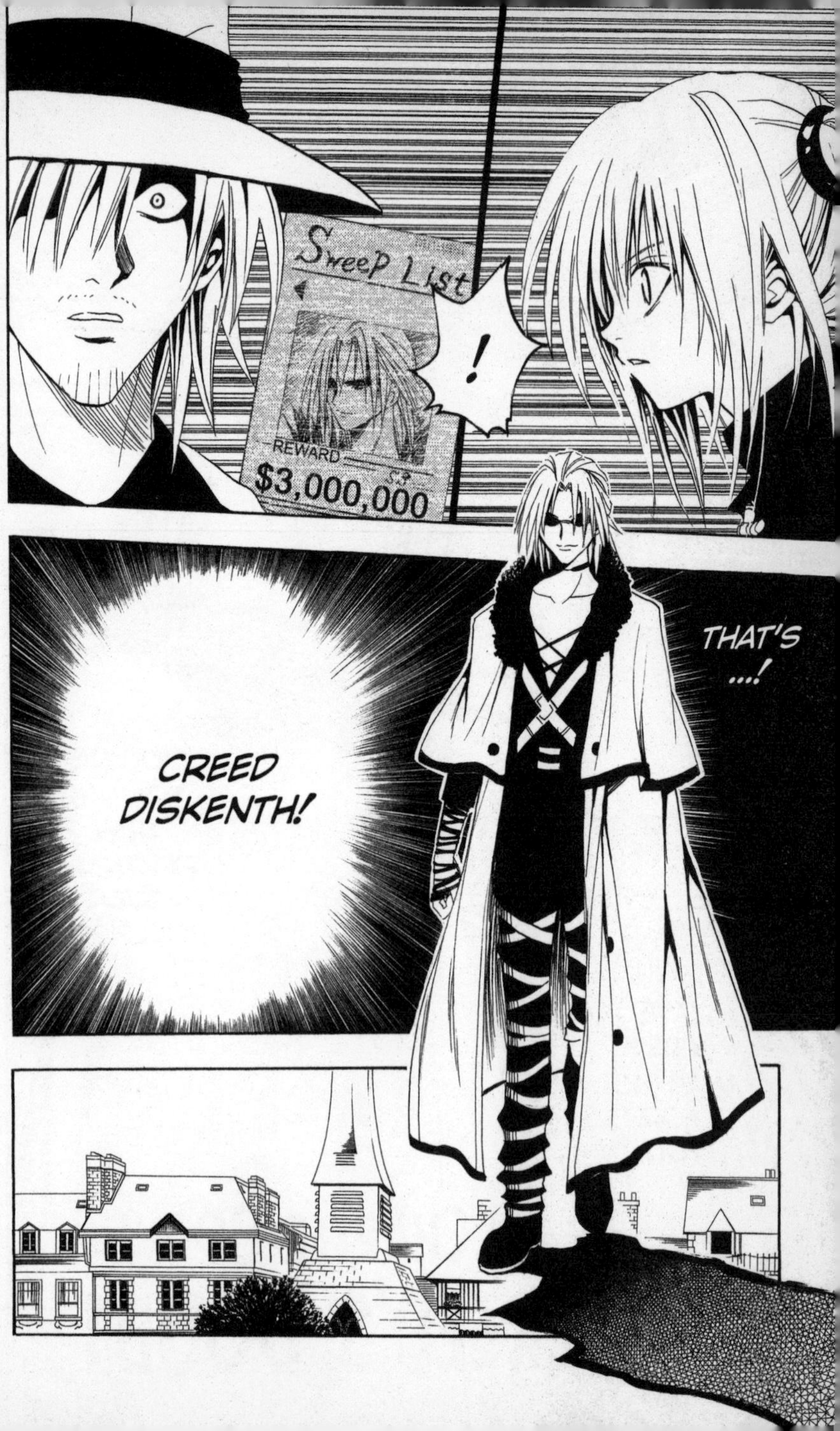
!
Sweep List
REWARD
$3,000,000
THAT'S ...!
CREED DISKENTH!

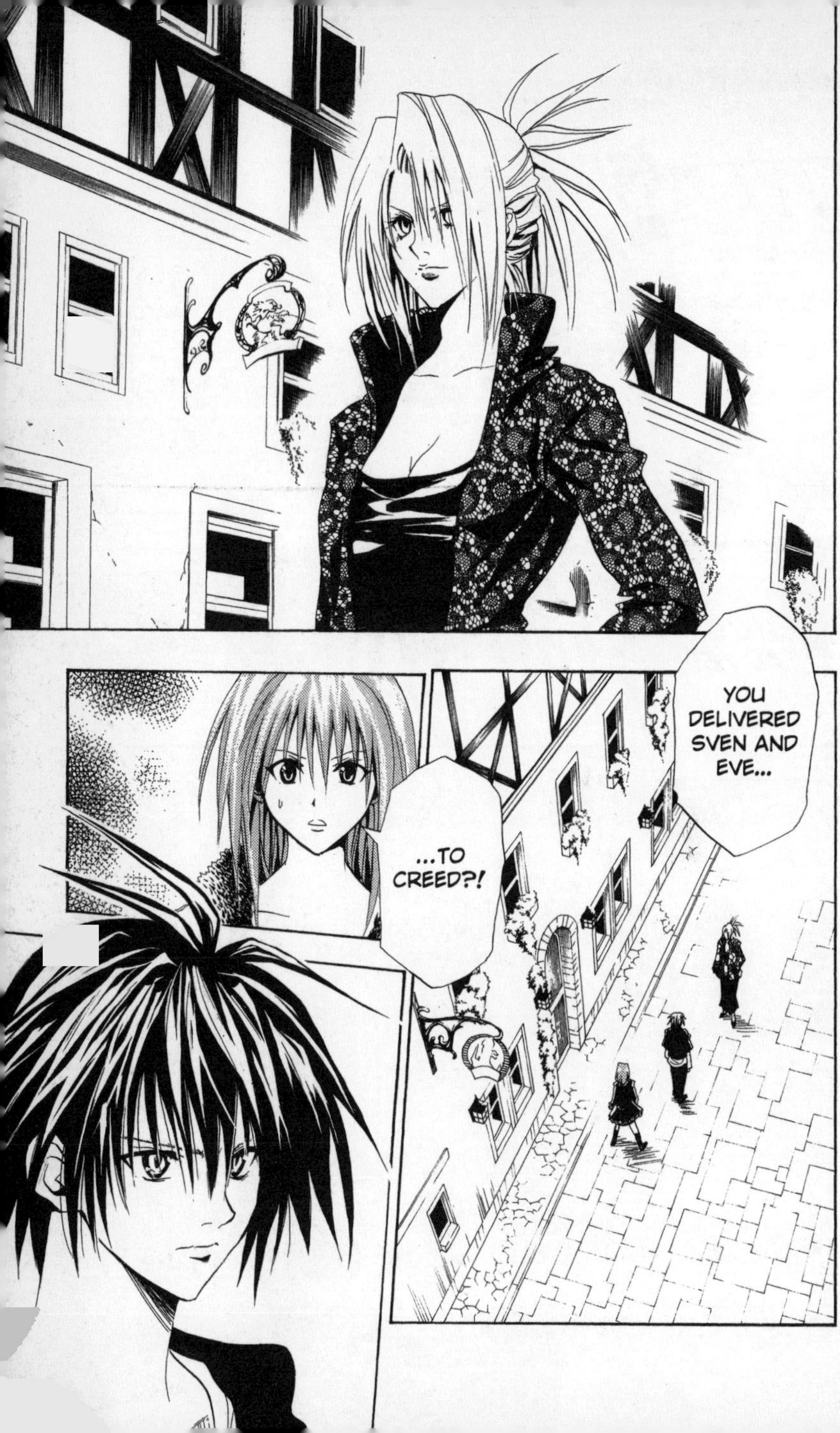
YOU DELIVERED SVEN AND EVE...
...TO CREED?!

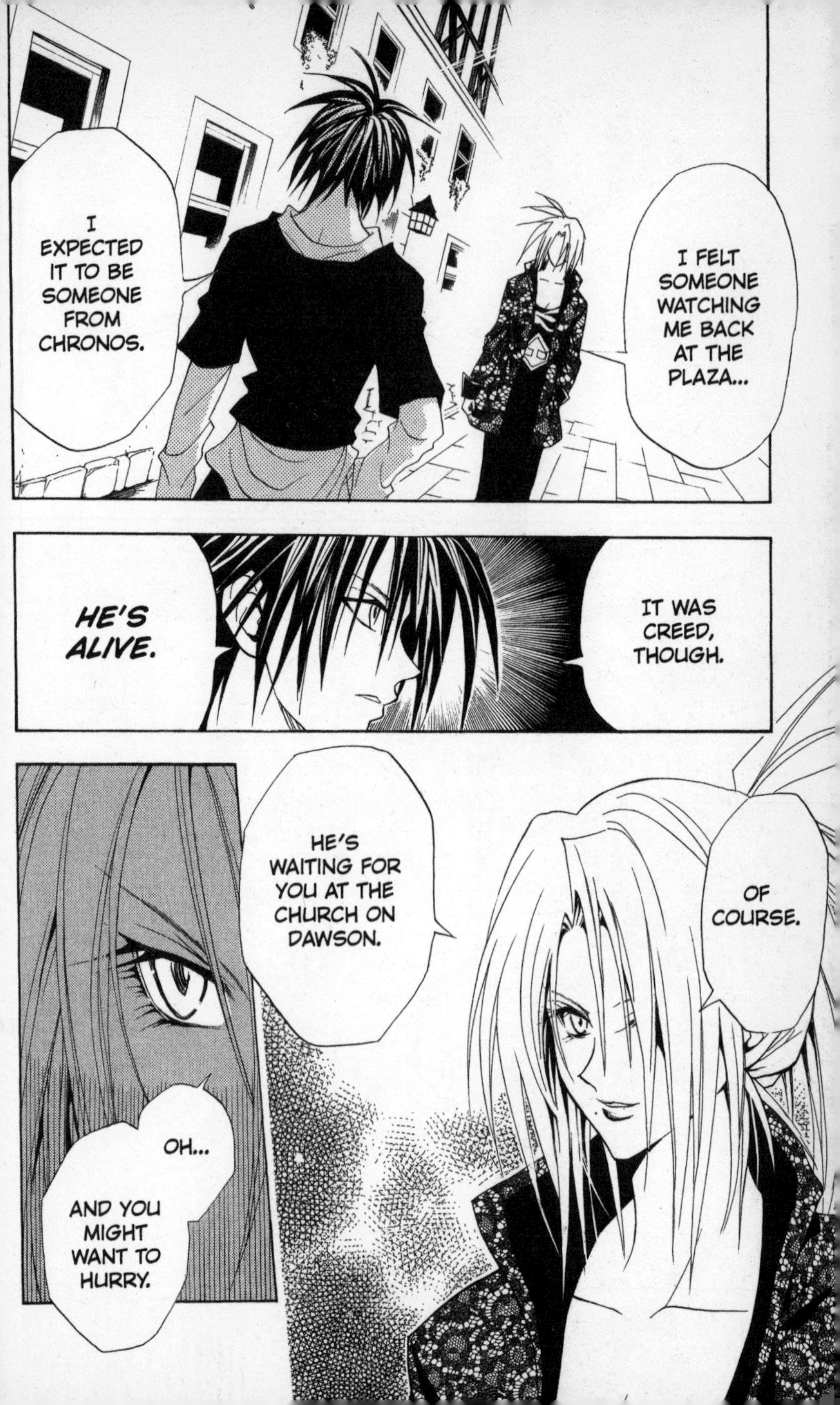
I FELT SOMEONE WATCHING ME BACK AT THE PLAZA...
I EXPECTED IT TO BE SOMEONE FROM CHRONOS.
IT WAS CREED, THOUGH.
HE'S ALIVE.
OF COURSE.
HE'S WAITING FOR YOU AT THE CHURCH ON DAWSON.
OH...
AND YOU MIGHT WANT TO HURRY.

READ THIS WAY

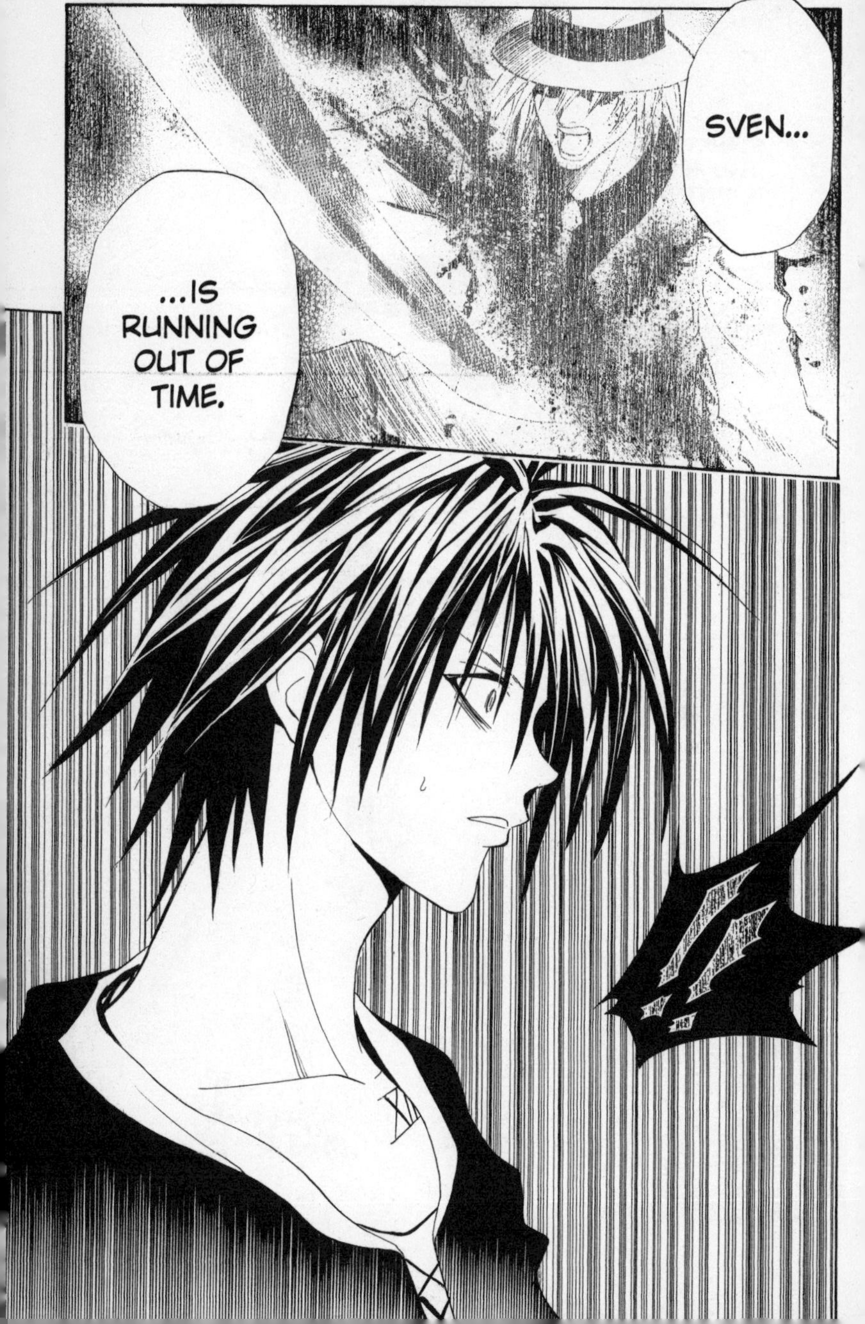
SVEN...
...IS RUNNING OUT OF TIME.

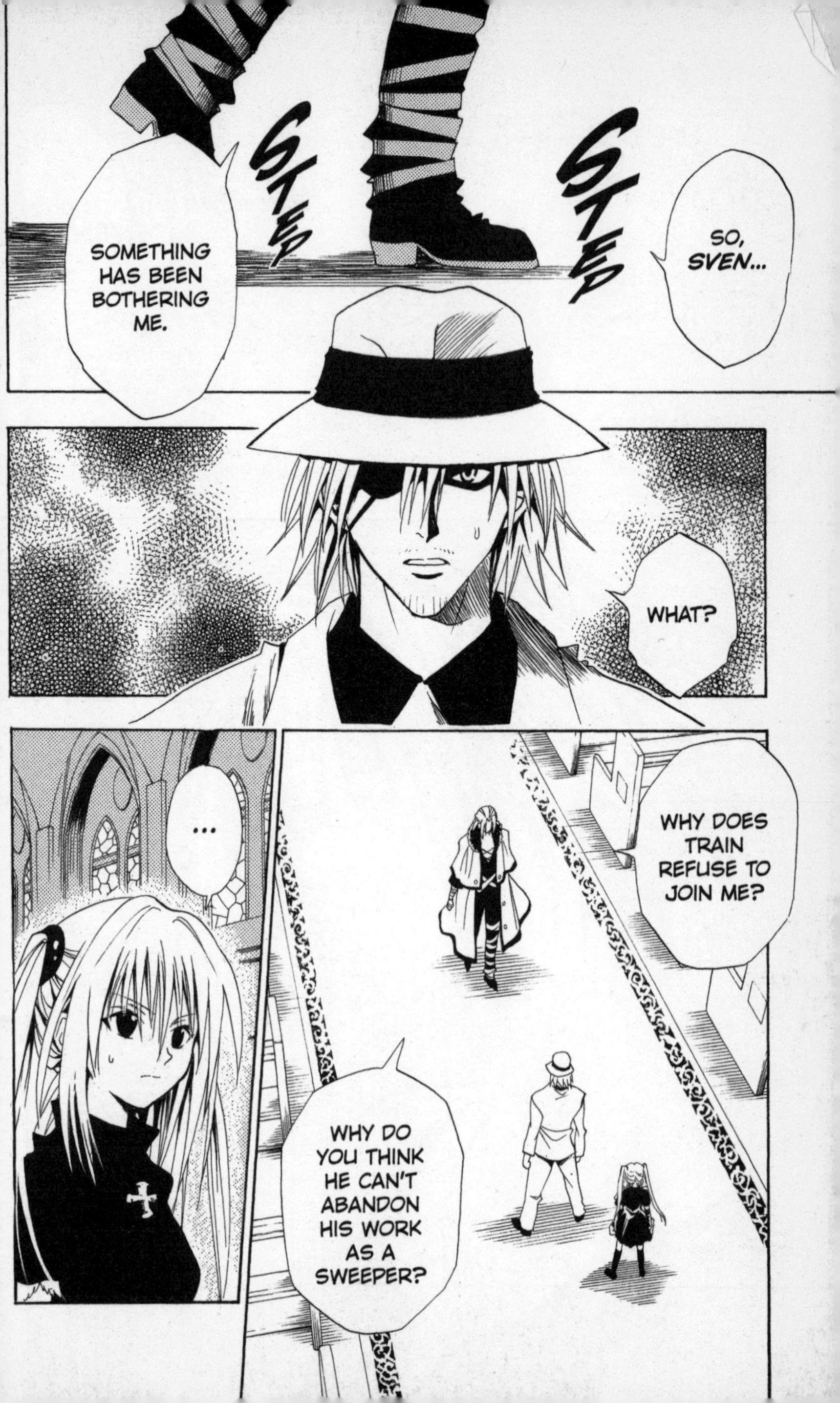
SO, SVEN...
STEP
STEP
SOMETHING HAS BEEN BOTHERING ME.
WHAT?
WHY DOES TRAIN REFUSE TO JOIN ME?
WHY DO YOU THINK HE CAN'T ABANDON HIS WORK AS A SWEEPER?
...

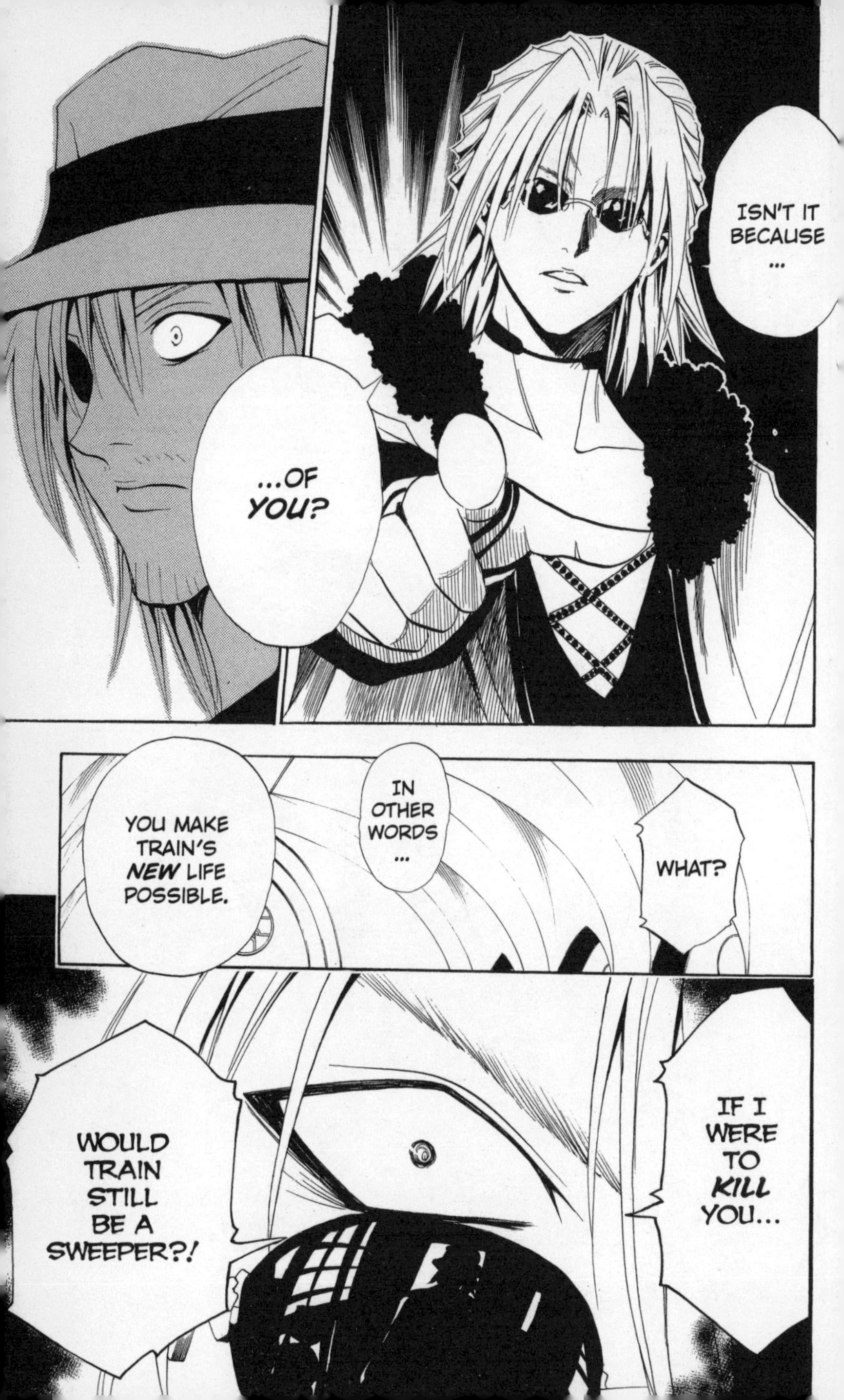
ISN'T IT BECAUSE ...
...OF *YOU?*
WHAT?
IN OTHER WORDS ...
YOU MAKE TRAIN'S *NEW* LIFE POSSIBLE.
IF I WERE TO *KILL* YOU...
WOULD TRAIN STILL BE A SWEEPER?!

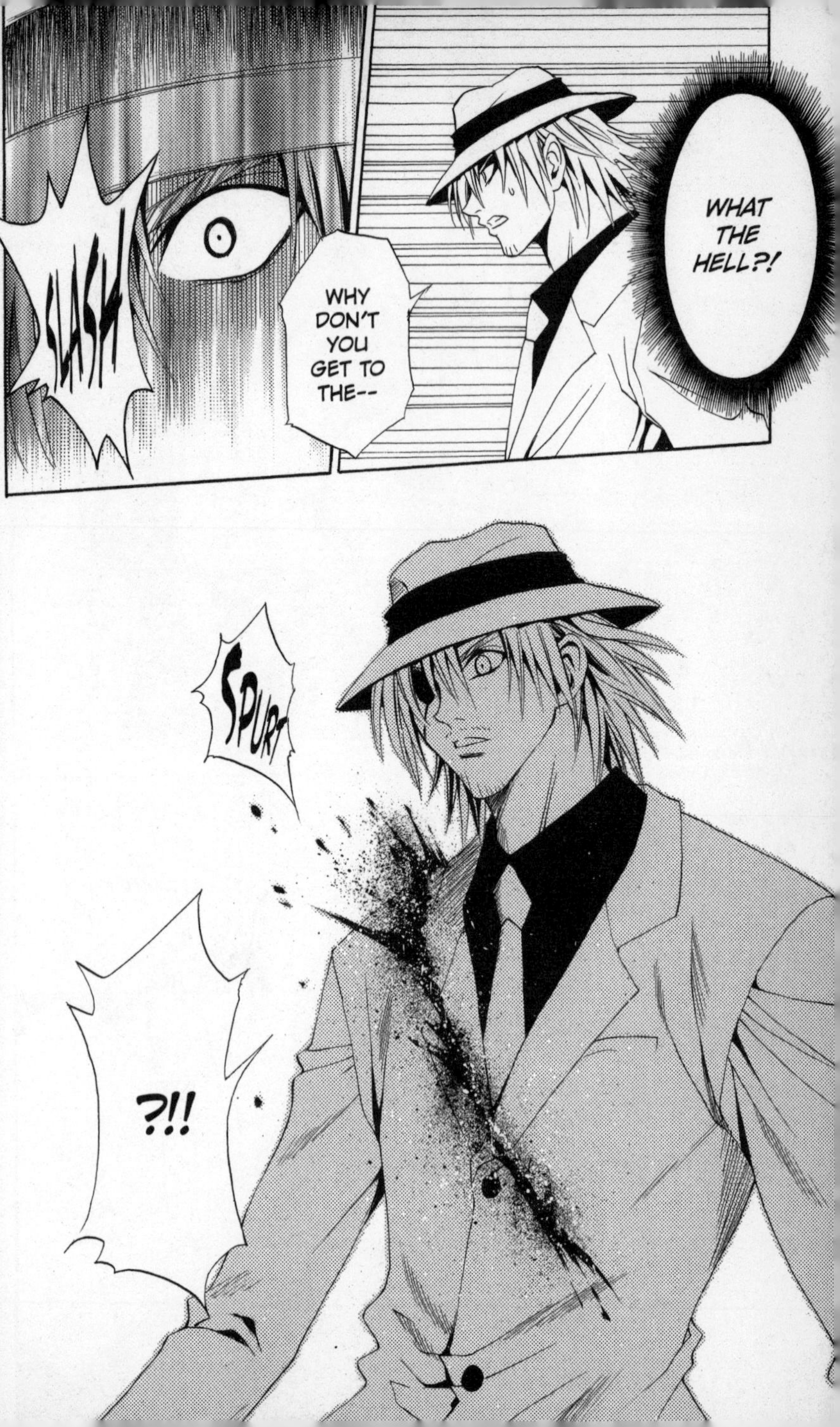
WHAT THE HELL?!
WHY DON'T YOU GET TO THE--
SLASH
SPURT
?!!

READ THIS WAY

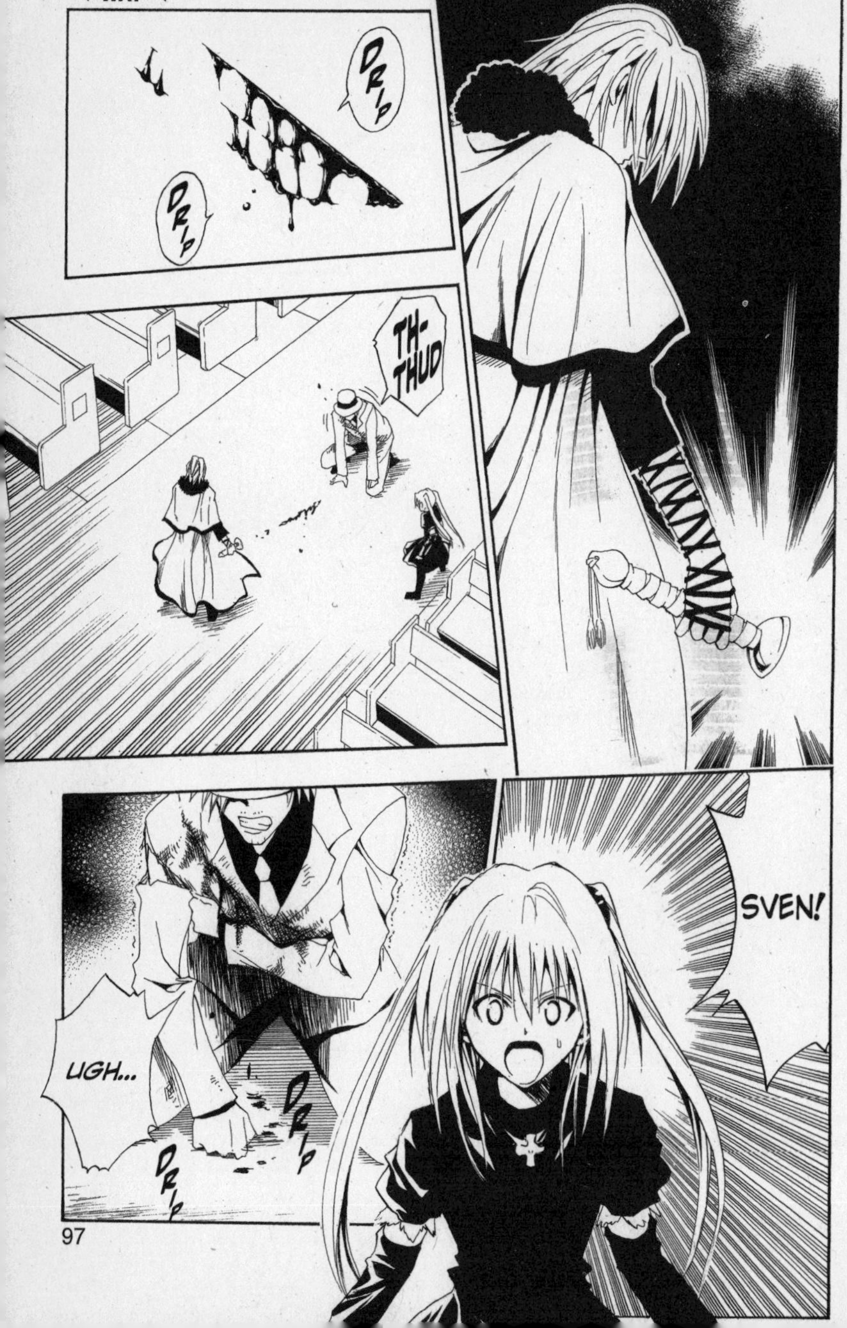

DRIP
DRIP
TH-THUD
SVEN!
UGH...
DRIP
DRIP

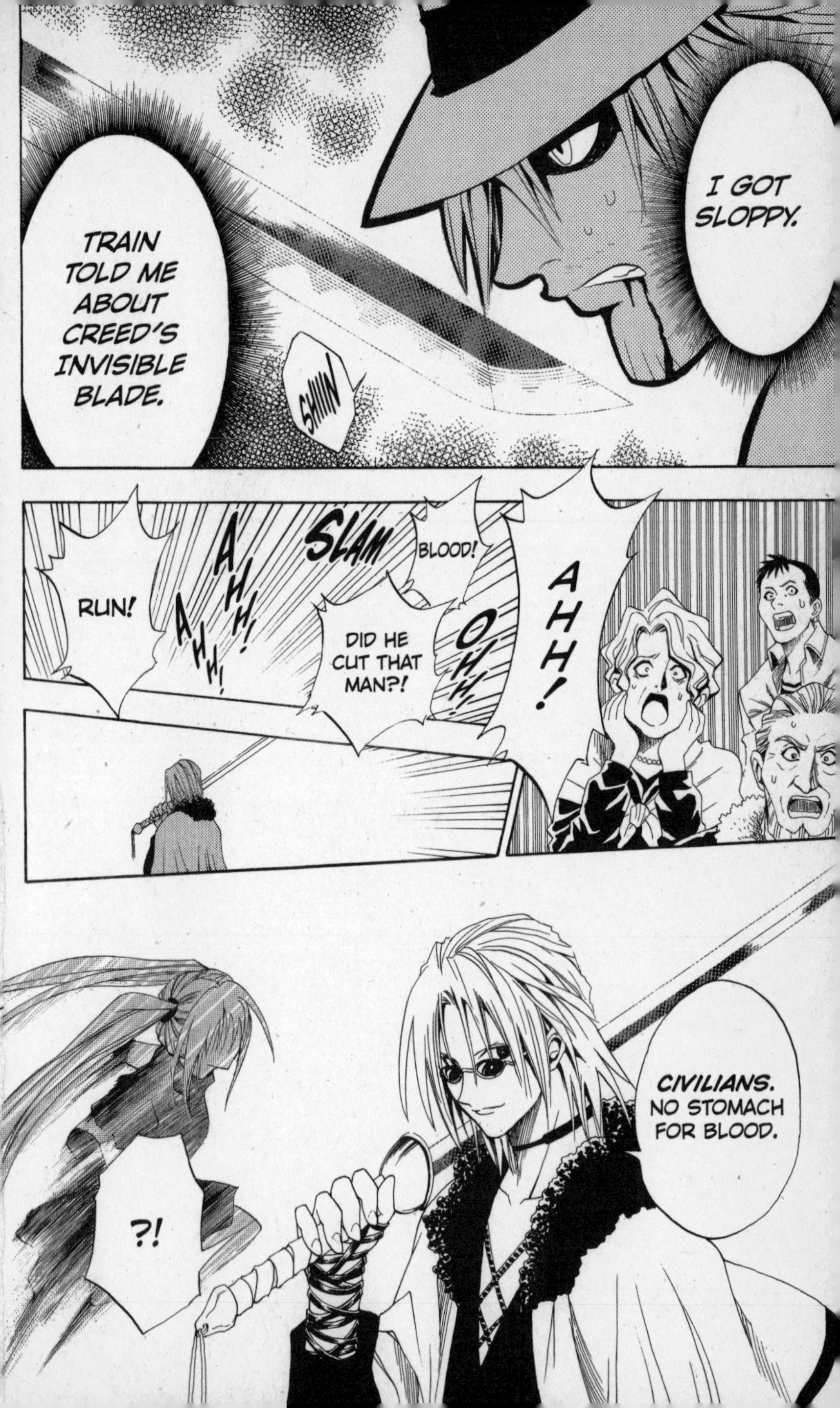
I GOT SLOPPY.
SHIIIN
TRAIN TOLD ME ABOUT CREED'S INVISIBLE BLADE.
AHH!
OHH!
DID HE CUT THAT MAN?!
BLOOD!
SLAM
AHH!
AHH!
RUN!
CIVILIANS. NO STOMACH FOR BLOOD.
?!

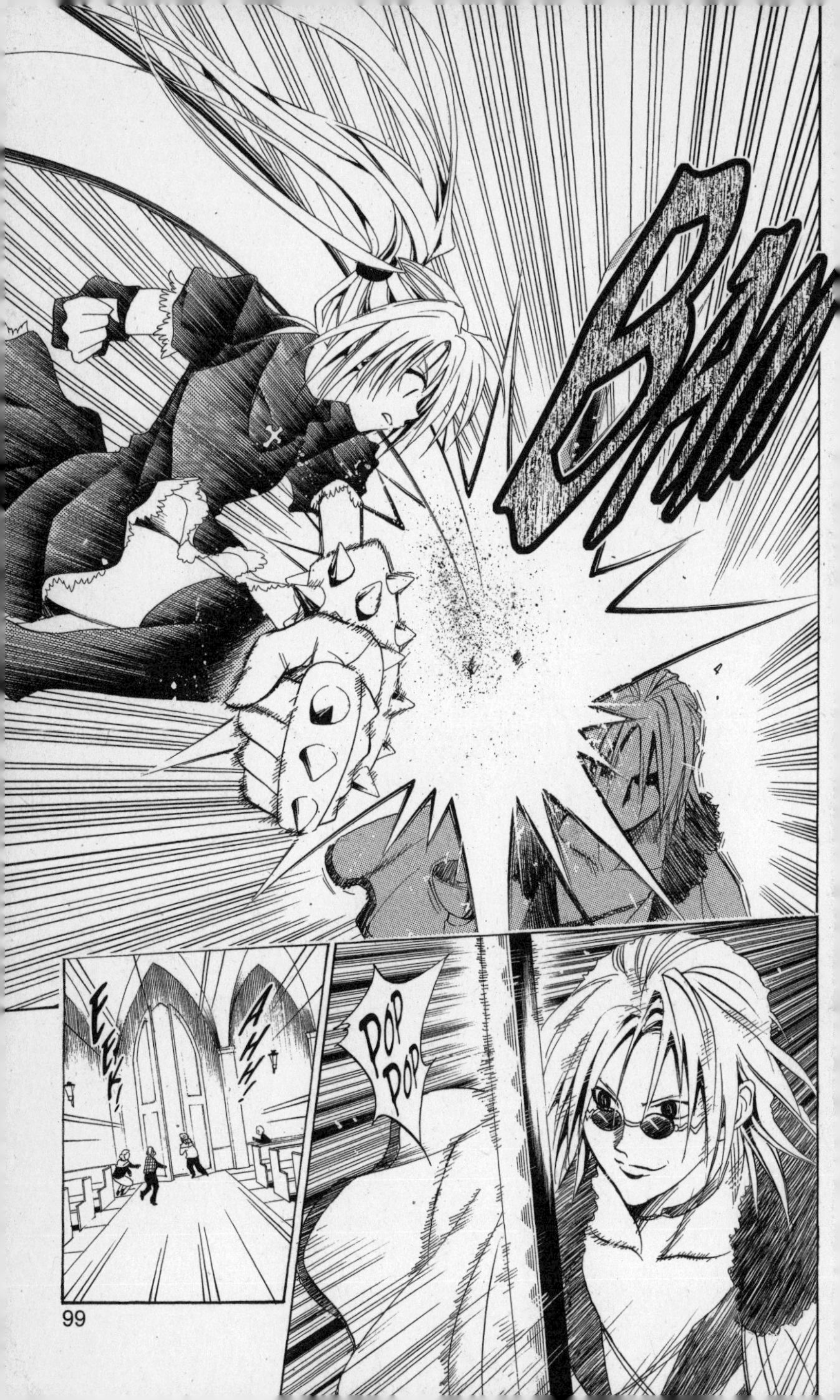
BAM
POP POP
AHH!!
EEK!!

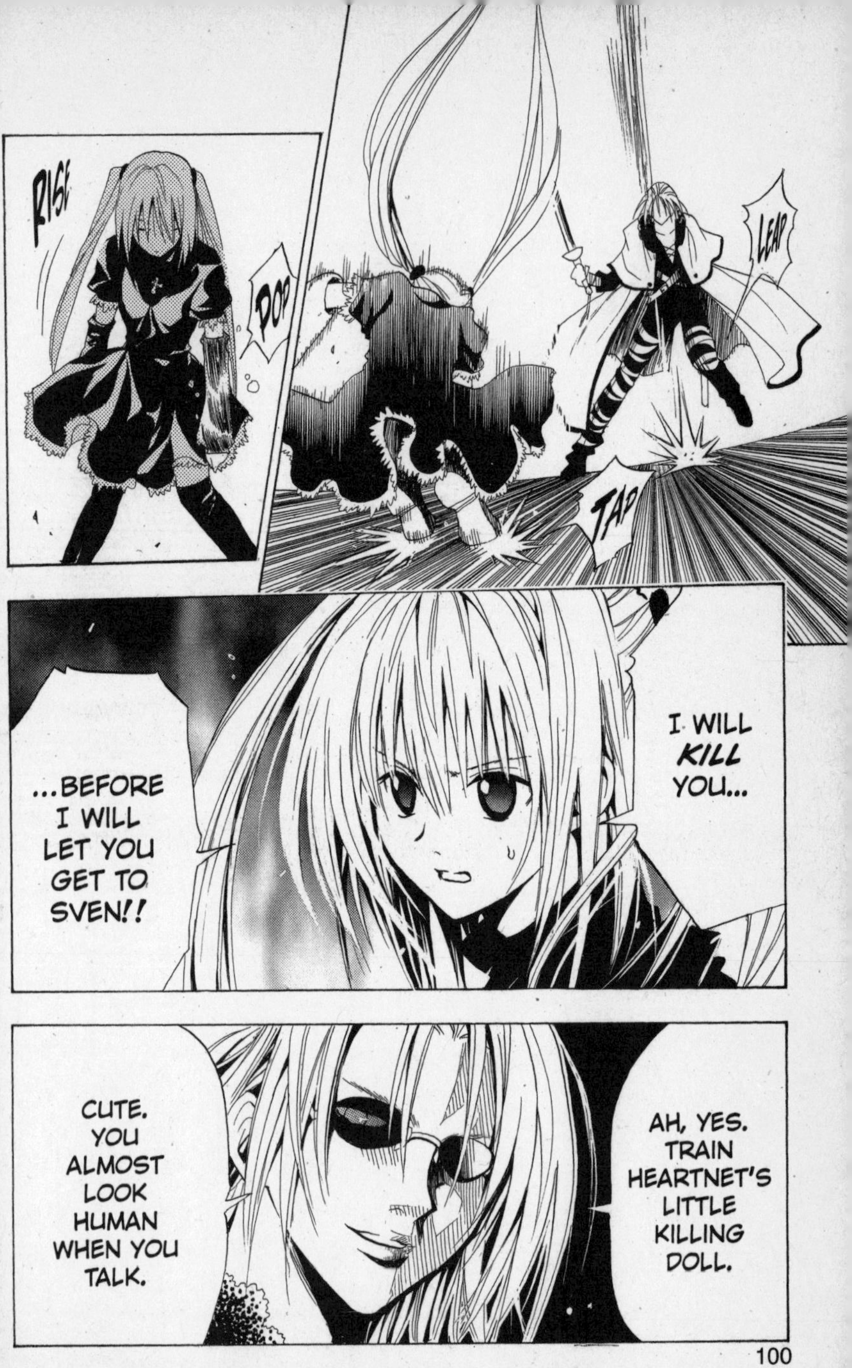
LEAP
POP
TAP
RISE
I WILL *KILL* YOU...
...BEFORE I WILL LET YOU GET TO SVEN!!
AH, YES. TRAIN HEARTNET'S LITTLE KILLING DOLL.
CUTE. YOU ALMOST LOOK HUMAN WHEN YOU TALK.

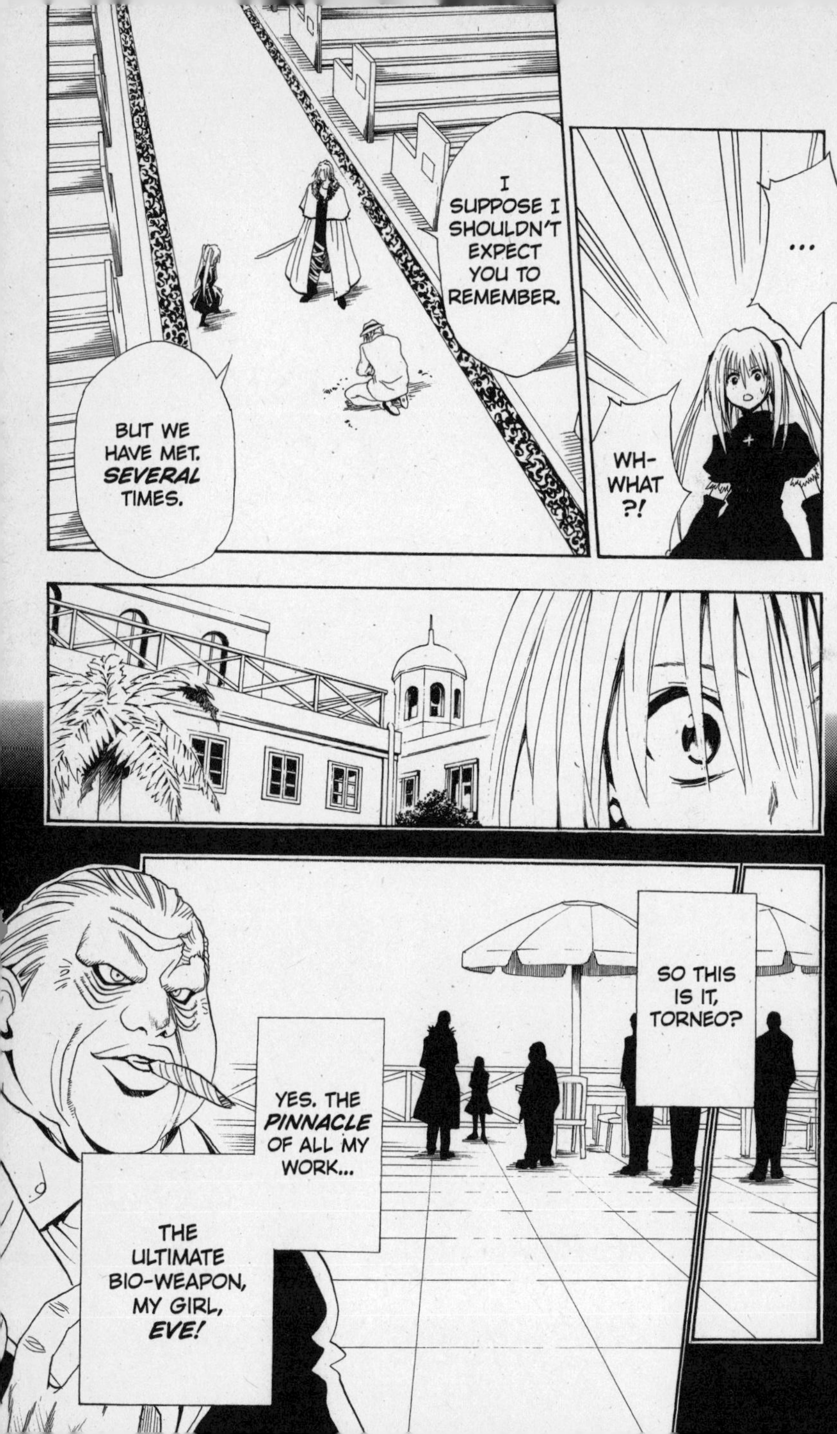
...
WH- WHAT ?!
I SUPPOSE I SHOULDN'T EXPECT YOU TO REMEMBER.
BUT WE HAVE MET. SEVERAL TIMES.
SO THIS IS IT, TORNEO?
YES. THE PINNACLE OF ALL MY WORK...
THE ULTIMATE BIO-WEAPON, MY GIRL, EVE!

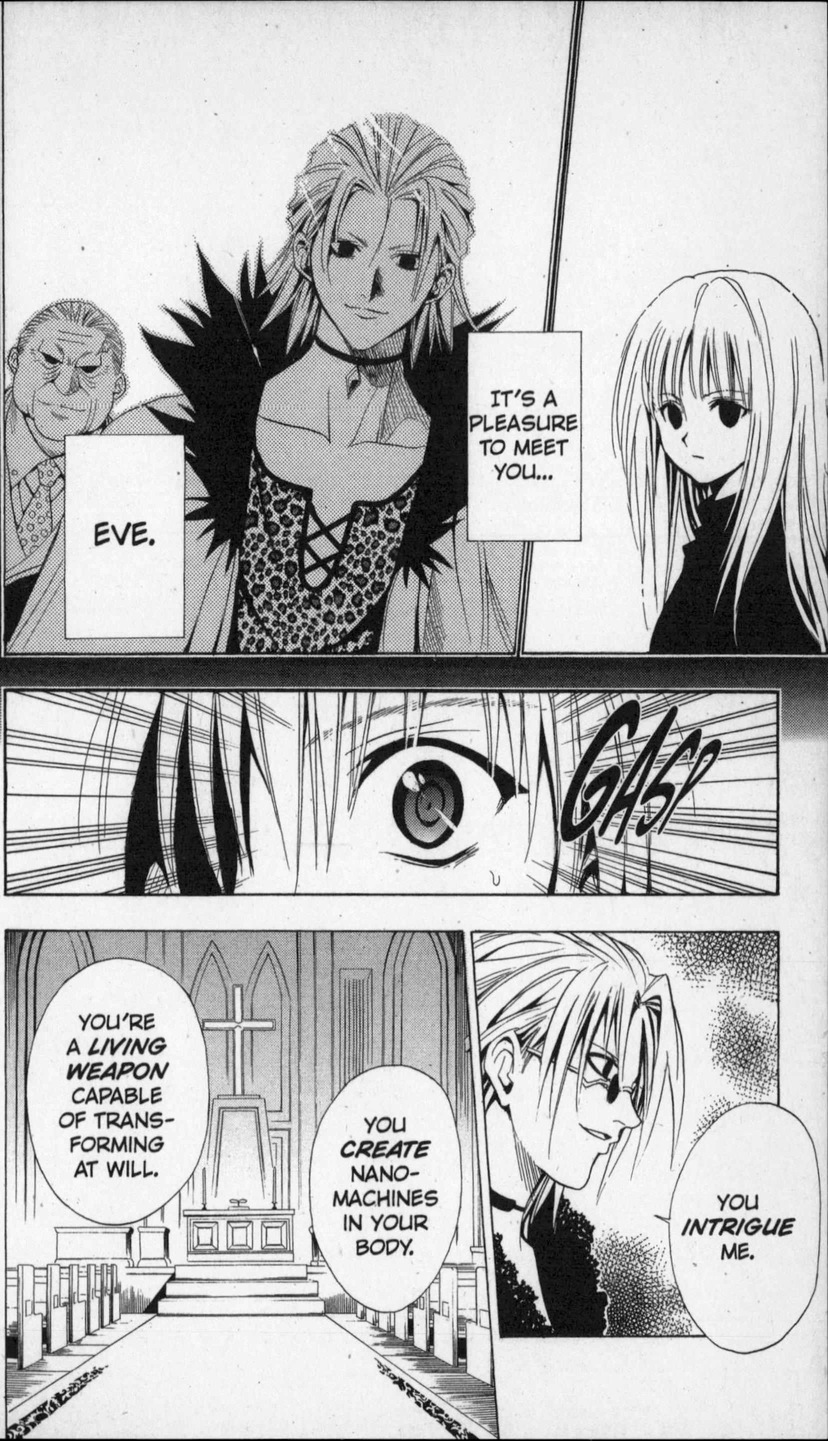
IT'S A PLEASURE TO MEET YOU...
EVE.
GASP
YOU INTRIGUE ME.
YOU CREATE NANO-MACHINES IN YOUR BODY.
YOU'RE A LIVING WEAPON CAPABLE OF TRANS-FORMING AT WILL.

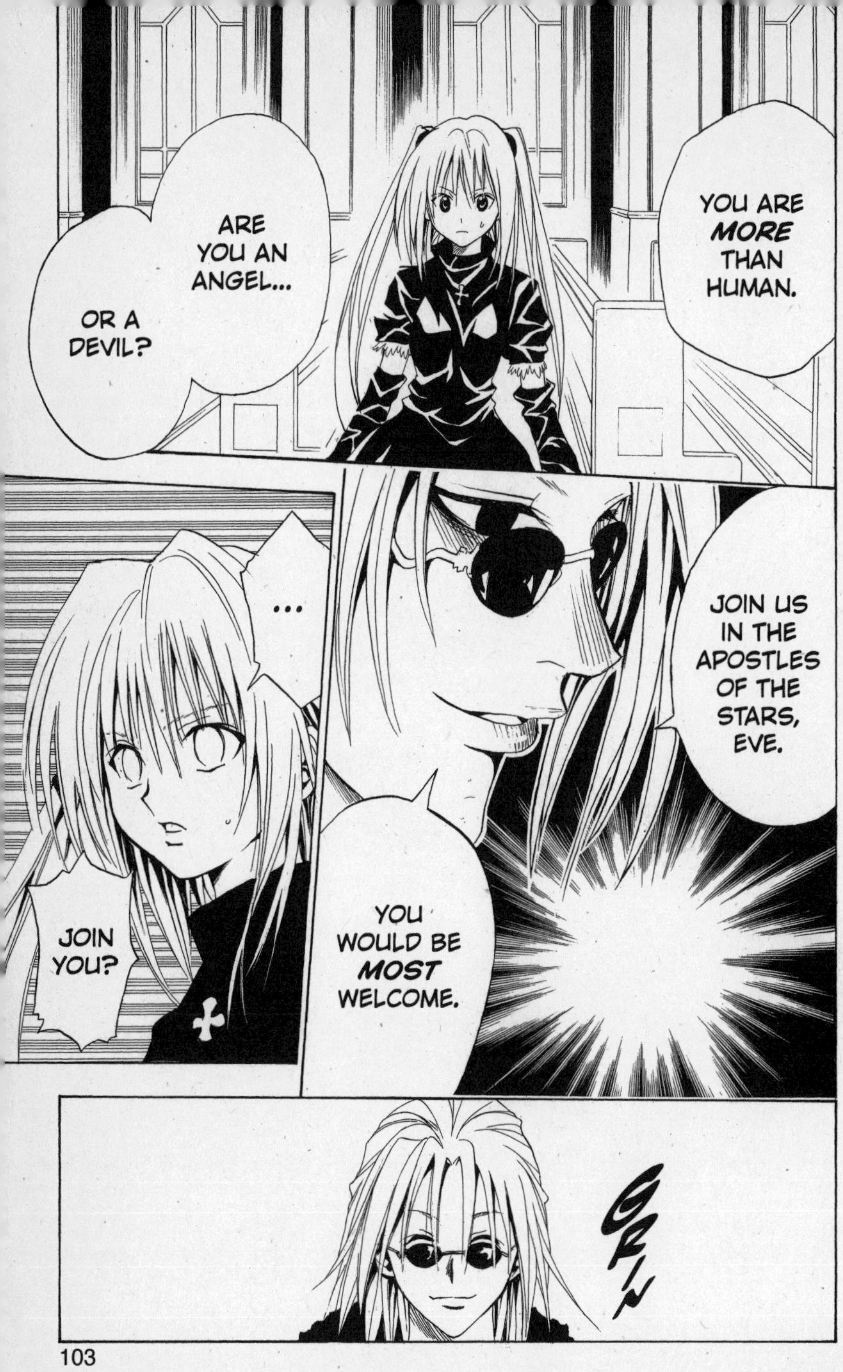
YOU ARE *MORE* THAN HUMAN.
ARE YOU AN ANGEL...
OR A DEVIL?
JOIN US IN THE APOSTLES OF THE STARS, EVE.
YOU WOULD BE *MOST* WELCOME.
...
JOIN YOU?
GRIN

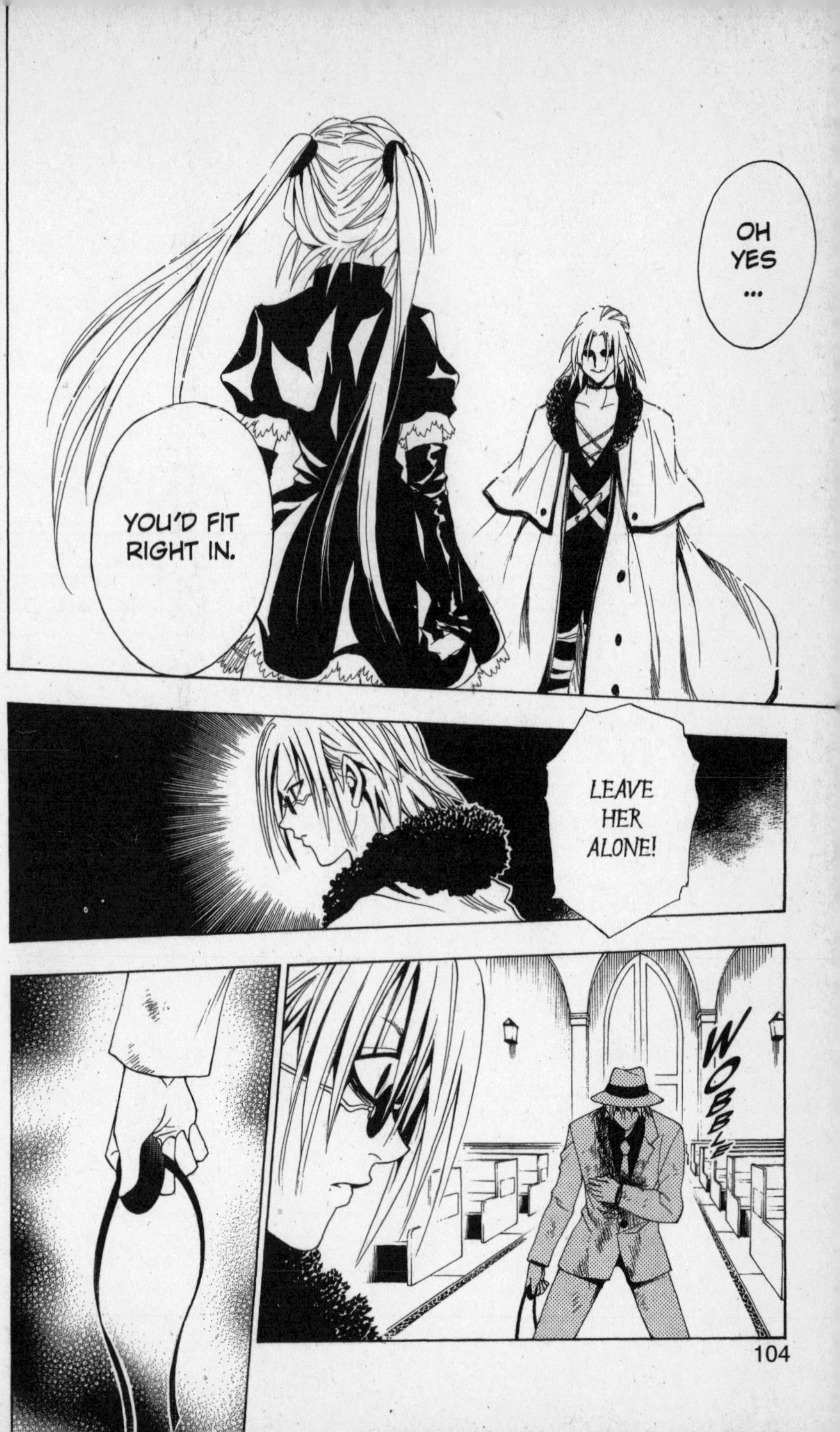
OH YES ...
YOU'D FIT RIGHT IN.
LEAVE HER ALONE!
WOBBLE

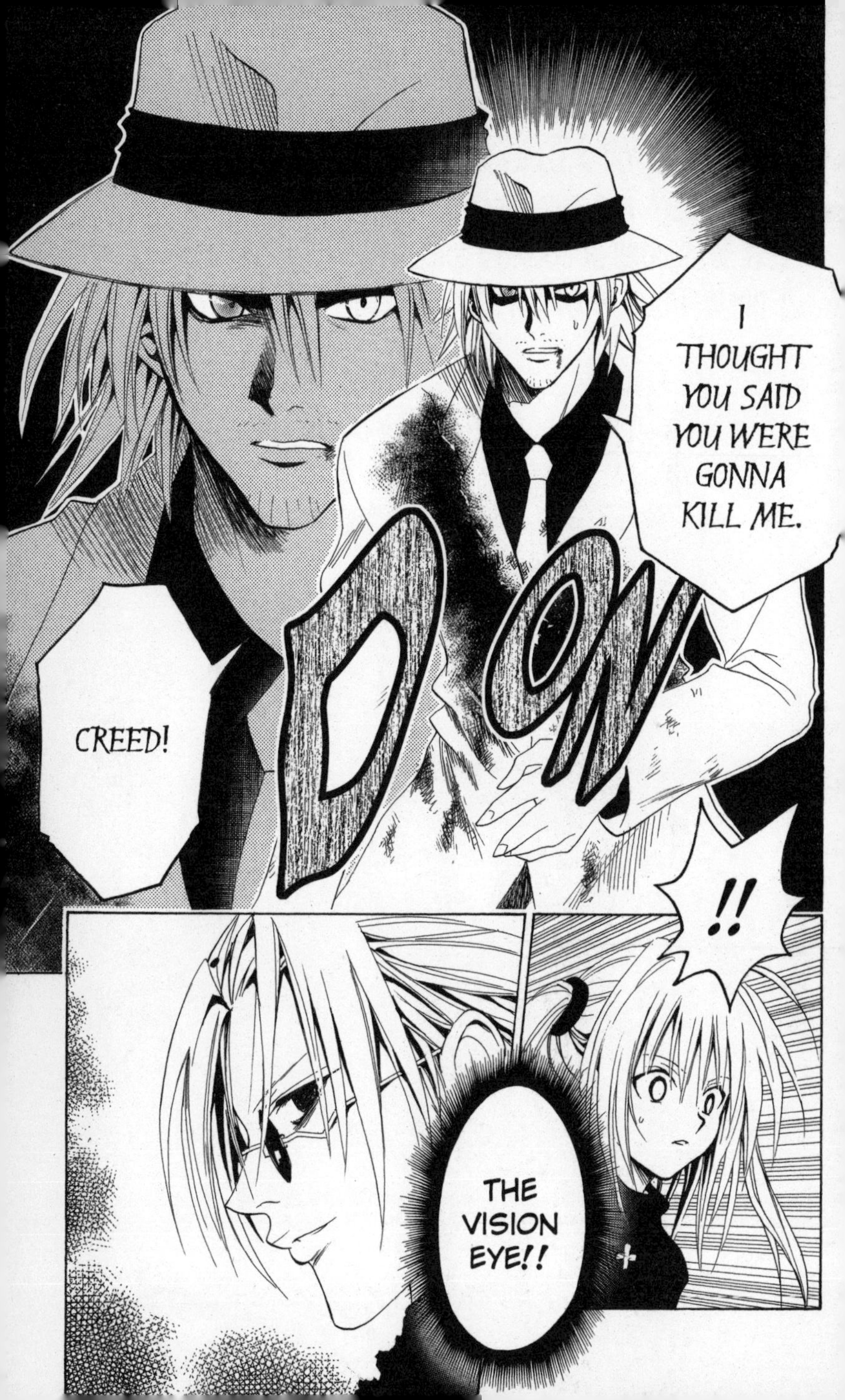
I THOUGHT YOU SAID YOU WERE GONNA KILL ME.
CREED!
!!
THE VISION EYE!!

◎ *Akamaru Jump* Cover Illustration of Eve and Train. They asked for a small illustration of a guy and a girl dressed for the beach.
(Eve was done in colored ink.
I drew Train with Copic markers.)

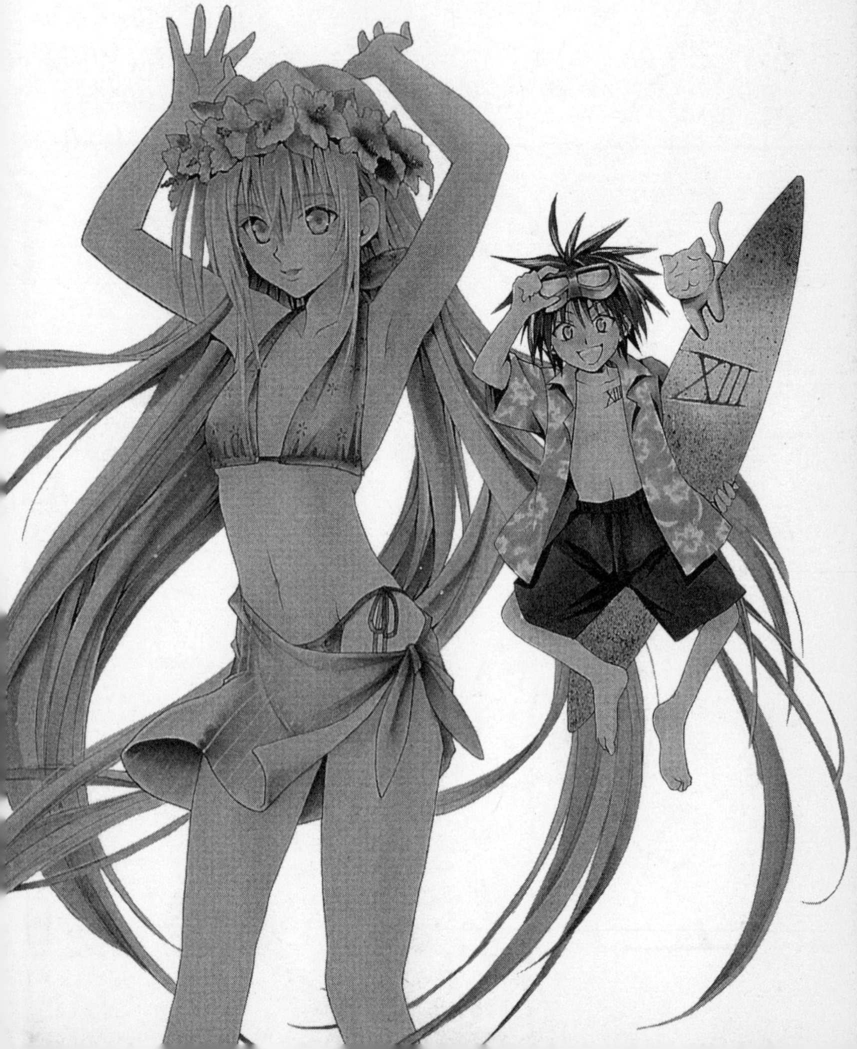
XIII

Chapter 90: Lucifer

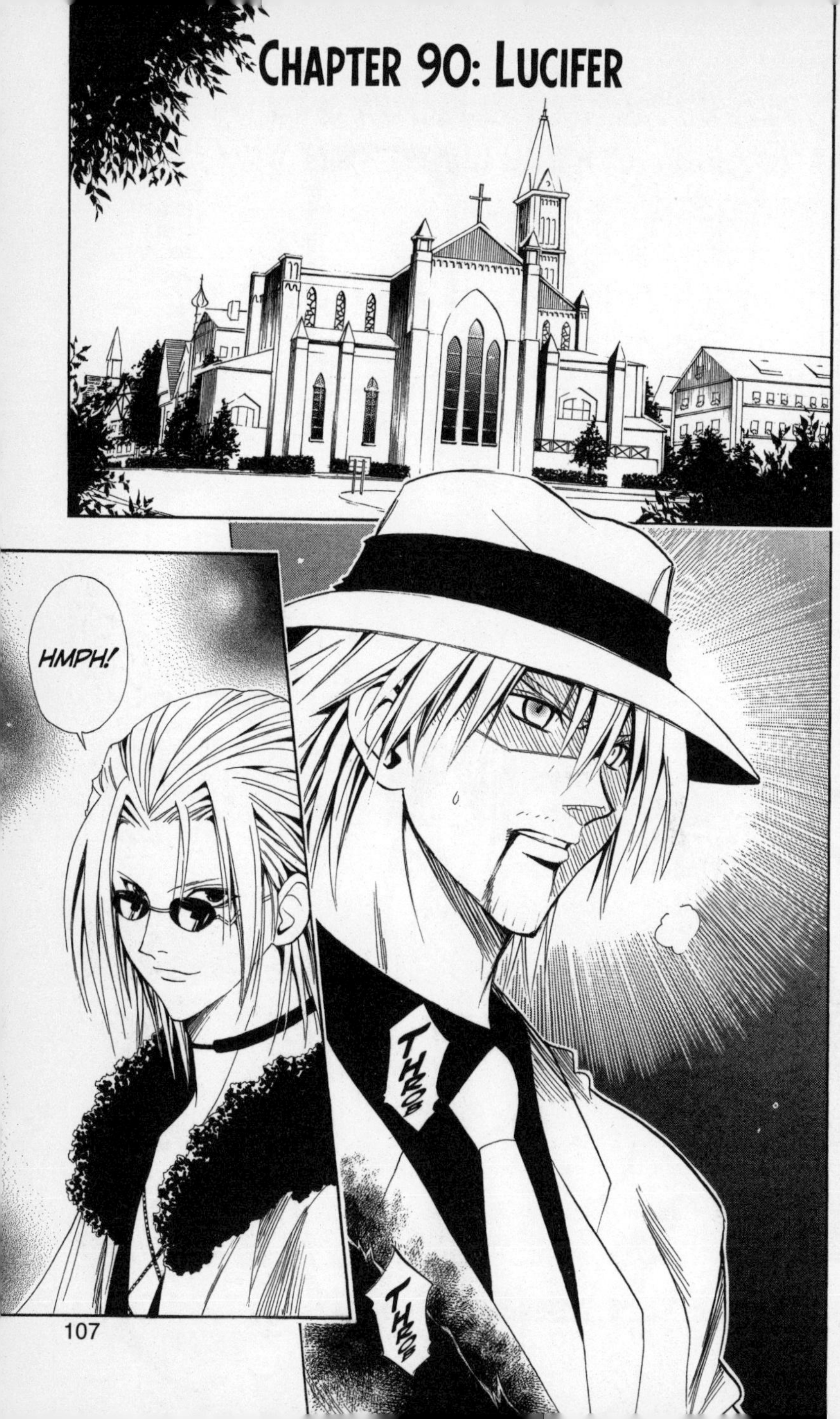
THROB
THROB
HMPH!

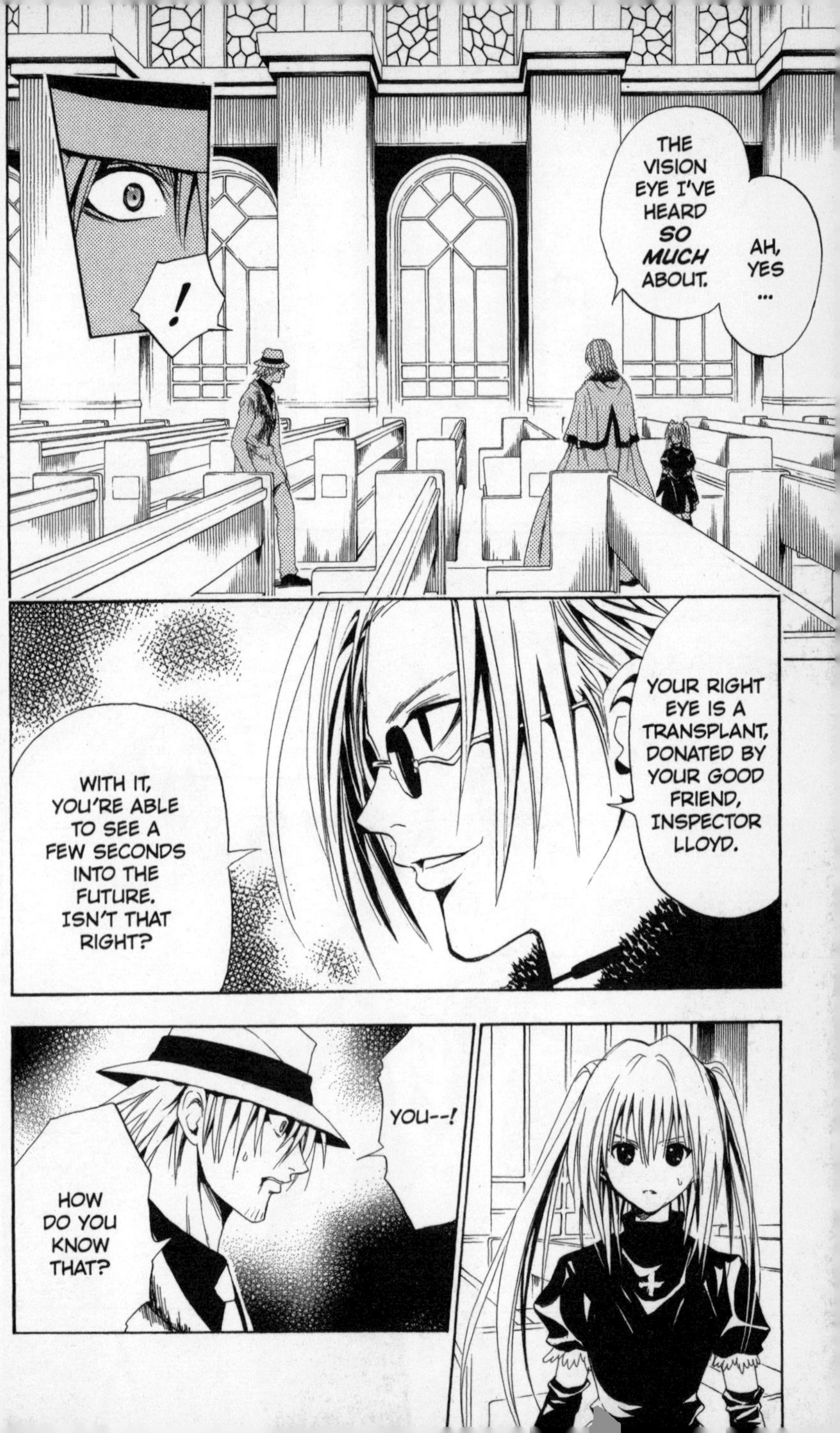
AH, YES ...
THE VISION EYE I'VE HEARD SO MUCH ABOUT.
!
YOUR RIGHT EYE IS A TRANSPLANT, DONATED BY YOUR GOOD FRIEND, INSPECTOR LLOYD.
WITH IT, YOU'RE ABLE TO SEE A FEW SECONDS INTO THE FUTURE. ISN'T THAT RIGHT?
YOU--!
HOW DO YOU KNOW THAT?

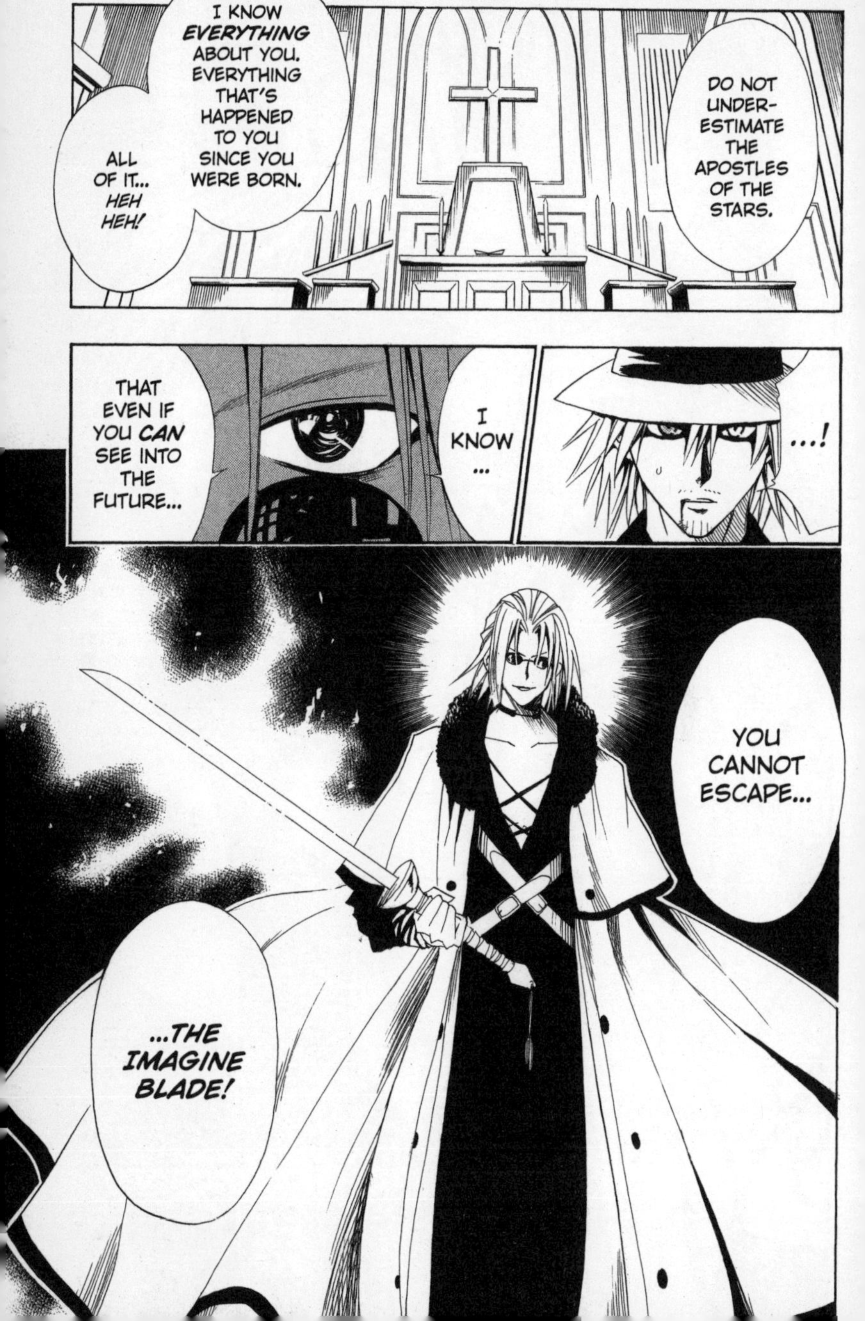
DO NOT UNDER-ESTIMATE THE APOSTLES OF THE STARS.
I KNOW *EVERYTHING* ABOUT YOU. EVERYTHING THAT'S HAPPENED TO YOU SINCE YOU WERE BORN.
ALL OF IT... *HEH HEH!*
...!
I KNOW ...
THAT EVEN IF YOU *CAN* SEE INTO THE FUTURE...
YOU CANNOT ESCAPE...
...THE IMAGINE BLADE!

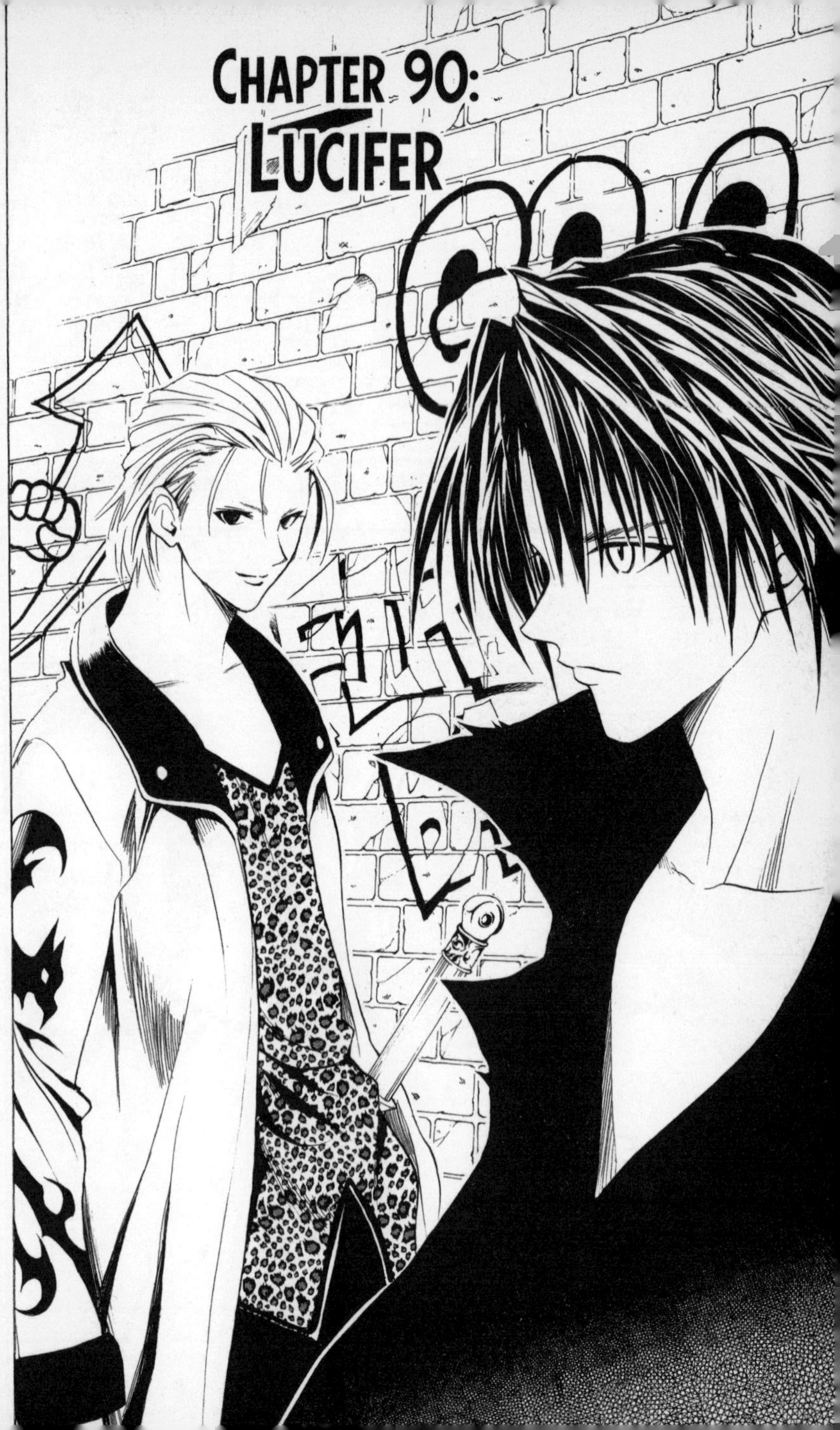
CHAPTER 90:
LUCIFER

READ THIS WAY

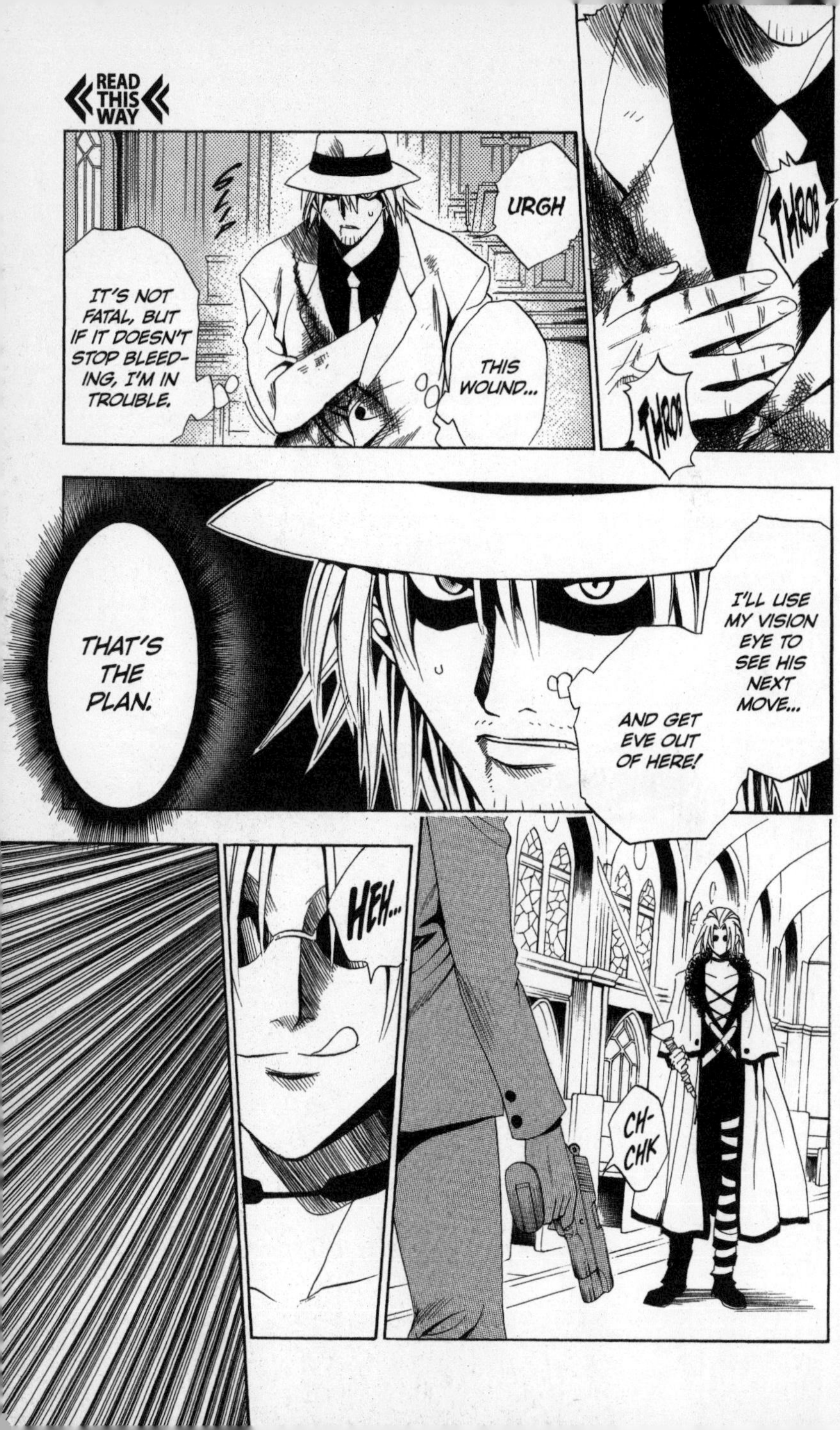
THROB
THROB
URGH
THIS WOUND...
IT'S NOT FATAL, BUT IF IT DOESN'T STOP BLEEDING, I'M IN TROUBLE.
I'LL USE MY VISION EYE TO SEE HIS NEXT MOVE...
AND GET EVE OUT OF HERE!
THAT'S THE PLAN.
CH-CHK
HEH...

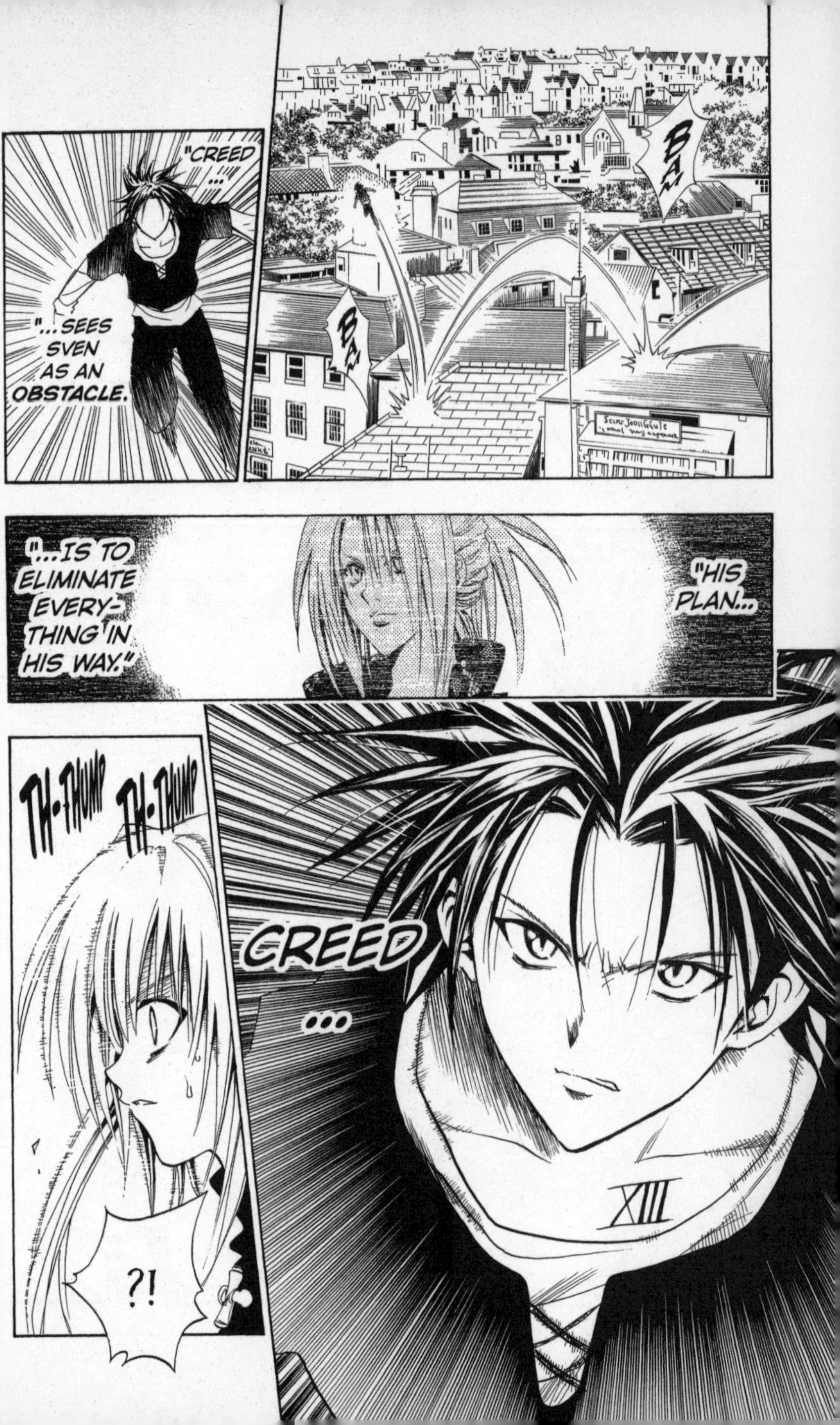
BAM
BAM
"CREED ...
"... SEES SVEN AS AN OBSTACLE.
"HIS PLAN...
"...IS TO ELIMINATE EVERY-THING IN HIS WAY."
CREED ...
TH-THUMP TH-THUMP
?!

READ THIS WAY

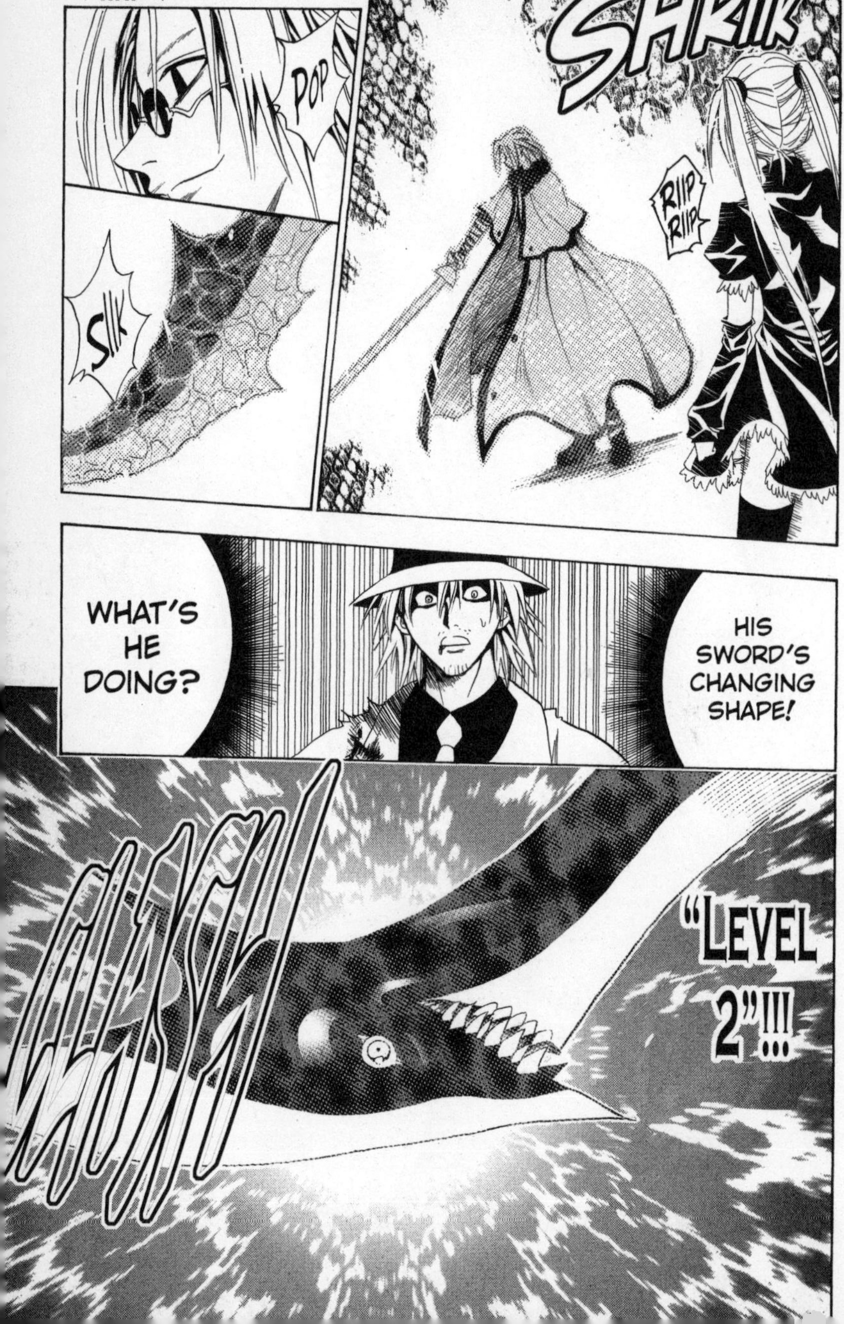
SHRIIK
RIIP RIIP
POP
SLIK
HIS SWORD'S CHANGING SHAPE!
WHAT'S HE DOING?
"LEVEL 2"!!!...

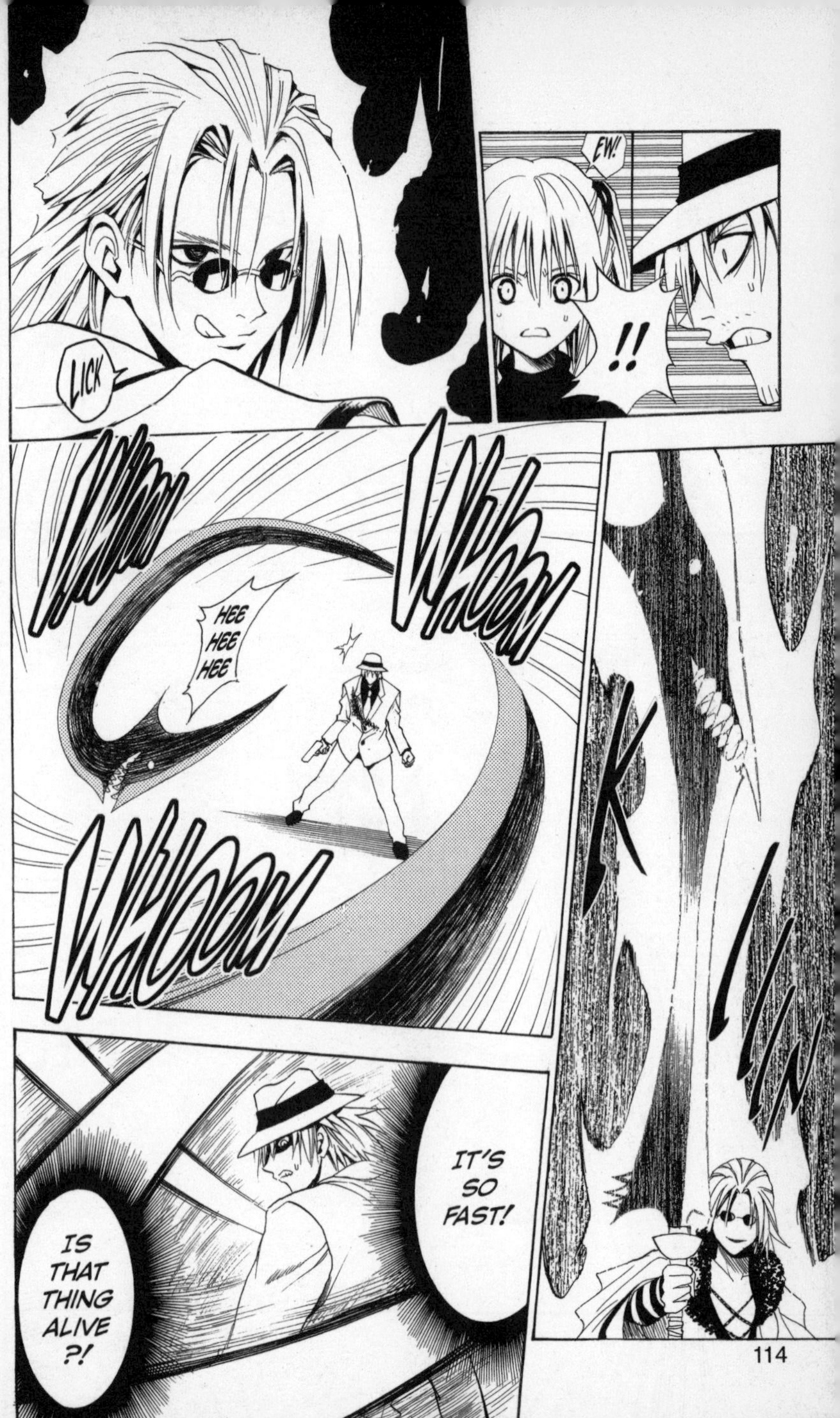

EW!
!!
LICK
HEE HEE HEE
IT'S SO FAST!
IS THAT THING ALIVE ?!

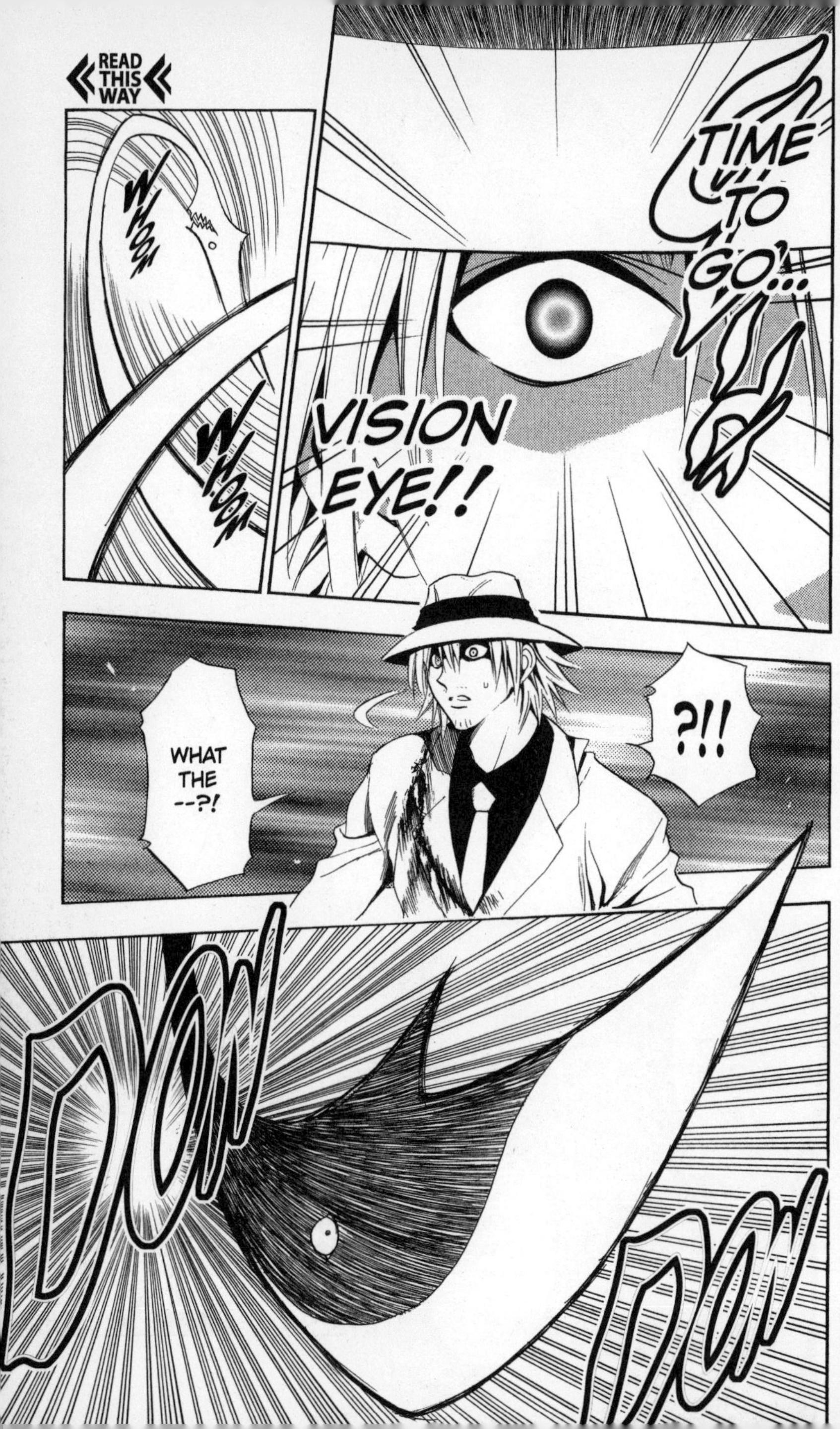
READ THIS WAY
TIME TO GO...
VISION EYE!!
WHOOM
WHOOM
?!!
WHAT THE --?!
DON
DON

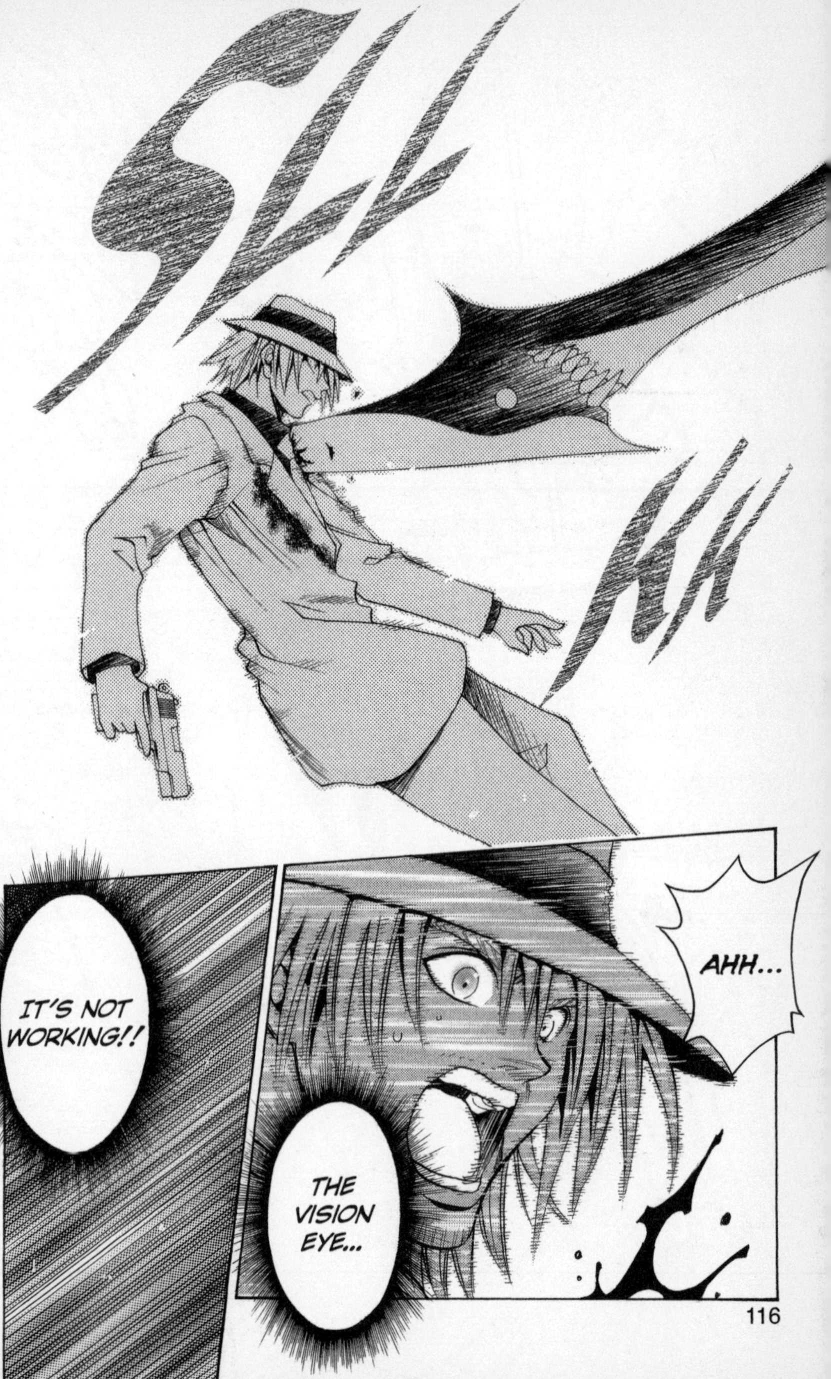

AHH...
THE VISION EYE...
IT'S NOT WORKING!!

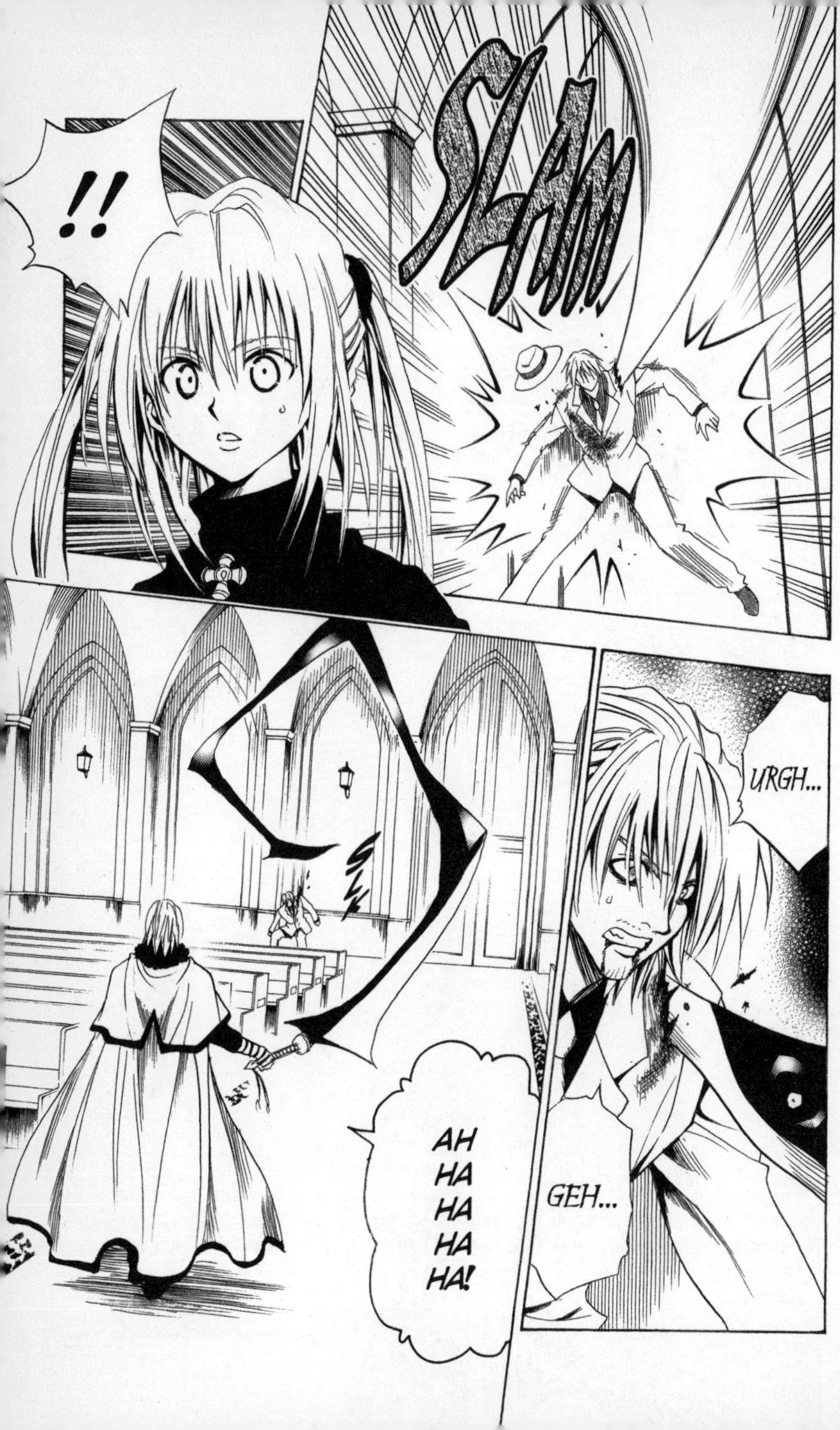
SLAM
!!
URGH...
GEH...
AH HA HA HA HA!

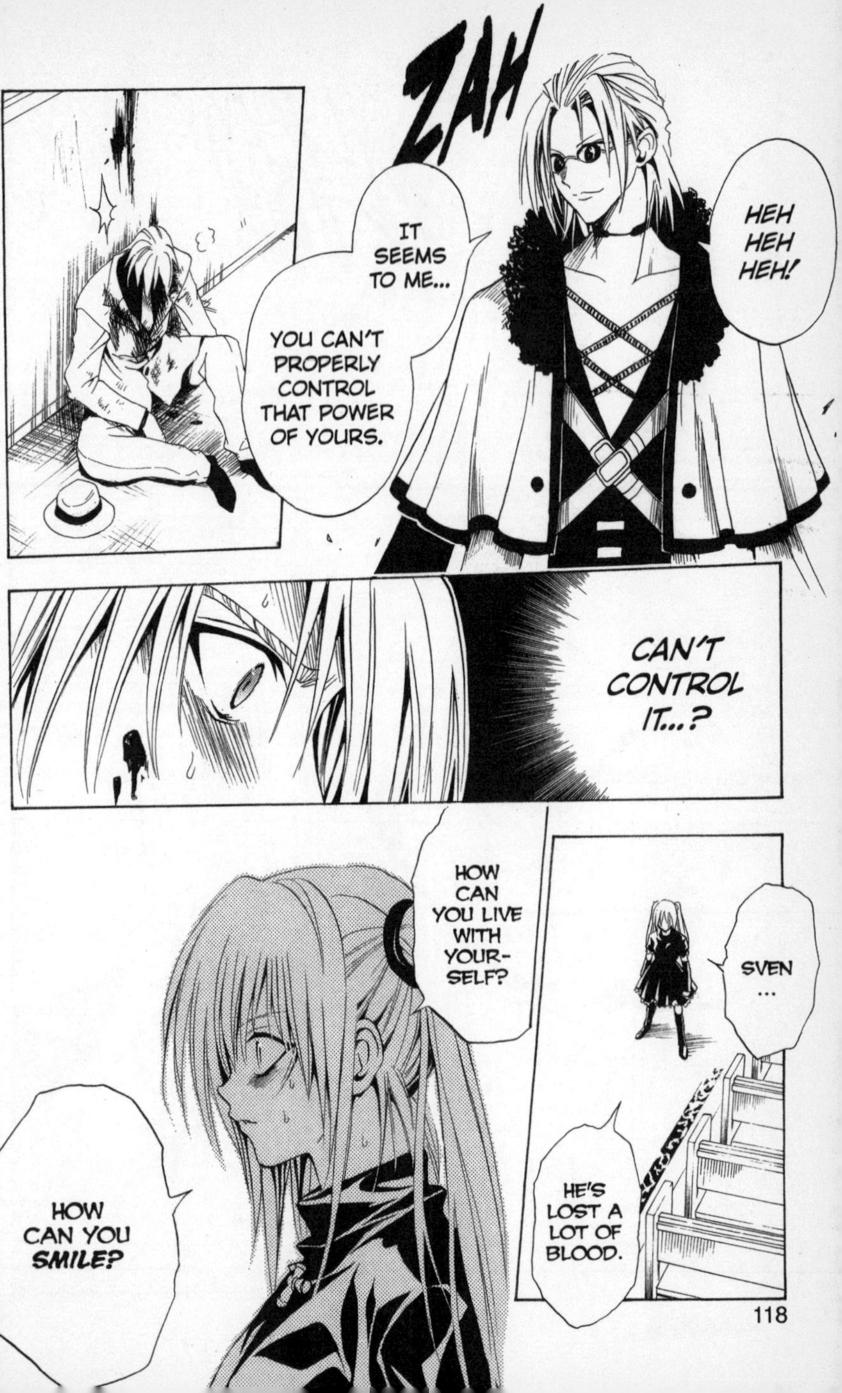
ZAH
HEH HEH HEH!
IT SEEMS TO ME...
YOU CAN'T PROPERLY CONTROL THAT POWER OF YOURS.
CAN'T CONTROL IT...?
SVEN...
HE'S LOST A LOT OF BLOOD.
HOW CAN YOU LIVE WITH YOURSELF?
HOW CAN YOU SMILE?

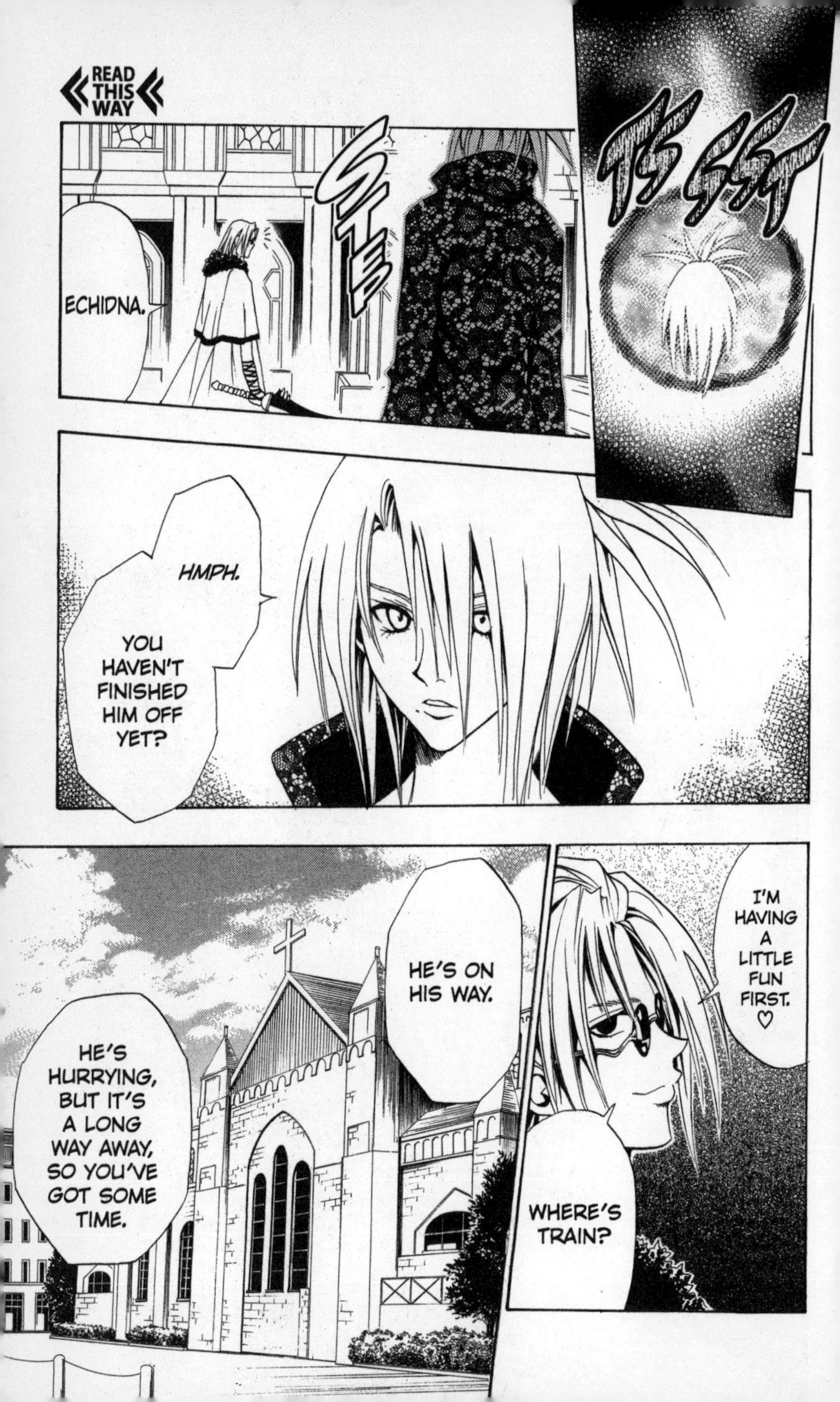
READ THIS WAY
TSSST
STEP
ECHIDNA.
HMPH.
YOU HAVEN'T FINISHED HIM OFF YET?
I'M HAVING A LITTLE FUN FIRST. ♡
WHERE'S TRAIN?
HE'S ON HIS WAY.
HE'S HURRYING, BUT IT'S A LONG WAY AWAY, SO YOU'VE GOT SOME TIME.

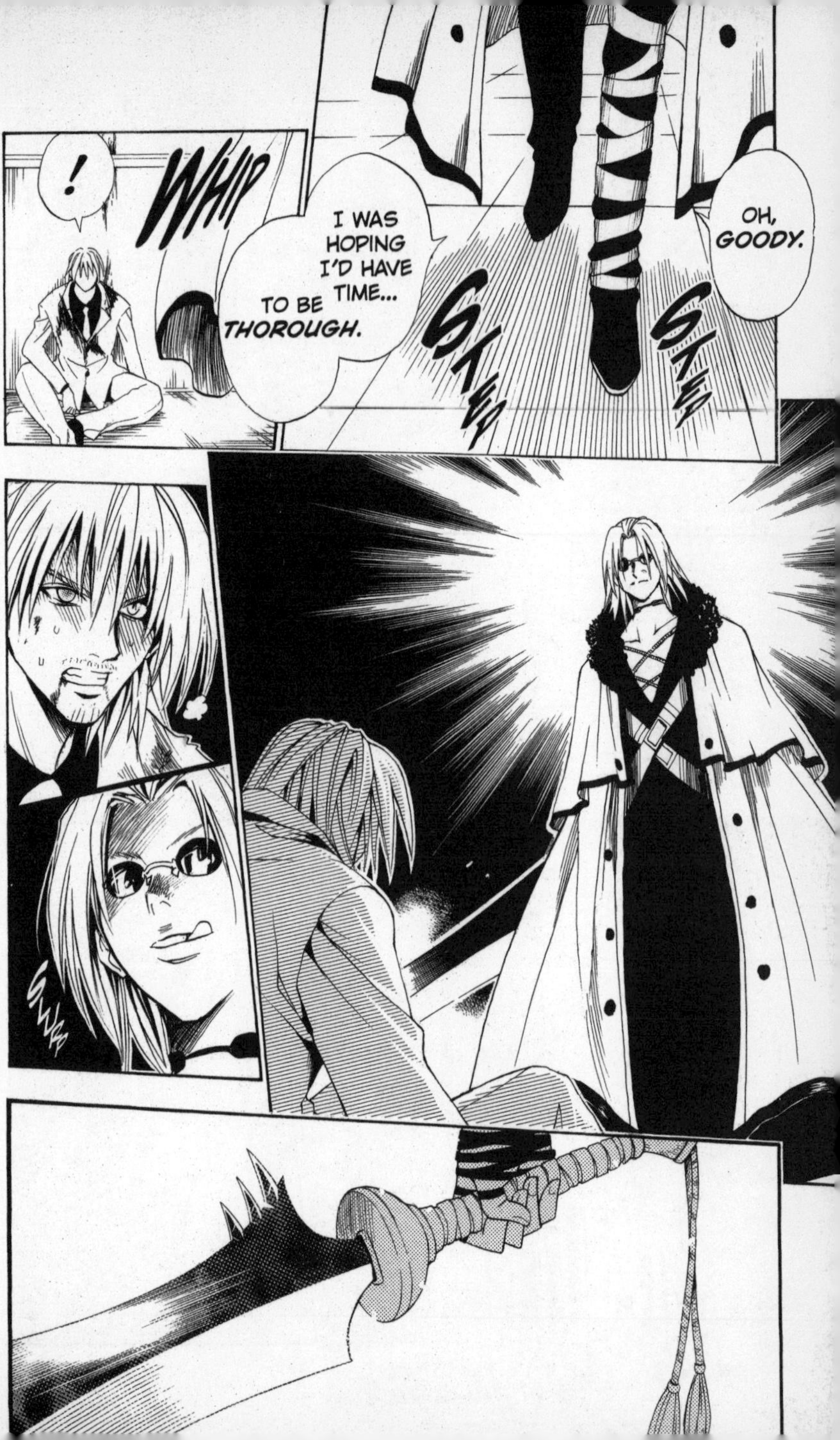
OH, GOODY.
I WAS HOPING I'D HAVE TIME...
TO BE THOROUGH.
!
WHIP

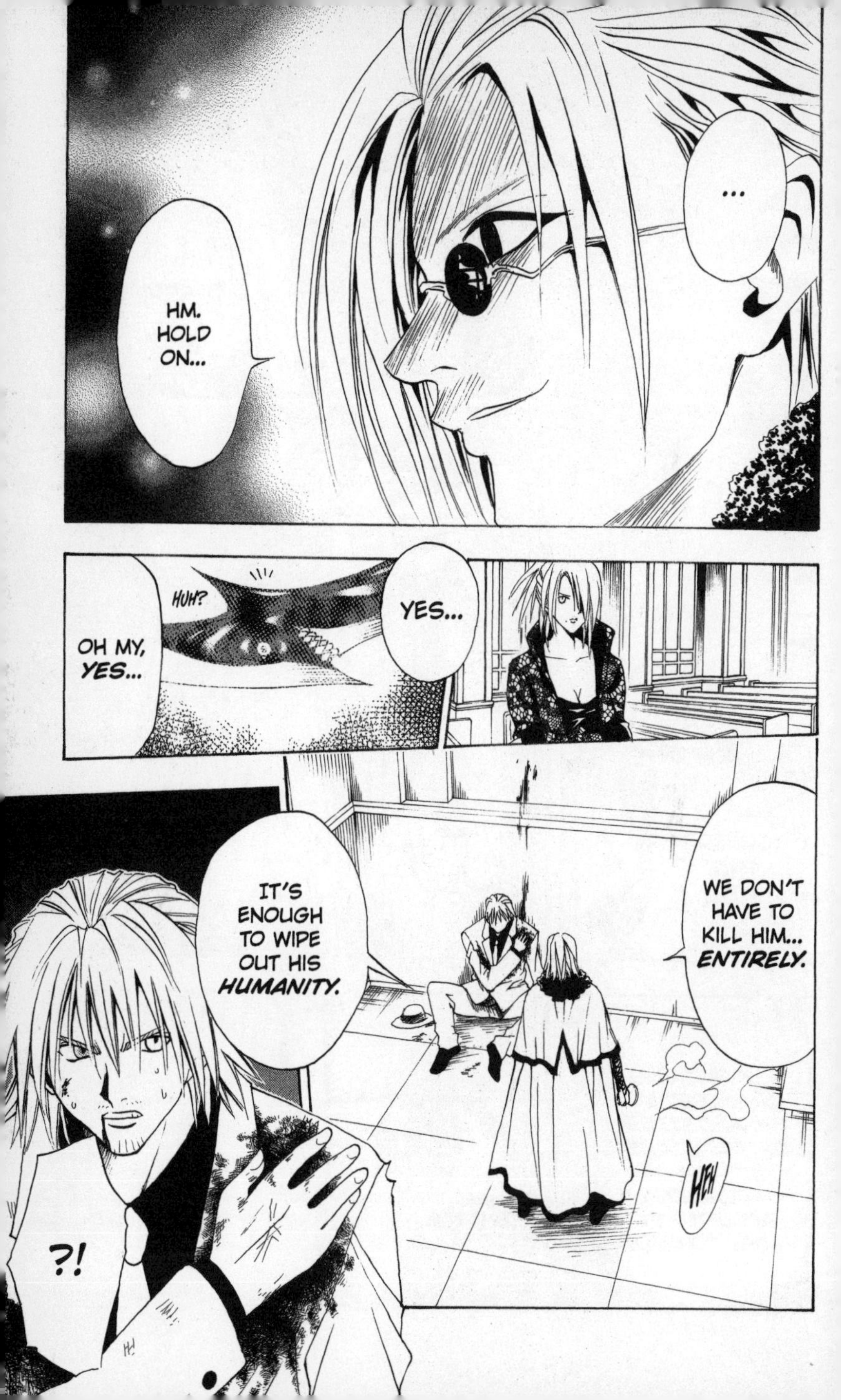
...
HM. HOLD ON...
YES...
HUH?
OH MY, *YES*...
WE DON'T HAVE TO KILL HIM... *ENTIRELY.*
HEH
IT'S ENOUGH TO WIPE OUT HIS *HUMANITY.*
?!

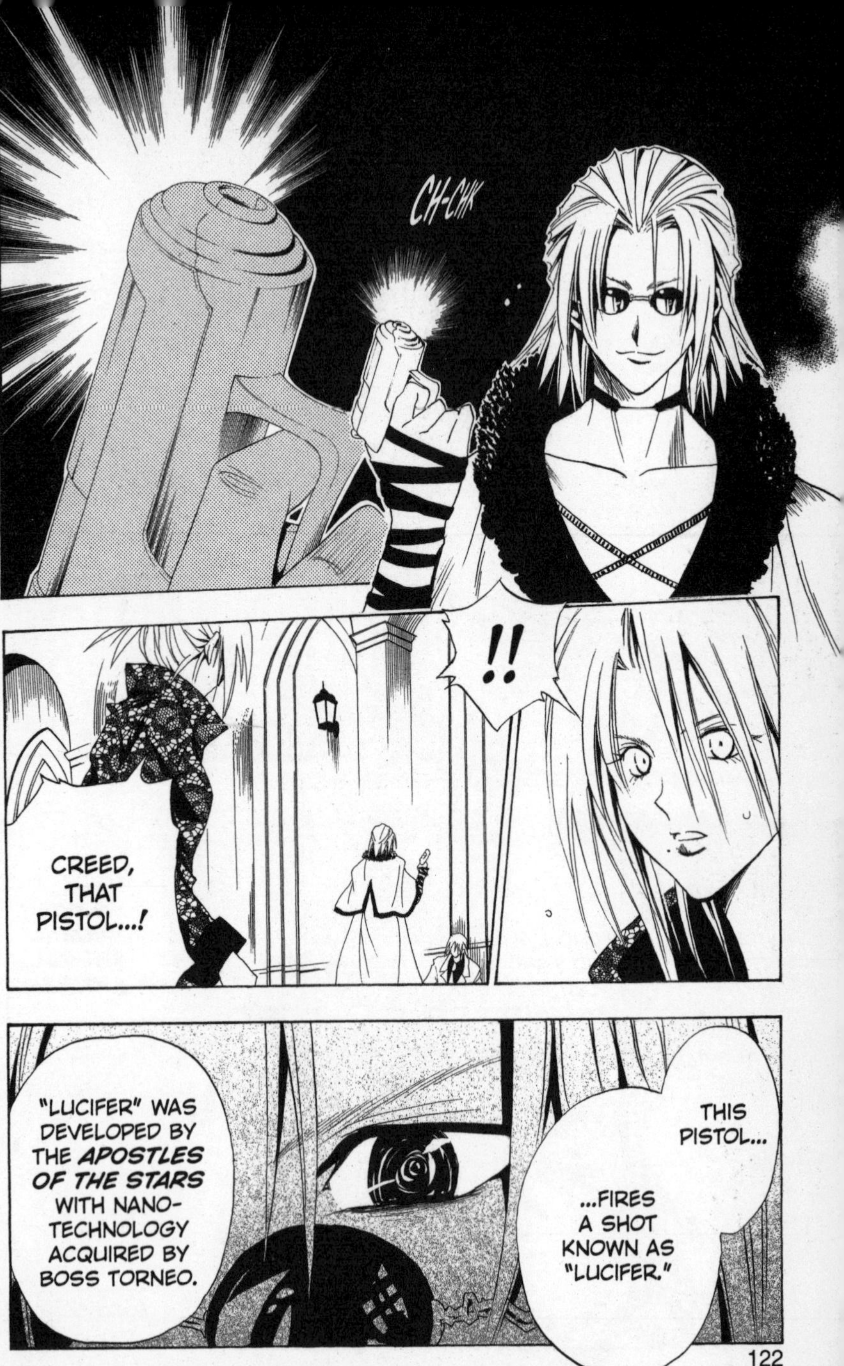
CH-CHK
!!
CREED, THAT PISTOL...!
THIS PISTOL...
...FIRES A SHOT KNOWN AS "LUCIFER."
"LUCIFER" WAS DEVELOPED BY THE *APOSTLES OF THE STARS* WITH NANO-TECHNOLOGY ACQUIRED BY BOSS TORNEO.

READ THIS WAY

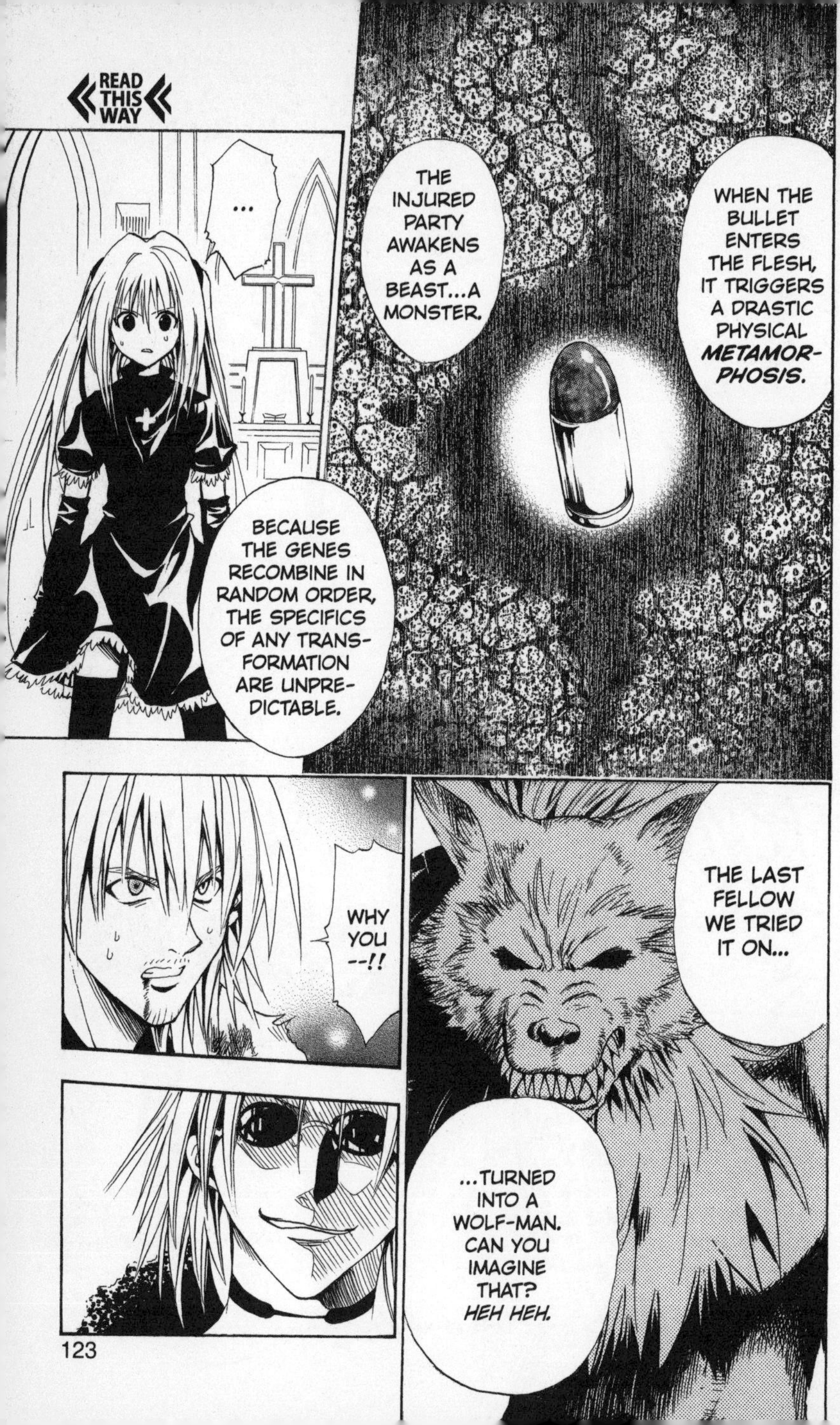
WHEN THE BULLET ENTERS THE FLESH, IT TRIGGERS A DRASTIC PHYSICAL *METAMORPHOSIS.*
THE INJURED PARTY AWAKENS AS A BEAST...A MONSTER.
...
BECAUSE THE GENES RECOMBINE IN RANDOM ORDER, THE SPECIFICS OF ANY TRANSFORMATION ARE UNPREDICTABLE.
THE LAST FELLOW WE TRIED IT ON...
...TURNED INTO A WOLF-MAN. CAN YOU IMAGINE THAT? *HEH HEH.*
WHY YOU --!!

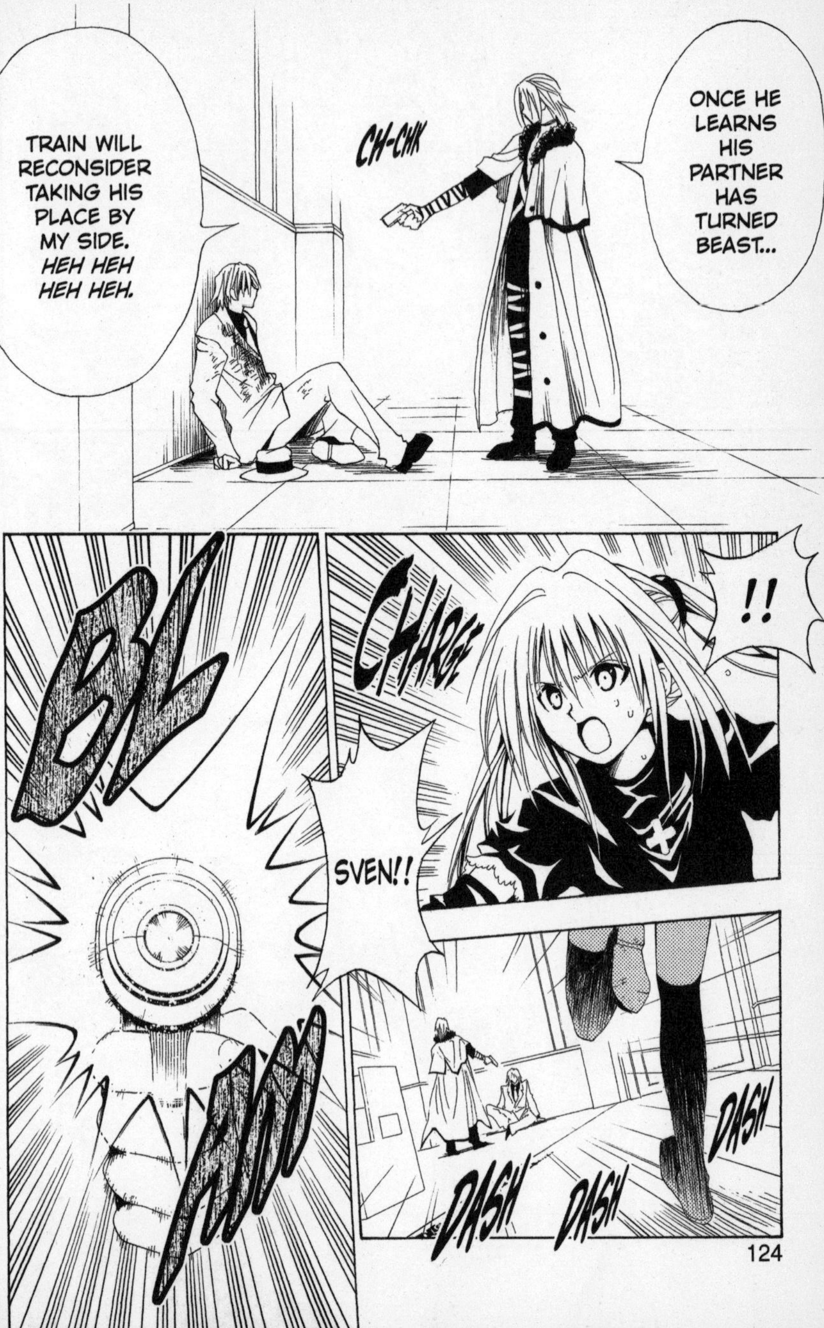
ONCE HE LEARNS HIS PARTNER HAS TURNED BEAST...
CH-CHK
TRAIN WILL RECONSIDER TAKING HIS PLACE BY MY SIDE. *HEH HEH HEH HEH.*
CHARGE
!!
SVEN!!
DASH
DASH
DASH
BL

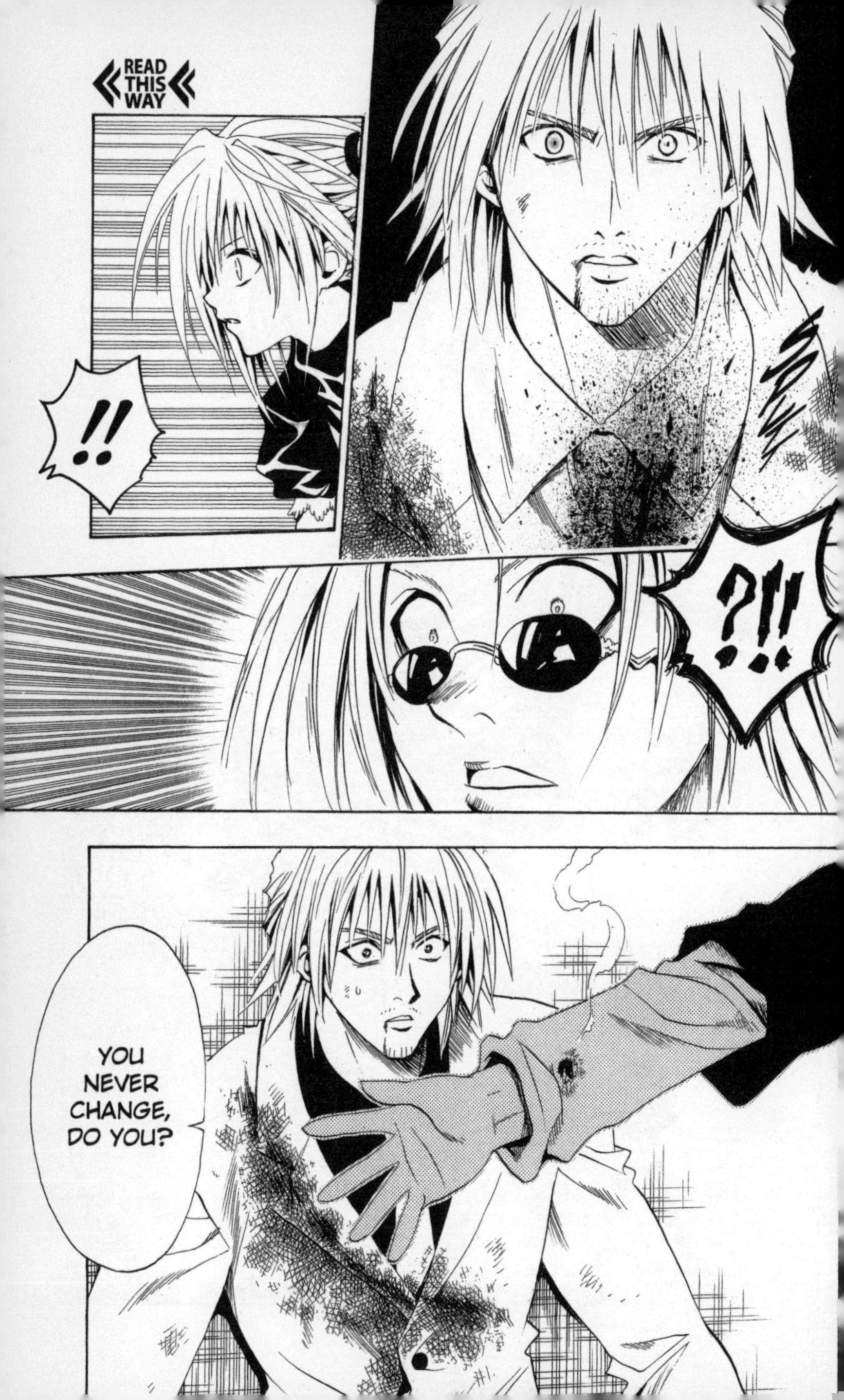
READ THIS WAY
!!
?!!
YOU NEVER CHANGE, DO YOU?

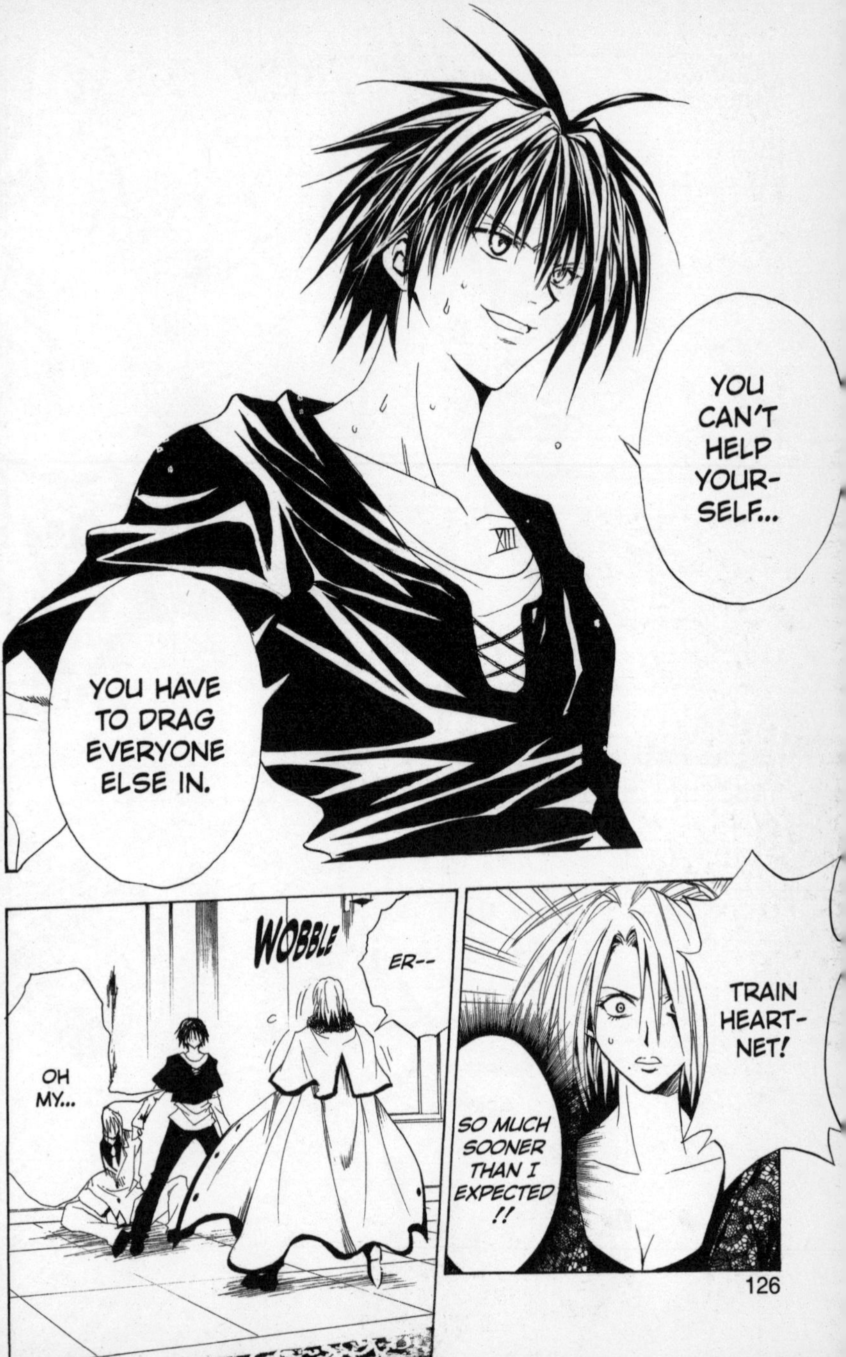
YOU CAN'T HELP YOURSELF...
YOU HAVE TO DRAG EVERYONE ELSE IN.
TRAIN HEARTNET!
SO MUCH SOONER THAN I EXPECTED!!
WOBBLE
ER--
OH MY...

READ THIS WAY

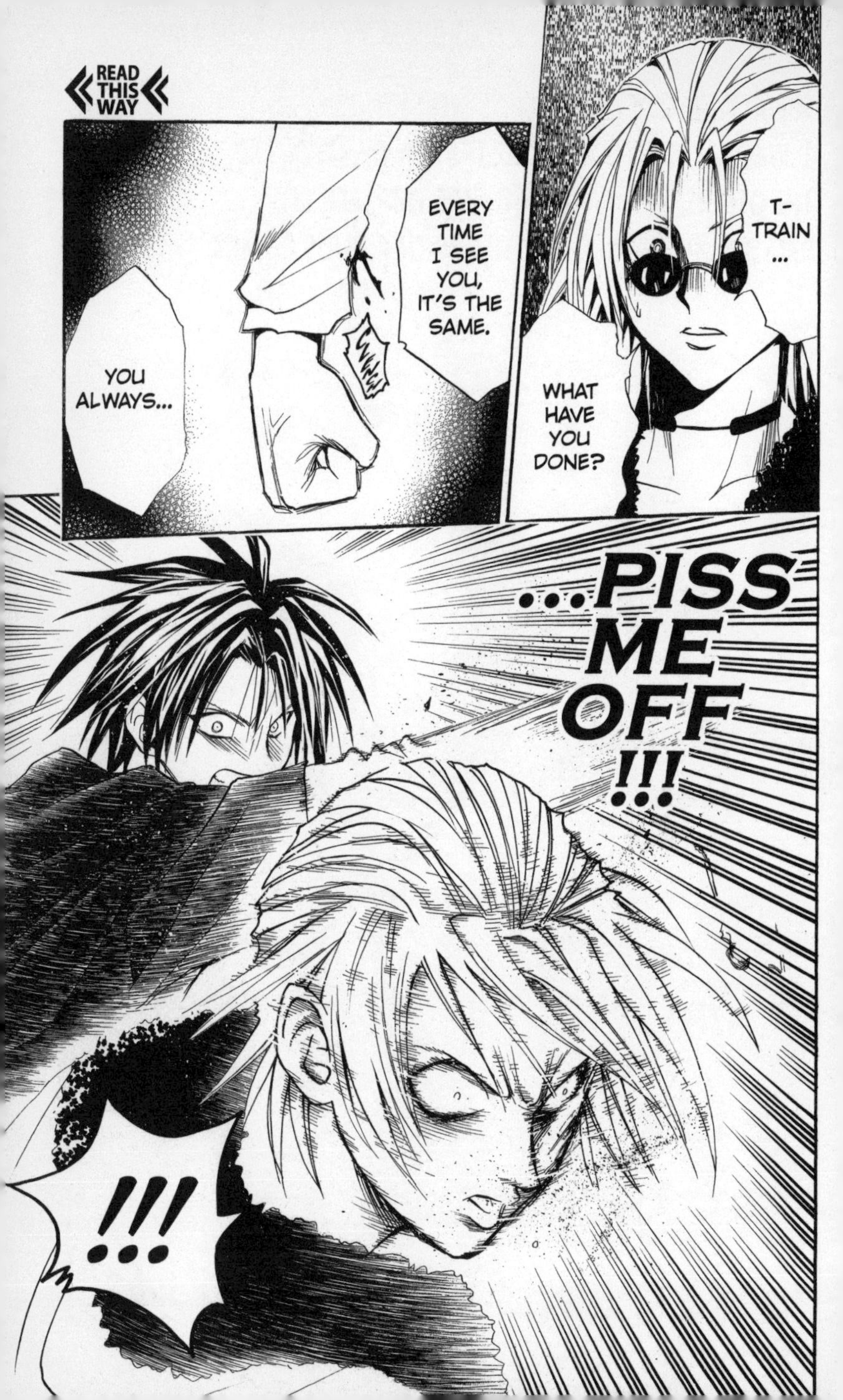
T-TRAIN ...
WHAT HAVE YOU DONE?
EVERY TIME I SEE YOU, IT'S THE SAME.
YOU ALWAYS...
...PISS ME OFF !!!
!!!

Weekly Shonen Jump Cover Illustration 1

I was asked to do an illustration of Train and the others at a party. So here they are all dressed up. Train is toasting with a glass of milk.

Chapter 91: Big Changes

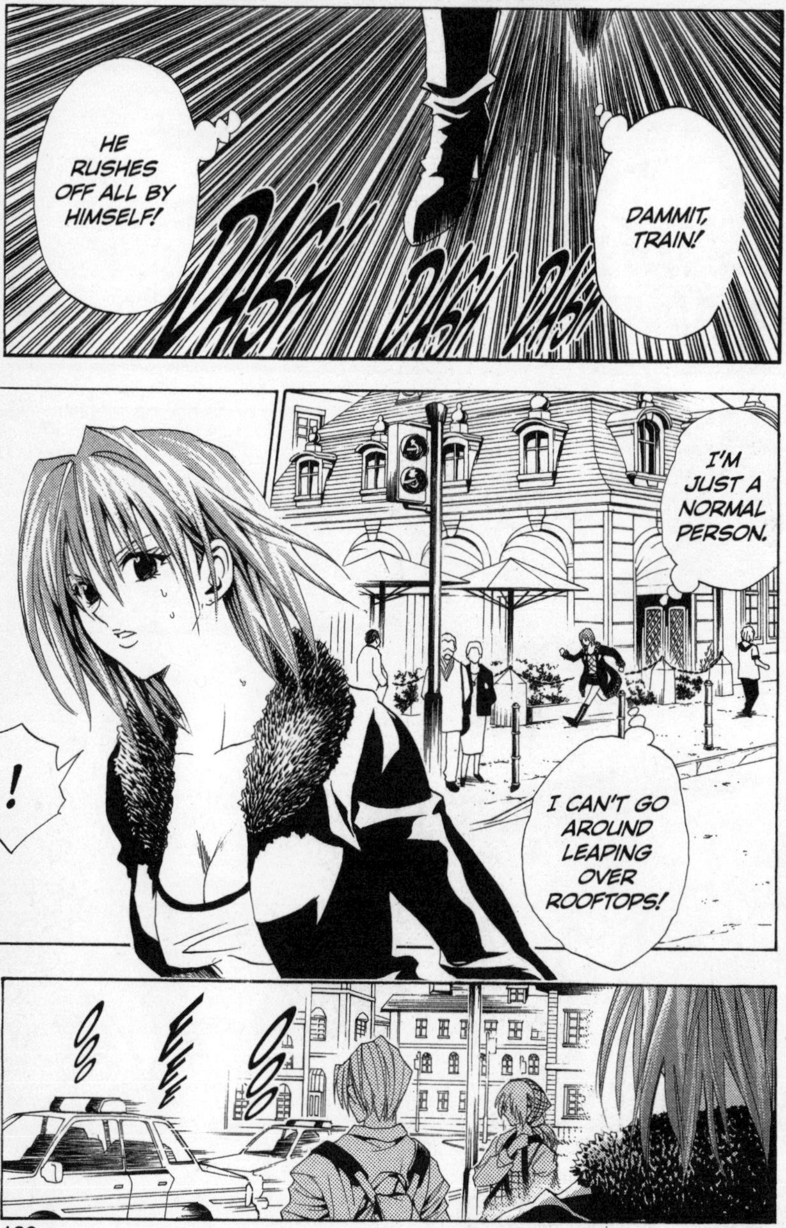
DAMMIT, TRAIN!
HE RUSHES OFF ALL BY HIMSELF!
DASH DASH DASH
I'M JUST A NORMAL PERSON.
I CAN'T GO AROUND LEAPING OVER ROOFTOPS!
!

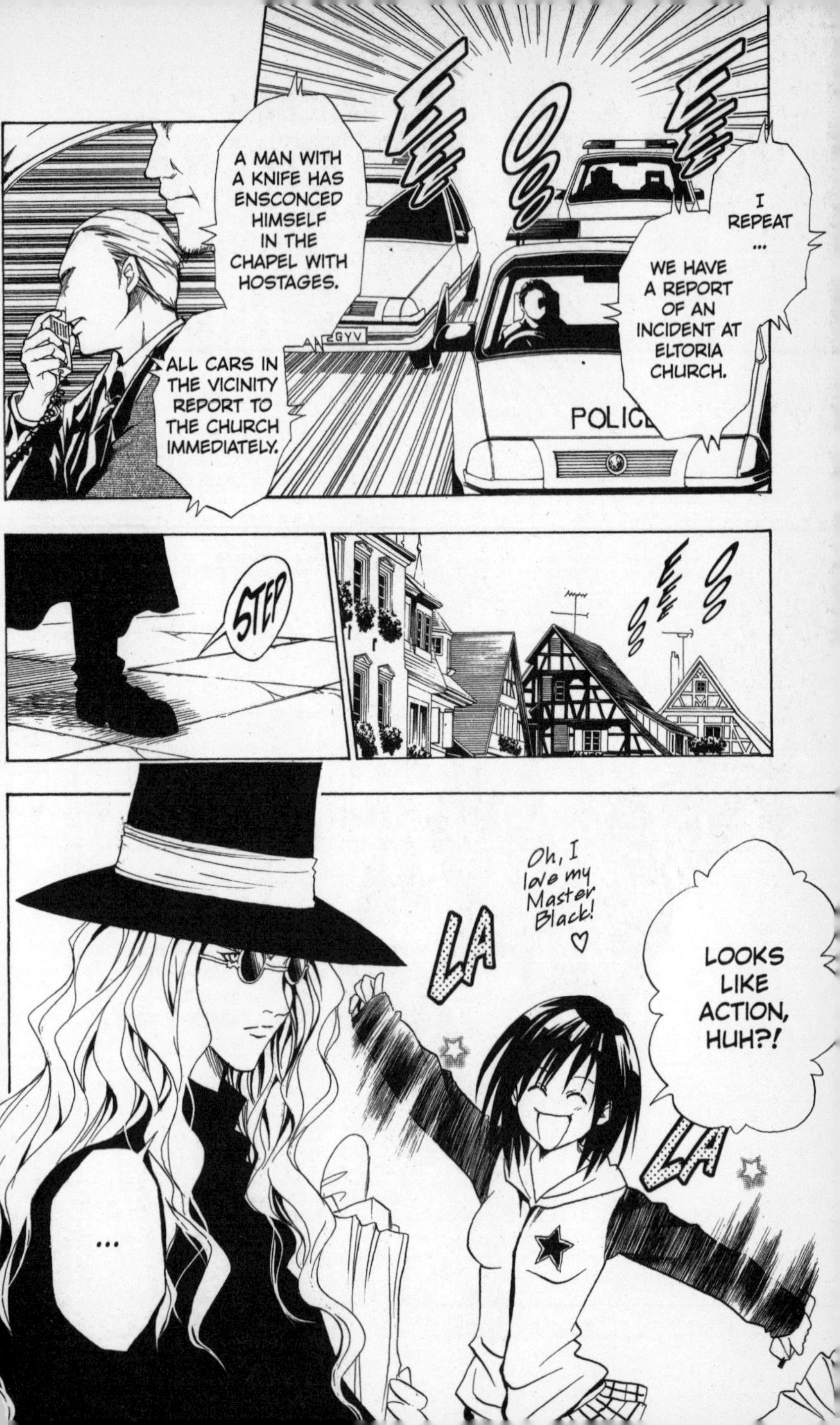
I REPEAT ...
WE HAVE A REPORT OF AN INCIDENT AT ELTORIA CHURCH.
POLICE
A MAN WITH A KNIFE HAS ENSCONCED HIMSELF IN THE CHAPEL WITH HOSTAGES.
ALL CARS IN THE VICINITY REPORT TO THE CHURCH IMMEDIATELY.
STEP
LOOKS LIKE ACTION, HUH?!
LA
LA
Oh, I love my Master Black! ♥
...

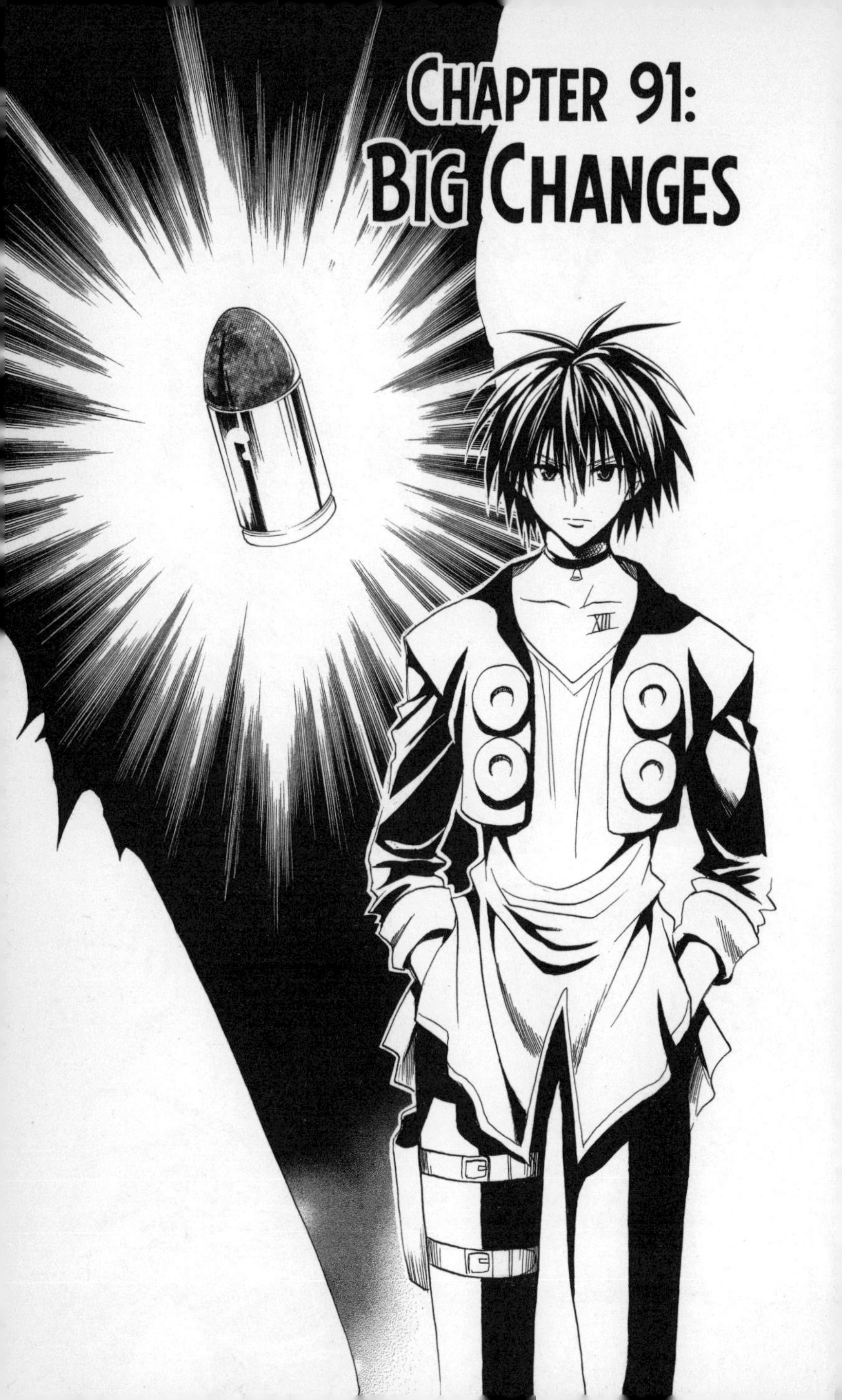
Chapter 91:
Big Changes

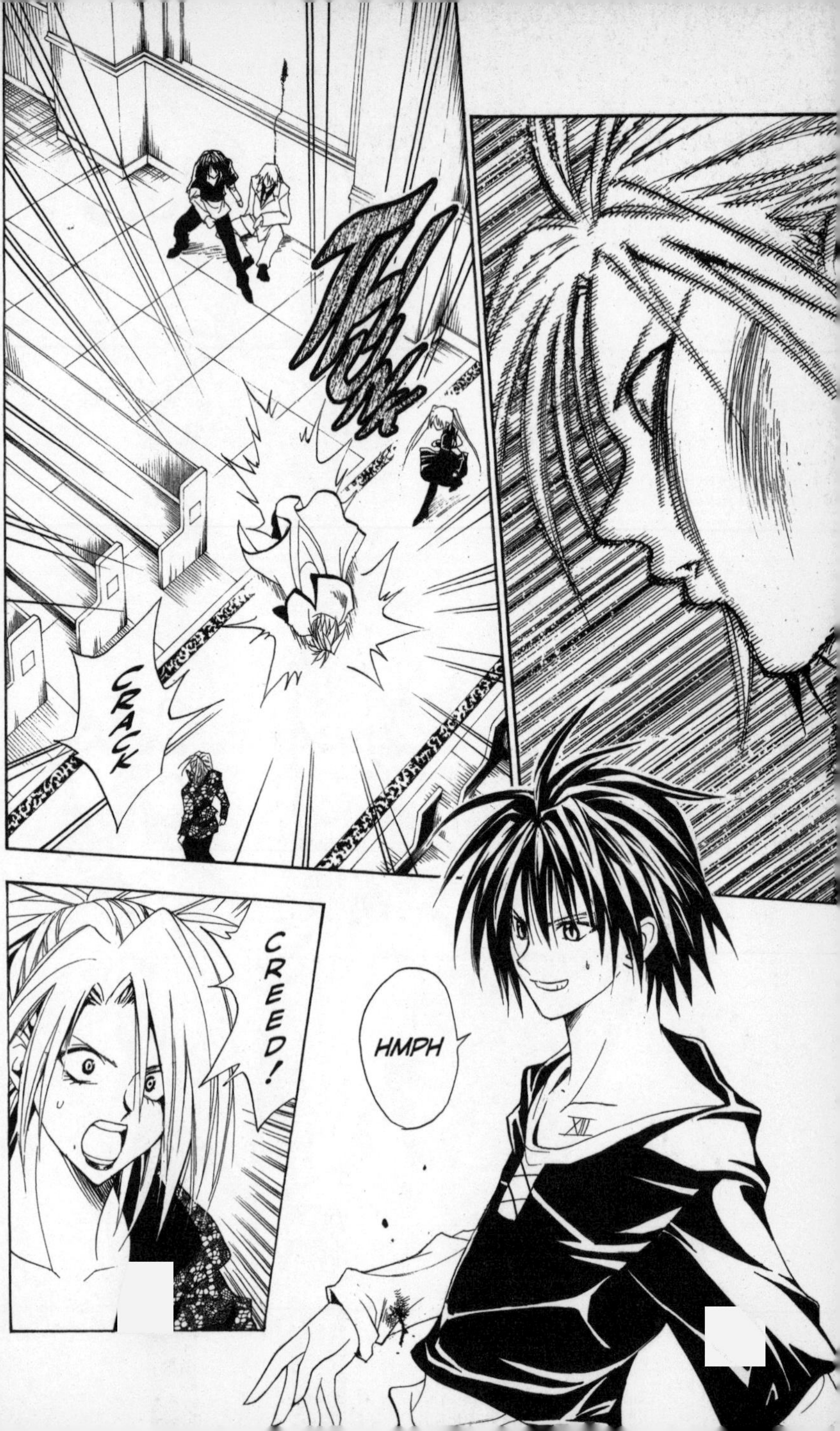
THUNK
CRACK
HMPH
CREEED!

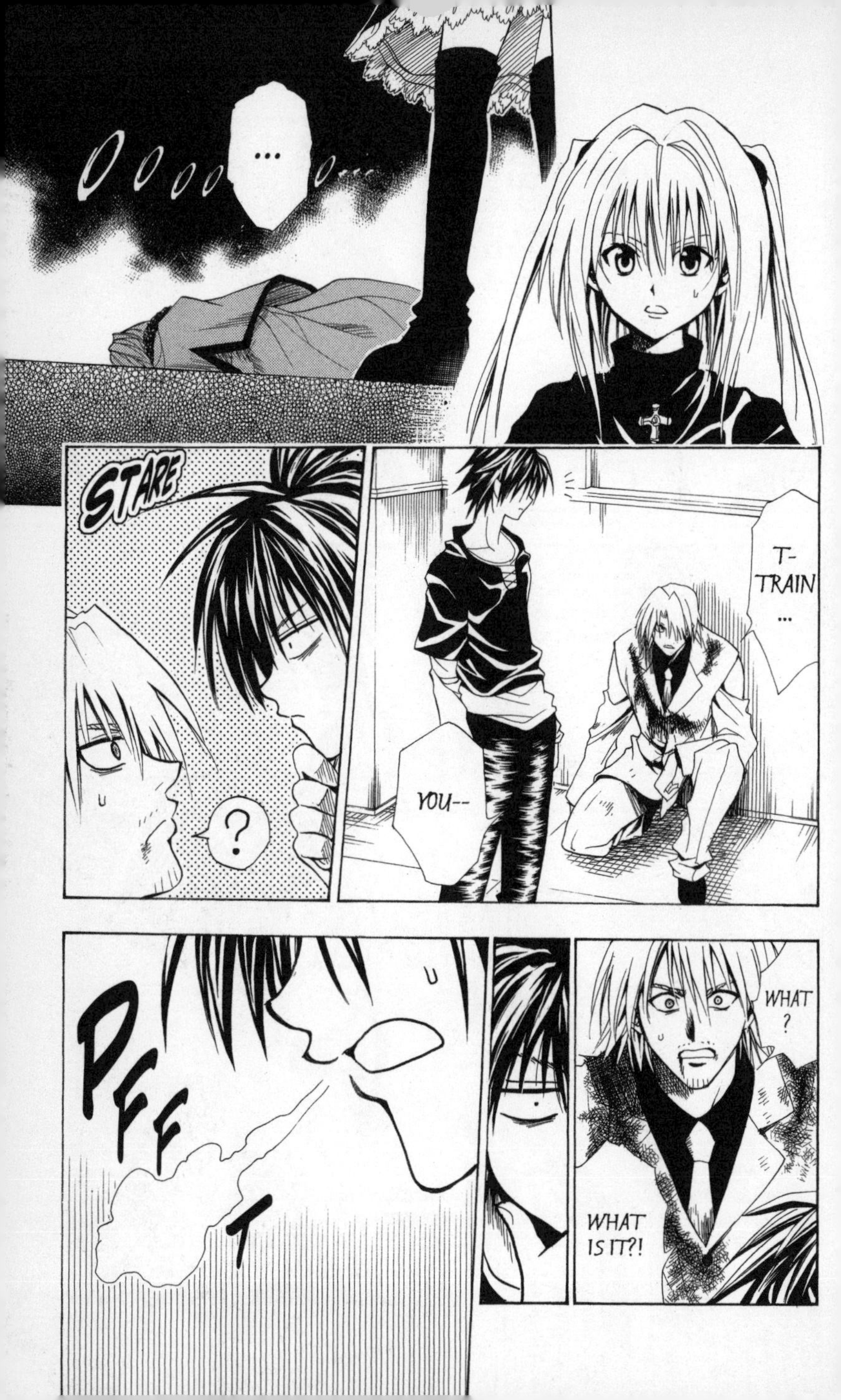

OOOOOO...
...
T-TRAIN...
YOU--
STARE
?
WHAT?
WHAT IS IT?!
PFFT

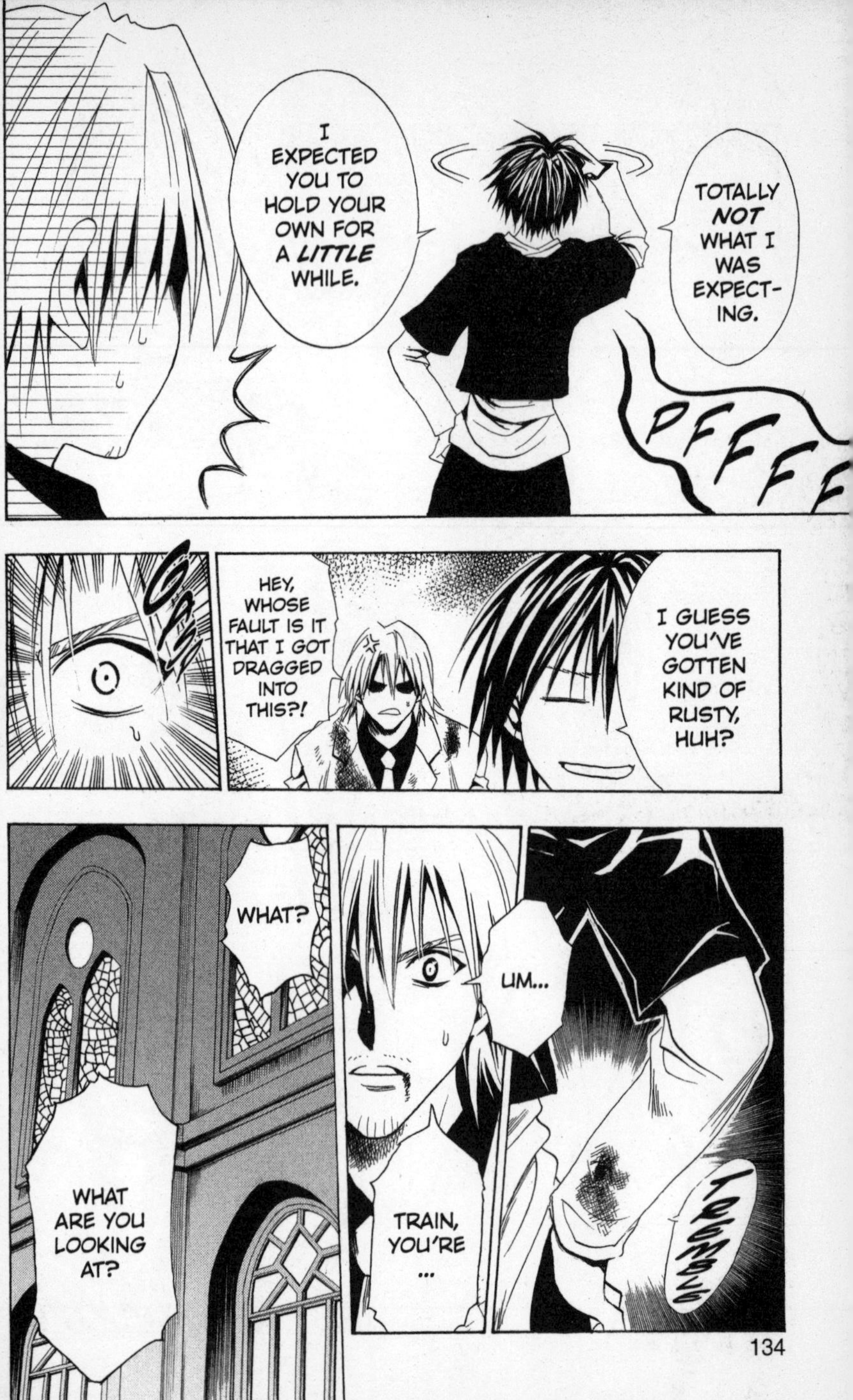

TOTALLY *NOT* WHAT I WAS EXPECT-ING.
I EXPECTED YOU TO HOLD YOUR OWN FOR A *LITTLE* WHILE.
PFFFF
I GUESS YOU'VE GOTTEN KIND OF RUSTY, HUH?
HEY, WHOSE FAULT IS IT THAT I GOT DRAGGED INTO THIS?!
UM...
TRAIN, YOU'RE ...
TREMBLE
WHAT?
WHAT ARE YOU LOOKING AT?

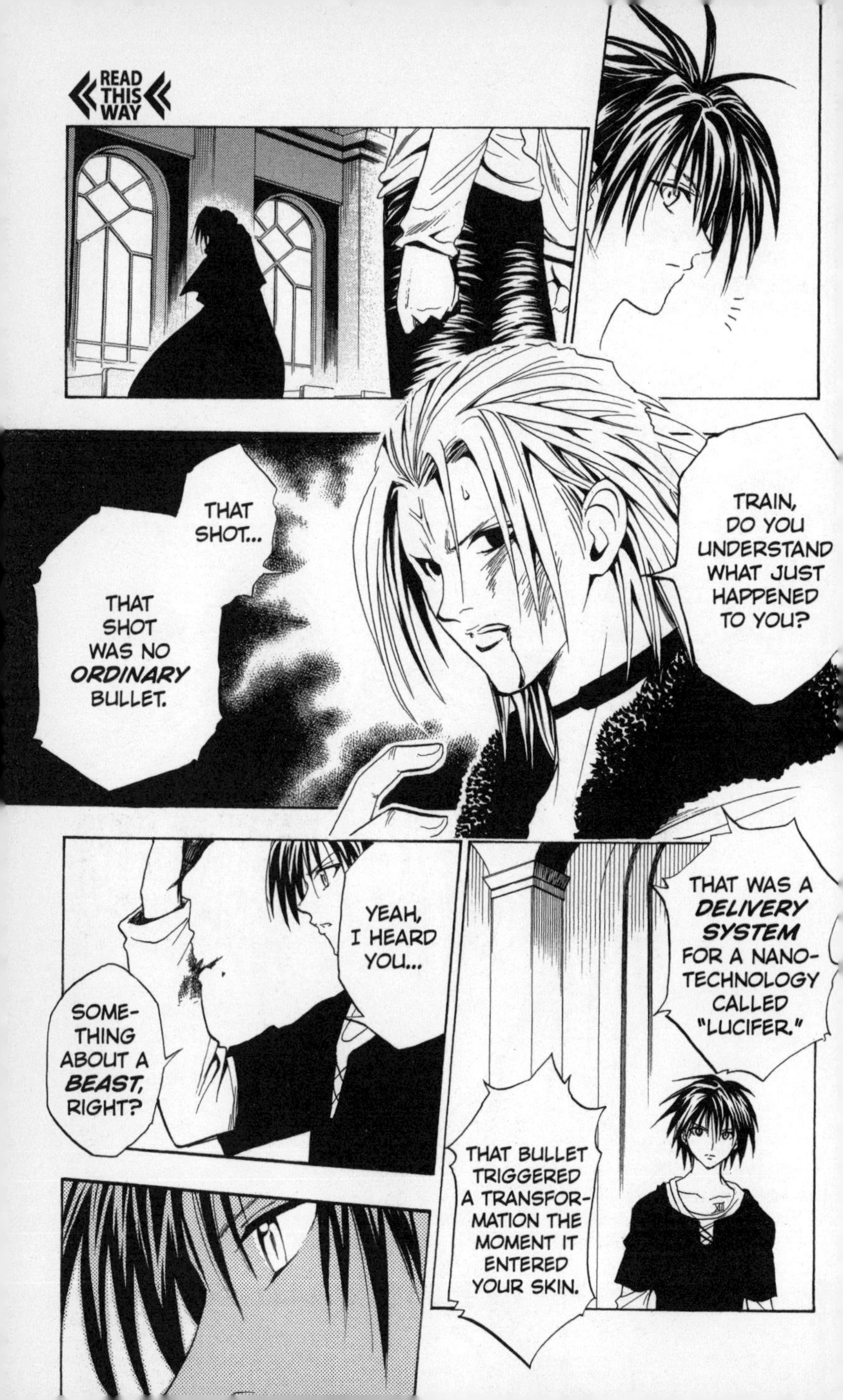
READ THIS WAY
TRAIN, DO YOU UNDERSTAND WHAT JUST HAPPENED TO YOU?
THAT SHOT...
THAT SHOT WAS NO *ORDINARY* BULLET.
THAT WAS A *DELIVERY SYSTEM* FOR A NANO-TECHNOLOGY CALLED "LUCIFER."
THAT BULLET TRIGGERED A TRANSFOR-MATION THE MOMENT IT ENTERED YOUR SKIN.
YEAH, I HEARD YOU...
SOME-THING ABOUT A *BEAST,* RIGHT?

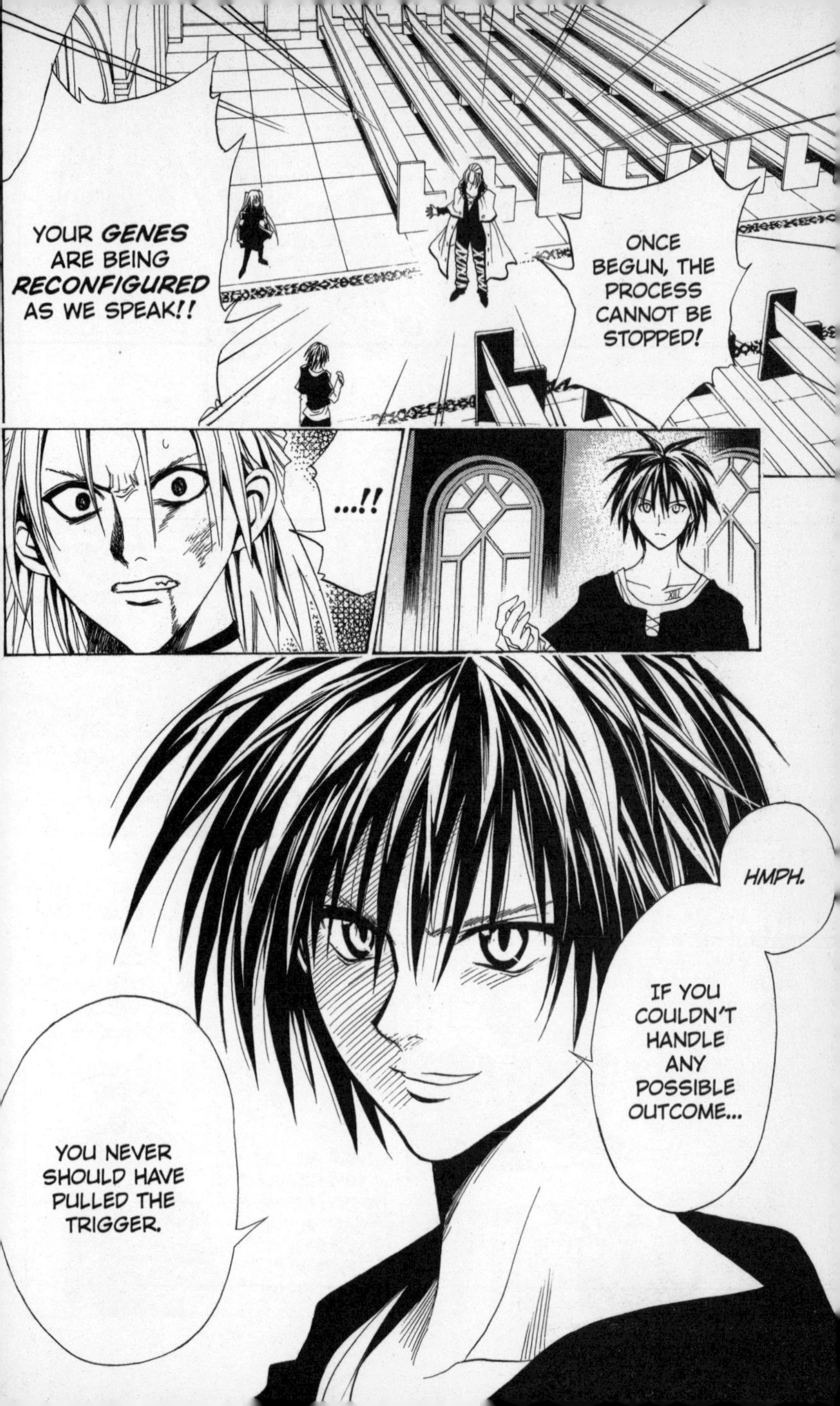
ONCE BEGUN, THE PROCESS CANNOT BE STOPPED!
YOUR GENES ARE BEING RECONFIGURED AS WE SPEAK!!
...!!
HMPH.
IF YOU COULDN'T HANDLE ANY POSSIBLE OUTCOME...
YOU NEVER SHOULD HAVE PULLED THE TRIGGER.

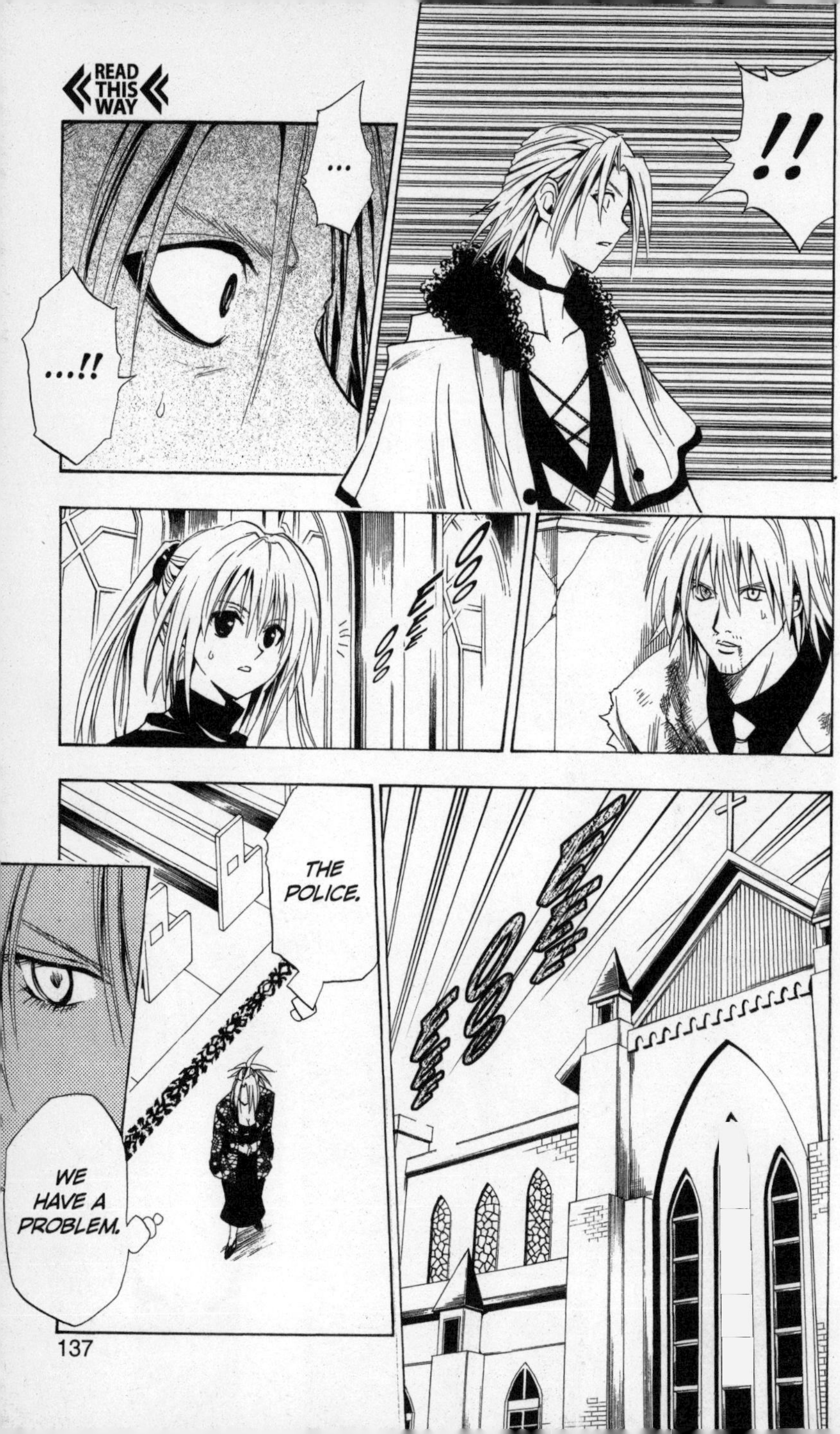
READ THIS WAY
!!
...
...!!
THE POLICE.
WE HAVE A PROBLEM.

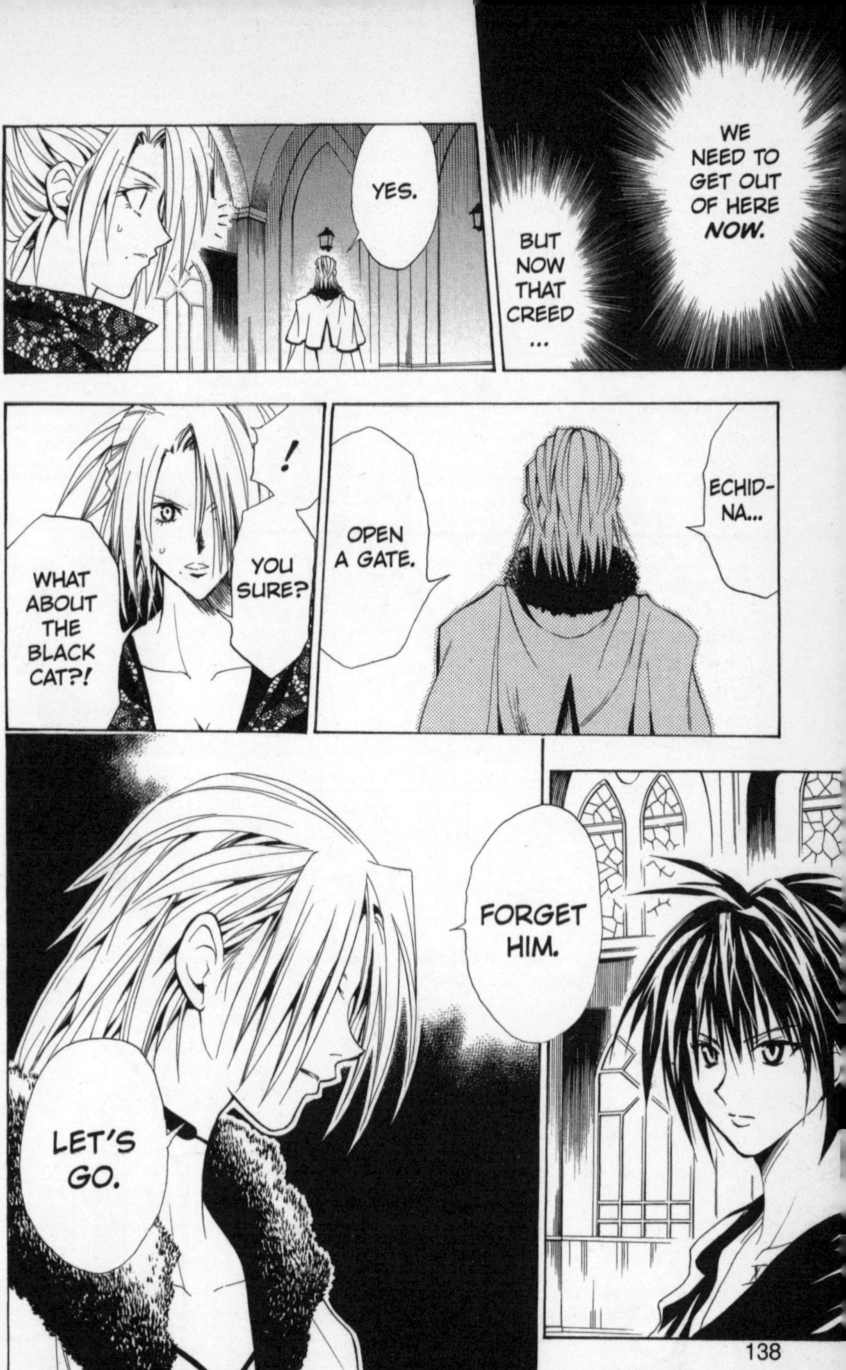
WE NEED TO GET OUT OF HERE NOW.
BUT NOW THAT CREED ...
YES.
ECHID-NA...
OPEN A GATE.
!
YOU SURE?
WHAT ABOUT THE BLACK CAT?!
FORGET HIM.
LET'S GO.

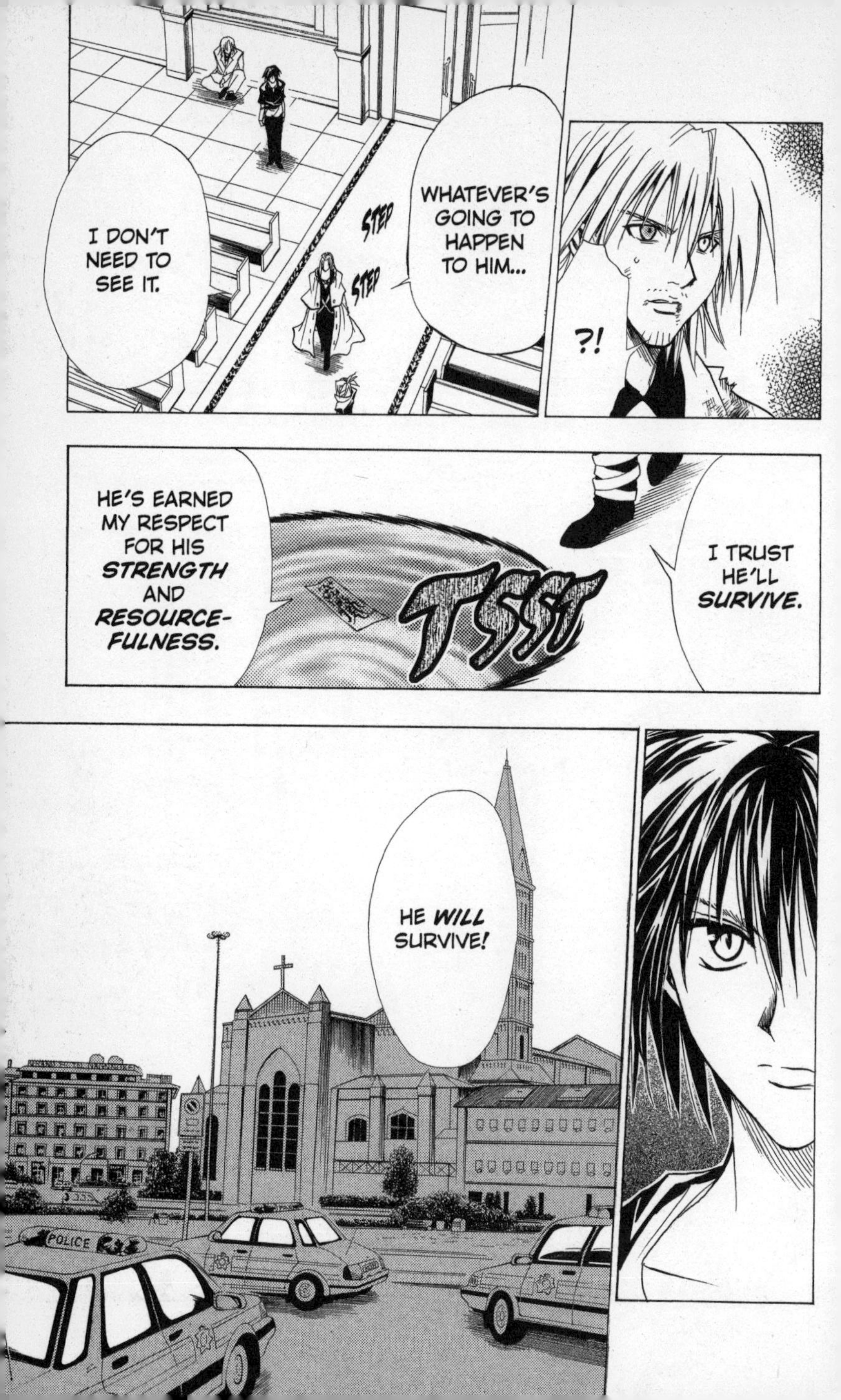
?!
WHATEVER'S GOING TO HAPPEN TO HIM...
STEP
STEP
I DON'T NEED TO SEE IT.
I TRUST HE'LL *SURVIVE.*
TSST
HE'S EARNED MY RESPECT FOR HIS *STRENGTH* AND *RESOURCE-FULNESS.*
HE *WILL* SURVIVE!
POLICE

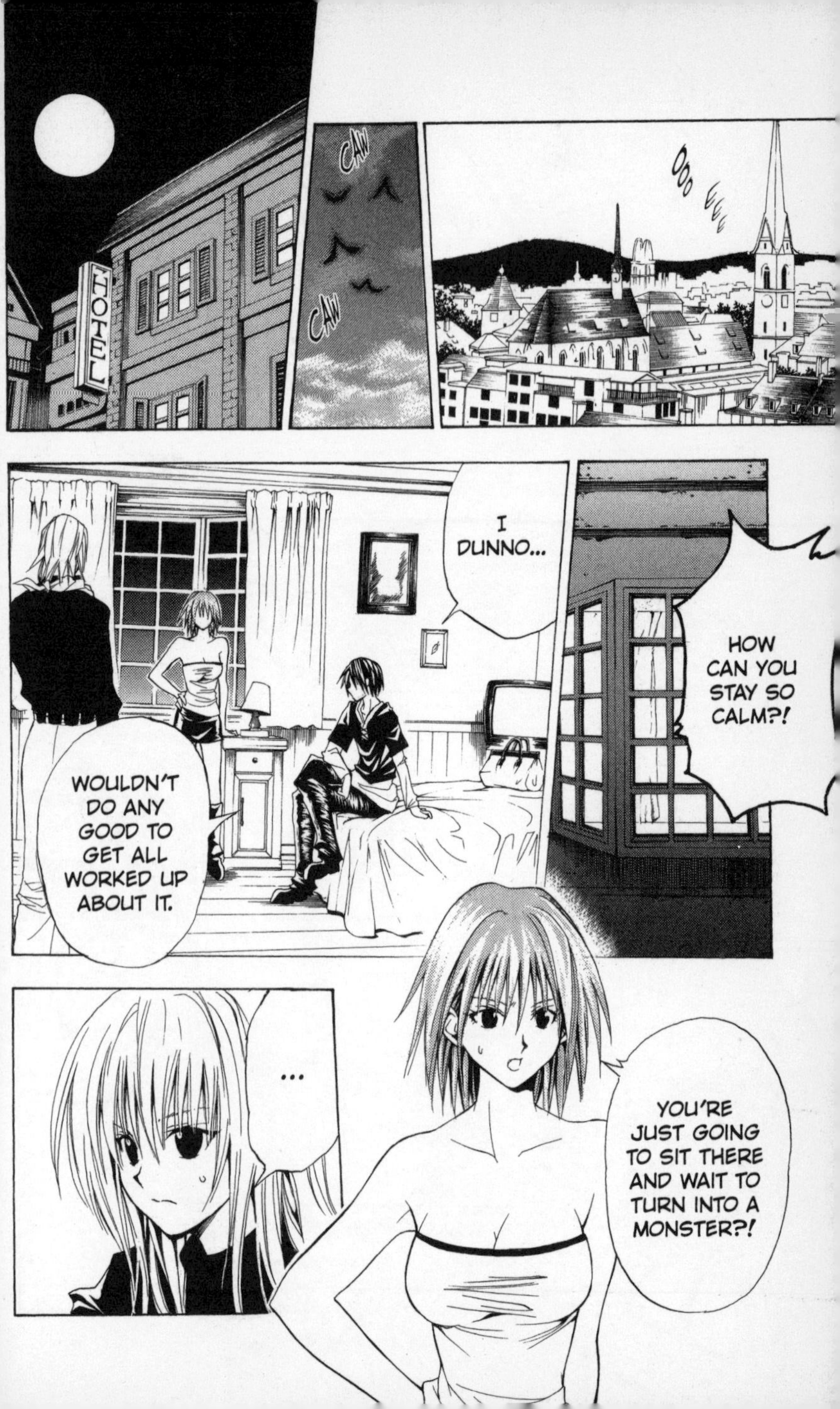
OOO UUU
CAW
CAW
HOTEL
HOW CAN YOU STAY SO CALM?!
I DUNNO...
WOULDN'T DO ANY GOOD TO GET ALL WORKED UP ABOUT IT.
YOU'RE JUST GOING TO SIT THERE AND WAIT TO TURN INTO A MONSTER?!
...

READ THIS WAY

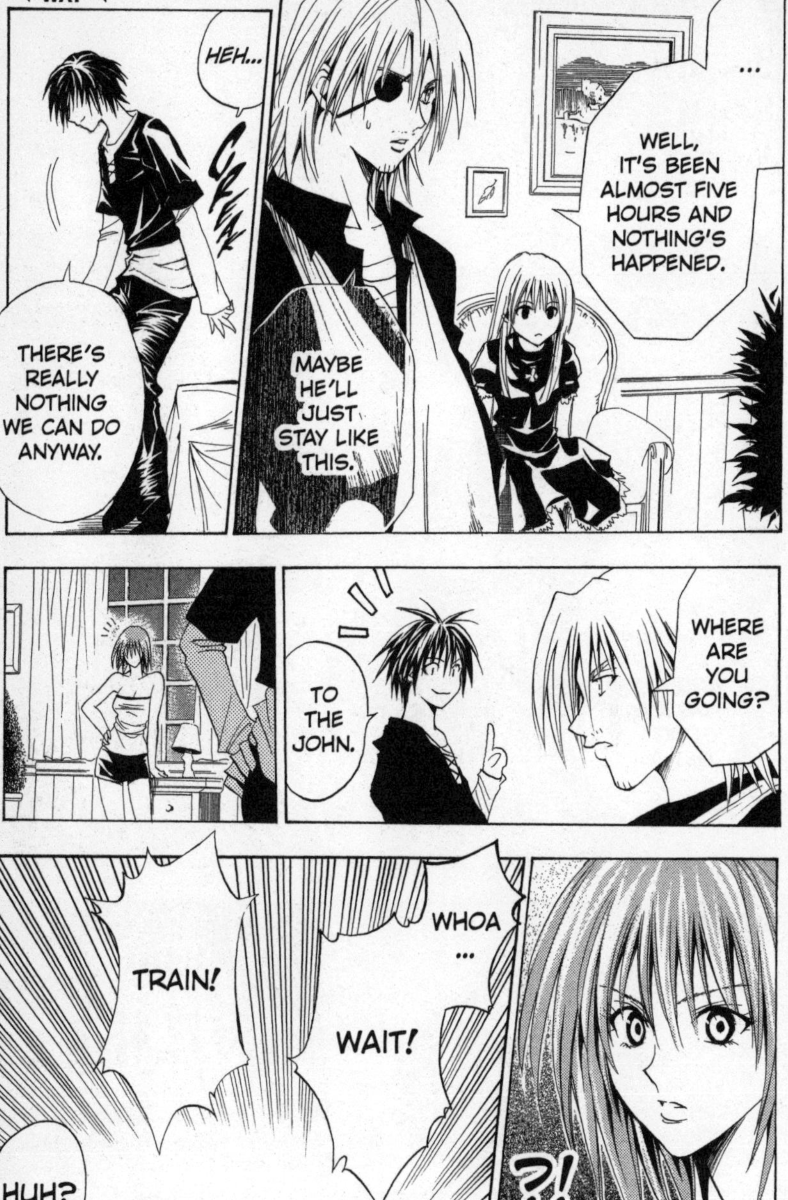
...
WELL, IT'S BEEN ALMOST FIVE HOURS AND NOTHING'S HAPPENED.
MAYBE HE'LL JUST STAY LIKE THIS.
HEH...
THERE'S REALLY NOTHING WE CAN DO ANYWAY.
WHERE ARE YOU GOING?
TO THE JOHN.
?!
WHOA ...
WAIT!
TRAIN!
HUH?

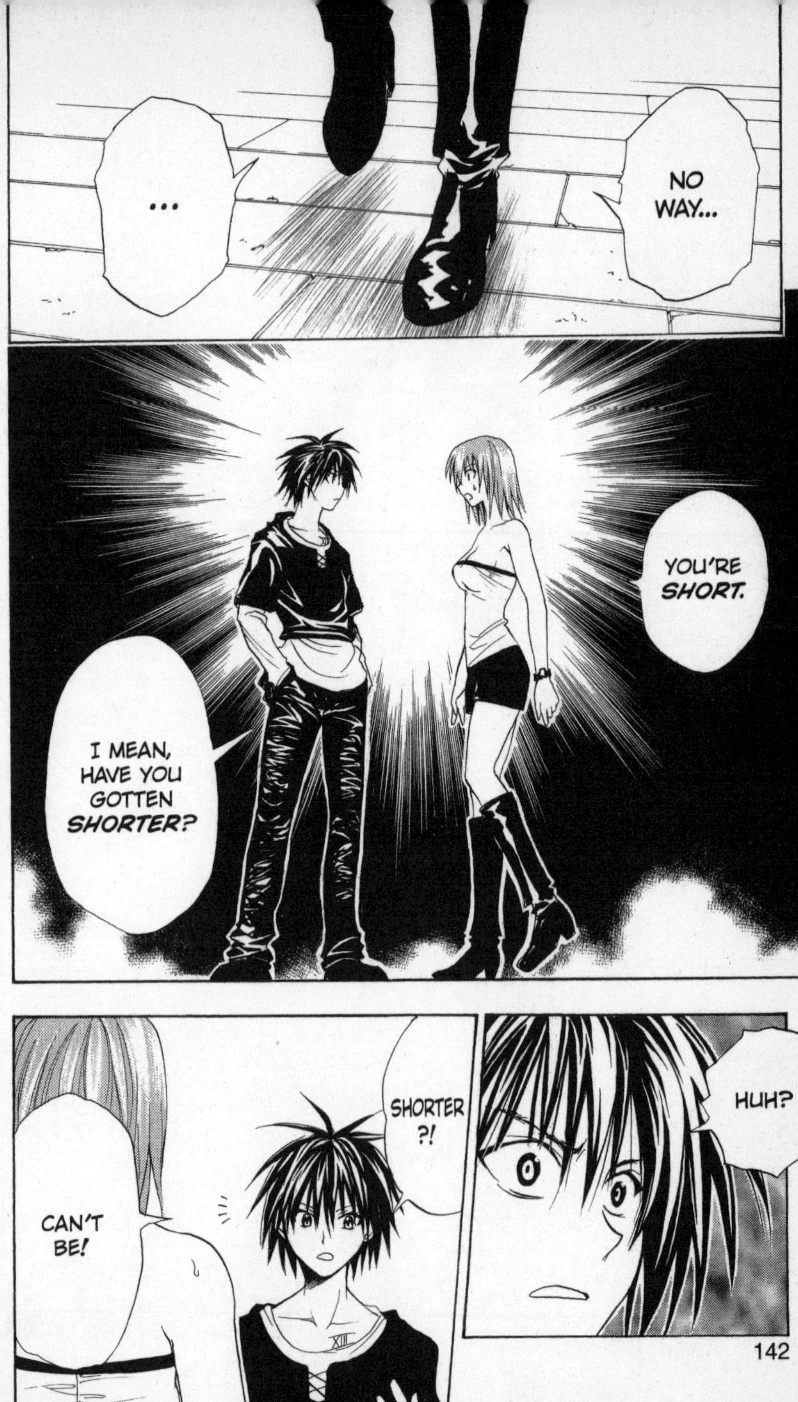
NO WAY...
...
YOU'RE *SHORT.*
I MEAN, HAVE YOU GOTTEN *SHORTER?*
HUH?
SHORTER ?!
CAN'T BE!

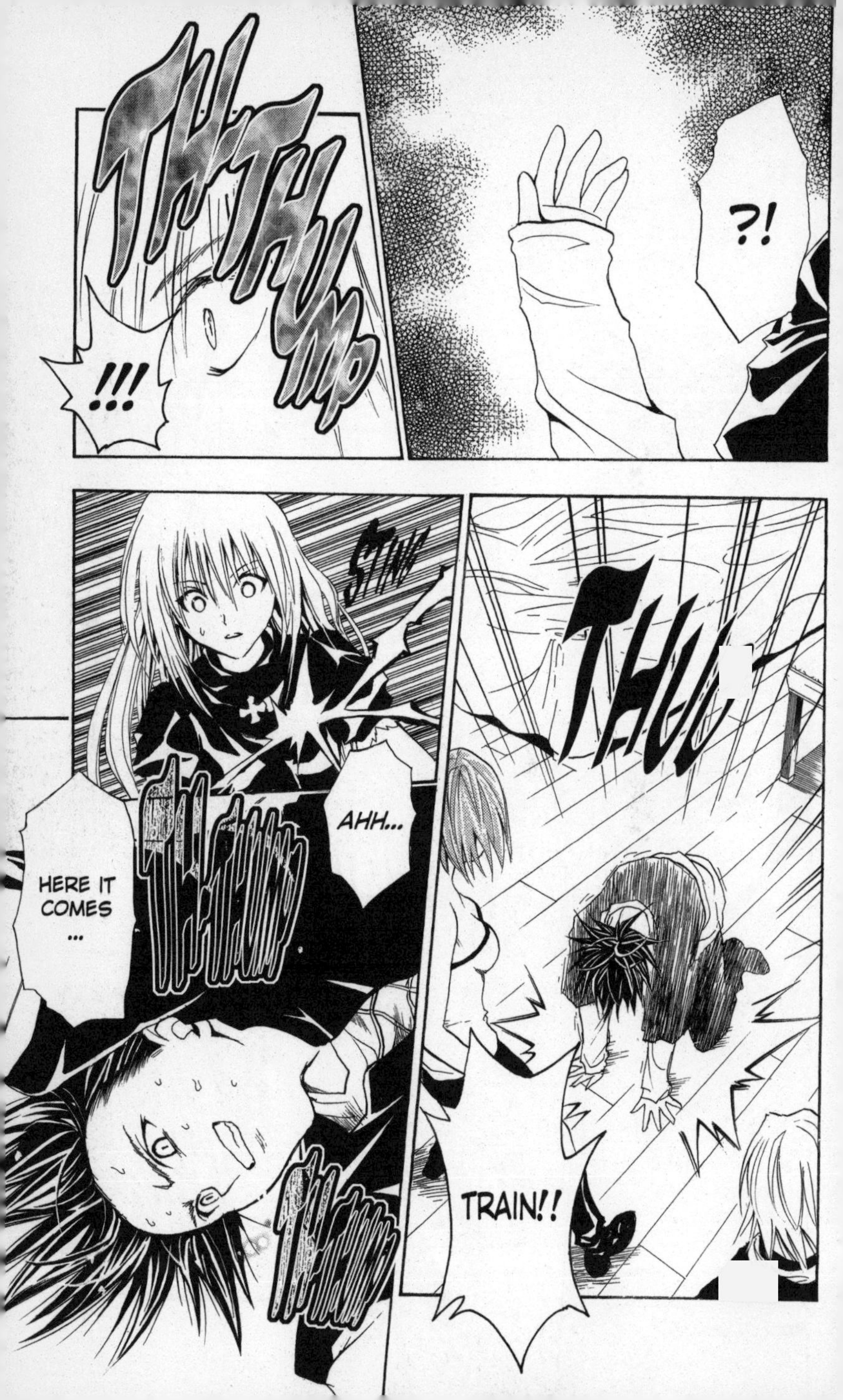
?!
TH-THUMP
!!!
TRAIN!!
AHH...
HERE IT COMES ...

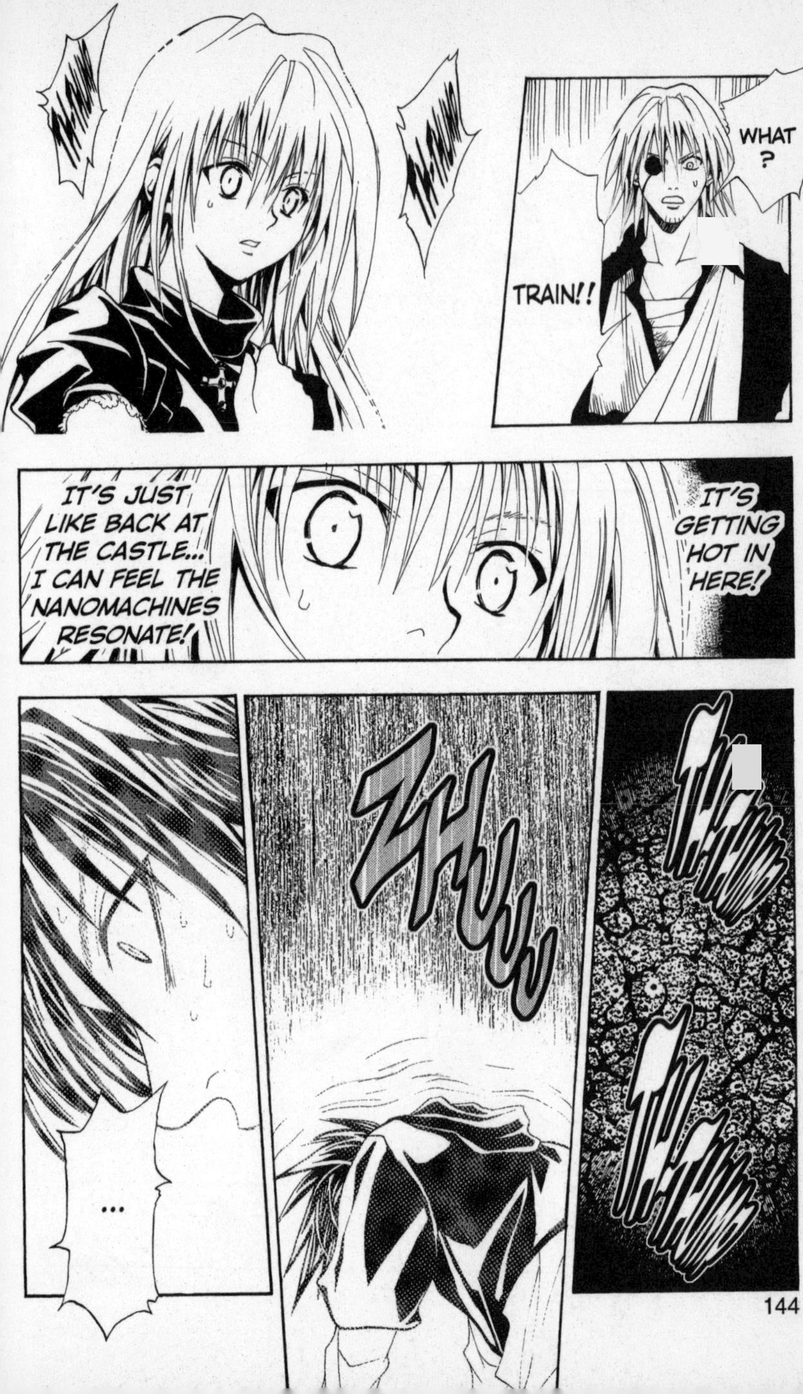
WHAT?
TRAIN!!
IT'S GETTING HOT IN HERE!
IT'S JUST LIKE BACK AT THE CASTLE... I CAN FEEL THE NANOMACHINES RESONATE!
ZHUUU
...

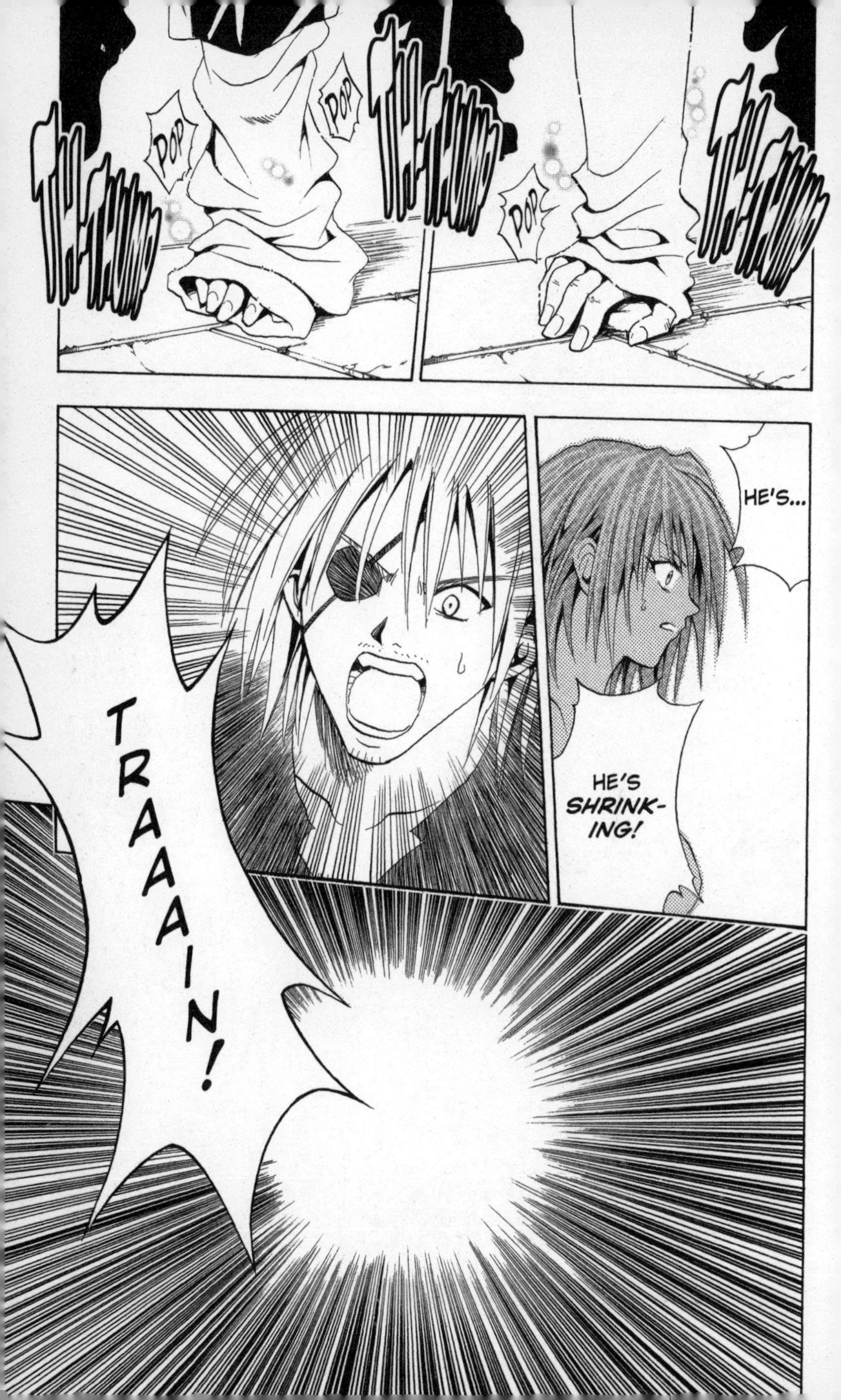
POP
POP
POP
HE'S...
HE'S SHRINKING!
TRAAAIN!

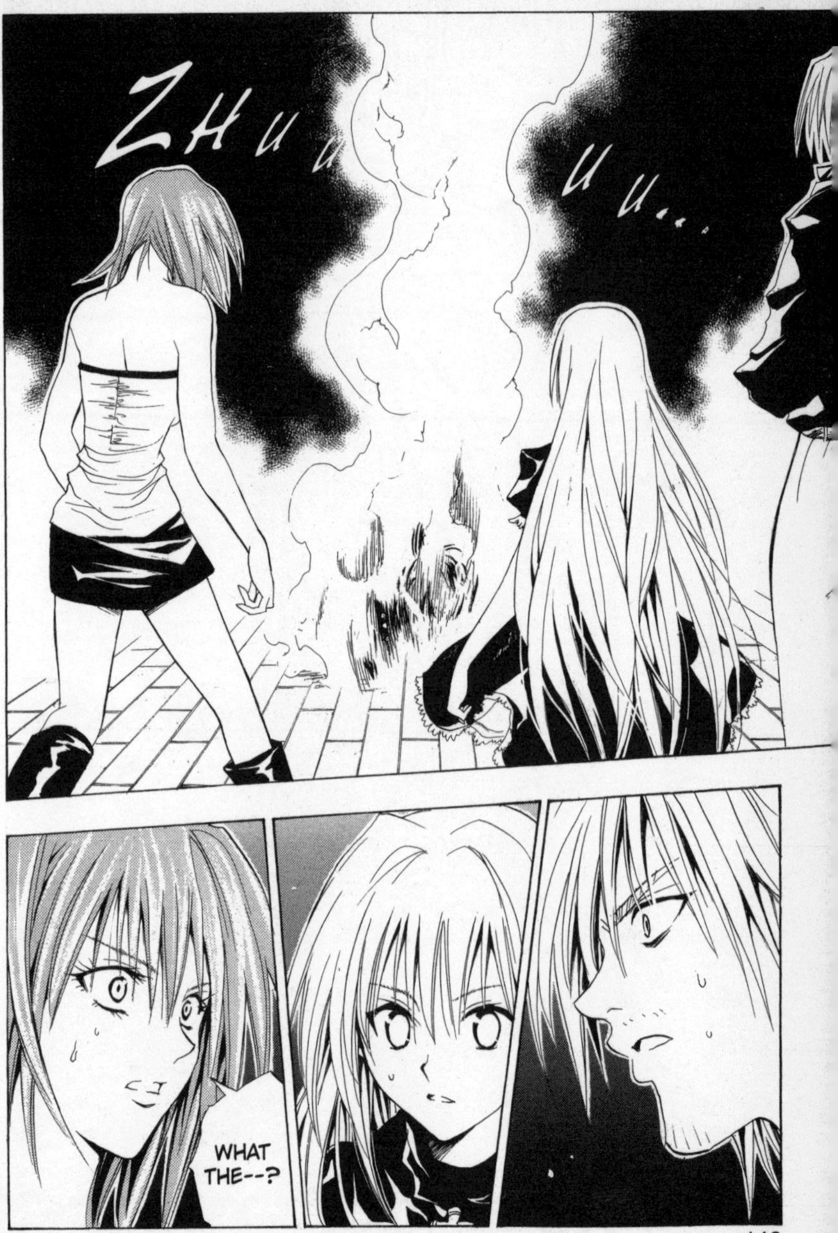
ZHUU UUU...
WHAT THE--?

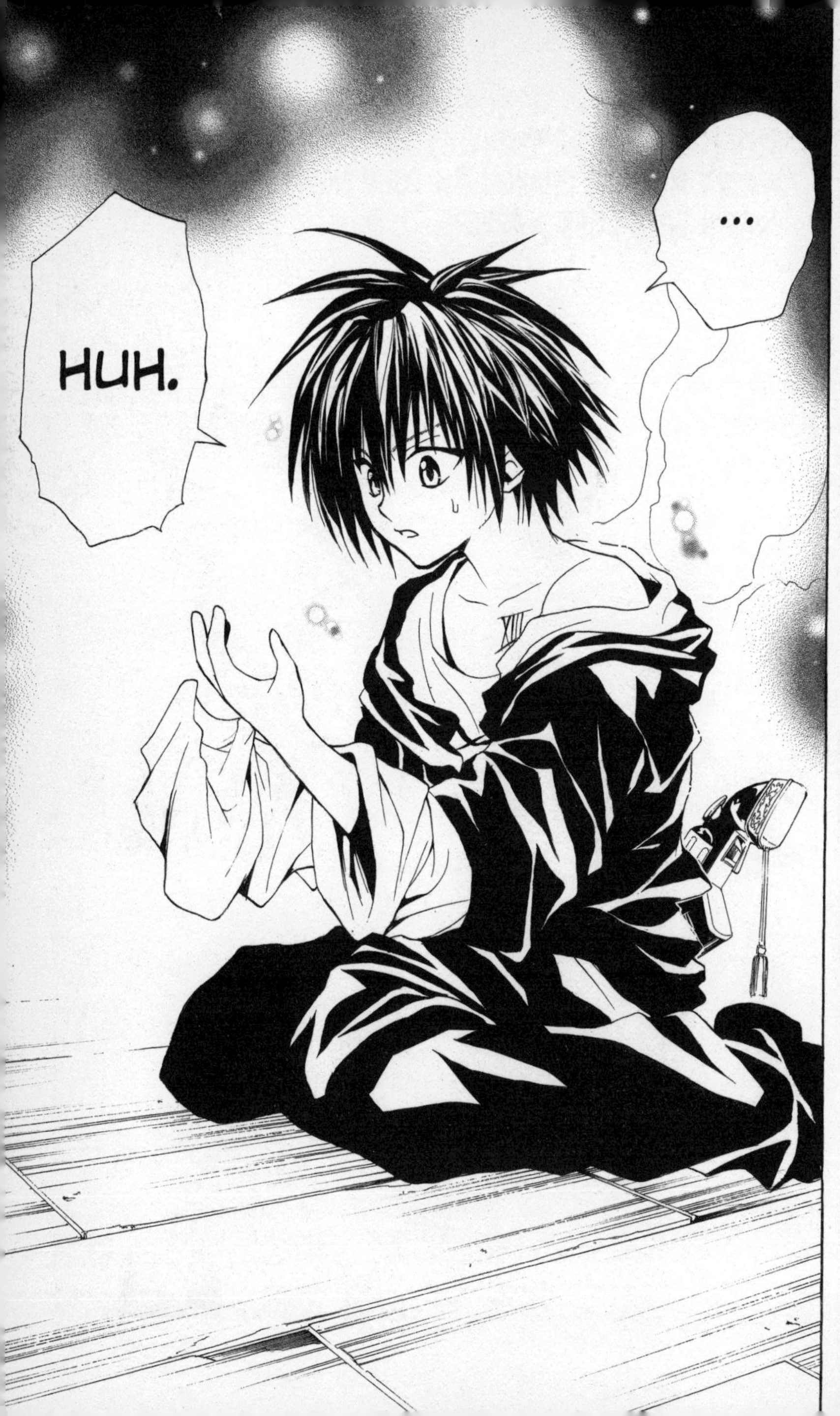
...
HUH.

◎ *WEEKLY SHONEN JUMP* COVER ILLUSTRATION 2
SVEN IS USUALLY DRESSED VERY NATTILY, SO THERE WASN'T MUCH TO CHANGE. ALL FOUR FIGURES WERE DRAWN WITH COPIC MARKERS.

Chapter 92: Dr. Tearju

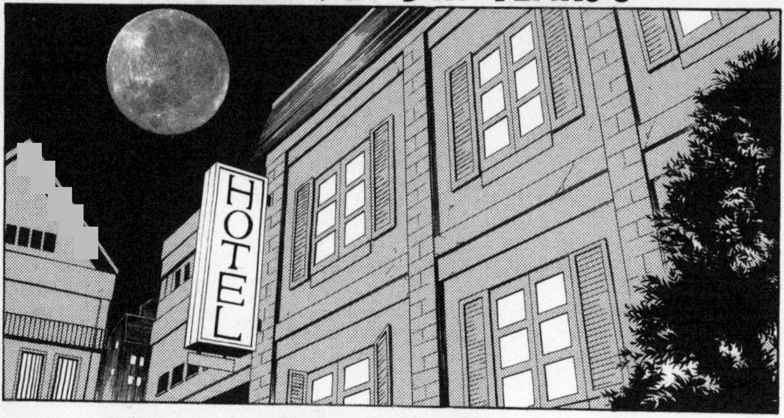
HOTEL

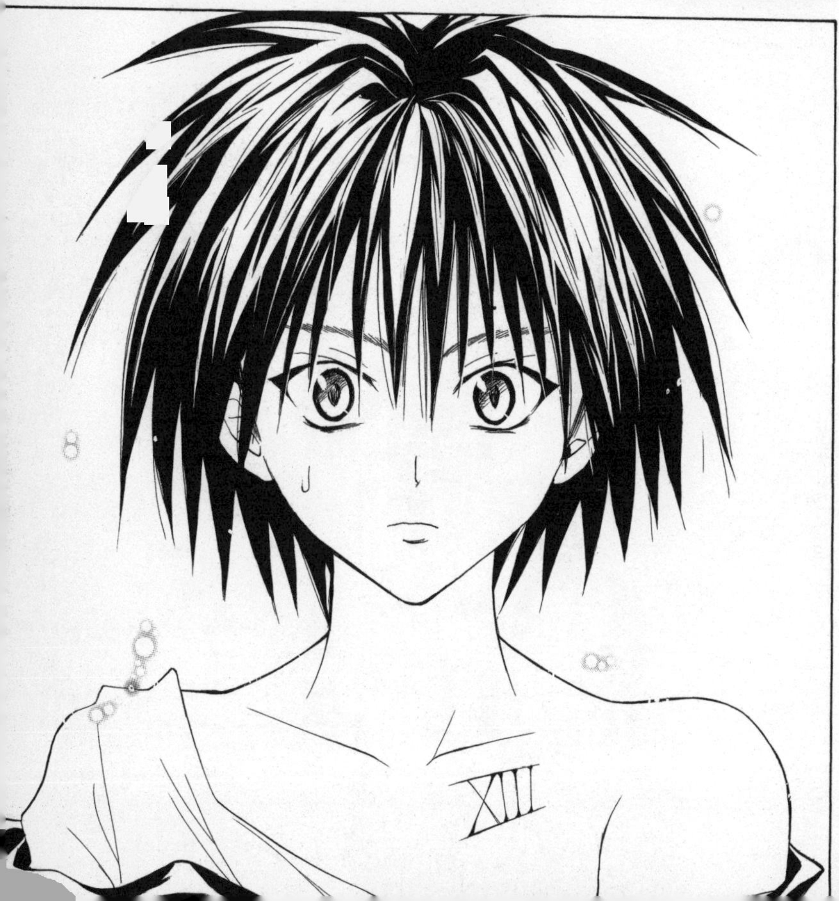
XIII

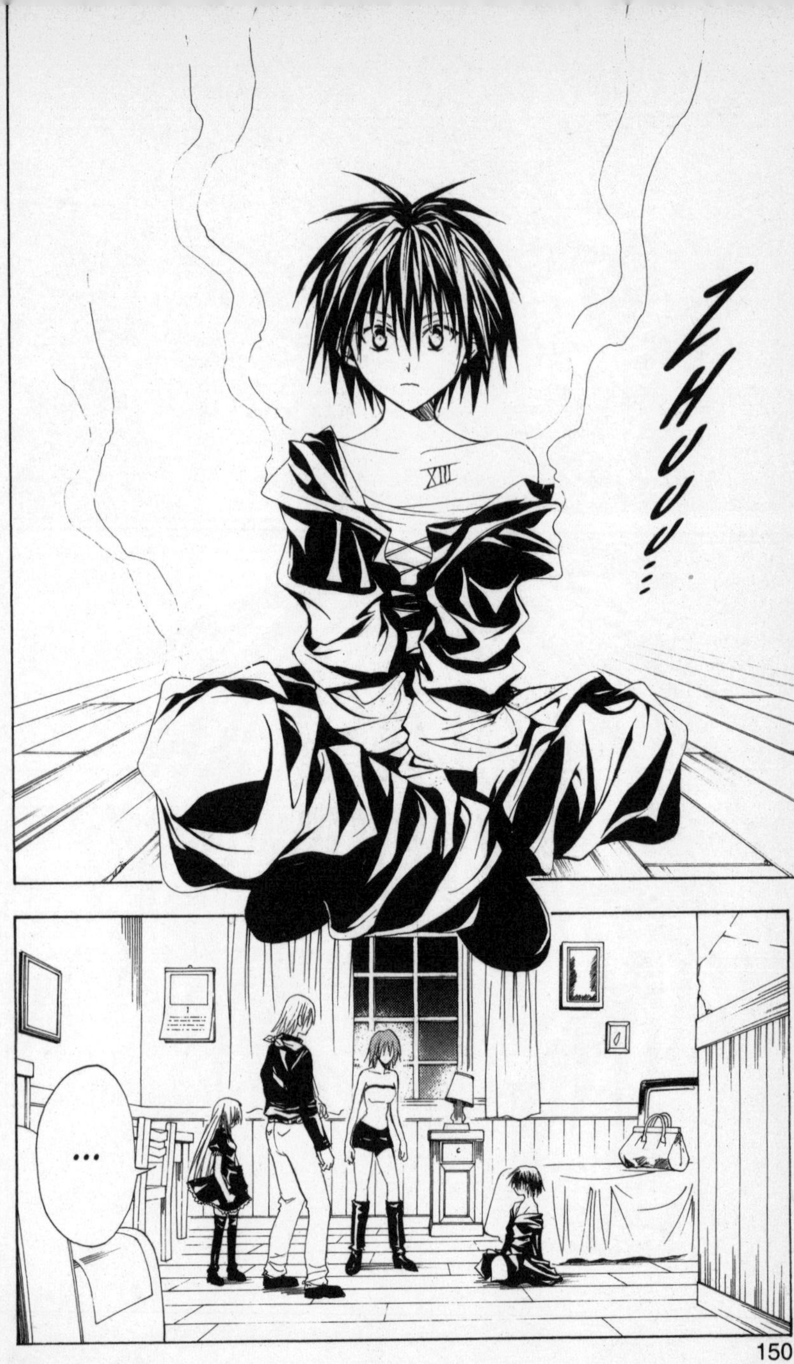
ZHUUUU...
...

READ THIS WAY

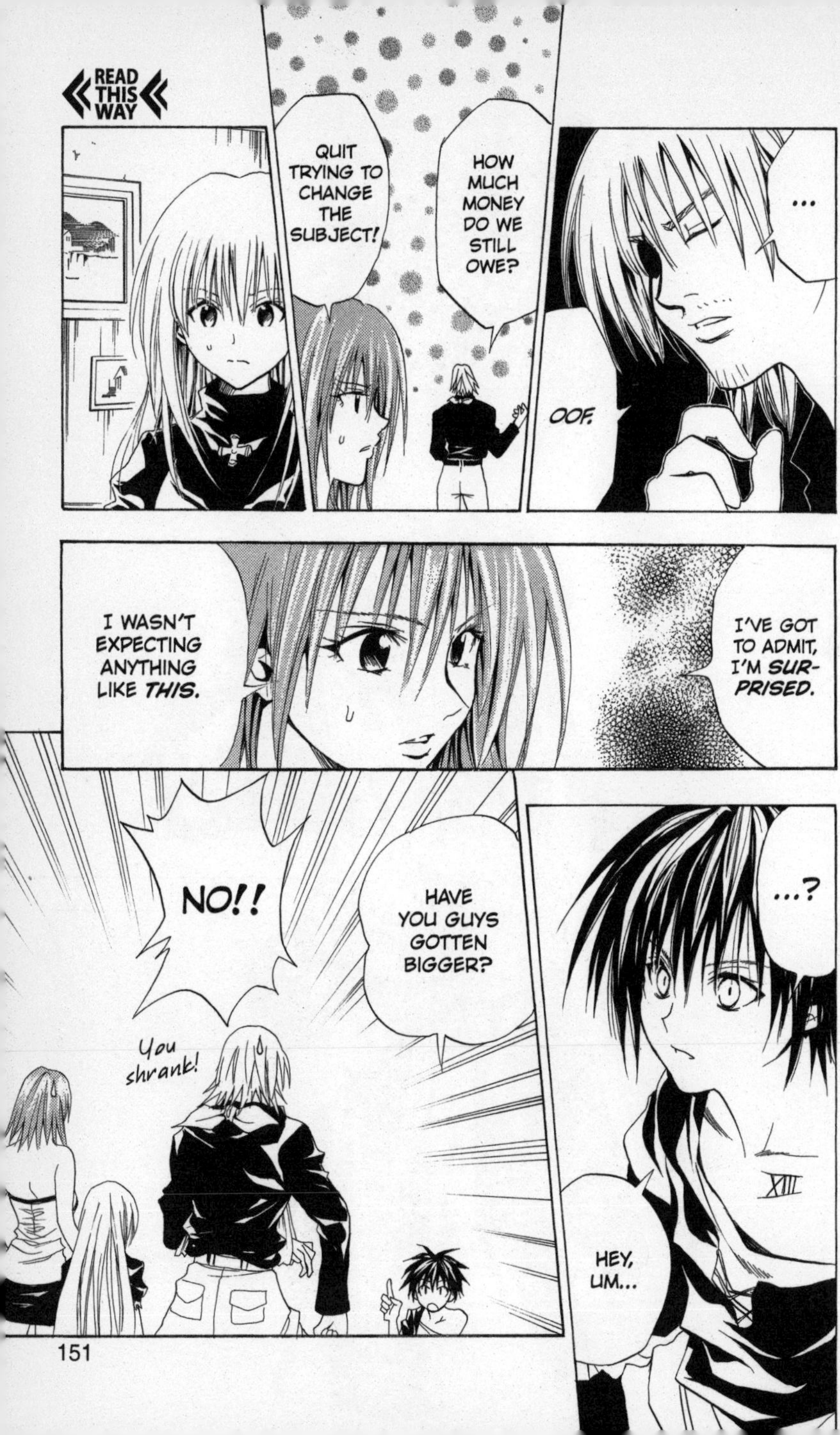
...
OOF.
HOW MUCH MONEY DO WE STILL OWE?
QUIT TRYING TO CHANGE THE SUBJECT!
I'VE GOT TO ADMIT, I'M *SURPRISED.*
I WASN'T EXPECTING ANYTHING LIKE *THIS.*
...?
HEY, UM...
HAVE YOU GUYS GOTTEN BIGGER?
NO!!
You shrank!

Chapter 92:
Dr. Tearju

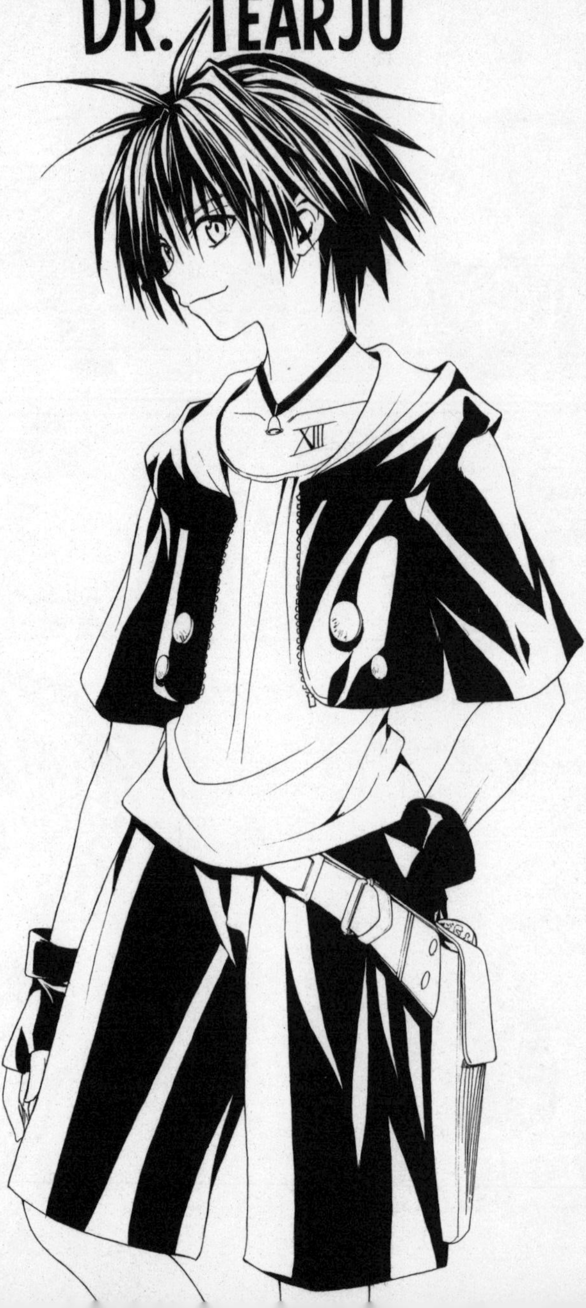
XIII

READ THIS WAY

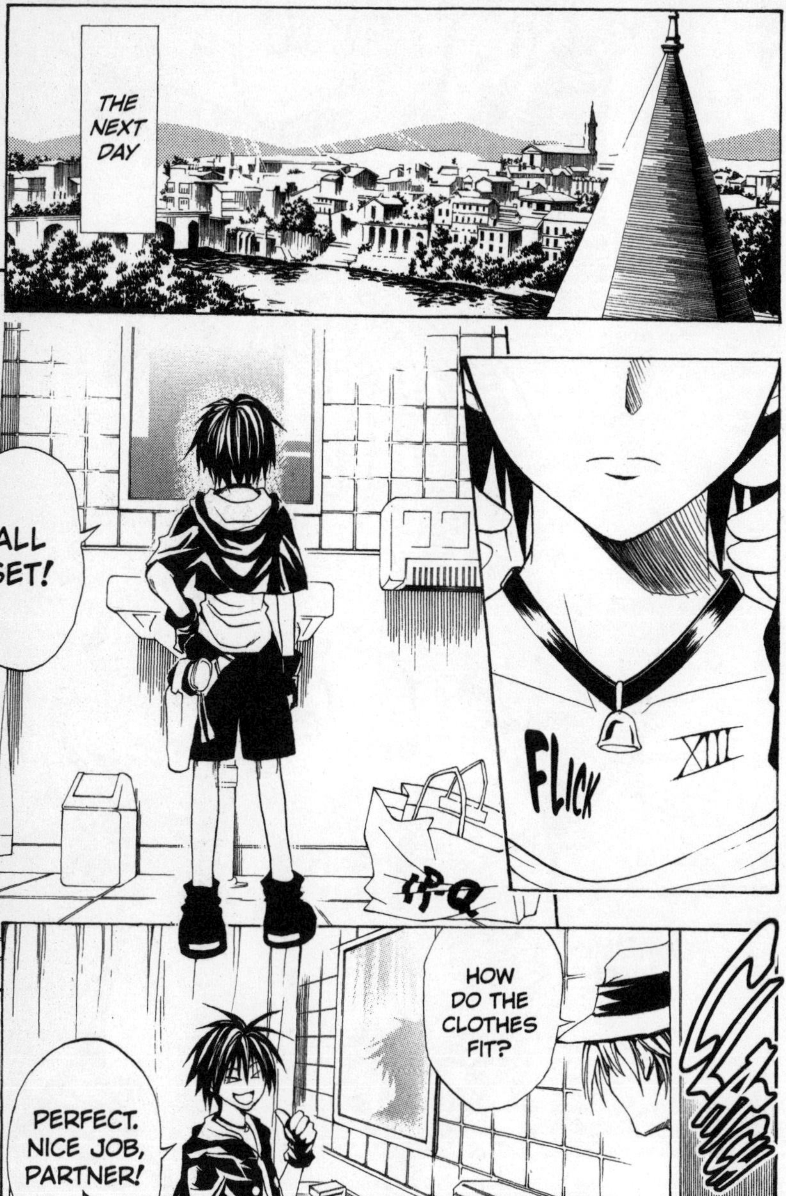
THE NEXT DAY
FLICK
XIII
ALL SET!
IP-Q
HOW DO THE CLOTHES FIT?
PERFECT. NICE JOB, PARTNER! ♪

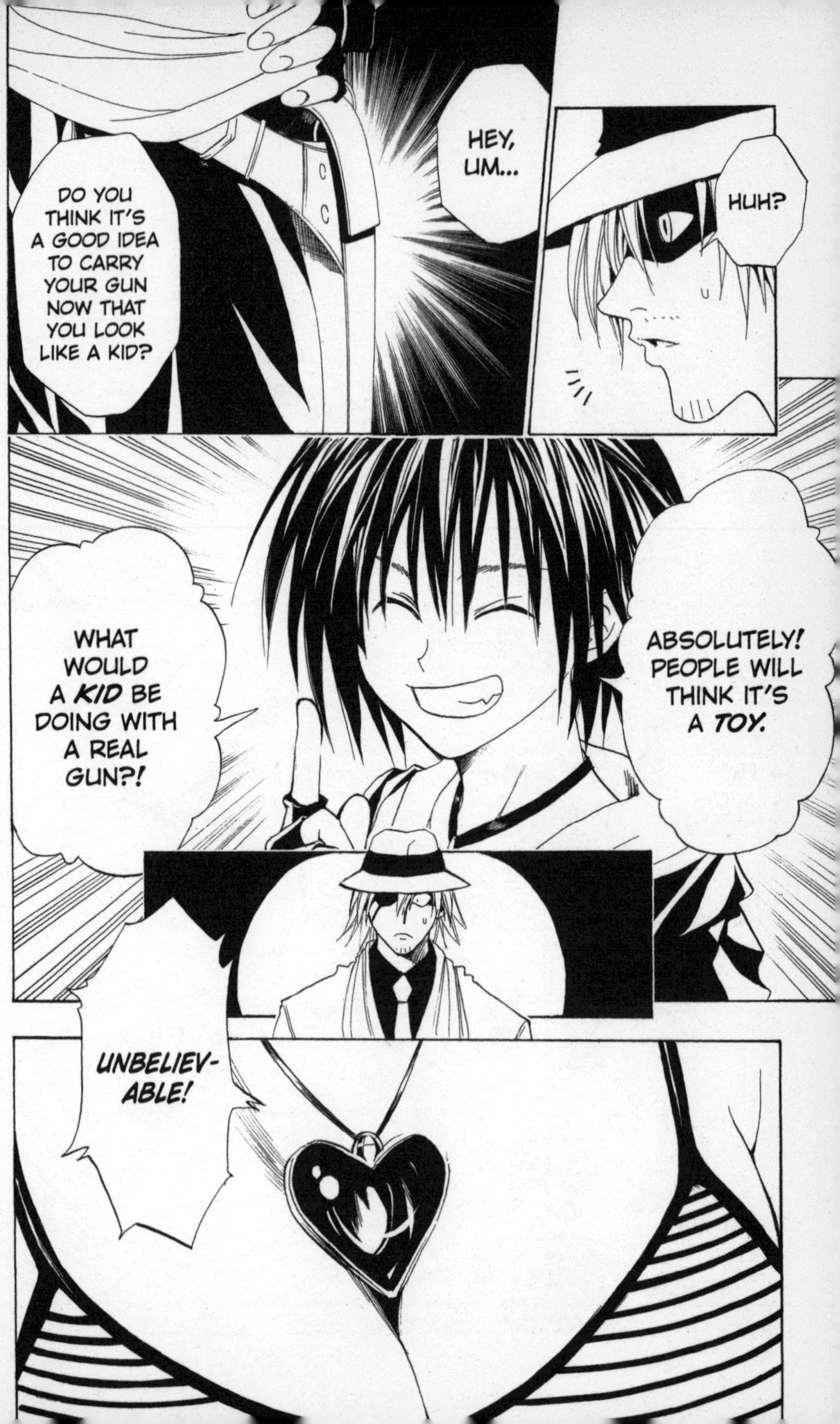
HUH?
HEY, UM...
DO YOU THINK IT'S A GOOD IDEA TO CARRY YOUR GUN NOW THAT YOU LOOK LIKE A KID?
ABSOLUTELY! PEOPLE WILL THINK IT'S A *TOY.*
WHAT WOULD A *KID* BE DOING WITH A REAL GUN?!
UNBELIEV-ABLE!

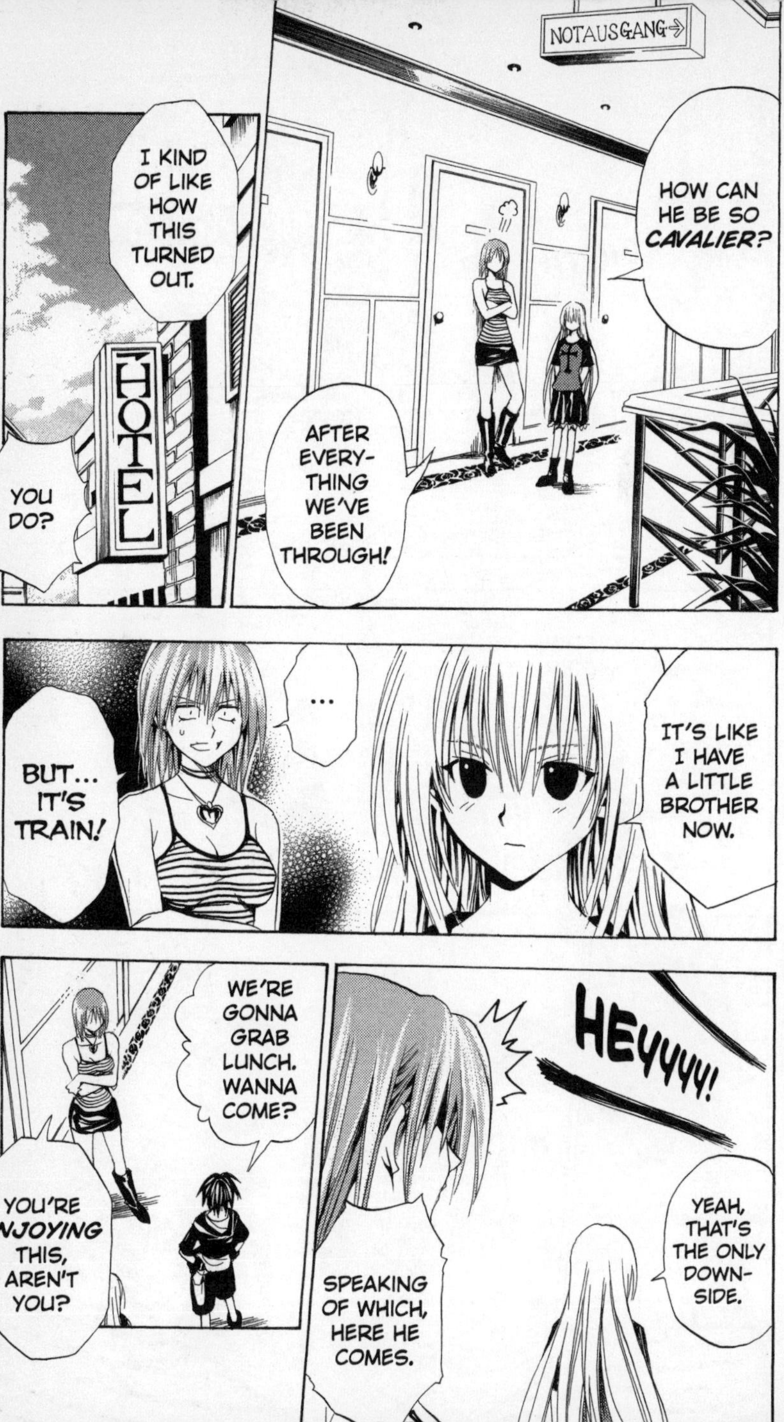
NOTAUSGANG→
HOW CAN HE BE SO CAVALIER?
AFTER EVERY-THING WE'VE BEEN THROUGH!
I KIND OF LIKE HOW THIS TURNED OUT.
HOTEL
YOU DO?
IT'S LIKE I HAVE A LITTLE BROTHER NOW.
...
BUT... IT'S TRAIN!
HEYYYY!
YEAH, THAT'S THE ONLY DOWN-SIDE.
SPEAKING OF WHICH, HERE HE COMES.
WE'RE GONNA GRAB LUNCH. WANNA COME?
YOU'RE ENJOYING THIS, AREN'T YOU?

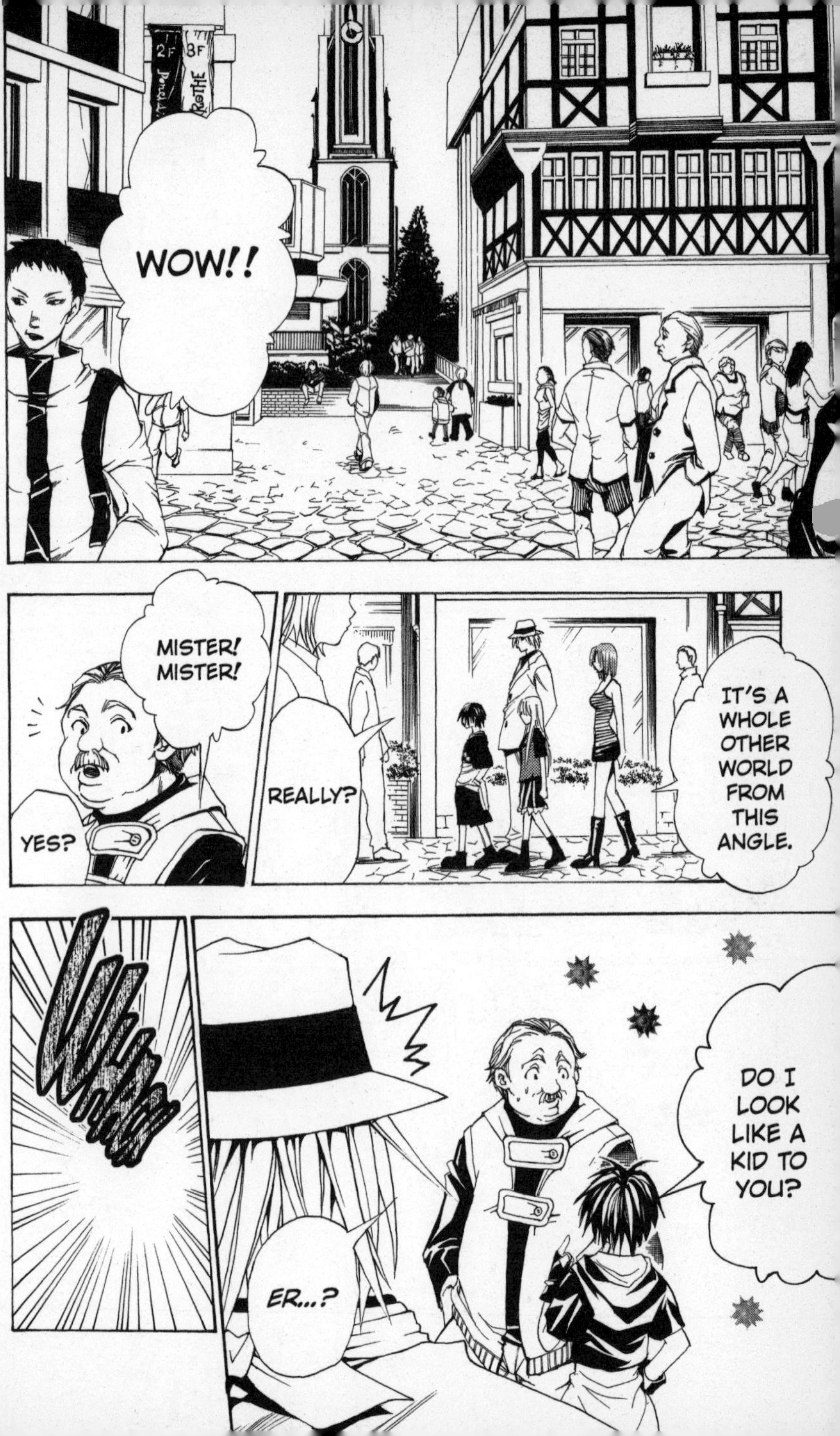
WOW!!
IT'S A WHOLE OTHER WORLD FROM THIS ANGLE.
REALLY?
MISTER! MISTER!
YES?
DO I LOOK LIKE A KID TO YOU?
ER...?

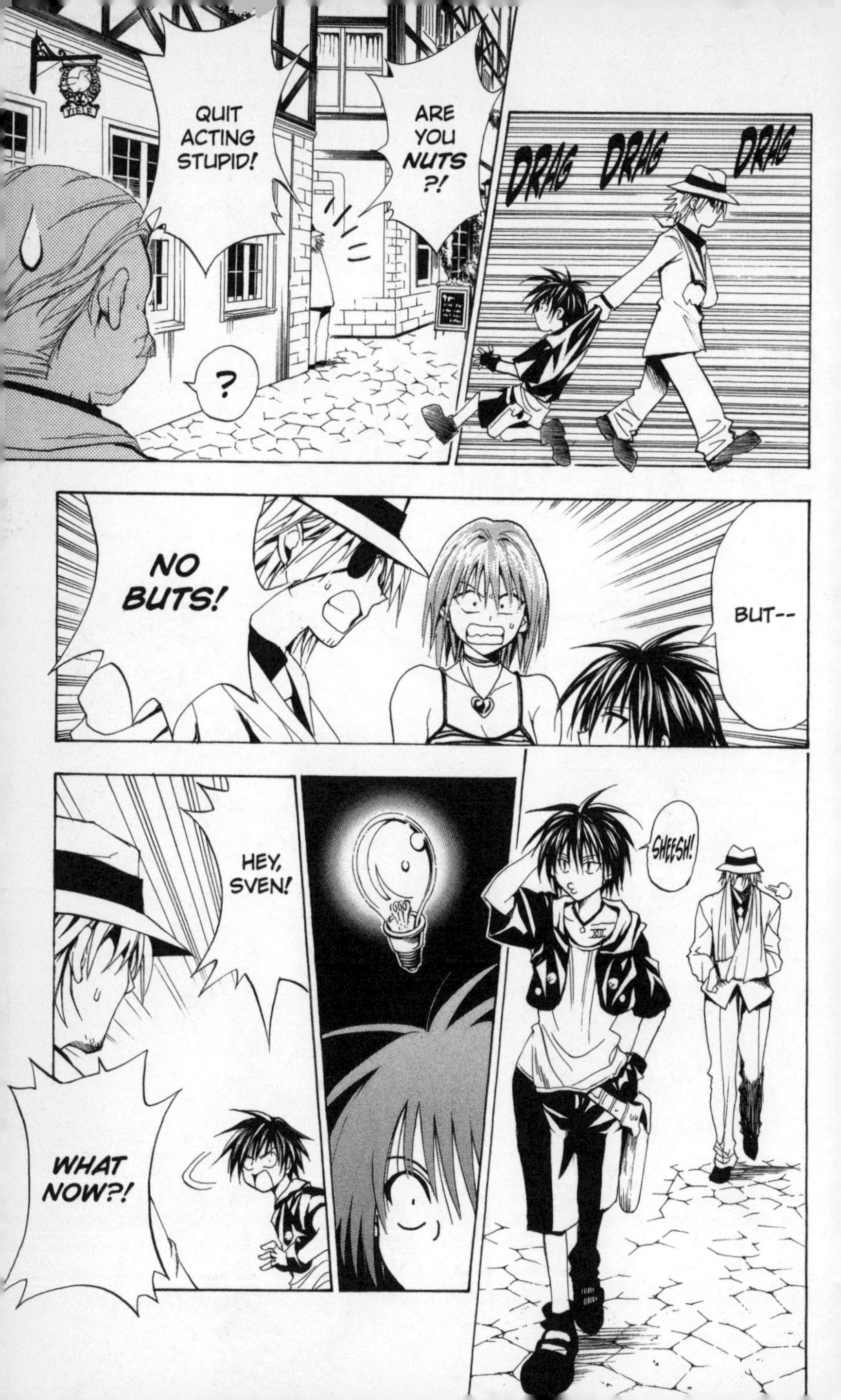
DRAG DRAG DRAG
ARE YOU NUTS?!
QUIT ACTING STUPID!
?
BUT--
NO BUTS!
SHEESH!
HEY, SVEN!
WHAT NOW?!

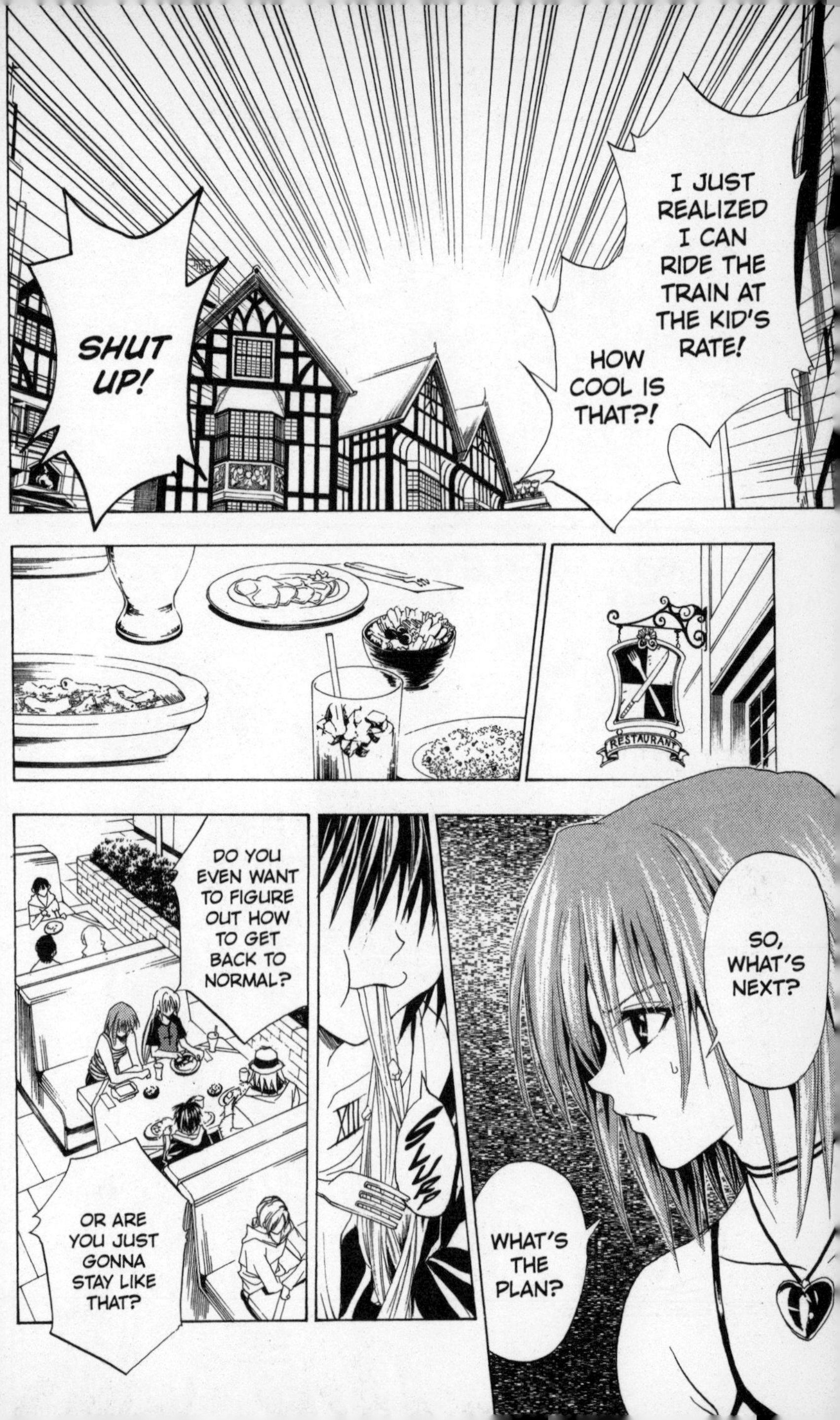
I JUST REALIZED I CAN RIDE THE TRAIN AT THE KID'S RATE!
HOW COOL IS THAT?!
SHUT UP!
RESTAURANT
SO, WHAT'S NEXT?
WHAT'S THE PLAN?
DO YOU EVEN WANT TO FIGURE OUT HOW TO GET BACK TO NORMAL?
OR ARE YOU JUST GONNA STAY LIKE THAT?

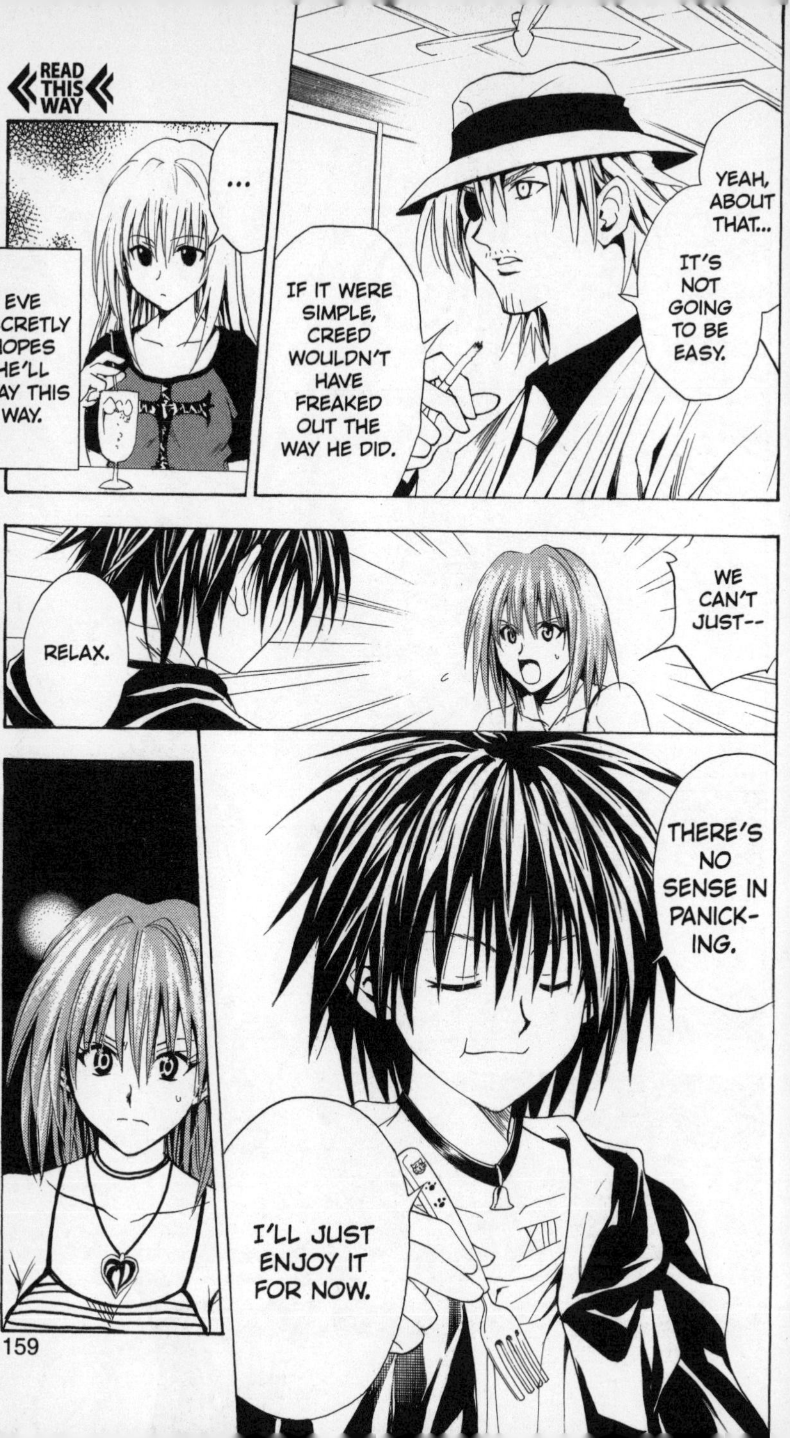
READ THIS WAY
YEAH, ABOUT THAT...
IT'S NOT GOING TO BE EASY.
IF IT WERE SIMPLE, CREED WOULDN'T HAVE FREAKED OUT THE WAY HE DID.
...
EVE SECRETLY HOPES HE'LL STAY THIS WAY.
WE CAN'T JUST--
RELAX.
THERE'S NO SENSE IN PANICK-ING.
I'LL JUST ENJOY IT FOR NOW.

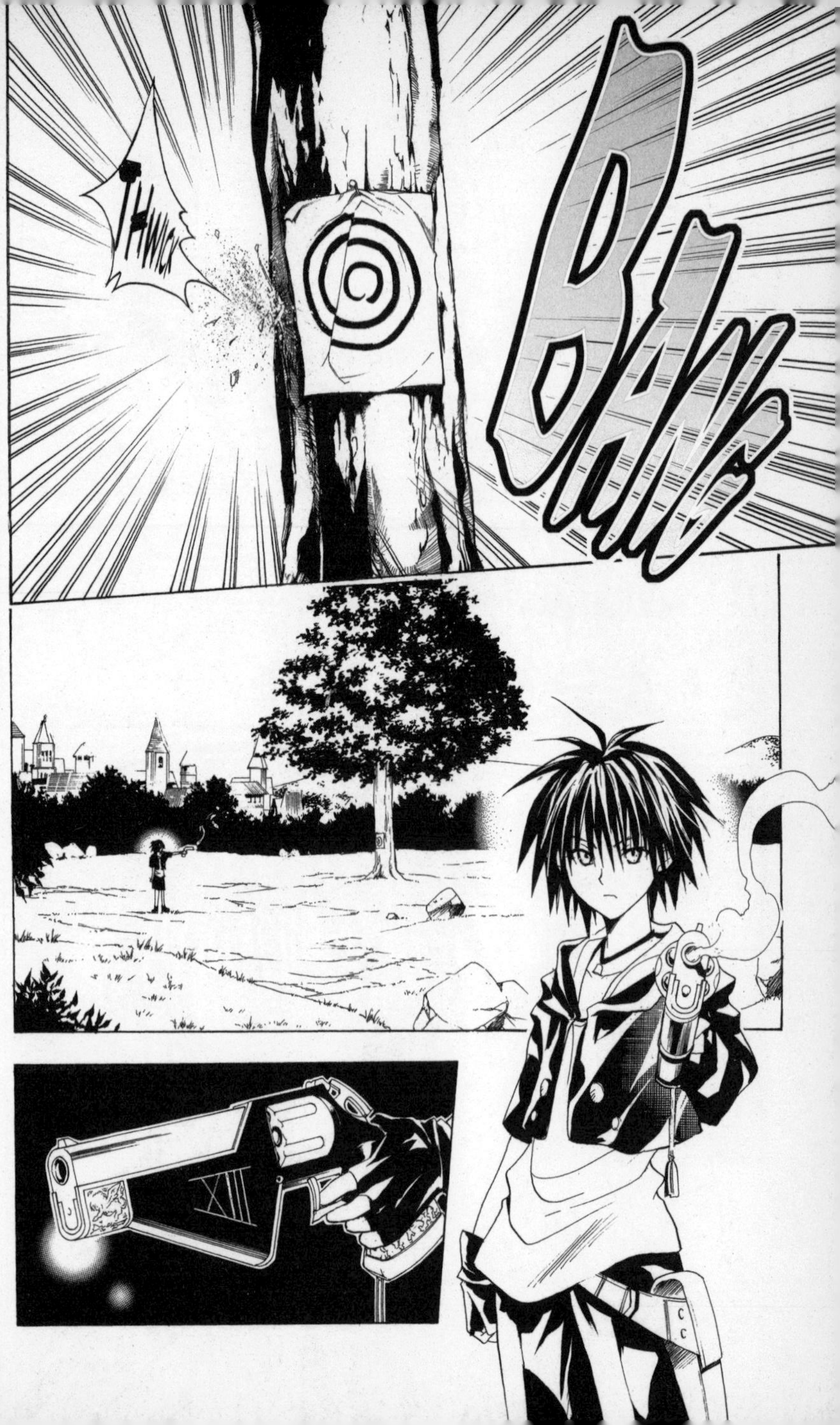
BAM
THWICK

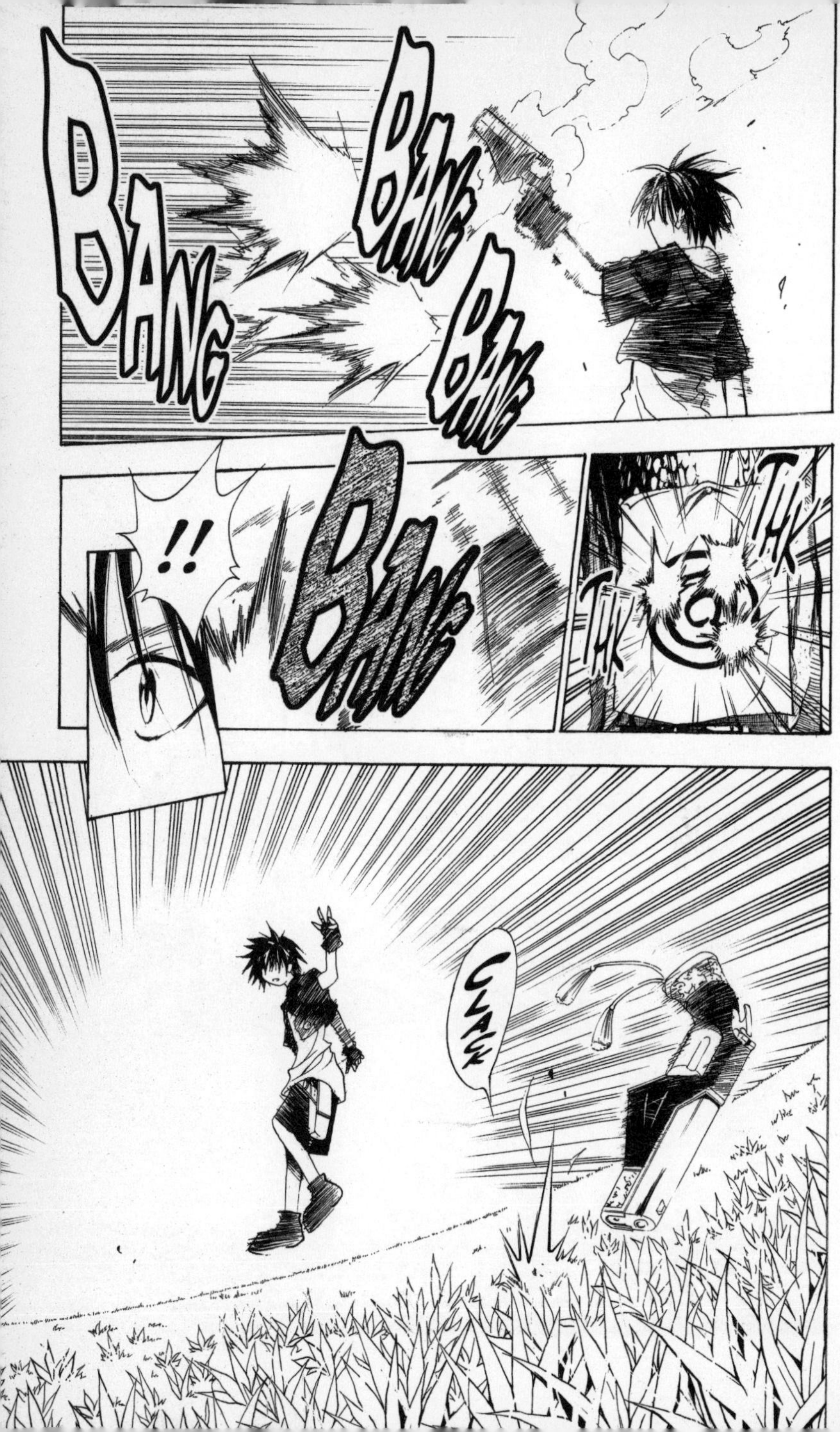
BANG
BANG
BANG
THK
THK
BANG
!!
CLACK

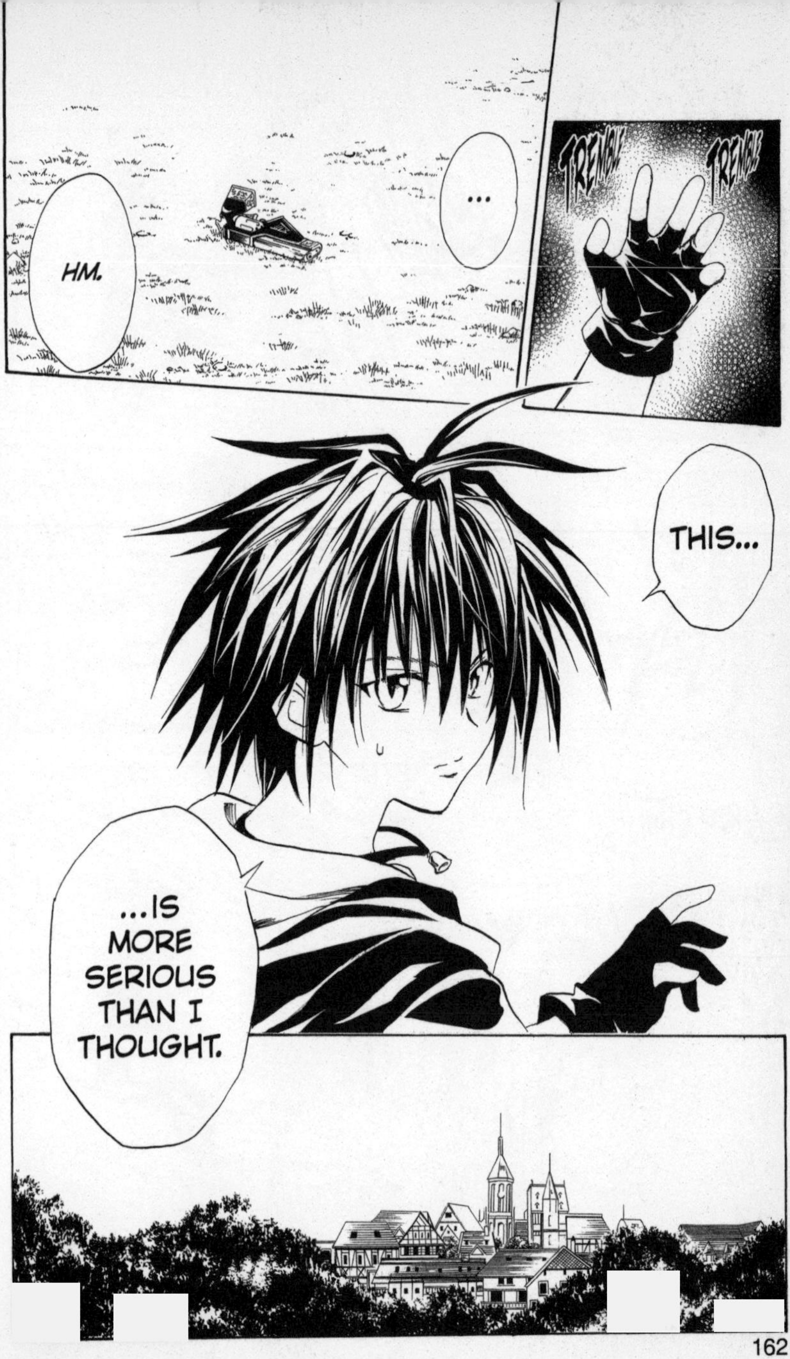
TREMBLE
TREMBLE
...
HM.
THIS...
...IS MORE SERIOUS THAN I THOUGHT.

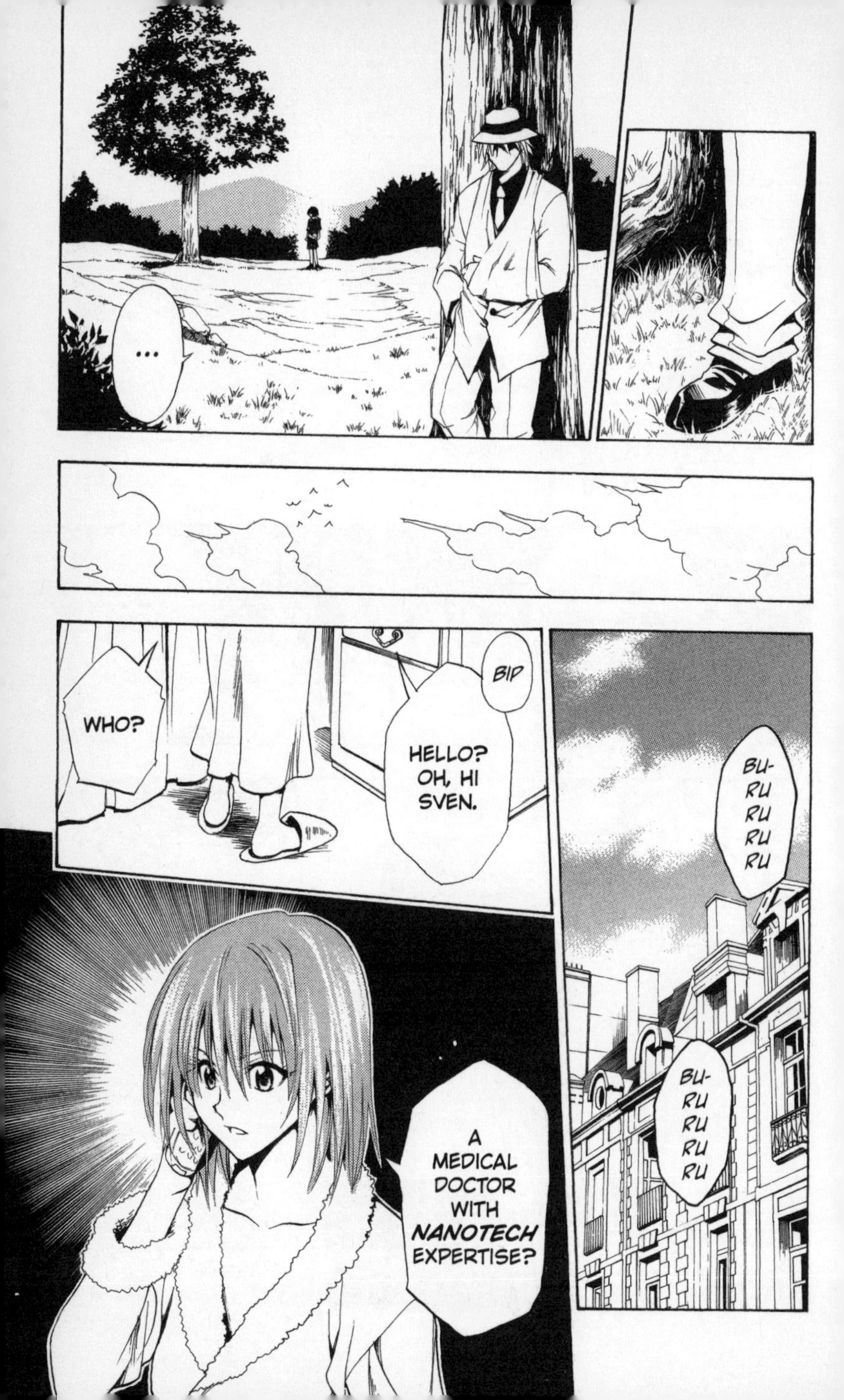
...
BU-RU RU RU RU
BU-RU RU RU RU RU
BIP
HELLO? OH, HI SVEN.
WHO?
A MEDICAL DOCTOR WITH *NANOTECH* EXPERTISE?

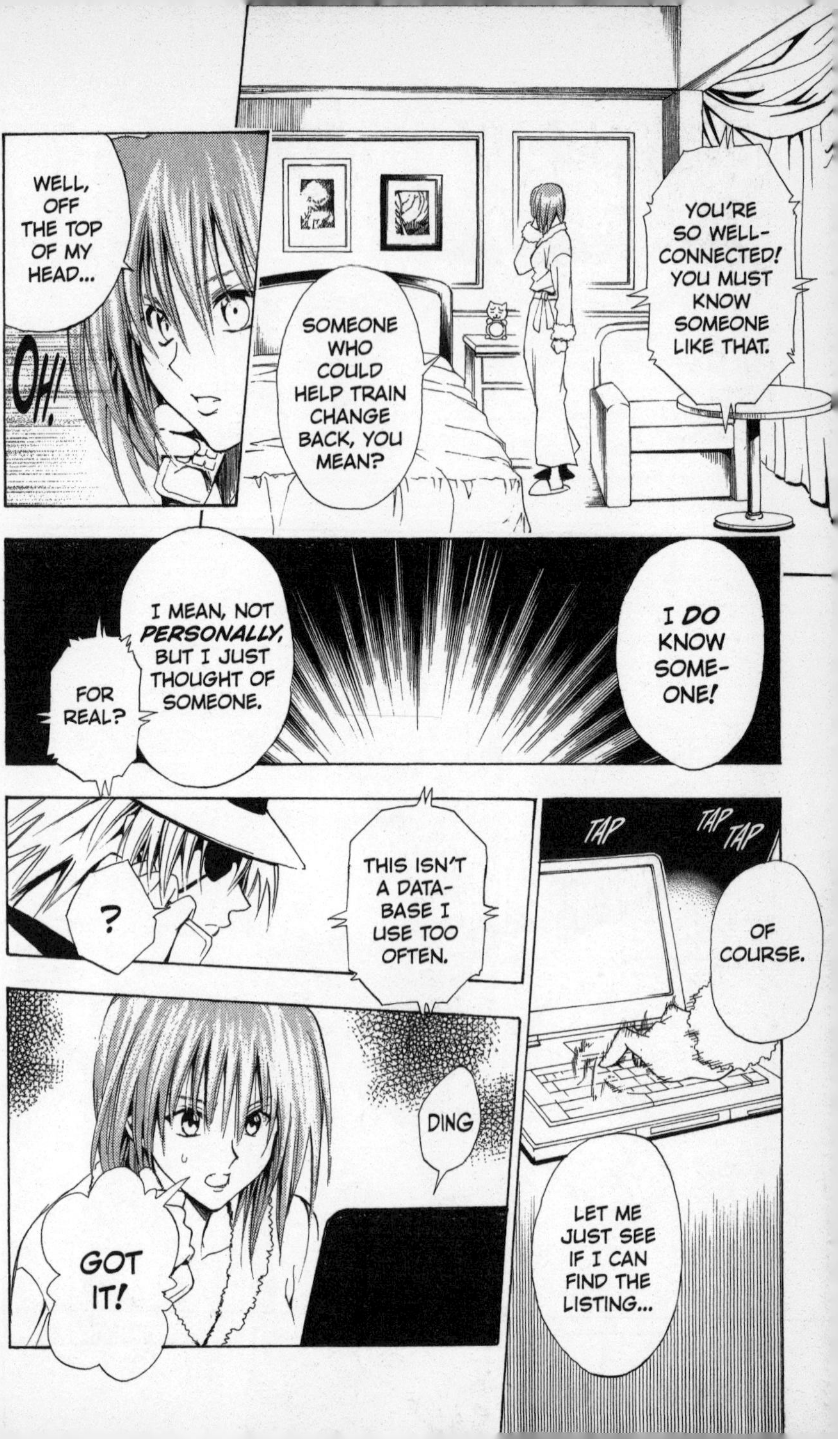
YOU'RE SO WELL-CONNECTED! YOU MUST KNOW SOMEONE LIKE THAT.
SOMEONE WHO COULD HELP TRAIN CHANGE BACK, YOU MEAN?
WELL, OFF THE TOP OF MY HEAD...
OH!
I *DO* KNOW SOME-ONE!
I MEAN, NOT ***PERSONALLY,*** BUT I JUST THOUGHT OF SOMEONE.
FOR REAL?
TAP
TAP TAP
OF COURSE.
LET ME JUST SEE IF I CAN FIND THE LISTING...
THIS ISN'T A DATA-BASE I USE TOO OFTEN.
?
DING
GOT IT!

READ THIS WAY

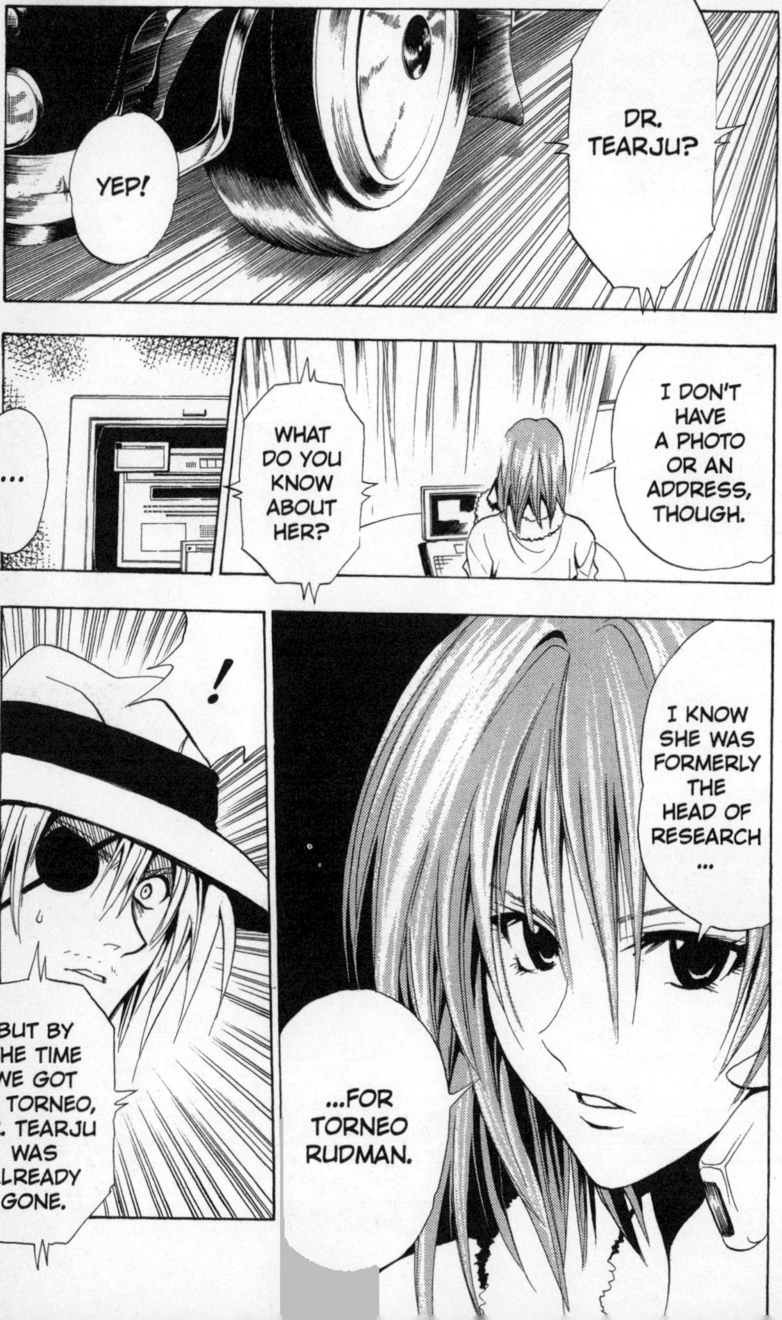
DR. TEARJU?
YEP!
I DON'T HAVE A PHOTO OR AN ADDRESS, THOUGH.
WHAT DO YOU KNOW ABOUT HER?
...
I KNOW SHE WAS FORMERLY THE HEAD OF RESEARCH...
...FOR TORNEO RUDMAN.
!
BUT BY THE TIME WE GOT TO TORNEO, DR. TEARJU WAS ALREADY GONE.

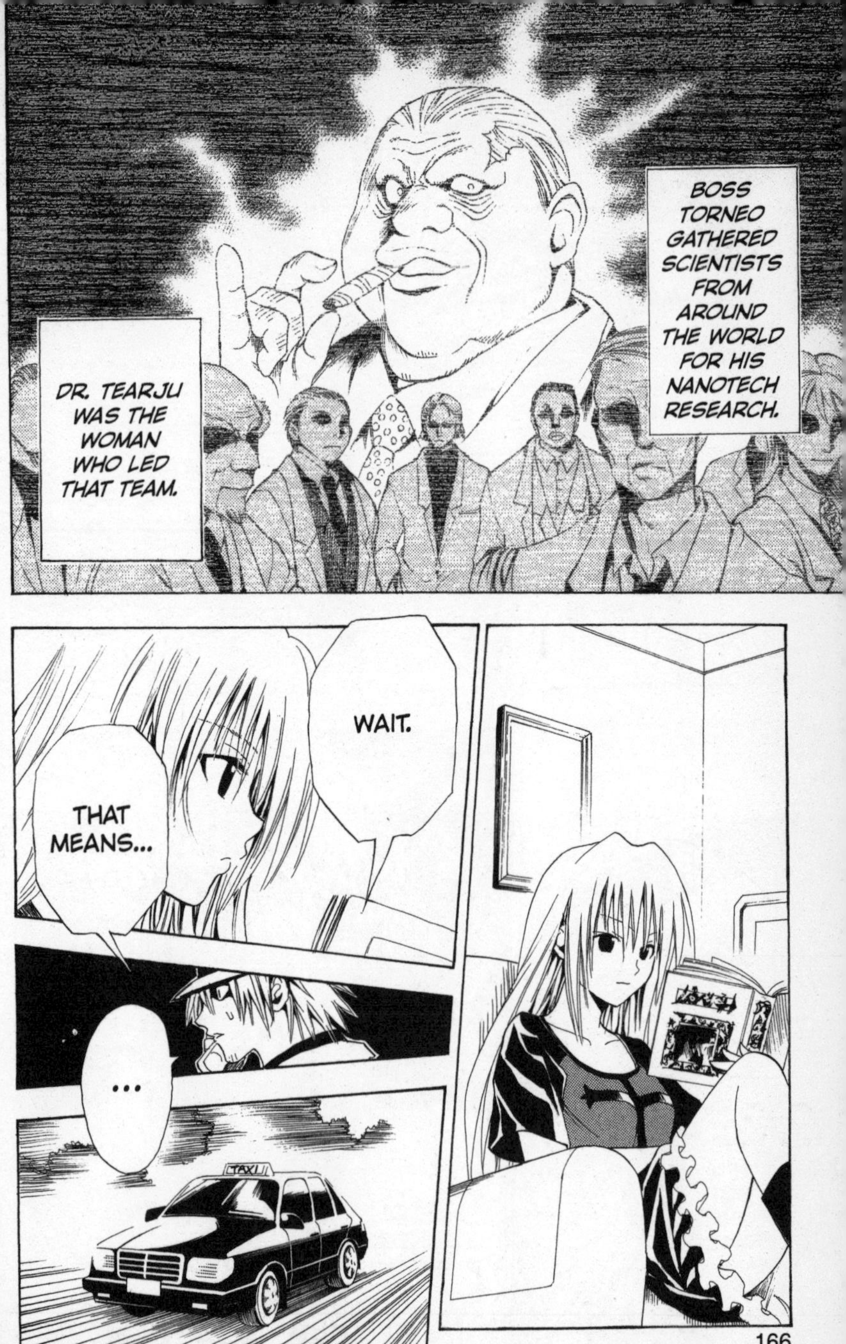
BOSS TORNEO GATHERED SCIENTISTS FROM AROUND THE WORLD FOR HIS NANOTECH RESEARCH.
DR. TEARJU WAS THE WOMAN WHO LED THAT TEAM.
WAIT.
THAT MEANS...
...
TAXI

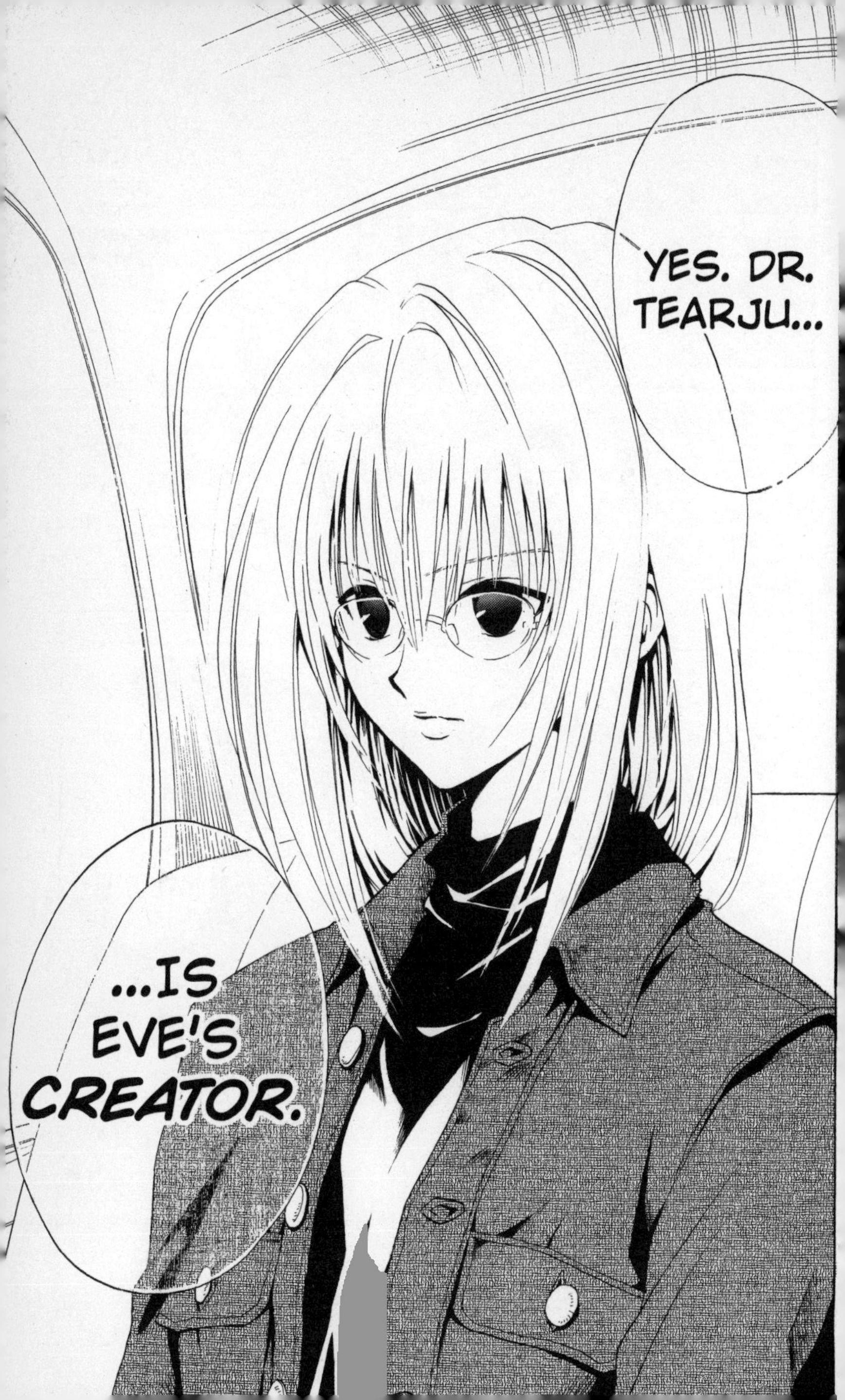
YES. DR. TEARJU...
...IS EVE'S CREATOR.

Bonus Drama

"Kyoko's Confusion"

※Please read Chapter 93 first!

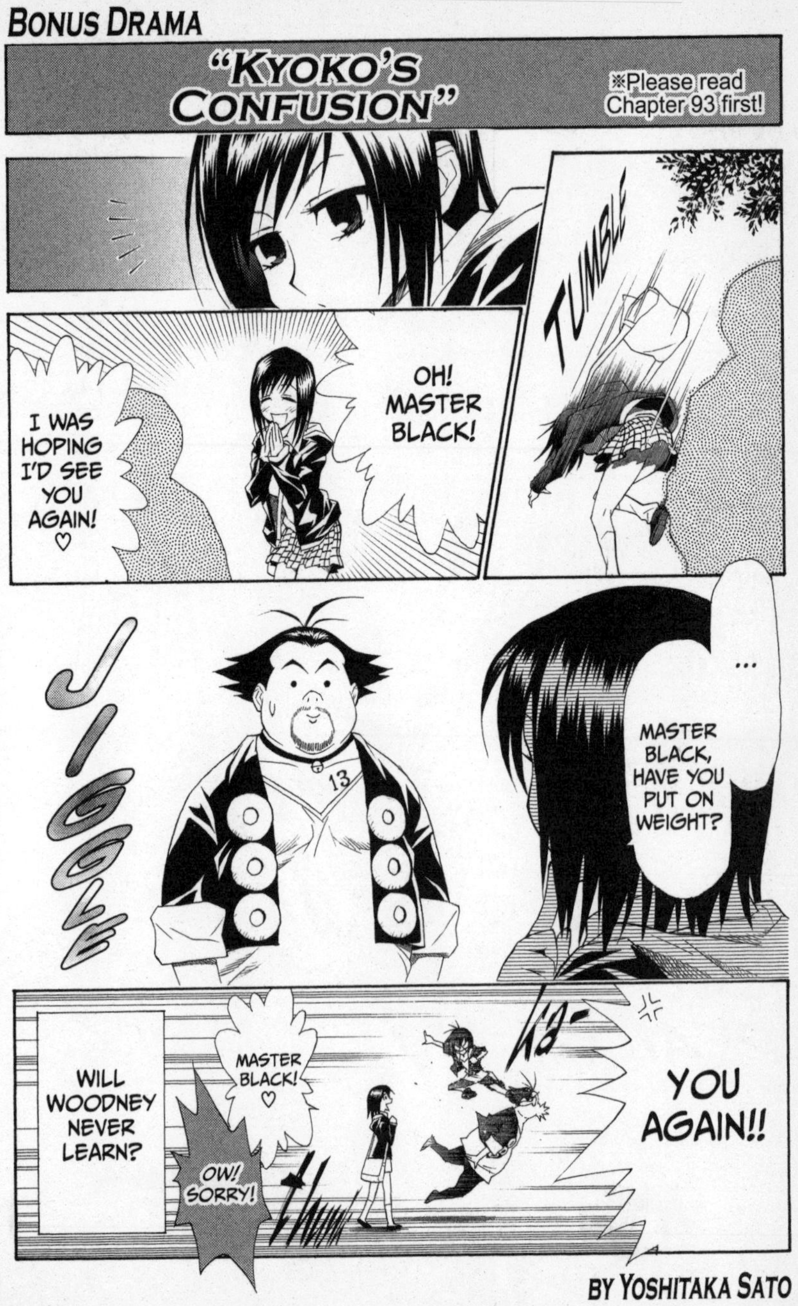
TUMBLE
OH! MASTER BLACK!
I WAS HOPING I'D SEE YOU AGAIN! ♡
...
MASTER BLACK, HAVE YOU PUT ON WEIGHT?
JIGGLE
YOU AGAIN!!
MASTER BLACK! ♡
OW! SORRY!
WILL WOODNEY NEVER LEARN?

By Yoshitaka Sato

Chapter 93: Surprise Attack

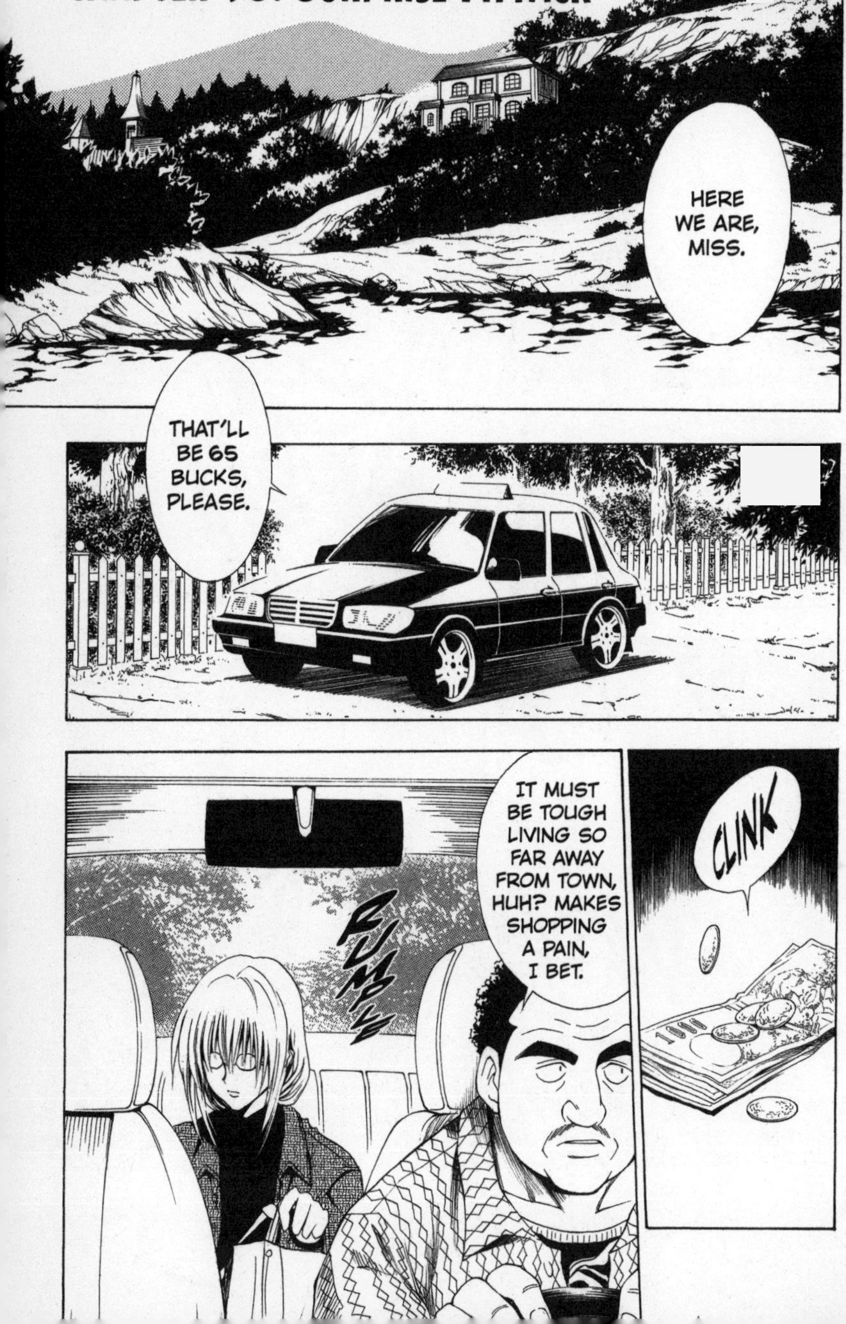
HERE WE ARE, MISS.
THAT'LL BE 65 BUCKS, PLEASE.
CLINK
IT MUST BE TOUGH LIVING SO FAR AWAY FROM TOWN, HUH? MAKES SHOPPING A PAIN, I BET.
RUMPLE

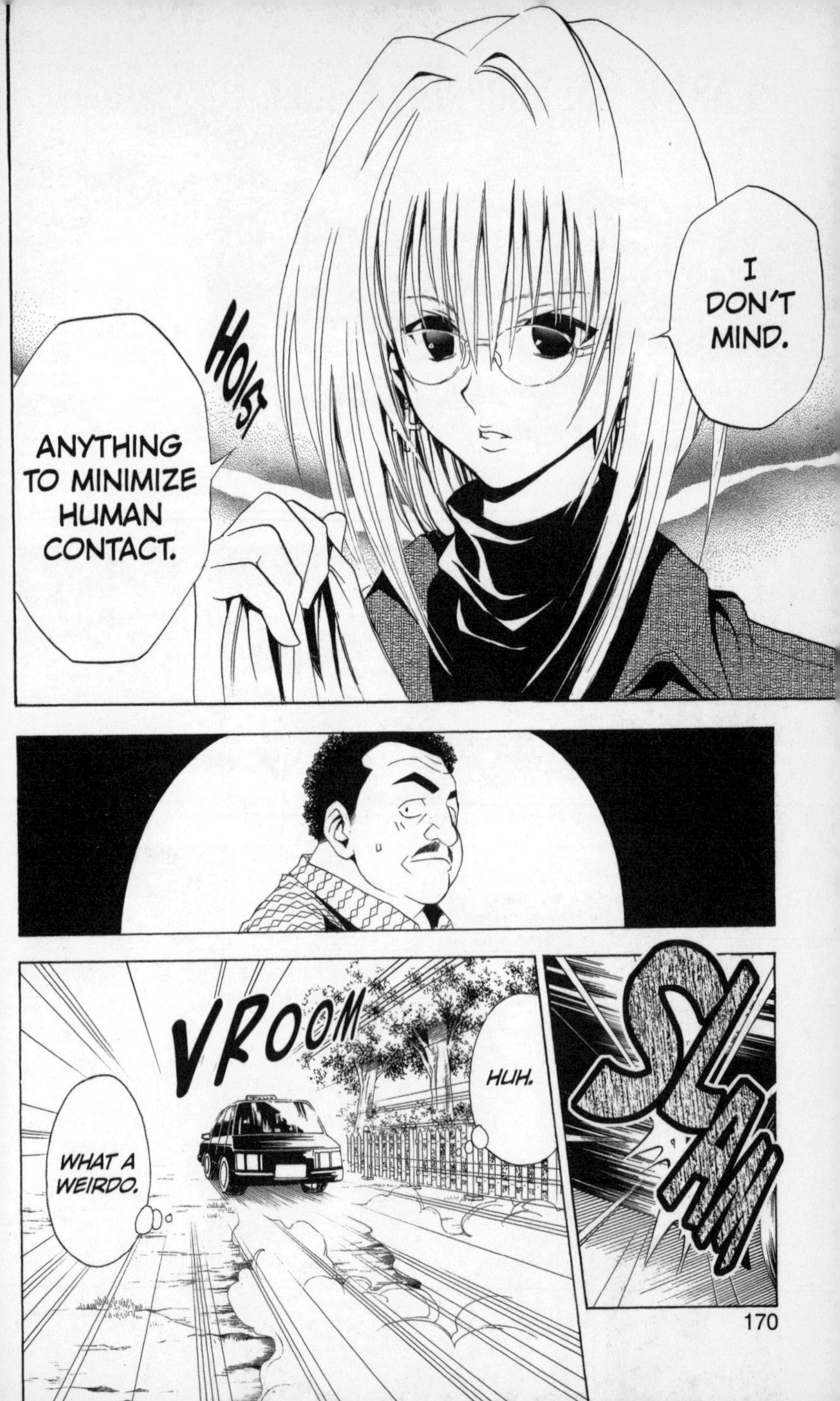
I DON'T MIND.
HOIST
ANYTHING TO MINIMIZE HUMAN CONTACT.
SLAM
HUH.
VROOM
WHAT A WEIRDO.

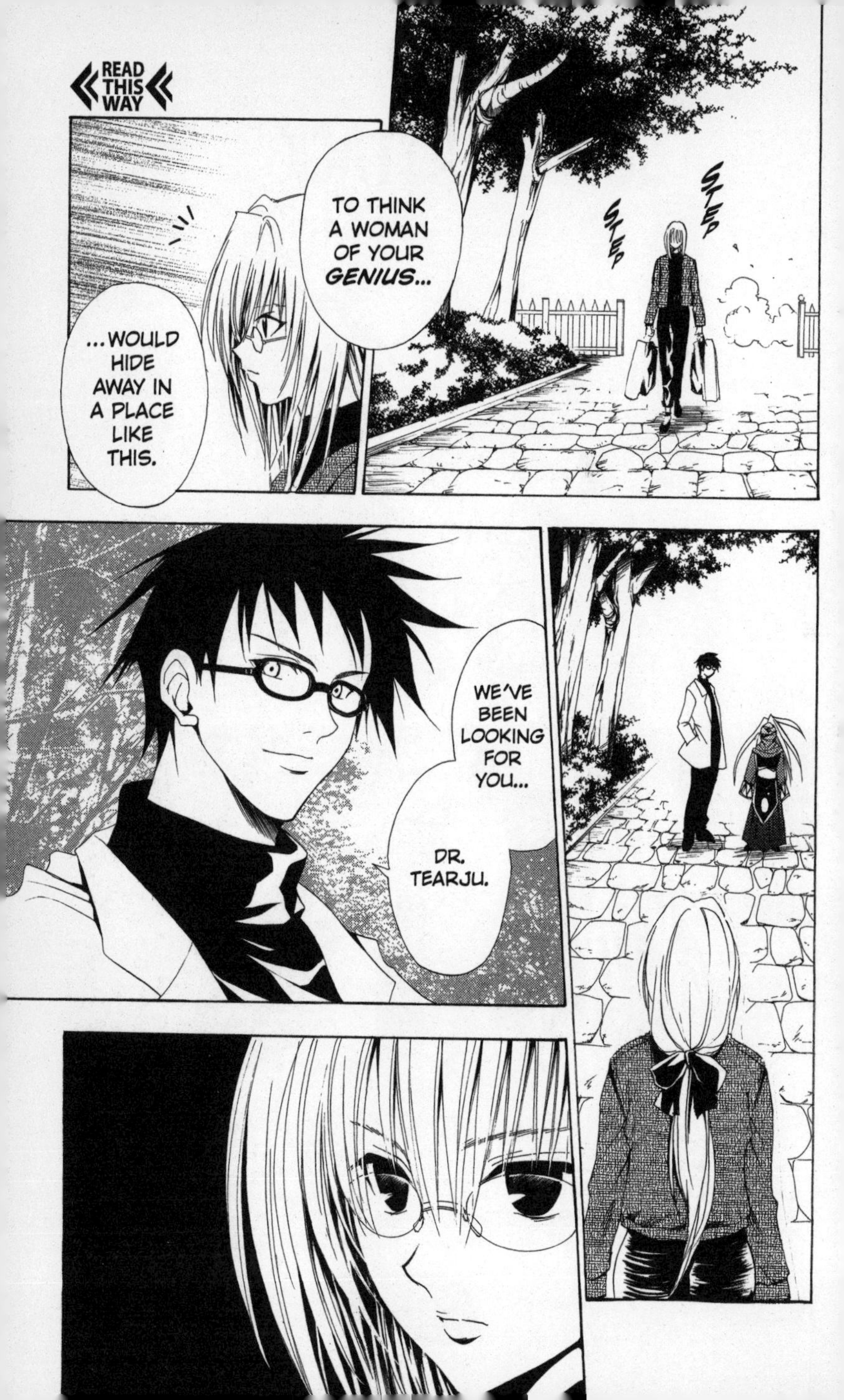
READ THIS WAY
STEP
STEP
TO THINK A WOMAN OF YOUR *GENIUS*...
...WOULD HIDE AWAY IN A PLACE LIKE THIS.
WE'VE BEEN LOOKING FOR YOU...
DR. TEARJU.

Chapter 93:
Sudden Attack

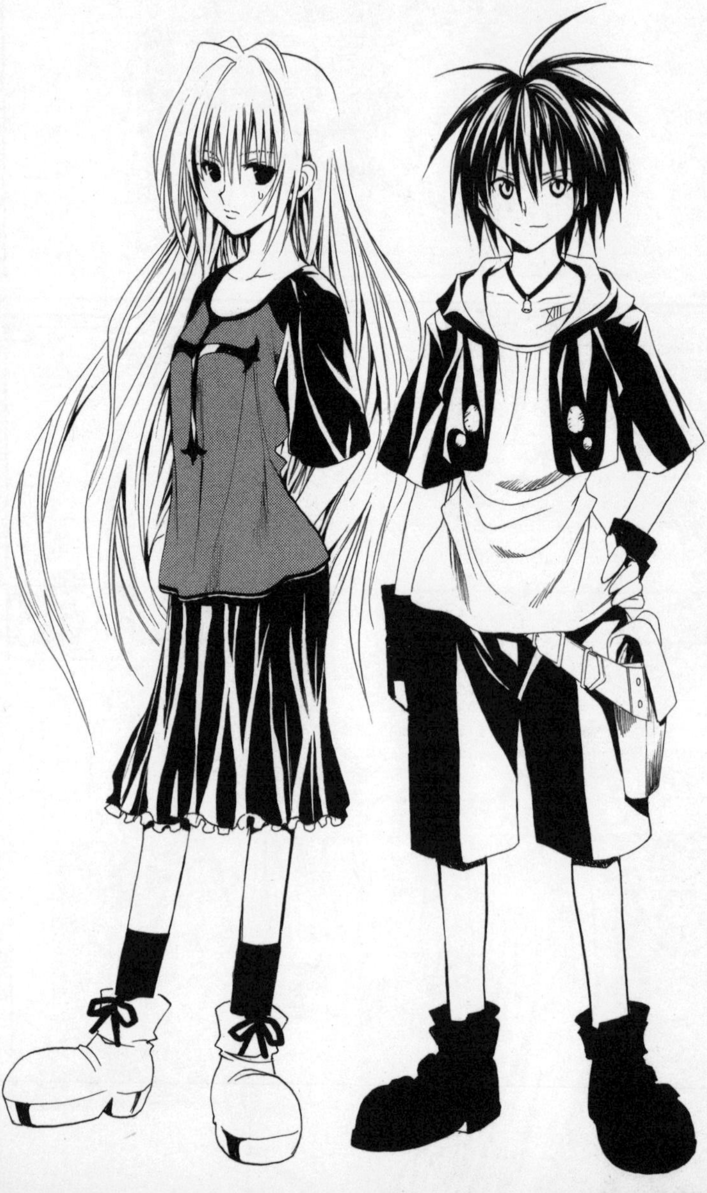

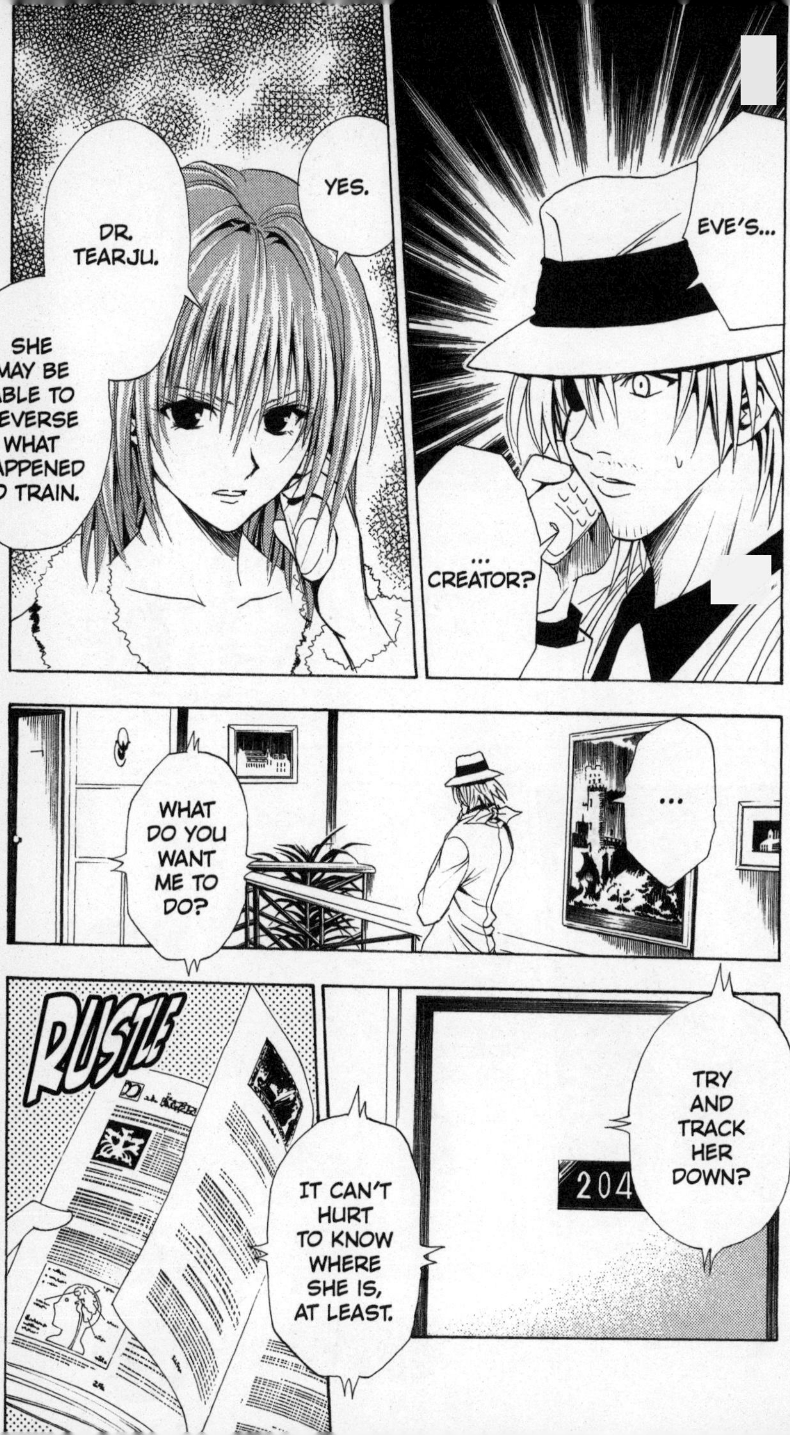
EVE'S...
...CREATOR?
YES.
DR. TEARJU.
SHE MAY BE ABLE TO REVERSE WHAT HAPPENED TO TRAIN.
...
WHAT DO YOU WANT ME TO DO?
TRY AND TRACK HER DOWN?
204
RUSTLE
IT CAN'T HURT TO KNOW WHERE SHE IS, AT LEAST.

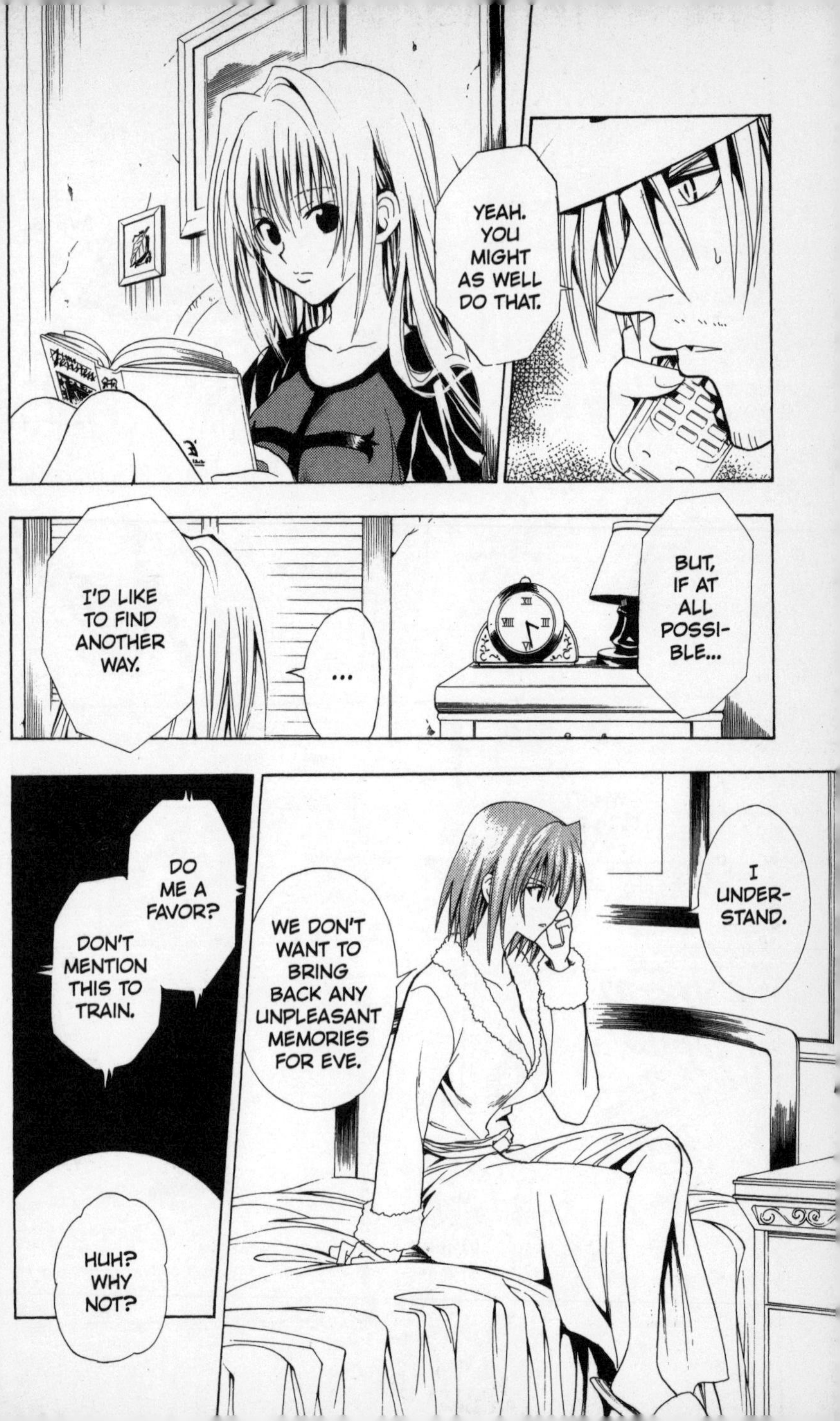
YEAH. YOU MIGHT AS WELL DO THAT.
BUT, IF AT ALL POSSIBLE...
...
I'D LIKE TO FIND ANOTHER WAY.
I UNDERSTAND.
WE DON'T WANT TO BRING BACK ANY UNPLEASANT MEMORIES FOR EVE.
DO ME A FAVOR?
DON'T MENTION THIS TO TRAIN.
HUH? WHY NOT?

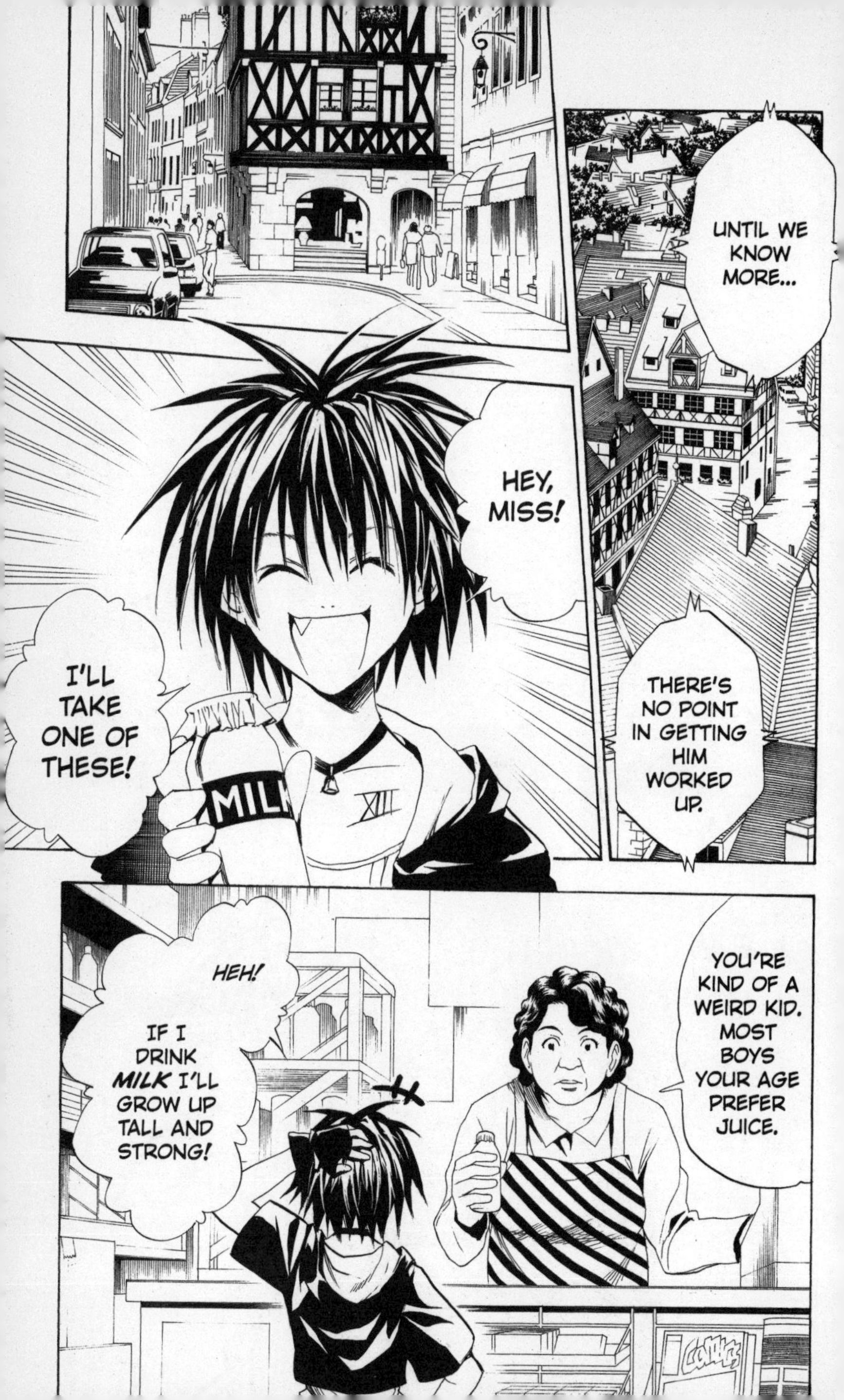
UNTIL WE KNOW MORE...
THERE'S NO POINT IN GETTING HIM WORKED UP.
HEY, MISS!
I'LL TAKE ONE OF THESE!
MILK
YOU'RE KIND OF A WEIRD KID. MOST BOYS YOUR AGE PREFER JUICE.
HEH!
IF I DRINK *MILK* I'LL GROW UP TALL AND STRONG!

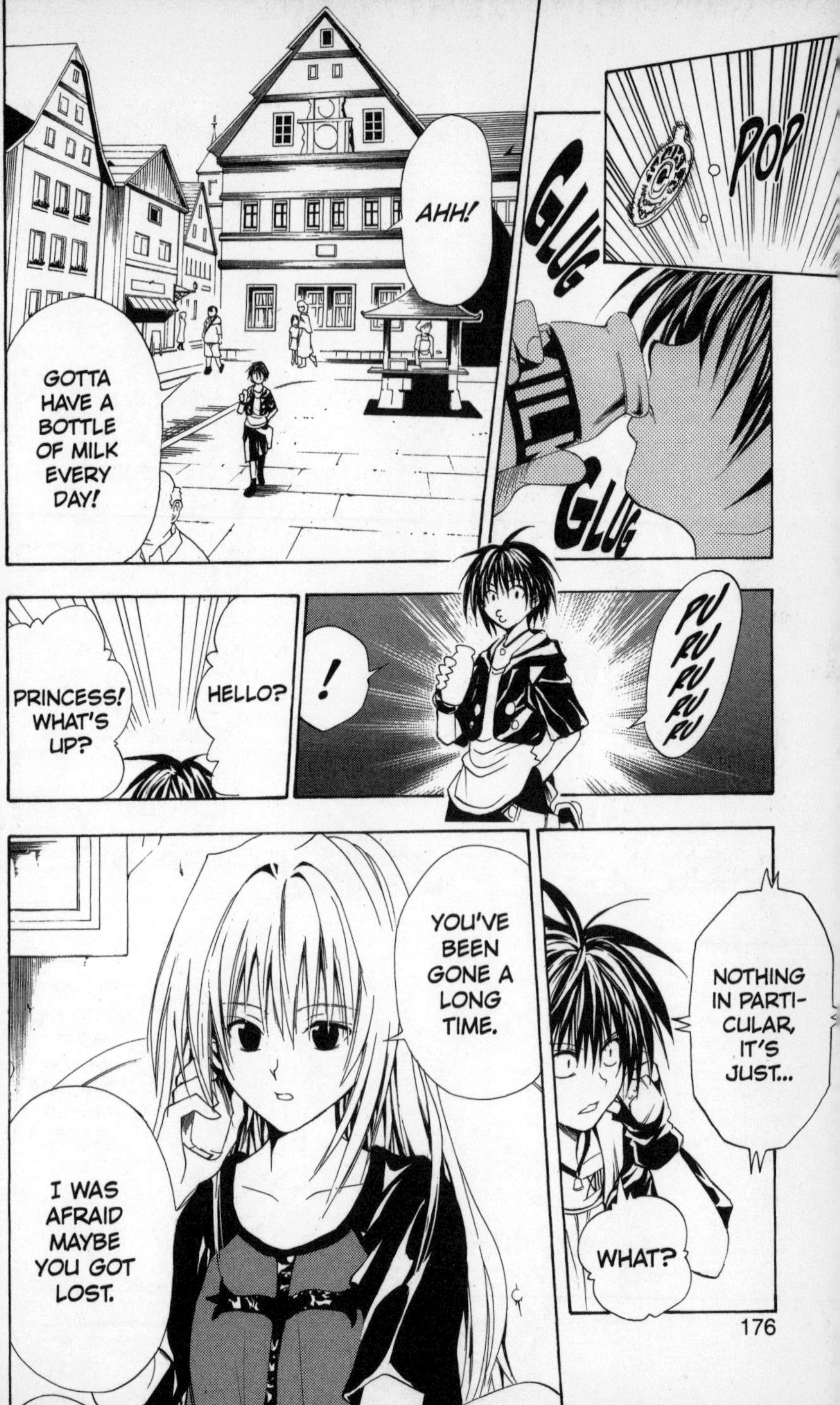
POP
GLUG
GLUG
AHH!
GOTTA HAVE A BOTTLE OF MILK EVERY DAY!
PURURURURU
!
HELLO?
PRINCESS! WHAT'S UP?
NOTHING IN PARTI-CULAR, IT'S JUST...
WHAT?
YOU'VE BEEN GONE A LONG TIME.
I WAS AFRAID MAYBE YOU GOT LOST.

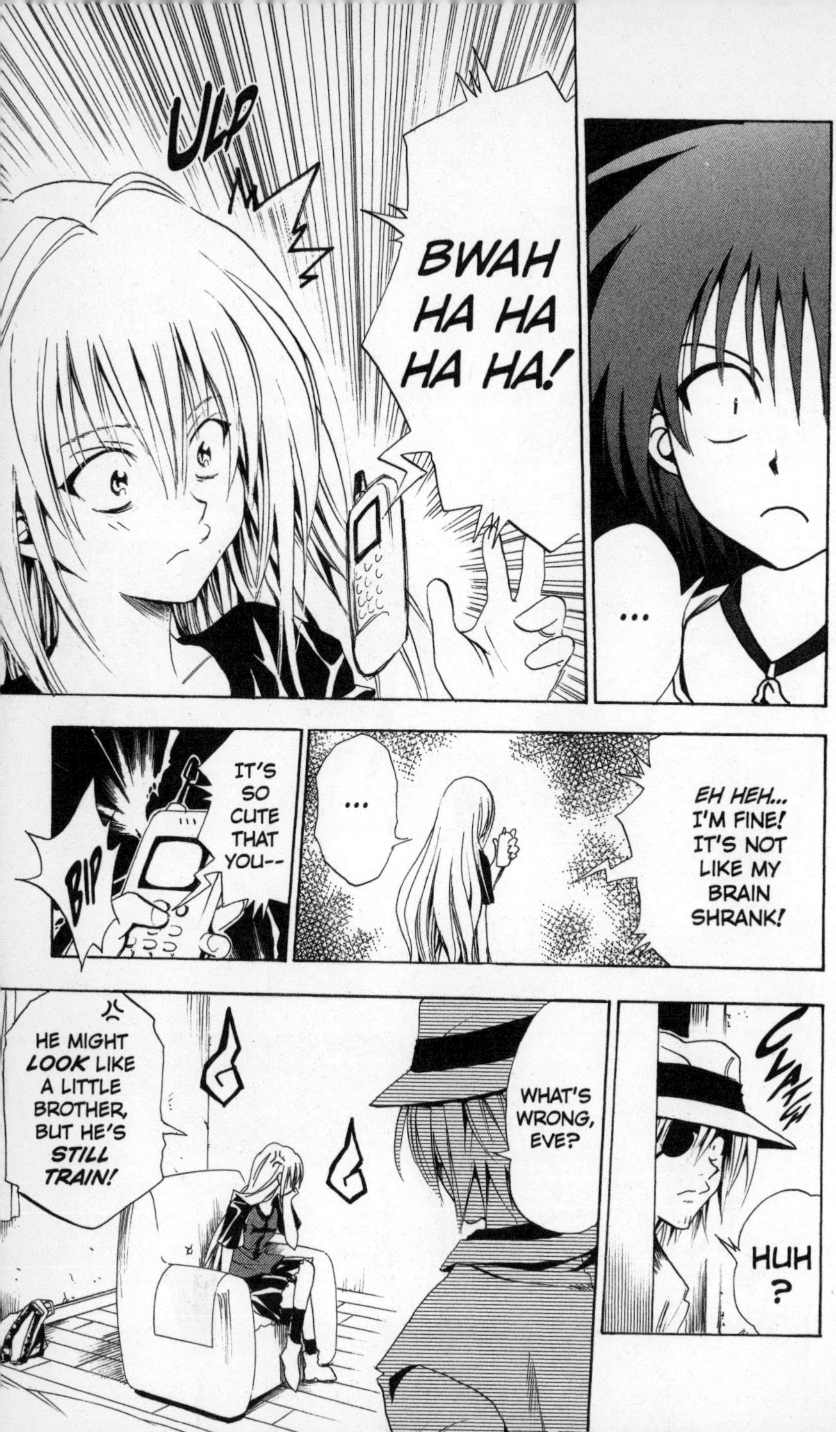
...
BWAH HA HA HA HA!
ULP
EH HEH... I'M FINE! IT'S NOT LIKE MY BRAIN SHRANK!
...
IT'S SO CUTE THAT YOU--
BIP
HUH ?
WHAT'S WRONG, EVE?
HE MIGHT LOOK LIKE A LITTLE BROTHER, BUT HE'S STILL TRAIN!

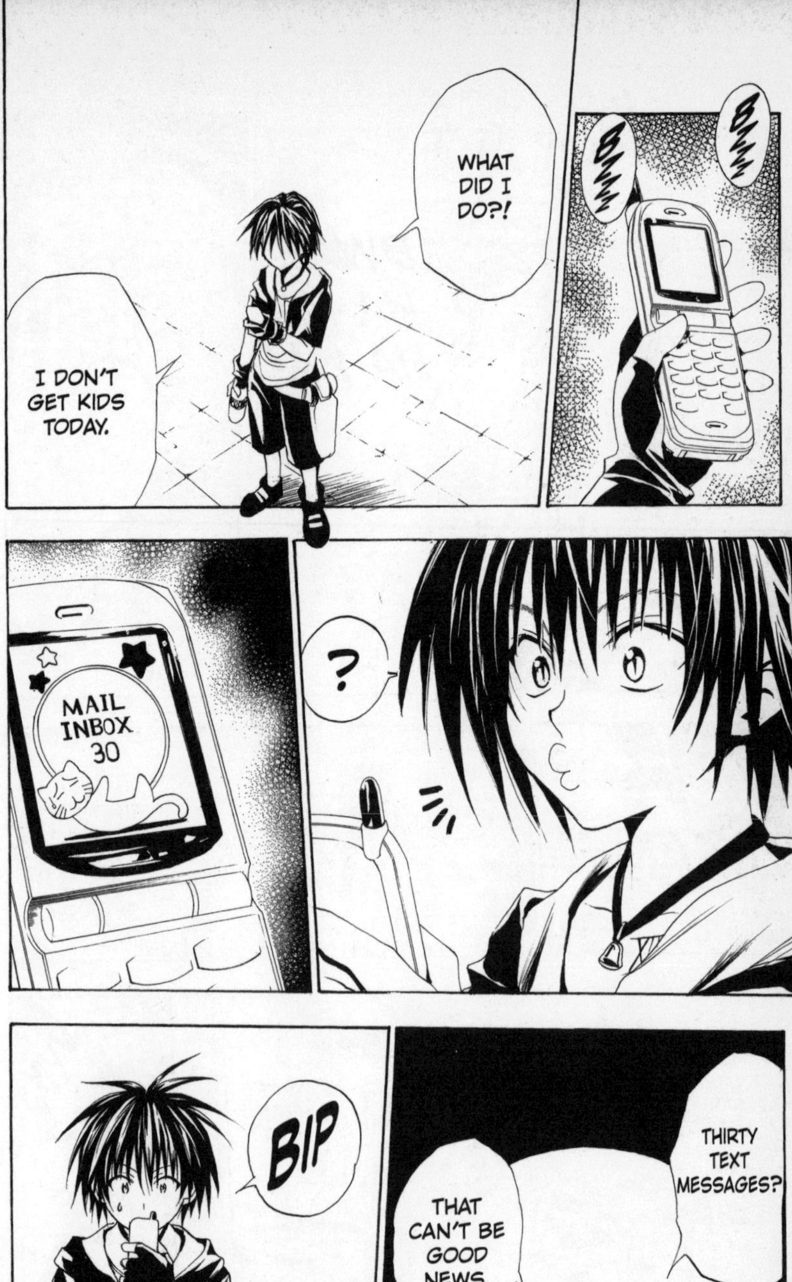
WHAT DID I DO?!
I DON'T GET KIDS TODAY.
?
MAIL INBOX 30
THIRTY TEXT MESSAGES?
THAT CAN'T BE GOOD NEWS.
BIP

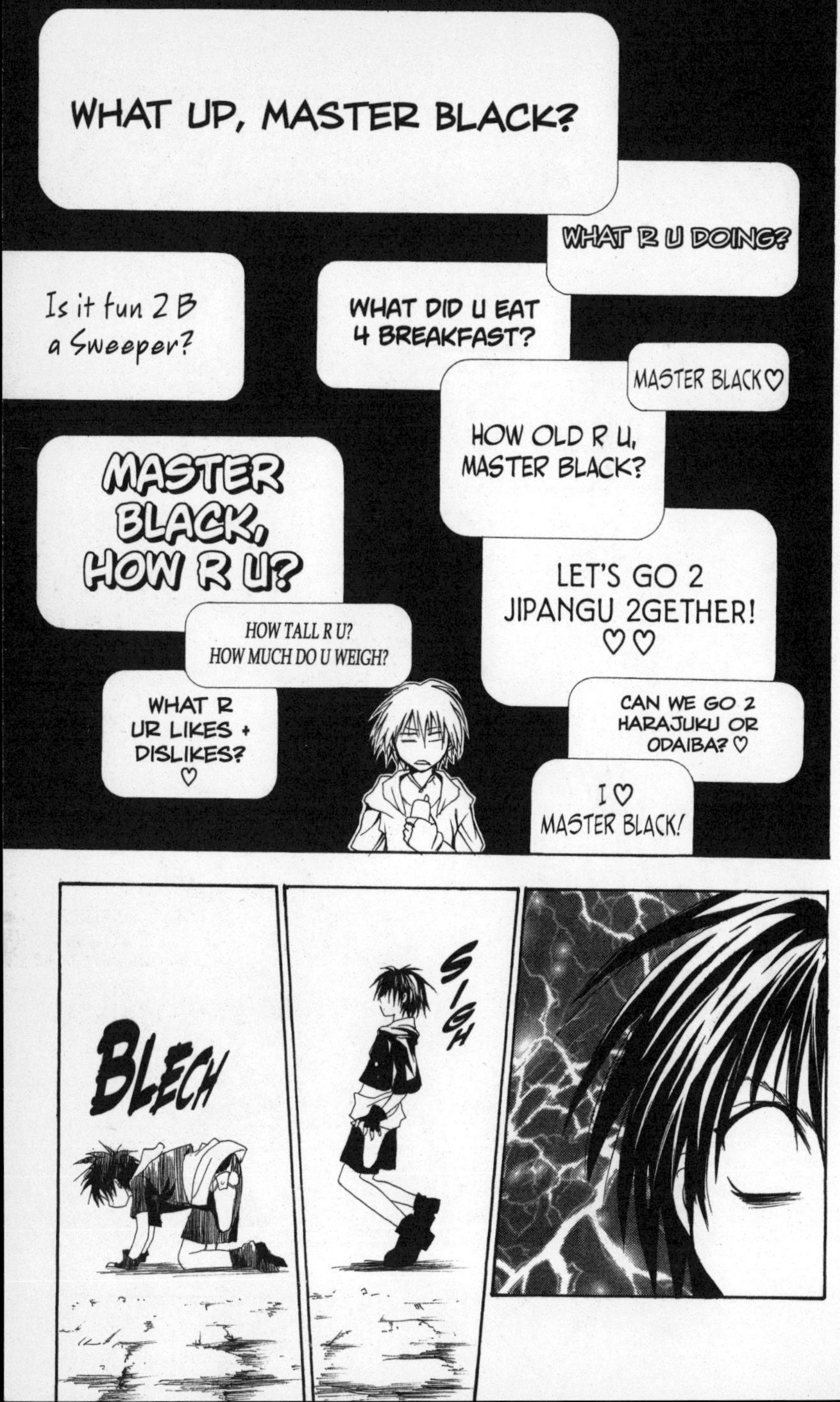
WHAT UP, MASTER BLACK?
WHAT R U DOING?
WHAT DID U EAT 4 BREAKFAST?
Is it fun 2 B a Sweeper?
MASTER BLACK♡
HOW OLD R U, MASTER BLACK?
MASTER BLACK, HOW R U?
LET'S GO 2 JIPANGU 2GETHER! ♡♡
HOW TALL R U? HOW MUCH DO U WEIGH?
CAN WE GO 2 HARAJUKU OR ODAIBA? ♡
WHAT R UR LIKES + DISLIKES? ♡
I ♡ MASTER BLACK!
SIGH
BLECH

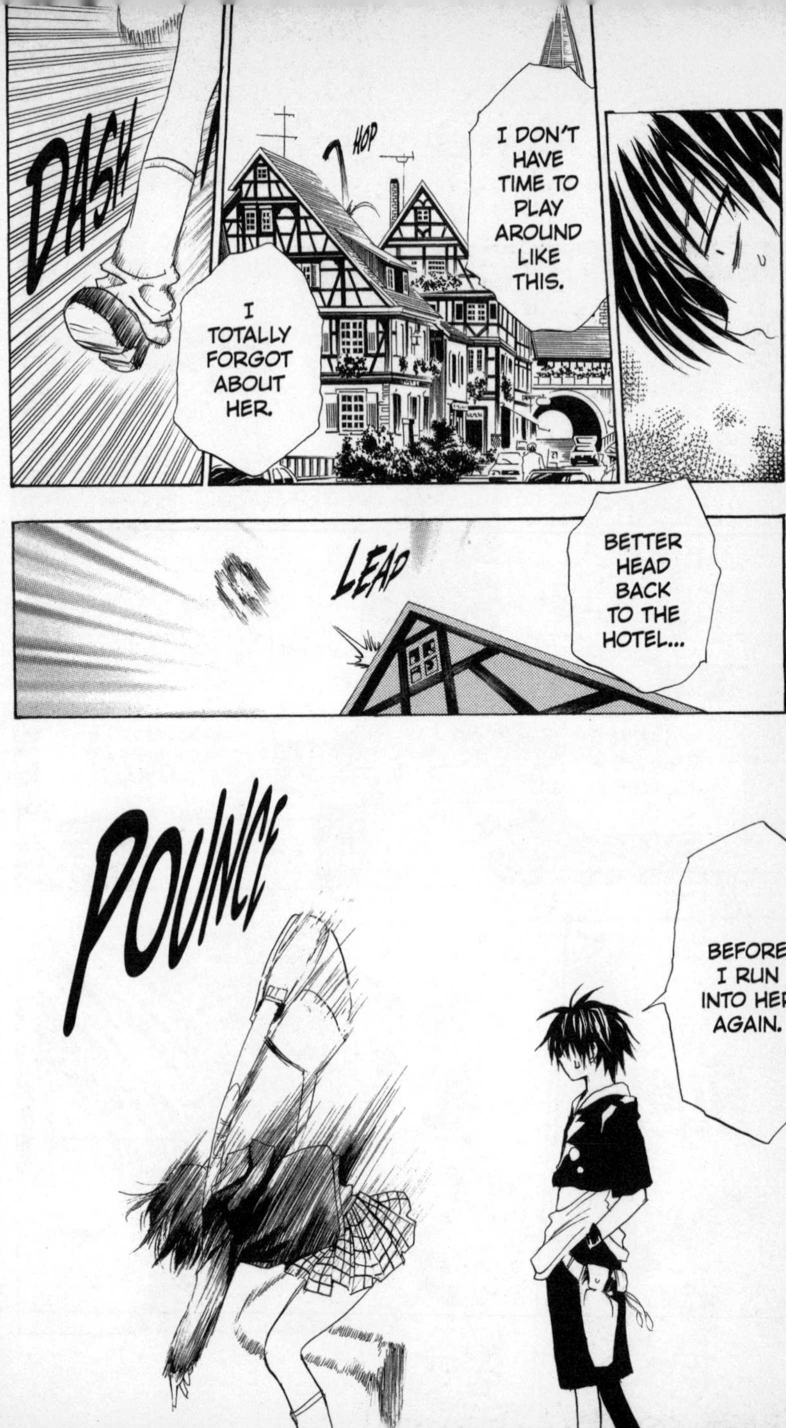
I DON'T HAVE TIME TO PLAY AROUND LIKE THIS.
HOP
I TOTALLY FORGOT ABOUT HER.
DASH
BETTER HEAD BACK TO THE HOTEL...
LEAP
BEFORE I RUN INTO HER AGAIN.
POUNCE

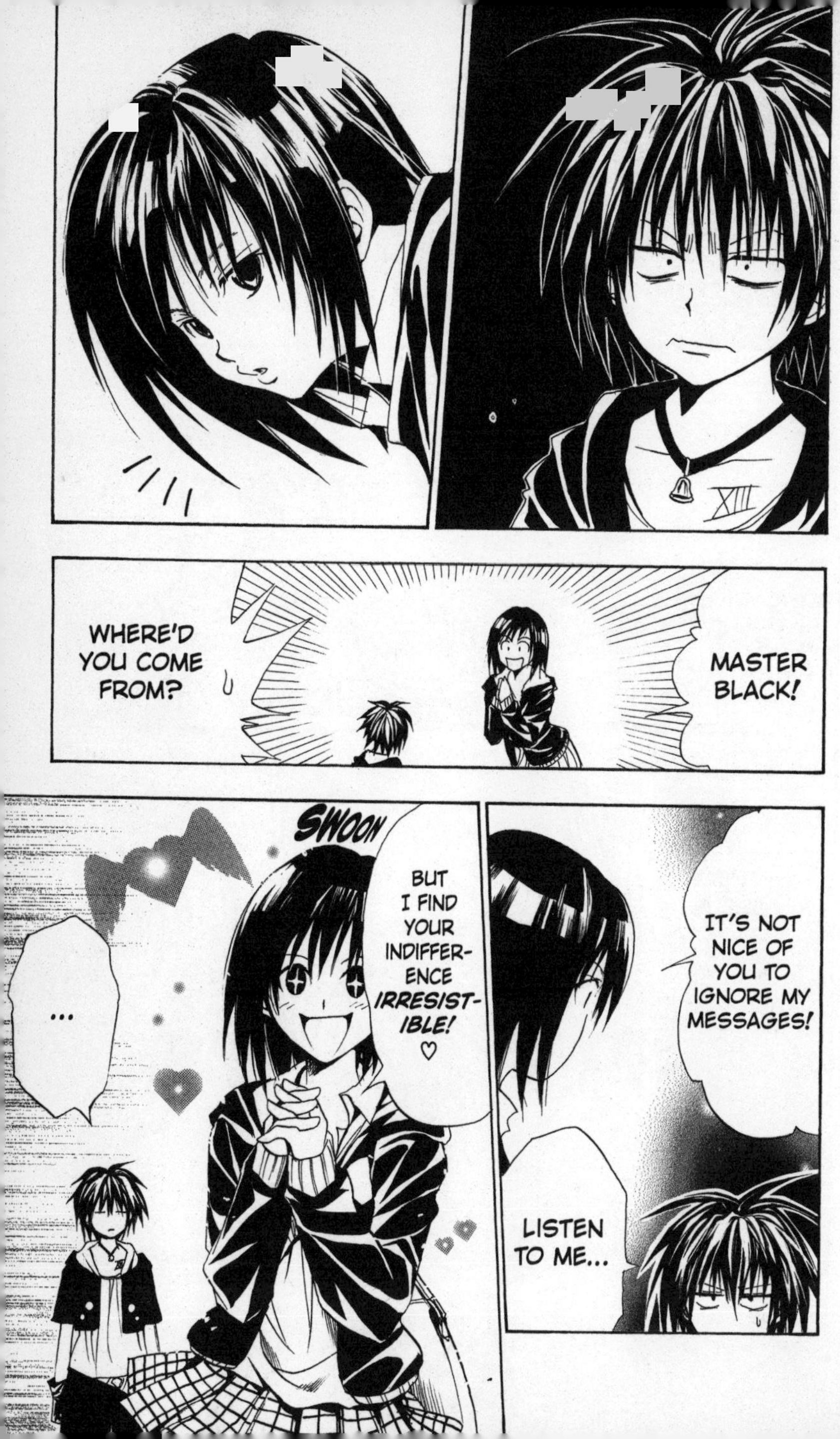
MASTER BLACK!
WHERE'D YOU COME FROM?
IT'S NOT NICE OF YOU TO IGNORE MY MESSAGES!
LISTEN TO ME...
SWOON
BUT I FIND YOUR INDIFFERENCE IRRESISTIBLE! ♡
...

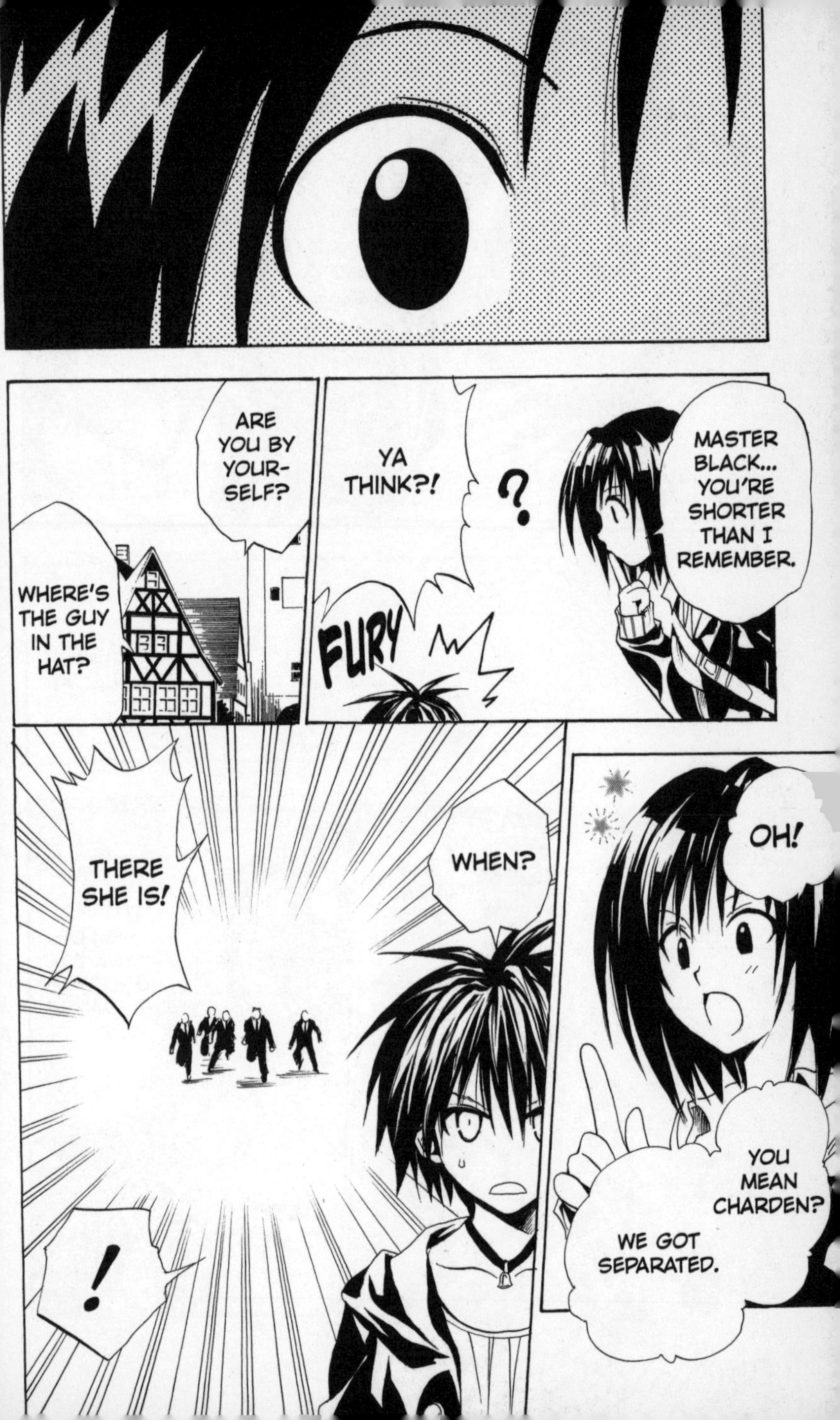
MASTER BLACK... YOU'RE SHORTER THAN I REMEMBER.
?
YA THINK?!
FURY
ARE YOU BY YOUR-SELF?
WHERE'S THE GUY IN THE HAT?
OH!
YOU MEAN CHARDEN?
WE GOT SEPARATED.
WHEN?
THERE SHE IS!
!

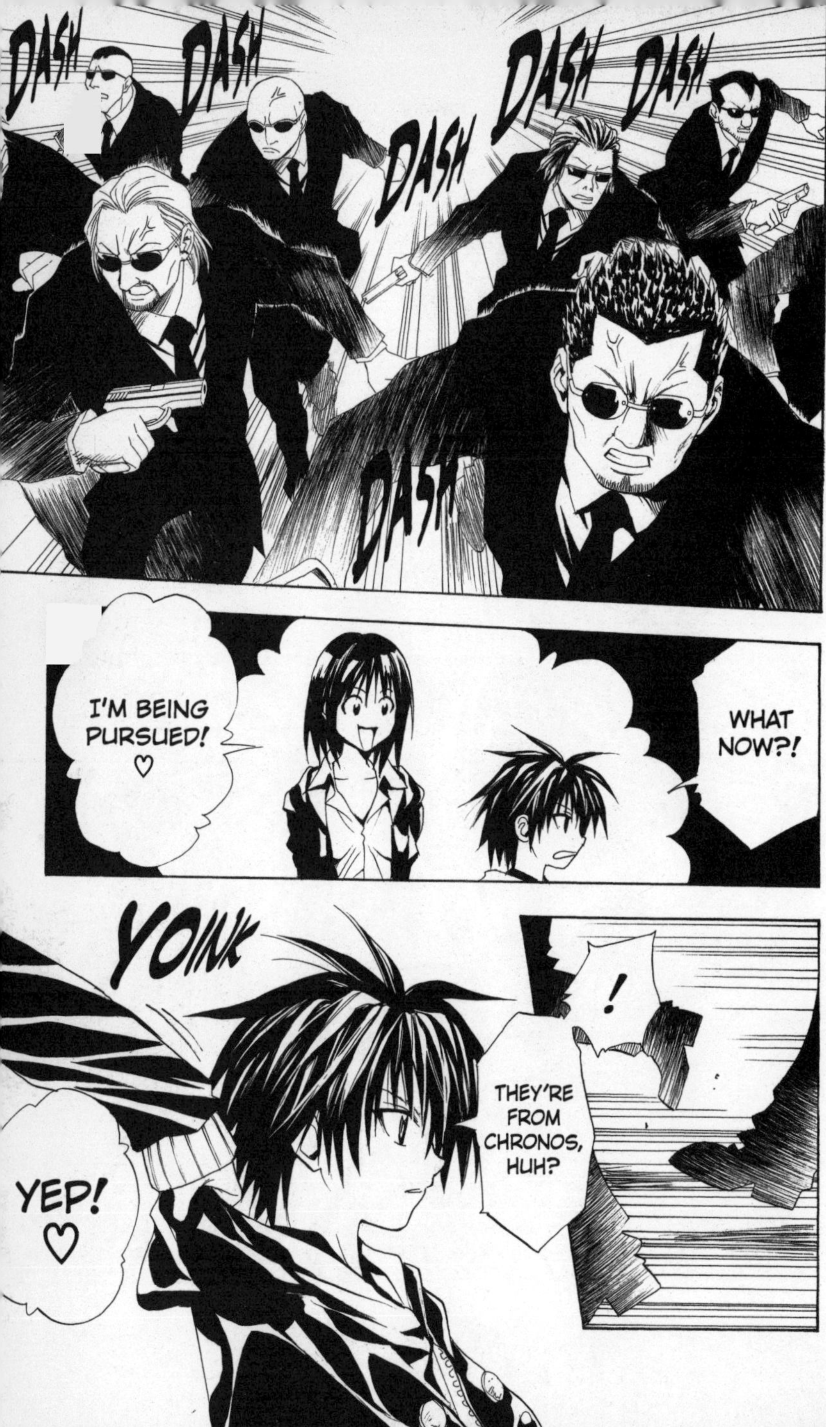
DASH
DASH
DASH
DASH
DASH
DASH
WHAT NOW?!
I'M BEING PURSUED! ♡
!
YOINK
THEY'RE FROM CHRONOS, HUH?
YEP! ♡

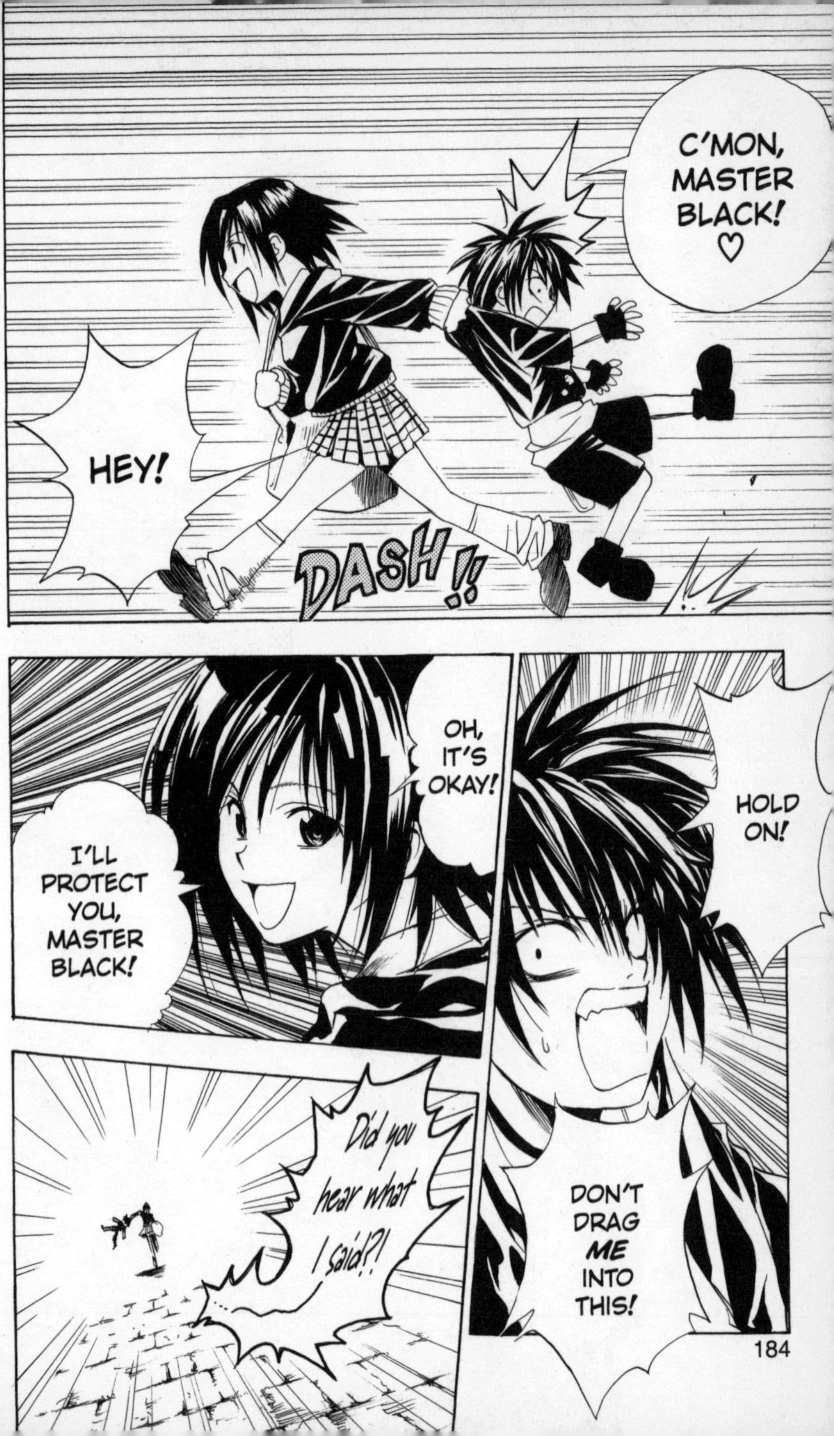
C'MON, MASTER BLACK! ♡
HEY!
DASH!!
HOLD ON!
DON'T DRAG *ME* INTO THIS!
OH, IT'S OKAY!
I'LL PROTECT YOU, MASTER BLACK!
Did you hear what I said?!

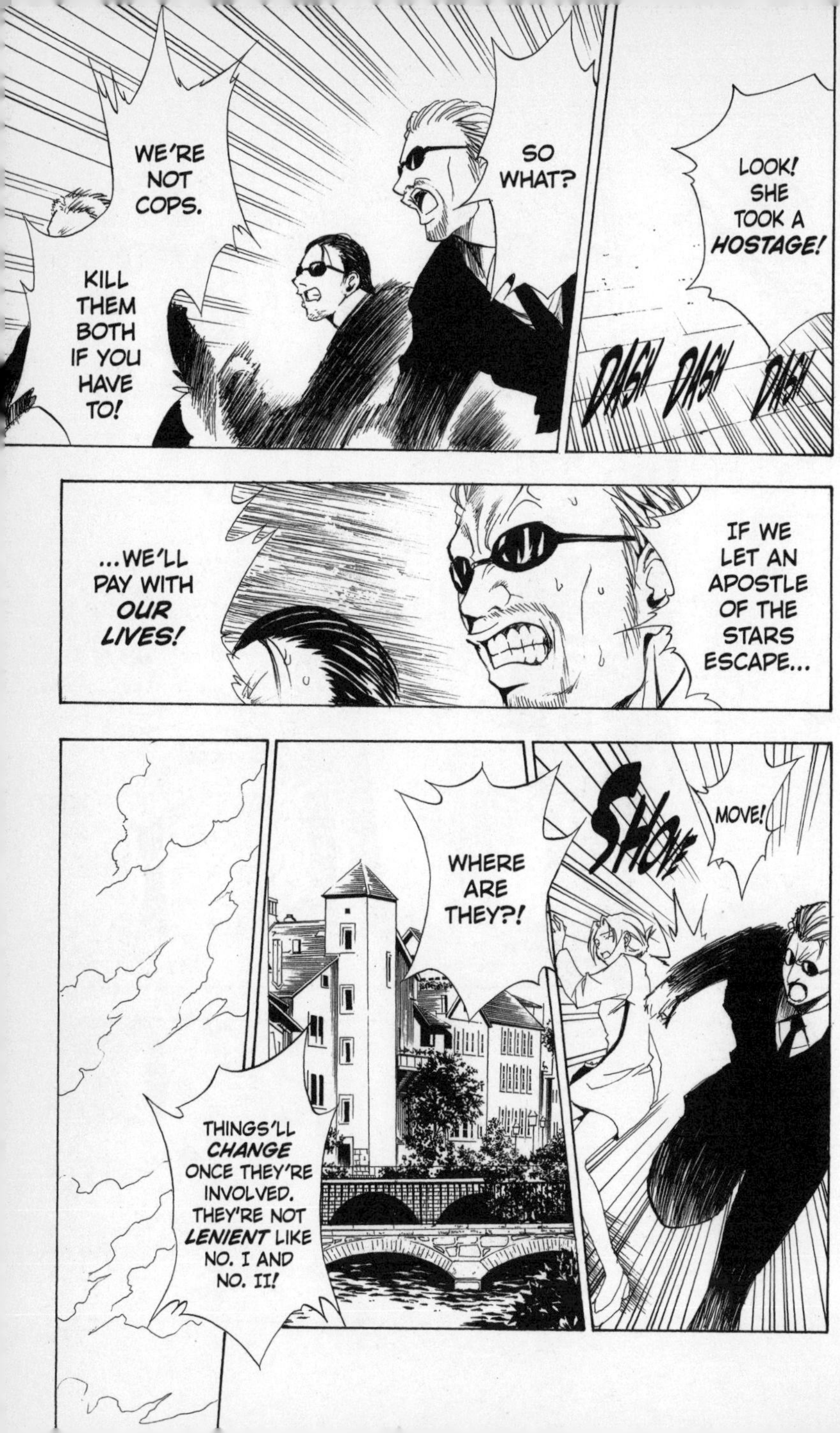
LOOK! SHE TOOK A HOSTAGE!
DASH DASH DASH
SO WHAT?
WE'RE NOT COPS.
KILL THEM BOTH IF YOU HAVE TO!
IF WE LET AN APOSTLE OF THE STARS ESCAPE...
...WE'LL PAY WITH OUR LIVES!
SHOVE
MOVE!
WHERE ARE THEY?!
THINGS'LL CHANGE ONCE THEY'RE INVOLVED. THEY'RE NOT LENIENT LIKE NO. I AND NO. II!

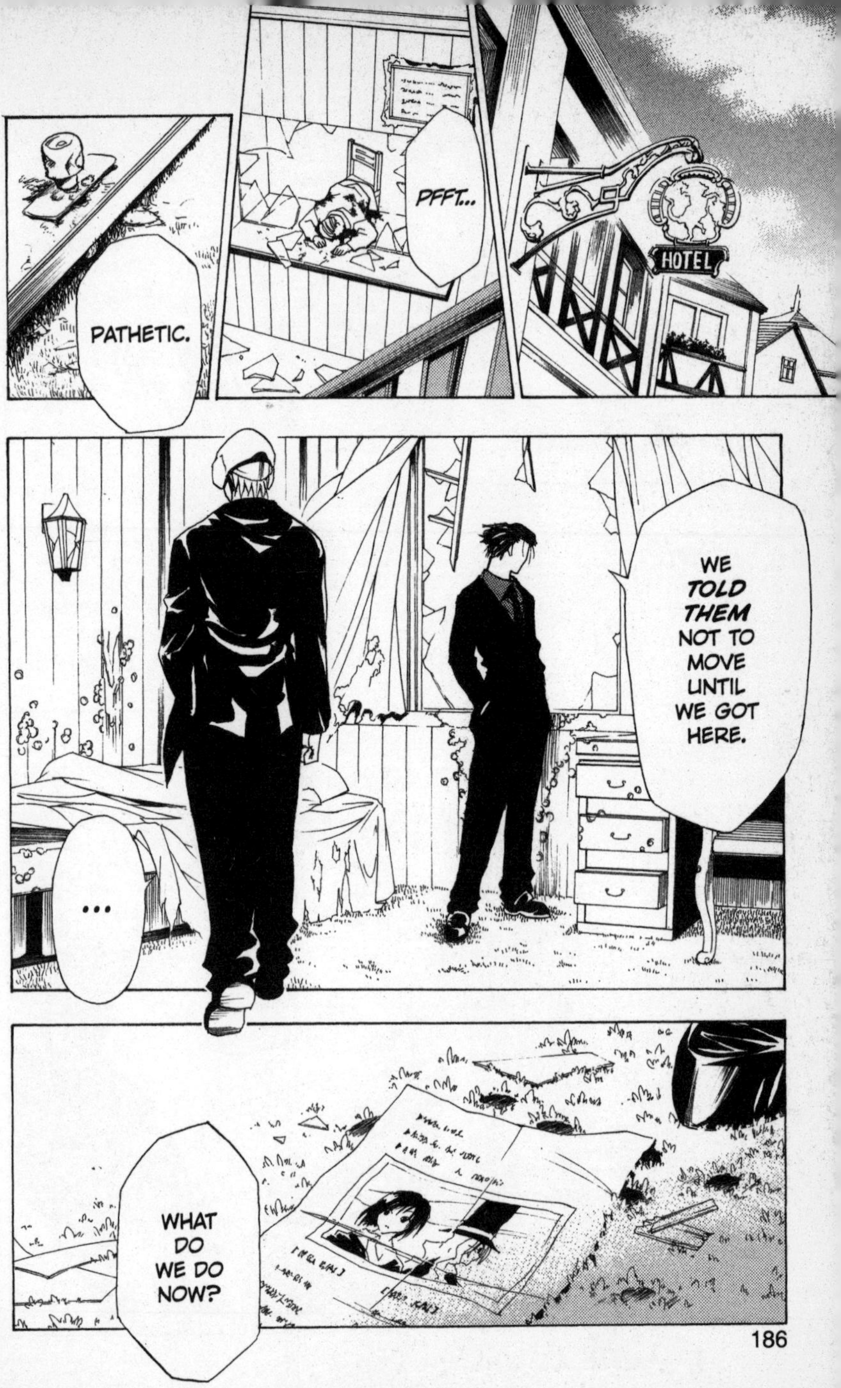
PFFT...
PATHETIC.
WE TOLD THEM NOT TO MOVE UNTIL WE GOT HERE.
...
WHAT DO WE DO NOW?

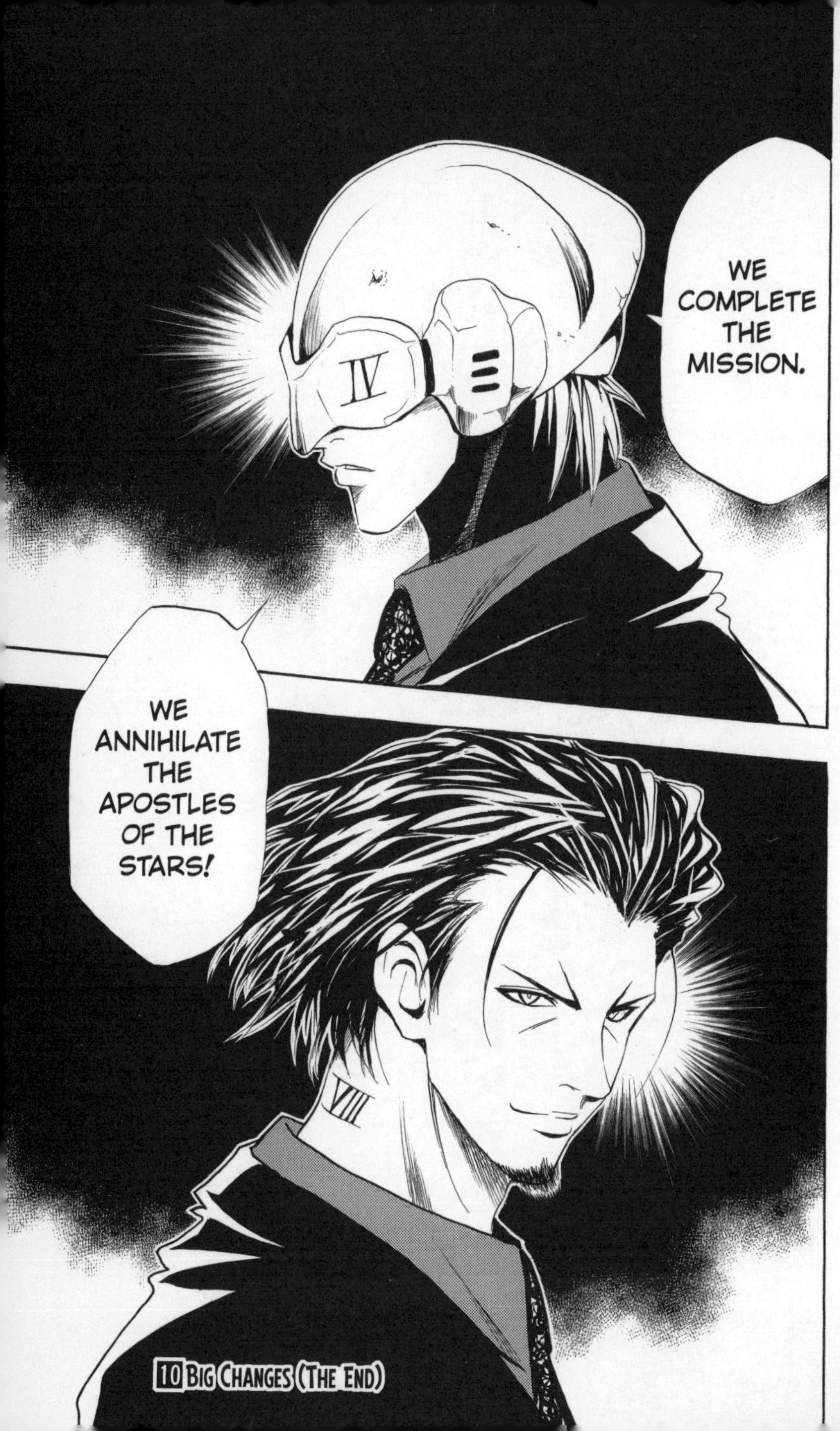
WE COMPLETE THE MISSION.
WE ANNIHILATE THE APOSTLES OF THE STARS!
10 BIG CHANGES (THE END)

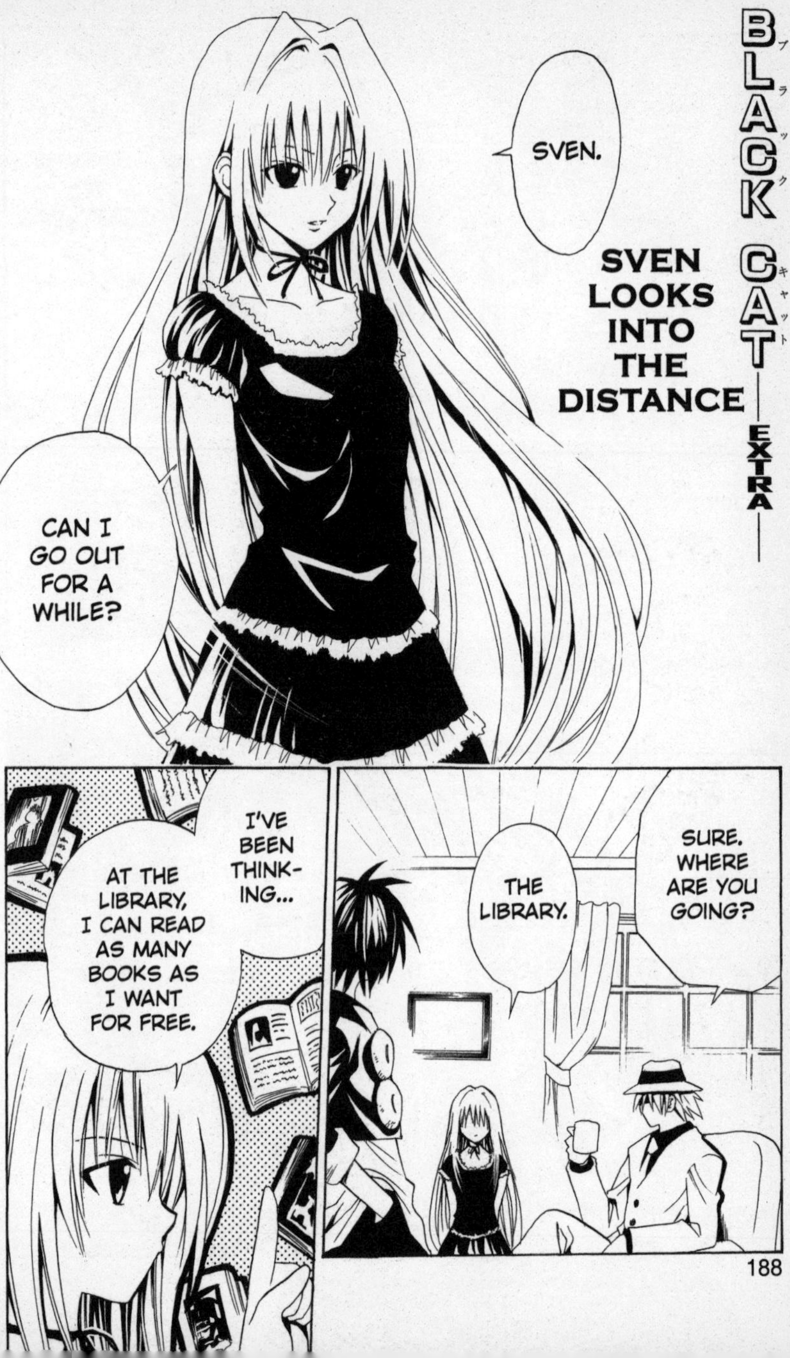
BLACK CAT
EXTRA
SVEN LOOKS INTO THE DISTANCE
SVEN.
CAN I GO OUT FOR A WHILE?
SURE. WHERE ARE YOU GOING?
THE LIBRARY.
I'VE BEEN THINKING...
AT THE LIBRARY, I CAN READ AS MANY BOOKS AS I WANT FOR FREE.

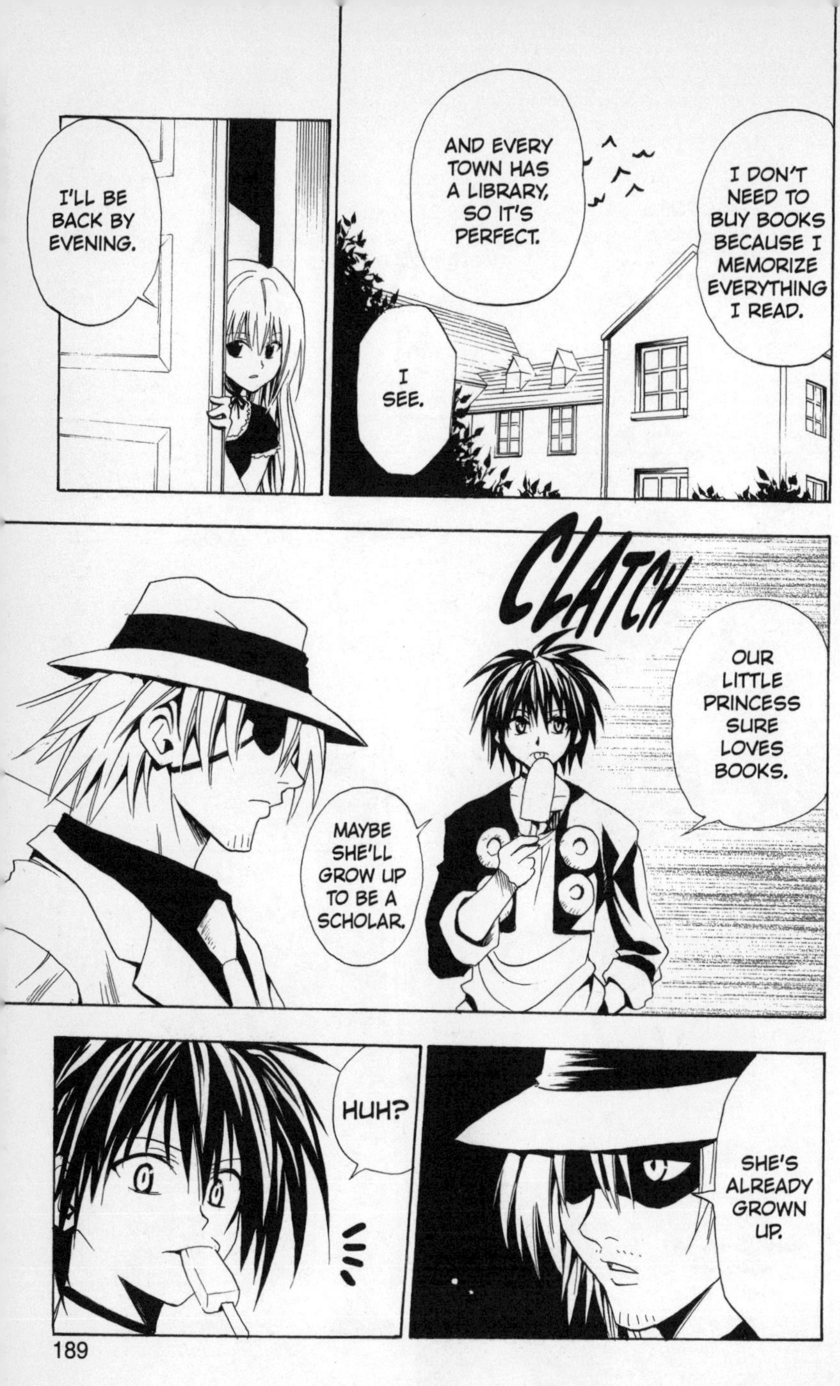

I DON'T NEED TO BUY BOOKS BECAUSE I MEMORIZE EVERYTHING I READ.
AND EVERY TOWN HAS A LIBRARY, SO IT'S PERFECT.
I SEE.
I'LL BE BACK BY EVENING.
CLATCH
OUR LITTLE PRINCESS SURE LOVES BOOKS.
MAYBE SHE'LL GROW UP TO BE A SCHOLAR.
SHE'S ALREADY GROWN UP.
HUH?

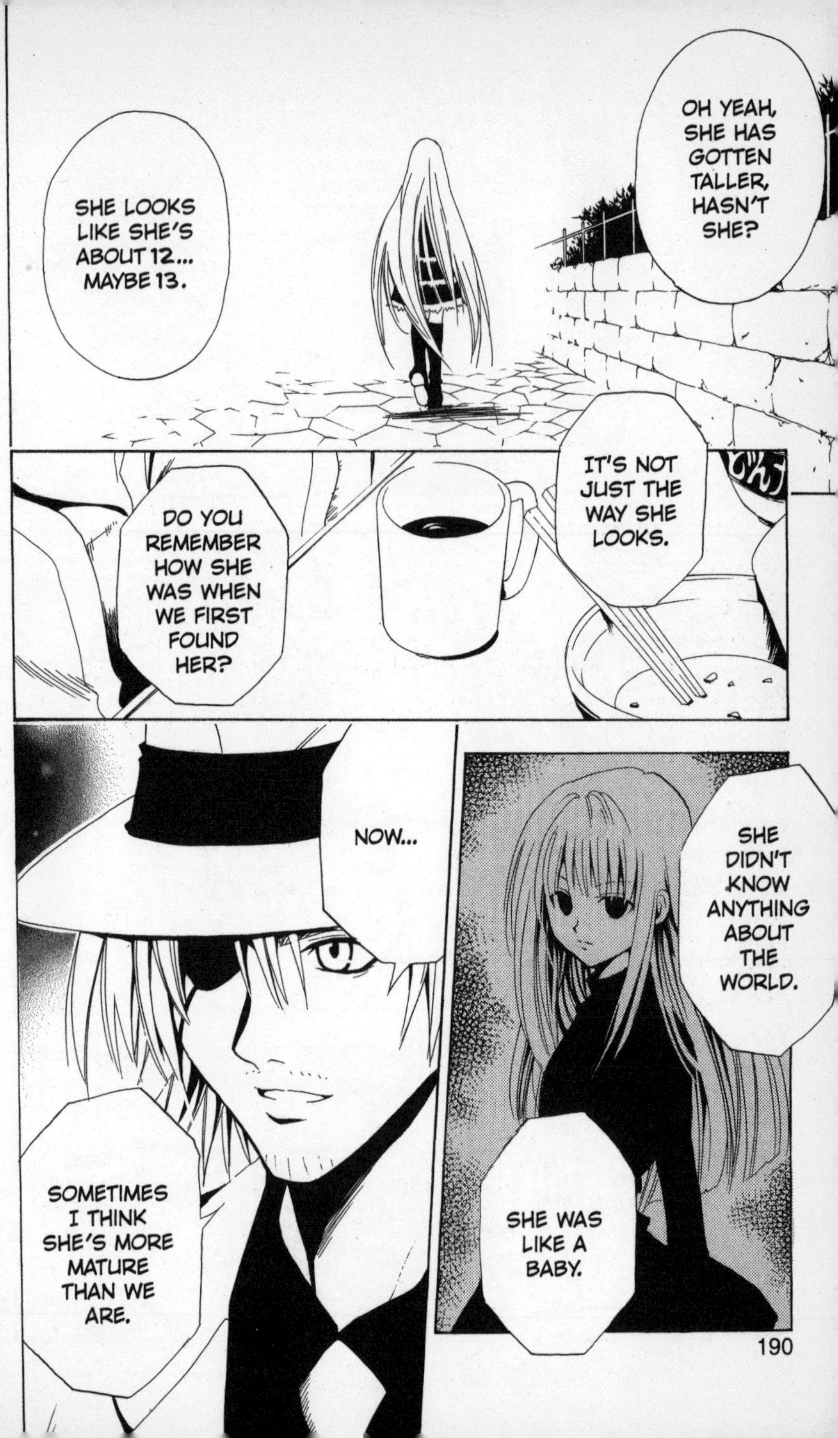
OH YEAH, SHE HAS GOTTEN TALLER, HASN'T SHE?
SHE LOOKS LIKE SHE'S ABOUT 12... MAYBE 13.
IT'S NOT JUST THE WAY SHE LOOKS.
DO YOU REMEMBER HOW SHE WAS WHEN WE FIRST FOUND HER?
SHE DIDN'T KNOW ANYTHING ABOUT THE WORLD.
SHE WAS LIKE A BABY.
NOW...
SOMETIMES I THINK SHE'S MORE MATURE THAN WE ARE.

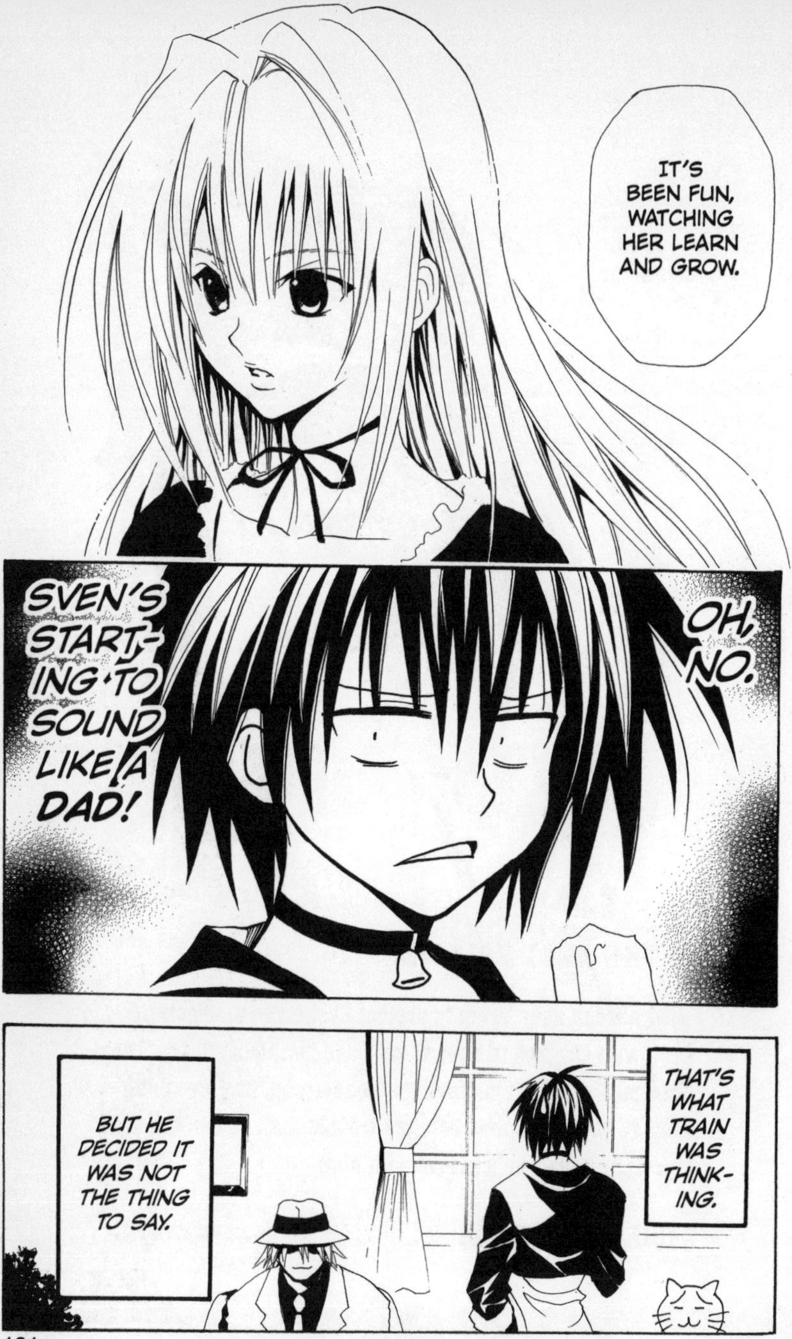
IT'S BEEN FUN, WATCHING HER LEARN AND GROW.
OH, NO.
SVEN'S START-ING TO SOUND LIKE A DAD!
THAT'S WHAT TRAIN WAS THINK-ING.
BUT HE DECIDED IT WAS NOT THE THING TO SAY.

BLACK CAT —EXTRA— "SVEN LOOKS INTO THE DISTANCE" THE END

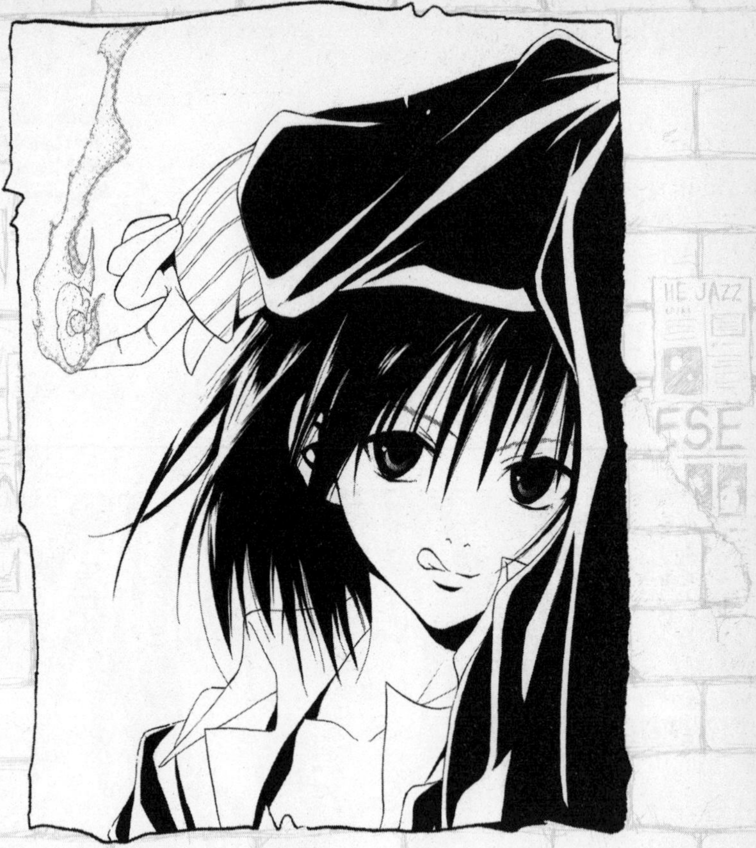
HE JAZZ
FSE

IN THE NEXT VOLUME...

Charden asks Train to protect Kyoko and to negotiate with Chronos to have them leave her alone. But for the pint-sized Train, having a headstrong, fire-breathing teenage girl in tow may be more trouble than he can handle, especially since she's in love with him!

AVAILABLE NOVEMBER 2007!

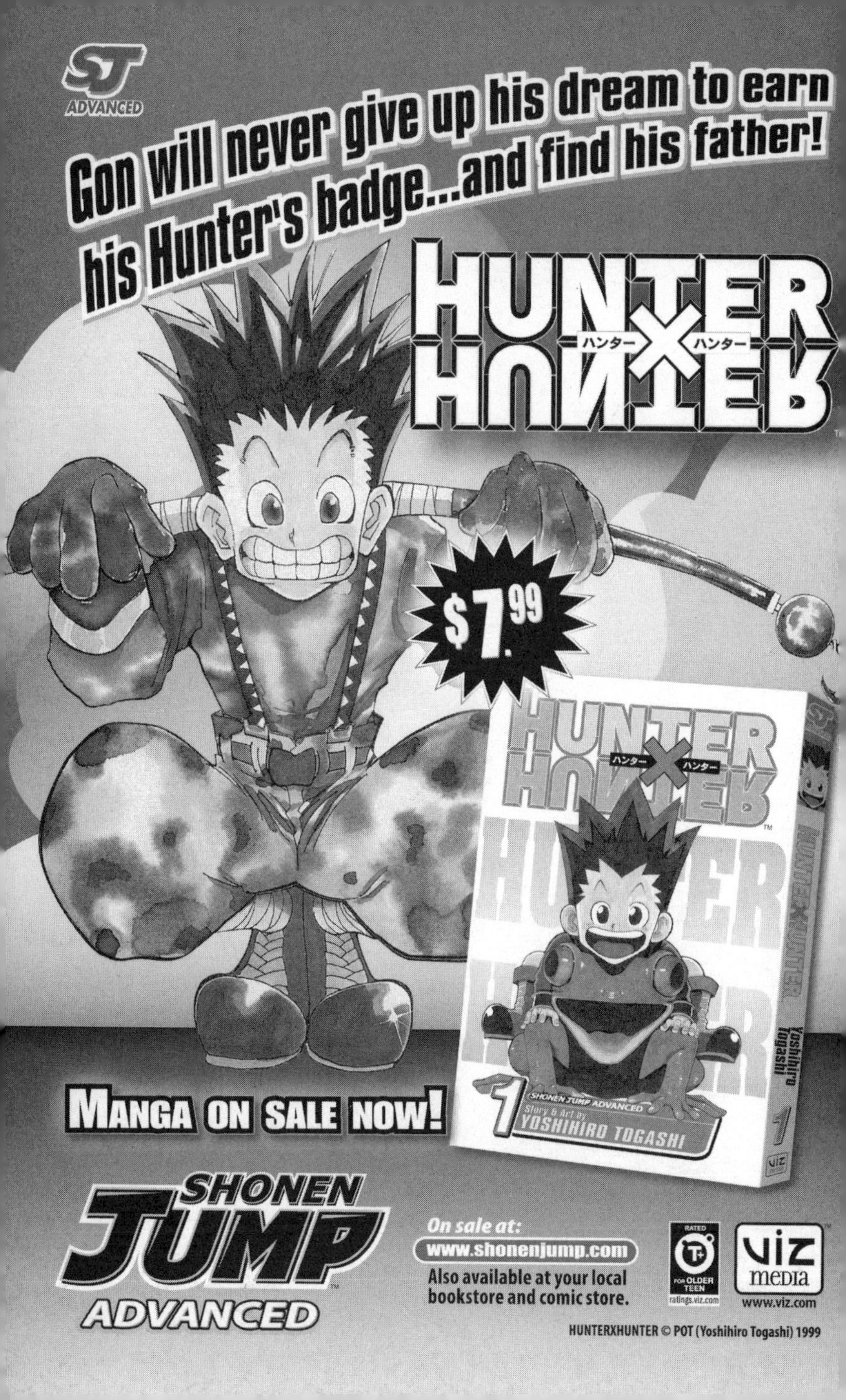

ADVANCED
Gon will never give up his dream to earn his Hunter's badge...and find his father!
HUNTER ハンター × ハンター HUNTER
$7.99
HUNTER × HUNTER
1 SHONEN JUMP ADVANCED
Story & Art by YOSHIHIRO TOGASHI
Yoshihiro Togashi
MANGA ON SALE NOW!
SHONEN JUMP ADVANCED
On sale at:
www.shonenjump.com
Also available at your local bookstore and comic store.
RATED T+ FOR OLDER TEEN
ratings.viz.com
viz media
www.viz.com
HUNTERXHUNTER © POT (Yoshihiro Togashi) 1999

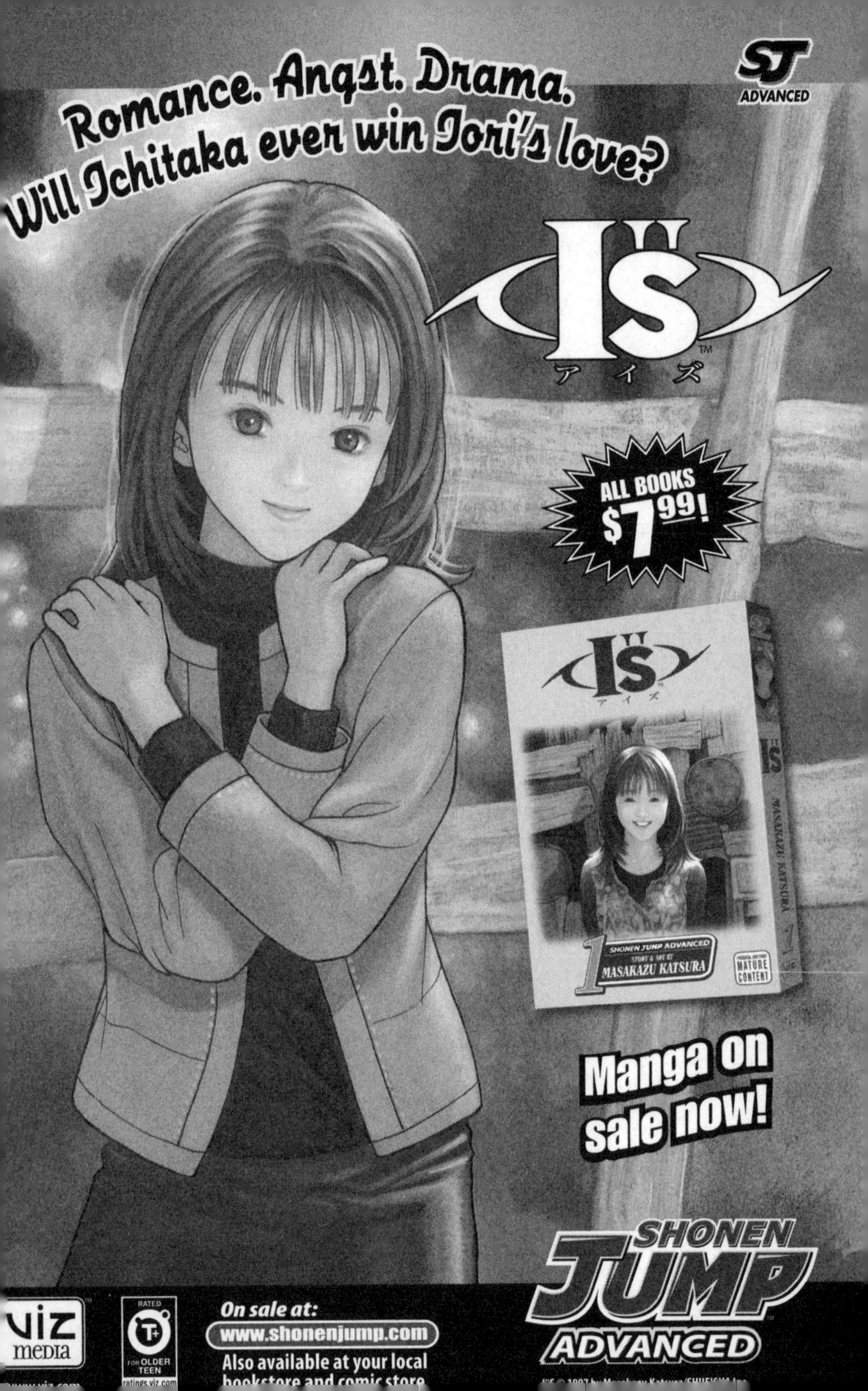

SJ ADVANCED
Romance. Angst. Drama.
Will Ichitaka ever win Iori's love?
I"S
アイズ
ALL BOOKS $7.99!
I"S
アイズ
1
SHONEN JUMP ADVANCED
STORY & ART BY
MASAKAZU KATSURA
MATURE CONTENT
Manga on sale now!
SHONEN JUMP ADVANCED
viz media
RATED T+ FOR OLDER TEEN
ratings.viz.com
On sale at:
www.shonenjump.com
Also available at your local bookstore and comic store

Tell us what you think about SHONEN JUMP manga!

Our survey is now available online.
Go to: www.*SHONENJUMP*.com/*mangasurvey*

Help us make our product offering better!

THE REAL ACTION STARTS IN...

www.shonenjump.com

ADVANCED

media

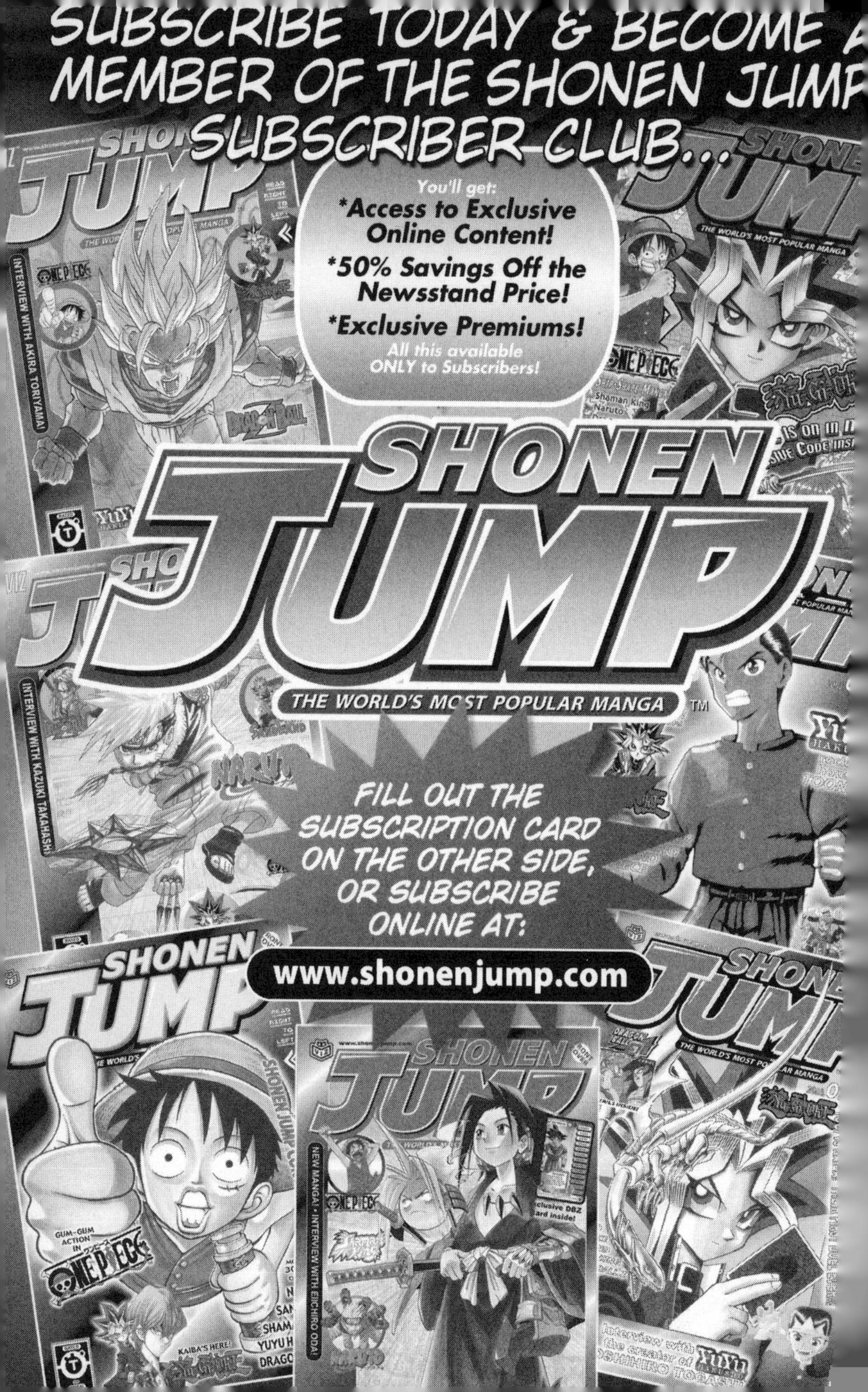
SUBSCRIBE TODAY & BECOME A MEMBER OF THE SHONEN JUMP SUBSCRIBER CLUB...
You'll get:
*Access to Exclusive Online Content!
*50% Savings Off the Newsstand Price!
*Exclusive Premiums!
All this available ONLY to Subscribers!
SHONEN JUMP
THE WORLD'S MOST POPULAR MANGA ™
FILL OUT THE SUBSCRIPTION CARD ON THE OTHER SIDE, OR SUBSCRIBE ONLINE AT:
www.shonenjump.com